INTO THE LIGHT

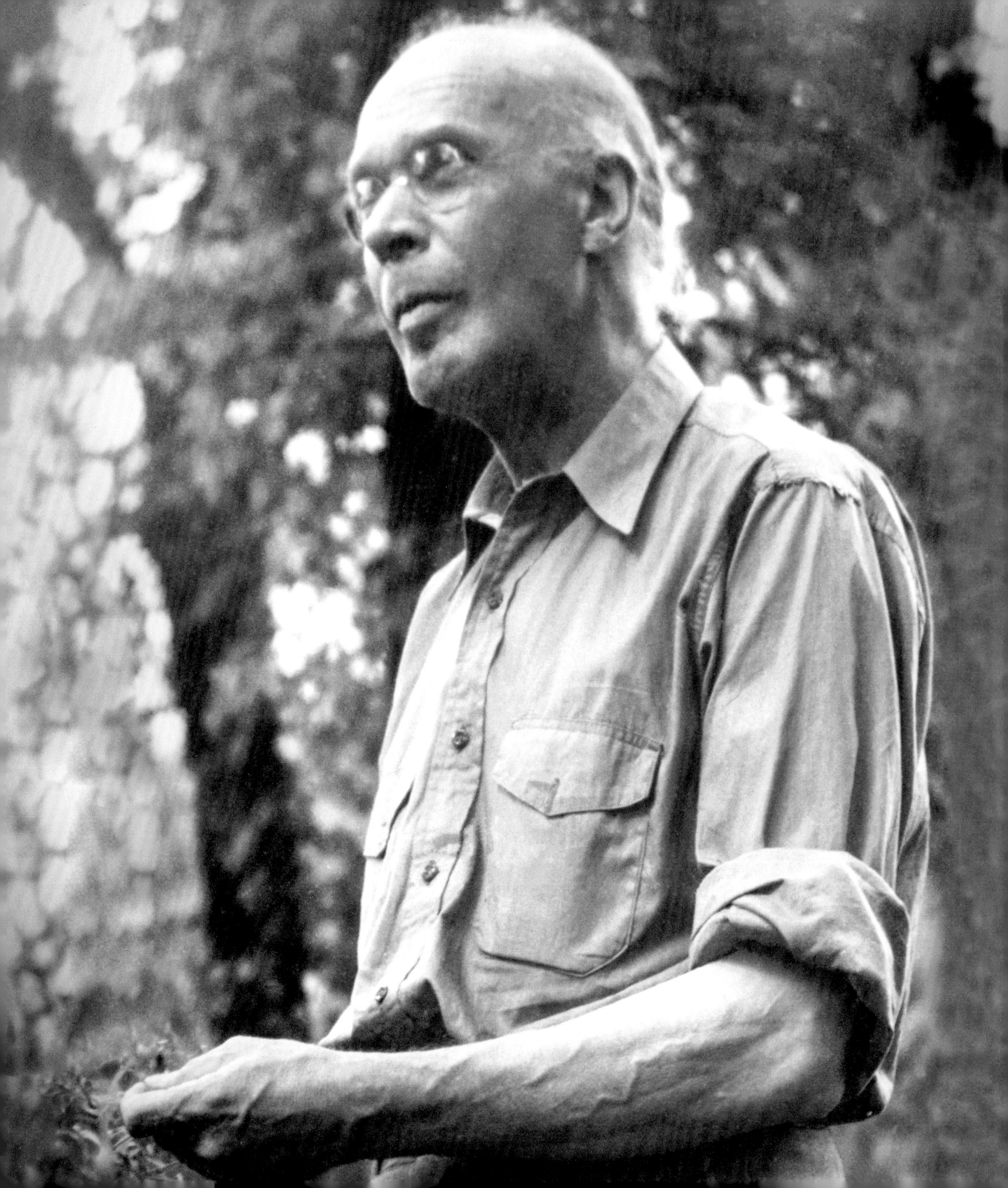

SARAH MILROY, IAN A.C. DEJARDIN,
AND MICHAEL PARKE-TAYLOR

INTO THE LIGHT

Lionel LeMoine FitzGerald

Figure.1
Vancouver / Berkeley / London

McMichael
CANADIAN ART COLLECTION D'ART CANADIEN

wag Winnipeg Art Gallery

Contents

Director's Foreword

IAN A.C. DEJARDIN
EXECUTIVE DIRECTOR
MCMICHAEL CANADIAN ART COLLECTION

FRONTISPIECE
L.L. FitzGerald, Winnipeg, July 28, 1954
Gift of Earl and Patsy Green from the Estate of Patricia Morrison / School of Art Gallery, University of Manitoba, Winnipeg / 17-014
Photo: Robert Ayre

Lionel LeMoine FitzGerald belonged to Winnipeg, and to the prairie, heart and soul, so it is particularly gratifying and appropriate that this project is a collaboration with our colleagues at the Winnipeg Art Gallery. Indeed, it could not have been otherwise. In his foreword, Director and CEO Stephen Borys spells out the artist's seminal role in the cultural history of his hometown, but a little piece of FitzGerald's legacy belongs to the McMichael as well, long considered the spiritual home of the Group of Seven. For a few short months, FitzGerald was a member of the Group, invited to join in 1932, during the Group's final year. This affiliation may have been a bit of a double-edged sword for his reputation, since FitzGerald was too much of an individual to gel with any group—his aesthetic was always unique. The undeniable quality of his work, recognized by the membership, does not alter the fact that his style seems to have little in common with theirs, despite the shared and unstinting commitment to art practice. It feels entirely right and proper that FitzGerald's ashes were scattered southwest of Winnipeg at his grandmother's farm in Snowflake, the fount and origin of his artistic awareness, rather than buried alongside his Group confreres in the Artists' Cemetery at the McMichael.

Researching for this exhibition, my colleague Sarah Milroy and I quickly realized that the bedrock of FitzGerald's art lies in his drawings. We sifted through literally thousands of them. Many, of course, were products of his long teaching career—exercises, in effect. But at its best, FitzGerald's draftsmanship is exquisitely delicate and precisely poetic. Like those of one of his idols, Paul Cézanne, FitzGerald's drawings are by no means incidental to an assessment of his achievement; they are in fact central to it.

This is the fourth exhibition that I have had the pleasure of co-curating with Sarah and the third to focus on a key Canadian artist, after *From the Forest to the Sea: Emily Carr in British Columbia* (2014) and *David Milne: Modern Painting* (2018). Sarah's commitment to Canadian art has been inspirational to me personally; her appointment in 2018 as Chief Curator at the McMichael has ushered in an exciting era at the gallery, and this exhibition is one of its first fruits.

Working with our colleagues in Manitoba has been a great pleasure, and we are grateful to them for their generosity in time, enthusiastic support, and—not least—loans. At the McMichael, the exhibitions team, headed by Jennifer Withrow, and the preparators, headed by Lorena Jurdana, have been models of professionalism, as always. Alexandra Cousins and Brittney Sproule have steered us through the many challenges presented by the publication and exhibition with a devoted attention to detail, and our Chief Registrar, Janine Butler, has worked skilfully on all aspects of securing the many loans. Thanks are due as well to Michael Parke-Taylor for his extraordinary scholarly generosity in all aspects of the development of this project. In the final stages of preparation for this exhibition and book we asked him to join us as our co-curator. We are deeply in his debt. Finally, Eric Pearson, the exhibition's designer, deserves honourable mention for his sensitive response to FitzGerald's art. My thanks to them all for their commitment and enthusiasm in helping us give this great Canadian modernist the full tribute he has long deserved. ■

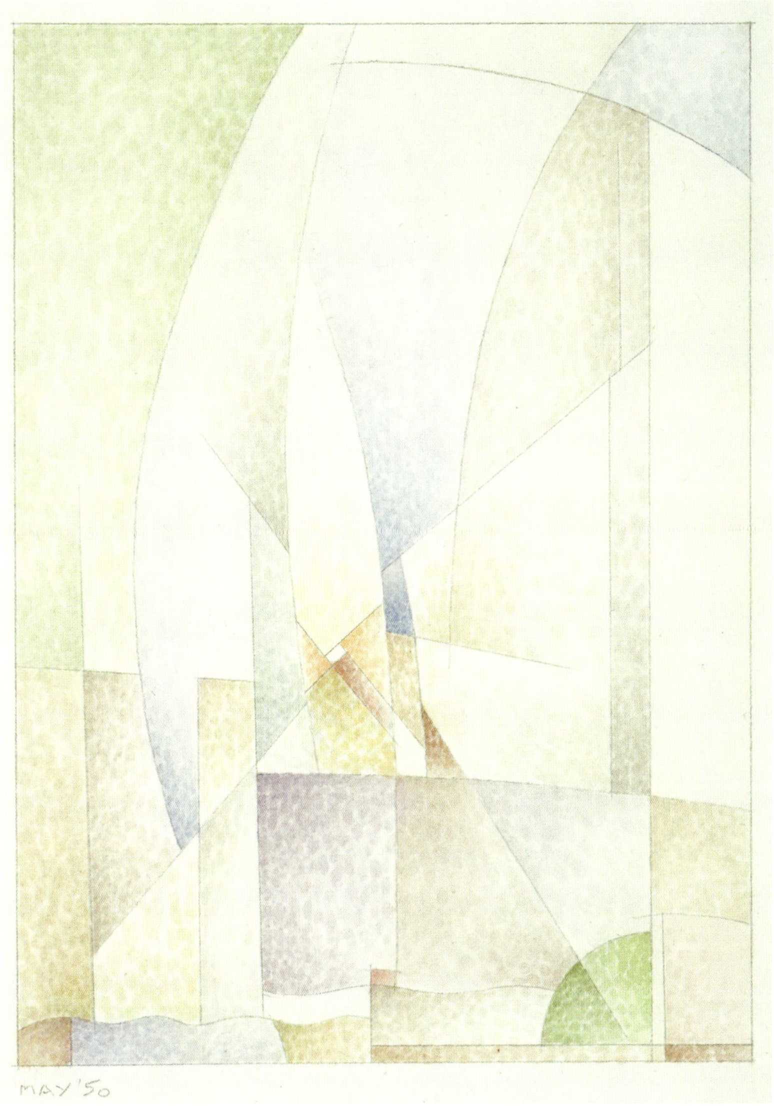

Abstract, 1950
watercolour over graphite on paper
20.5 × 15.3 cm

Director’s Foreword

STEPHEN BORYS

DIRECTOR AND CEO
WINNIPEG ART GALLERY

Undeniably, Lionel LeMoine FitzGerald contributed significantly to the development of modern art in Canada. His career is also remarkable for the way it pays loving tribute to his home. From flat fields and open prairie sky to the backyards and laneways of his St. James neighbourhood in Winnipeg, FitzGerald, much like his French hero, Paul Cézanne, tied artistic innovation to the particularities of place in his lived environment.

The Winnipeg Art Gallery (WAG) is one of Canada’s oldest civic galleries. L.L. FitzGerald, arguably Manitoba’s first truly modern painter, was only just beginning his professional artistic career when the then Winnipeg Museum of Fine Arts opened its doors in December 1912. His talent was recognized early in his hometown. FitzGerald was included in the museum’s inaugural Royal Canadian Academy of Arts exhibition and received his first solo exhibition there in 1921—the same year as the WAG’s purchase of its first FitzGerald for the permanent collection: *Summer Afternoon, The Prairie*, 1921.

Since that date, the WAG has become the primary and comprehensive public repository of FitzGerald’s work. Today, the WAG holds more than a thousand paintings, drawings, prints, and sculptures by the artist. We have been pleased to lend liberally to the current exhibition from our stores, providing a sense of the artist’s process that will be a revelation to audiences both here at home and beyond.

It is also noteworthy that FitzGerald played an integral role in growing the WAG collection in other significant ways. Beginning in 1924, he taught at the museum-run Winnipeg School of Art—the predecessor of today’s WAG Studio Programs. FitzGerald became principal in 1929, resigning twenty years later, in 1949. It was during his tenure at the School of Art that he, through his connections to his contemporaries, secured some of the earliest and most notable examples of Canadian art in the WAG collection today, including Lawren Harris’s *Lake McArthur, Rocky Mountains*, c. 1925; Emily Carr’s *Tree*

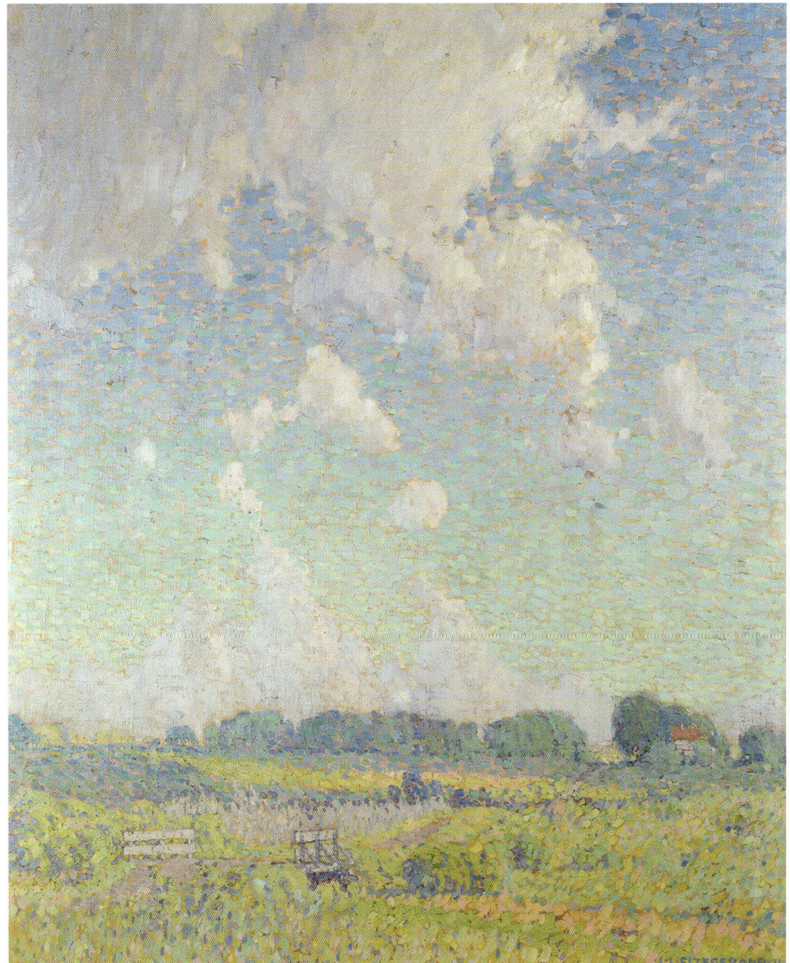

Summer Afternoon, The Prairie, 1921
oil on canvas
107.2 × 89.5 cm

Movement, 1937–38; and Bertram Brooker's *Sounds Assembling*, 1928. We remain in his debt for these important contributions to the development of the gallery.

The Winnipeg Art Gallery has staged fifteen solo exhibitions of FitzGerald's work—some in partnership with sister institutions such as the Vancouver Art Gallery, the National Gallery of Canada, and now the McMichael Canadian Art Collection. The last major FitzGerald survey was organized by the WAG in 1978. Now, more than forty years later, we have the opportunity to rethink and reappreciate FitzGerald's legacy in advancing modern art in Canada. The presentation of this exhibition in Winnipeg also coincides with the 150th anniversary of the Province of Manitoba and its entry into Confederation.

On behalf of the Winnipeg Art Gallery, I extend warm thanks and congratulations to Ian A.C. Dejardin, Executive Director of the McMichael Canadian Art Collection, and to Sarah Milroy, the McMichael's Chief Curator, as well as to Michael Parke-Taylor, for their intelligent reassessment of the art of L.L. FitzGerald. I also recognize Andrew Kear, former WAG Head of Collections and Exhibitions, now Head of Collections, Exhibitions and Programs at Museum London, for his important scholarly contributions and the role he took to make this exhibition a true partnership between the WAG and the McMichael. Finally, I would like to express my appreciation to our gallery teams in Winnipeg and Kleinburg for their professionalism and their dedication to this exhibition. ■

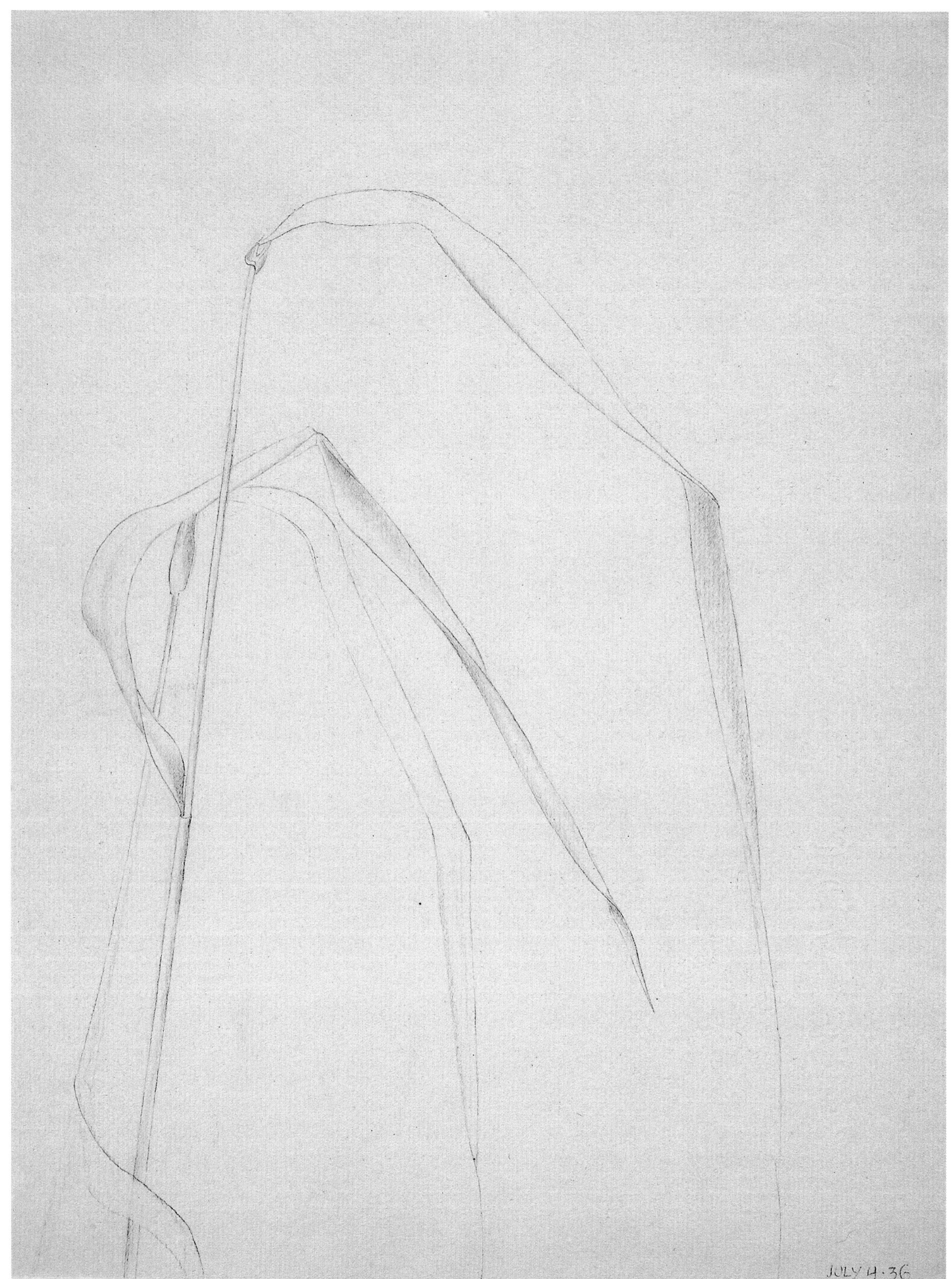
JULY 4 · 36

INTO THE LIGHT

SARAH MILROY

Let's start with two blades of grass. In this 1936 drawing by Lionel LeMoine FitzGerald, the slender leaves lift upward from a joint stem, the humblest of growing things. And yet, looking at them through the eyes of the artist, we pause to reconsider them, to see them for what they are: something exquisite, something elegantly expressive of both growth and decay, the blades reaching sunward, then delicately collapsing in entropy, the subtle crisp of desiccation setting in. FitzGerald famously said that a work of art is "a living thing," and here we catch his meaning as we witness the exploratory glide of his pencil on the paper, defining form, generating the tension between the subject and the space around it.

My colleague Ian Dejardin and I had seen many paintings and drawings by FitzGerald by the time I came face to face with this one. Our research had taken us through the collections of the Winnipeg Art Gallery, the Art Gallery of Ontario, the Vancouver Art Gallery, and numerous private collections across the country. But it was this drawing, seen in a light-filled viewing room at the National Gallery of Canada, that took my breath away. Outside the windows that morning the snow was blowing across the grey winter vista below, but here in front of me was life itself, the surging force of growth and change that was always fascinating to the artist.

Two Blades of Grass, 1936
graphite on laid paper
31.1 × 24 cm

As I think about FitzGerald's *Two Blades of Grass* now, more than a year later, several connections come to mind. What could be simpler and more quintessentially of the prairie than a blade of grass, and what more reflective of an artist celebrated for his ability to convey his connection to that pared-down, sky-canopied world? "Subconsciously the prairie and the skies get into most things I do no matter how abstracted they may be," FitzGerald wrote in 1954 to his friend Robert Ayre. "Occasionally," he continued, "I get out on the prairie just to wander and look, without making any notes other than mental ones

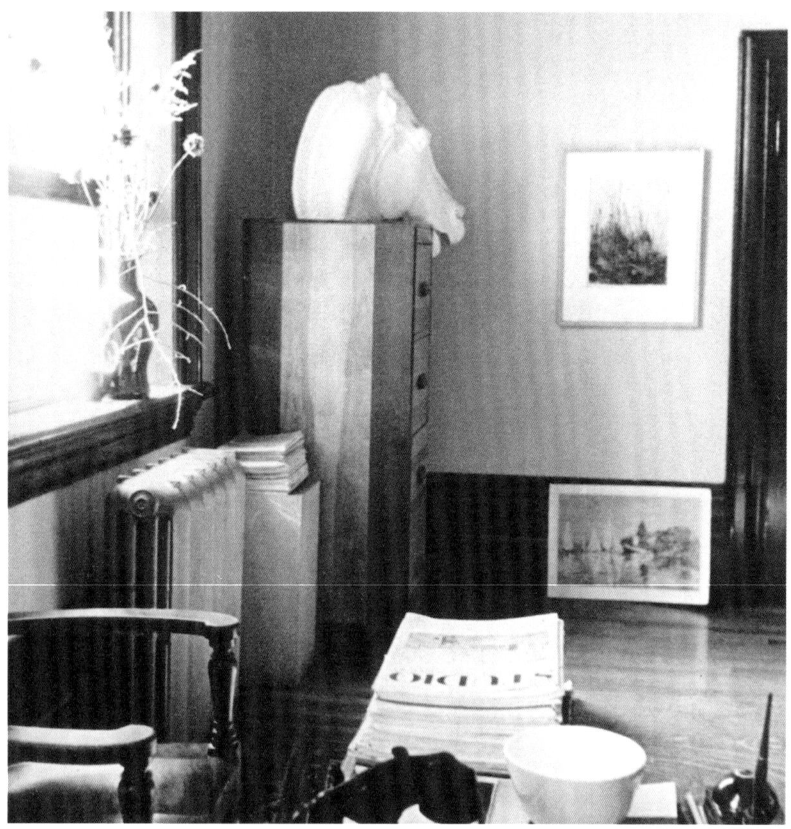

and always come back with an inner warmth from the familiar but always new feeling. Never a highly emotional reaction, just a sort of quiet contentment. And all this finally penetrates the drawings."[1]

Beyond its regional resonance, though, the drawing also reminds me of how FitzGerald kept a large reproduction of Albrecht Dürer's watercolour *The Great Piece of Turf*, 1503, framed on the wall of his office at the Winnipeg School of Art, a hyper-realized description of a hunk of sod sprouting grasses and weeds and a hymn to the wonder of the world at our (usually) heedless heel. In FitzGerald's office it kept company with a plaster cast of a horse's head from the Parthenon, a model of an Egyptian standing figure, and a reproduction of Claude Monet's *Regattas at Argenteuil*, c. 1872. In around 1939 FitzGerald posed for several photographs in this carefully constructed office-scenario, once with a book on Cézanne open before him (p. 14). In the view of his office here, a pile of back issues of *The Studio* is seen stacked on his desk—the source of much of his information on current art in Europe and the United States. I see these pictures now as documenting an act of self-portraiture by the artist. In creating these arrangements, he paid homage to the currents that flowed into his art, staking out his territory within both the history of art and the flow of time.

The drawing also reminds me that excerpts from Walt Whitman's *Leaves of Grass* were read aloud at FitzGerald's funeral—the words of the nineteenth-century American poet-sage who exalted nature and humankind's place within it in his rapturous verses. FitzGerald was a lover of poetry, and his archive at the University of Manitoba holds many clippings of verse by the British Romantic poets, particularly William Blake, with whom he also felt a special bond—so much so that he helped to curate an exhibition of Blake's etchings and drawings at the Winnipeg Art Gallery in 1942. In the same archive one finds FitzGerald's hardcover copy of the *Songs of Innocence*, inscribed inside by his artistic soulmate, Bertram Brooker: "To Lemoine [*sic*] in mutual reverence for Blake." In his "Auguries of Innocence," Blake famously invites his reader "To see a World in a Grain of Sand / And a Heaven in a Wild Flower / Hold Infinity in the palm of your hand . . ." Seeing nature's macrocosm in the microcosmic was a feature of FitzGerald's vision as well. These blades of grass speak of that same devotion to the tiniest gestures of the life force and its mysteries. Along with Turner, Ruskin, and Constable—beloved by FitzGerald for the atmospheric effects they achieved in paint and, in the case of Ruskin, for his close observation of nature—Blake served FitzGerald as a kind of thought companion across the ages.

Where does this kind of sensitivity and receptivity come from? After all, the Winnipeg he was born into was no fertile ground for budding aesthetes. Solace perhaps came from the soil itself. His boyhood was punctuated by summer visits to his grandmother's farm in Snowflake, Manitoba, near the US border, where he would spend long, unsupervised days exploring and dreaming in her barns and fields. He would look back on these happy months as the overture to his artistic life.

Work as an office boy in a Winnipeg brokerage firm and then as a commercial artist in an advertising firm led to his connection with artists who had been touched by Impressionism before their arrival in the city. Among them were Donald Macquarrie, Mary Ewart, and Augustus Vincent Tack, under whom he apprenticed, helping the older American artist to complete and install the murals for the Manitoba Legislative Building in 1920. Love came to this handsome and shy young man in the form of Felicia (Vally) Wright, a professional soprano whom he married in 1912, though their lack of emotional attunement would take its toll in the years to come.

A decade later he embarked for a short spell at the Art Students League of New York, an episode of conscientious study described by Andrew Kear in his essay on FitzGerald's early career for this publication. FitzGerald referred to this interlude as a "sudden jolt into everything,"[2] as he absorbed the work of the American Precisionist painters Charles Demuth and Charles Sheeler and the legacies of French modernism, particularly the work of Cézanne. The years that followed, though, were spent almost entirely in his hometown of Winnipeg, teaching and then leading the Winnipeg School of Art (1929 to 1949). Just one major trip during those teaching years, in 1930—a journey chronicled by Michael Parke-Taylor here—interrupted his embedded devotion to Manitoba.

Still, for all his staid commitment to work and home (he and Vally had a son and a daughter, Edward and Patricia), life would throw him curveballs. His student Irene Heywood, who later moved to Toronto and married the songwriter Wade Hemsworth, became his platonic love interest in the 1930s, their friendship finally evolving into a full-blown love affair in 1939, a relationship referenced in the essays here by Oliver Botar and Robert Enright. From his letters to Heywood, now housed in Library and Archives Canada, Ottawa, we can clearly see an eroticism unleashed that had previously emerged only in his art—principally in his depictions of trees and plants, as several writers in this volume note. The end of this affair precipitated a crisis that was resolved only in FitzGerald's immersion in the mystical landscapes of British Columbia in the 1940s and a new embrace of his own physical vitality. Like the Group of Seven's Lawren Harris and Frederick Varley, FitzGerald seems to have felt most fully alive on the West Coast, and his free flight into abstraction soon followed as he opened himself to new realms of experimentation.

In a way, FitzGerald's career is emblematic of a generation of Canadian pioneers who stood up for art as a sophisticated and serious undertaking—a pursuit requiring education, and worthy as an end in itself—in a settler culture that was still crude and mercenary. One thinks of the struggles of Emily Carr to be understood and to find

FitzGerald's office, c. 1939
Copies of *The Studio* are stacked on his desk, and in the background can be seen a plaster cast of a horse's head from the Parthenon and reproductions of *The Great Piece of Turf*, 1503, by Albrecht Dürer (Albertina, Vienna) and *Regattas at Argenteuil*, c. 1872, by Claude Monet (Musée d'Orsay, Paris)

her place in Victoria, British Columbia. Though the two appear never to have met, Carr and FitzGerald shared a love of poetry, a great facility with language, and an erotically charged experience of the natural world. (A dog-eared copy of her memoir *Klee Wyck* can be found in his archive.) Both artists also had a transformative visit to New York City in the summer of 1930, and I imagine them brushing past each other in Alfred Stieglitz's gallery 291, where the famous dealer of modern art was displaying the sexually charged Black Orchid paintings of Georgia O'Keeffe, or in the galleries of the Roerich Museum on 103rd Street and Riverside Drive, a mecca for artists drawn to then-current discussions of spirituality in art. (He would make a quick sketch of its exterior.)

There are similarities to be explored, as well, with David Milne, who holed himself up in his cabin—whether at Bishop's Pond, Baptiste Lake, or Temagami—the better to pursue his disciplined aesthetic program and tend to his musings on art and art history. Notwithstanding that FitzGerald held a public position for decades—a situation that would have been entirely untenable for Milne—both artists were bookish and somewhat introverted by nature, often revisiting their theories on art in draft after draft, or describing in vivid detail their experiences of the natural world. As Geoffrey James writes in his essay here, FitzGerald was an artist's artist, never quite receiving his due in his day. He would no doubt be moved to read the appreciations here by James, Wanda Koop, Robert Houle, and Pierre Dorion, artists from all parts of Canada who now hear the call of his enchanting works. This is a legacy that still lives and breathes.

Like Milne, FitzGerald stood apart from the apparatus of nation building extolled by the Group of Seven and their followers. FitzGerald became a member of the Group in 1932, largely due to his close professional affiliation with Lawren Harris, who took an interest in his work and his thought. But FitzGerald subtly distinguished himself from them when he quoted the Russian novelist Leo Tolstoy: "The feelings with which the artist infects others may be most various . . . feelings of love for native land, self devotion and submission to fate or to God expressed in a drama, raptures of lovers described in a novel, feelings of voluptuousness expressed in a picture."[3] The latter phrase perhaps describes his own calling, the first one the calling of the Group.

For both Milne and FitzGerald, the task of nation building had nothing to do with art, and the intimate subtlety of their modernism would result in their relative obscurity, perhaps even now. FitzGerald's is a quiet art, more akin to the more contemporary work of Jack Chambers than to that of the Group of Seven's A.Y. Jackson. The miracle of light falling on the textures of the windowsill, or on fruit in a bowl, or caressing the curve of a white metal jug, the billowing volumes of cloud becoming sky, the sheer geometries of a Winnipeg backyard under snow, or the dazzle of leaves blowing in the wind on the road to Snowflake—these are the epiphanies we look to FitzGerald for. And look we will in the pages that follow. ■

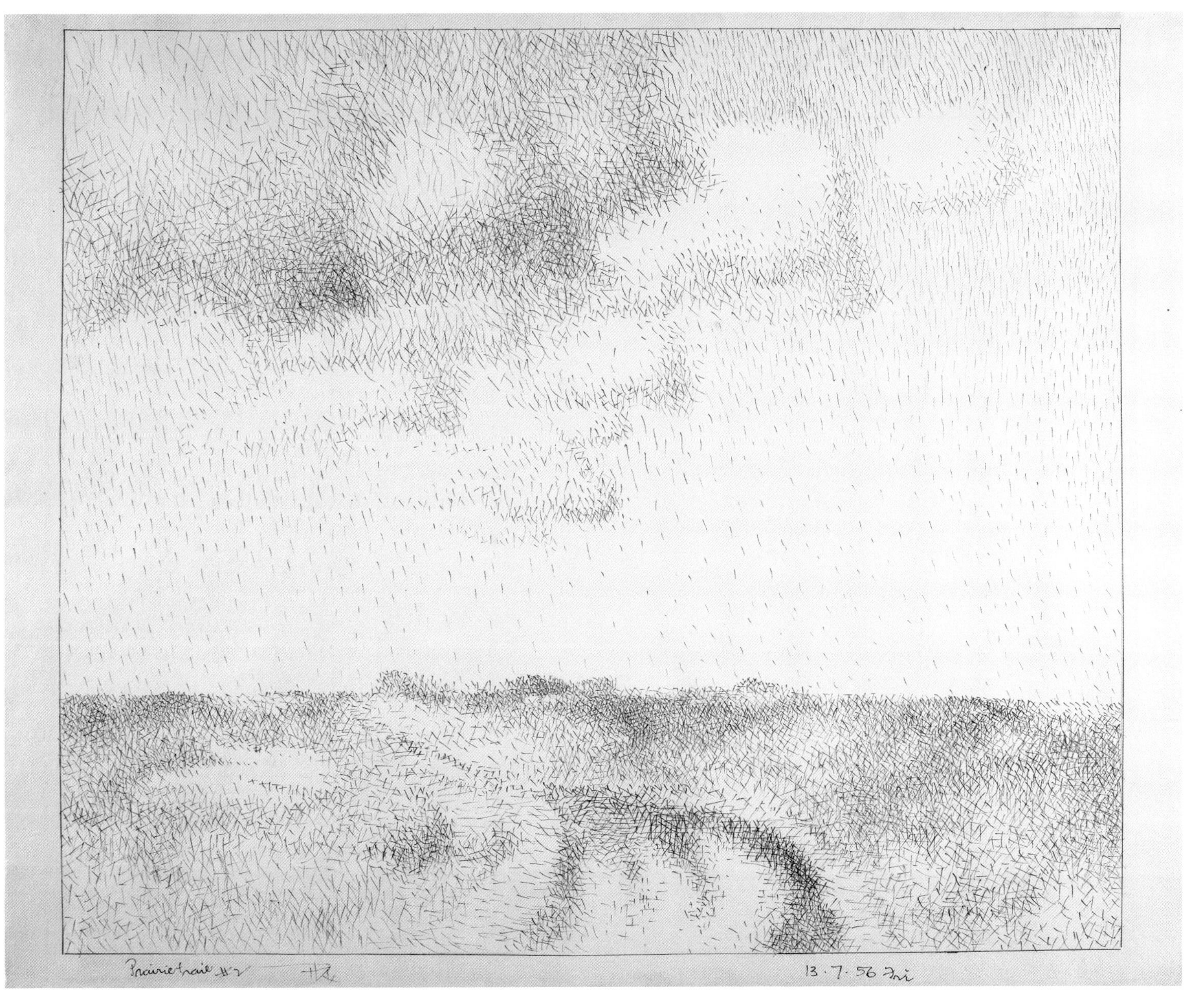

Prairie Trail
No. 2, 1956
ink on paper
45.7 × 57.1 cm;
image: 43 × 50.5 cm

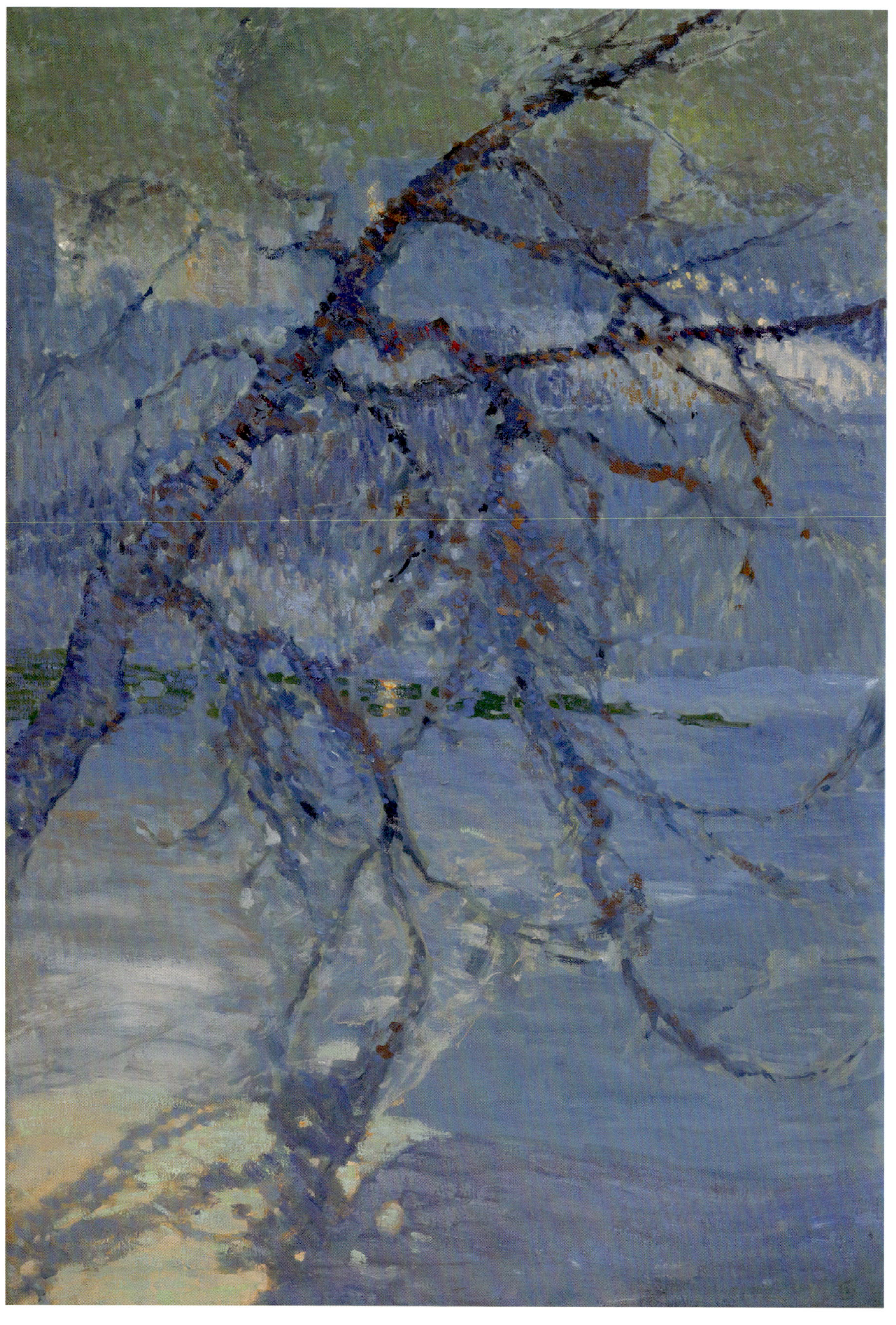

AN ART OF ADAPTATION

Rethinking FitzGerald's Early Career

ANDREW KEAR

Evening, The Red River, Winnipeg, c. 1920
oil on canvas
133.7 × 93.1 cm

Lionel LeMoine FitzGerald is often remembered as the "Painter of the Prairies," an artist who "found what he wanted in his own backyard."[1] At first glance, the characterization appears justified. During his lifetime, the Winnipegger never left continental American soil and rarely set foot outside Manitoba. FitzGerald held a deep affection for the subtle qualities of his home, its "intense light and feeling of great space," and the prairie features prominently in his work.[2]

What captivated him about "his own backyard," however, was not directly related to his regional loyalties. FitzGerald painted the prairies because he believed close observation of the details of the natural world to be the artist's essential starting point. The "study of nature" was the necessary raw material of creative expression through which artists, wherever they happen to live and whatever their subject matter, conceive and realize the work of art. As a mature artist, FitzGerald described a painting as an expression of something universal and ideational, "a living thing," "one great thought made up of many details . . . subordinate to the whole," a physical manifestation of artists' vision—of "what [they] have to say."[3] Even while its pictorial content is often grounded in the local, FitzGerald's work is never really about backyards.

Commentators, including FitzGerald himself, generally align the beginning of his artistic development with the time he spent studying at the Art Students League of New York between December 1921 and the end of March 1922.[4] His month-long tour of American art museums and institutions a decade later is generally seen to have rounded off his journey to artistic maturity. For all the celebration of his regional insularity, then, the consensus has held that the "Painter of the Prairies" achieved artistic significance by leaving home. However, a closer look reveals that FitzGerald's artistic interests were already informed by international influences prior to 1921, with the artist assimilating international ideas and inspiration as early as his teens.

FitzGerald's early career remains underexamined, with most commentators regarding the work of that period as superficial, derivative, and formulaic, albeit well received. As the critic Robert Ayre summarized, the artist "painted quickly and easily, developing a breezy Impressionism. People liked it and FitzGerald might have slipped into a formula and become a popular painter. But he wasn't satisfied. It was too easy. It had nothing to do with the thing inside that was struggling for expression."[5]

However, the work FitzGerald produced between 1915 and 1921 should be seen as important in itself and vital to an understanding of his later career. The significance resides not so much in the stylistic vocabulary of the work—Impressionism "employed without training"—but rather in how the untravelled and inexperienced artist behaved and coped in response to his local environment, making use of limited resources in the effort to expand his artistic knowledge and understanding.[6] Far from being simply a formulaic rehash, the self-described "hit and miss method" of FitzGerald's early career laid the groundwork for his later career, offering a fascinating case study of creative adaptation.[7]

FitzGerald was a devoted autodidact, his habit of mind established early on. In 1905, for example, just one year after the fifteen-year-old left public school, FitzGerald discovered John Ruskin's *Elements of Drawing* (1857) at Winnipeg's first public book-lending institution, the newly opened Carnegie Library on William Avenue. This book provided FitzGerald with practical guidance: "Here I had something definite, a plan of study, that might lead me into the way of doing things that promised possibilities in the future."[8] However, Ruskin dispenses much more than technical advice. *Elements* aimed to develop the aesthetic feelings and judgments of its reader. In the author's words, it provides "a delicate method of work such as may ensure [a student's] seeing truly" so "pupils may learn to love Nature" and not merely how to draw.[9]

Elements famously advances a theory of perception that begins with the raw empirical observation that "everything that you can see, in the world around you, presents itself to your eyes only as an arrangement of patches of different colour variously shaded." For Ruskin, "[t]he whole technical power of painting depends on our recovery of what may be called the innocence of the eye; that is to say, a sort of childish perception of these flat stains of colour, merely as such, without consciousness of what they signify, as a blind man would see them if suddenly gifted with sight."[10]

The American art critic and essayist Jonathan Crary points to Ruskin's "innocent eye," and to what Crary calls the theory's "primal opticality" as a harbinger of a modern vision witnessed in the painting of "Cézanne, Monet and others," paintings that would "[claim] for the eye a vantage point uncluttered by the weight of historical codes and conventions of seeing."[11] Indeed, it is a short step from the imperative to perceive the world as "flat stains of colour" to rendering the world that way in paint.

Although *Elements* was not translated into French in the nineteenth century, some artists in France were familiar with the publication by the 1880s. Ruskin's contention that "breaking one colour in small points through or over another is the most important of all processes in good modern... painting" was quoted by the American physicist Ogden Rood in *Modern Chromatics* (1879), a book embraced by the French art critic Félix Fénéon and the Neo-Impressionists after its translation in 1881.[12] One such painter, Paul Signac, expressed unalloyed admiration for *Elements* in several articles he wrote in 1898 for *La Revue blanche* and in his book *D'Eugène Delacroix au néo-impressionnisme.*[13] Even Monet, the patriarch of French Impressionism, is reported to have quoted Ruskin almost verbatim, stating that "he wished he had been born blind and then suddenly gained his sight so that he could have begun to paint in this way without knowing what the objects were that he saw before him."[14]

Ruskin was largely unfamiliar with modern French painting, and it is highly probable (given his antipathy to James McNeill Whistler's work) that he would have rejected Impressionism for its apparent concern for "life's visible surfaces" at the expense of "moral depth."[15] Nonetheless, in addition to providing FitzGerald with "a plan of study," Ruskin's *Elements* offered the young artist a possible way of understanding late nineteenth-century French painting.

FitzGerald was also exposed early on to modern artistic theories and to black-and-white reproductions of contemporary painting found in art periodicals of the day. His personal archive includes dozens of clipped articles and images, most of them taken from *The Studio*, a London-based magazine, and its American subsidiary, *The International Studio*. By 1914, *The Studio* had reproduced work by Manet, Monet, Pissarro, Degas, Cézanne, Cassatt, and Morisot. In *The International Studio*, American critics such as Willard Huntington Wright and Christian Brinton offered positive responses to leading international and American art. In March 1913, for instance, canvases by Van Gogh, Cézanne, and Gauguin appeared on pages alongside Brinton's informed discussion of Impressionism, Neo-Impressionism, Post-Impressionism, and Fauvism. His positive assessment of the modernist innovations he witnessed at the Armory Show of 1913, published a month later, drew special attention to the Cubist works: "call it optical music, emotional mathematics, or by whatever term you choose, the production of Picasso, Picabia, Braque, Duchamp and their colleagues cannot be dismissed as mere ingenious or impertinent pleasantry."[16] Wright's reviews from 1916 and 1917 single out, among others, John Marin, Max Weber, and Marsden Hartley, with the writer reproducing a pair of Cézannesque still lifes by Henry Lee McFee and Wright's brother (and co-founder of Synchromism), Stanton MacDonald-Wright.[17]

Of course, the mere fact that Ruskin may have provided FitzGerald the conceptual means through which to fully understand Impressionism or Neo-Impressionism does not mean FitzGerald necessarily did so. Neither did FitzGerald's reading of *The Studio* necessarily provide him with a thorough appreciation of the ideas then propelling the modern avant-garde. It's worth noting also that between 1910 and 1920 the majority of reproductions in *The International Studio* were of relatively conservative canvases by the American Impressionists and the Ashcan realists, among them Childe Hassam and George Bellows, respectively. This preponderance may explain FitzGerald's relatively conservative stylistic proclivities at the time, seen in works such as *Late Fall, Manitoba*, 1917 (p. 10), the first FitzGerald painting acquired by the National Gallery of Canada in 1918. It is also safe to argue that he was at least aware of both Neo- and Post-Impressionism in the 1910s through the writings of Brinton, Wright, and others.

Less than three years after discovering *Elements*, FitzGerald enrolled in local evening

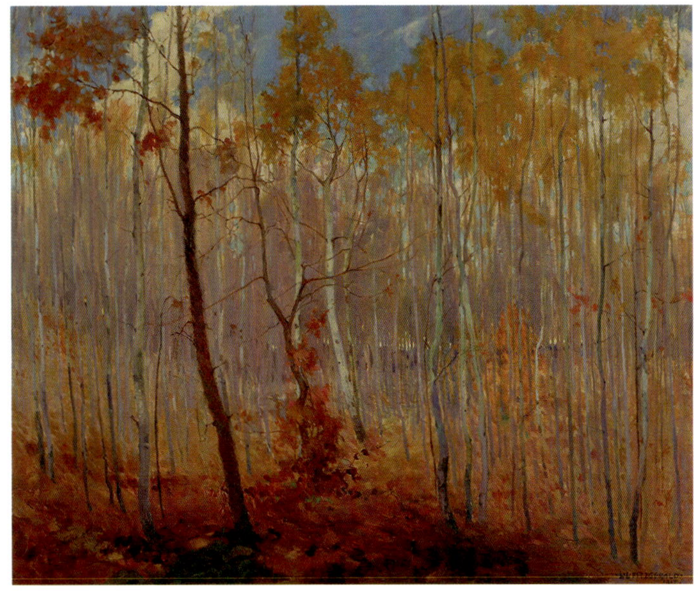

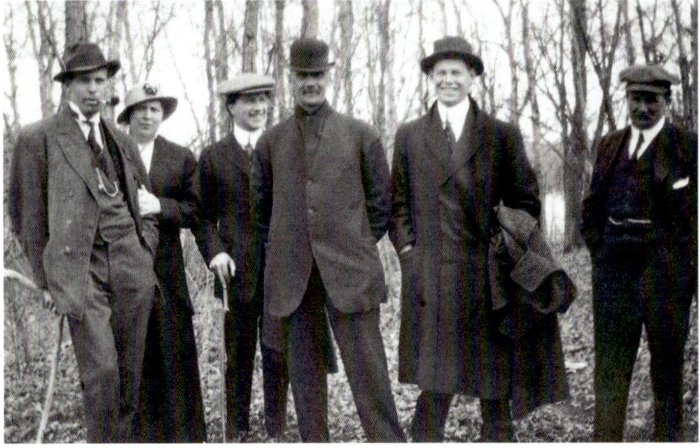

TOP
Late Fall, Manitoba, 1917
oil on canvas
76.7 × 91.7 cm

BOTTOM
L.L. FitzGerald, Mary Ewart, Arnold O. Brigden, Donald Macquarrie, F.H. Brigden, and an unidentified man at Sturgeon Creek, c. 1915
Lionel LeMoine FitzGerald fonds, PC 241 (A2009-016), / Box 1, Folder 12
University of Manitoba Archives & Special Collections, Winnipeg

art classes with Alexander Keszthelyi, who had taught at the Carnegie Institute in Pittsburgh.[18] While Keszthelyi's impact remains unclear, FitzGerald painted outdoors with oils for the first time under the Hungarian expatriate's instruction.[19] Another mentor who encouraged the young artist was the painter Mary Ewart (née Clay). The Philadelphian had studied with the American Impressionist William Merritt Chase in the 1890s,[20] and possibly with Whistler and John Singer Sargent.[21]

A third person provided FitzGerald with a technical understanding of early modern French painting: Donald Macquarrie, a Scottish artist working in the manner of Jean-Baptiste-Camille Corot. He arrived in Winnipeg in 1910 and served as the first curator of the civic art museum, opened in 1912. Macquarrie exhibited and shared a studio with FitzGerald and introduced the younger artist to monotype and *cliché verre* printmaking before leaving the city around 1914. Macquarrie's Barbizon school influence—inspiration taken from nature—is apparent in early canvases such as an untitled 1915 landscape that bears close similarities to the older artist's *Landscape with Crescent Moon*, 1913 (p. 11)—a painting that FitzGerald acquired for his personal collection.

Perhaps the most sympathetic modern painter FitzGerald encountered at this time was Augustus Tack. The American artist—whose work FitzGerald may have had prior familiarity with through *The International Studio*—arrived in Winnipeg in May 1920 to oversee the installation of his mural *Allegory of Law* in the dome of the Legislative Chamber at the newly constructed provincial Legislative Building.[22] FitzGerald worked as Tack's installation assistant in May and June. While Tack's commissioned work was conventional—allegorical depictions of Justice, Wisdom, and Knowledge—his studio interests and pursuits demonstrated a keen awareness and understanding of modern trends. Having studied under John Twachtman in New York, visited Monet at Giverny, and steeped himself in both French and American varieties of Impressionism since the mid-1880s, Tack by the early 1920s was moving decisively toward abstraction.[23] FitzGerald was clearly inspired by the man, if not exactly influenced by his work. Although FitzGerald acknowledged in his 1930 travel diary that he and Tack were not "by any means affinities," the fact that the two men reunited a decade later in New York suggests they had more in common than simply the provincial mural contract.[24]

FitzGerald was also able to develop an understanding of Impressionist and, to some degree, Post-Impressionist painting techniques indirectly, through periodic access to the canvases of Ontario- and Quebec-based artists who had trained in Europe and the United States. At the Winnipeg Museum of Fine Arts (today the Winnipeg Art Gallery), paintings by Florence Carlyle, William Clapp, Laura Muntz, Maurice Cullen, Helen McNicoll, Marc-Aurèle de Foy Suzor-Coté, and William Brymner appeared in touring exhibitions mounted by the Royal Canadian Academy of Arts and the Ontario Society of Artists. The offerings of younger, more stylistically daring artists such as A.Y. Jackson, Arthur Lismer, and Kathleen Munn were also displayed during the art museum's first decade. In 1912, FitzGerald had been invited to present a landscape painting in the RCA exhibition that opened the museum. By 1921, following his first solo exhibition there, FitzGerald was being lauded as a self-made Impressionist. "L.L. FitzGerald. Winnipeg's native son," reads one exhibition brochure, "whose studies have

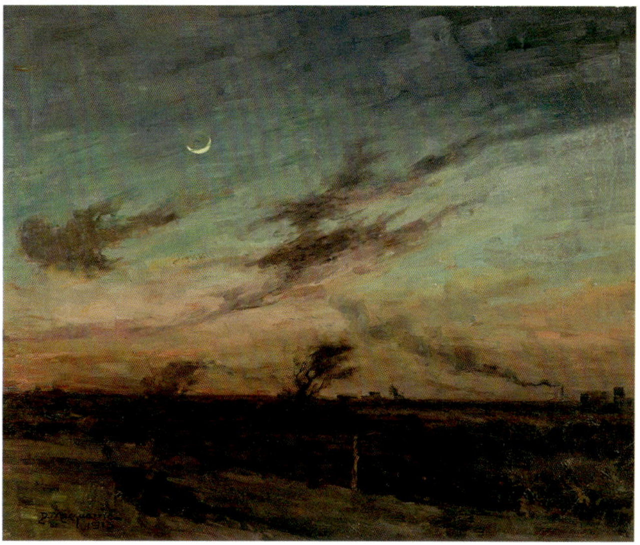

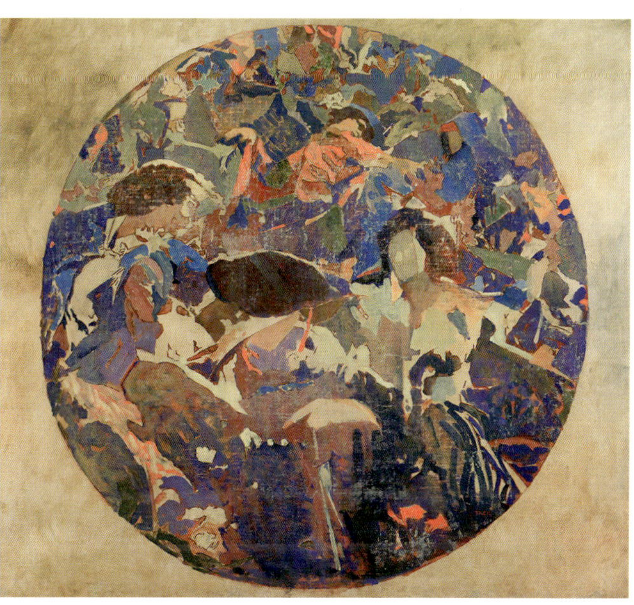

TOP
DONALD MACQUARRIE (1872–after 1934)
Landscape with Crescent Moon, 1913
oil on canvas
50.4 × 61.3 cm
Gift of Mrs. Hugh Morrison
Collection of the Winnipeg Art Gallery / G-64-22 / Photo: Lianed Marcoleta, courtesy of the Winnipeg Art Gallery

BOTTOM
AUGUSTUS VINCENT TACK (1870–1949)
Passacaglia, between 1922 and 1923
oil on canvas on plywood panel
111.44 × 126.37 cm
Acquired 1924 / The Phillips Collection, Washington, DC

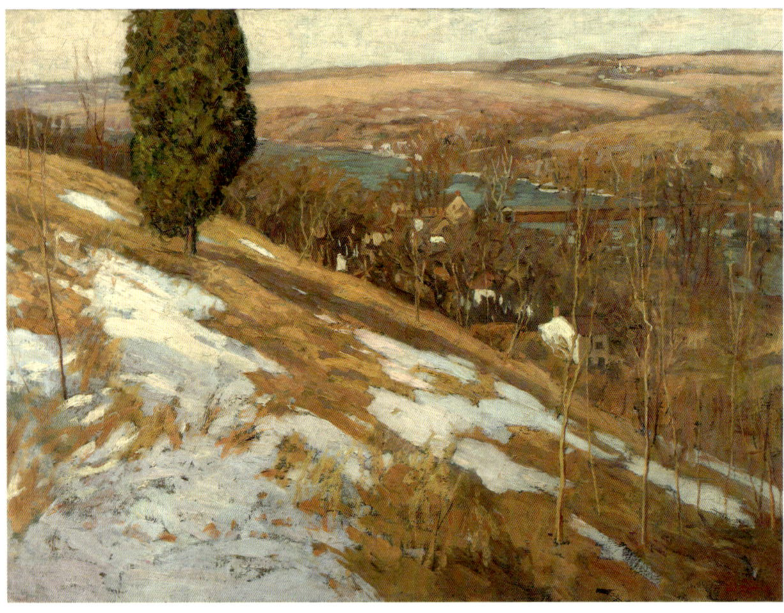

TOP
EDWARD WILLIS REDFIELD (1869–1965)
Centre Bridge, 1904
oil on canvas
91.4 × 127 cm
W. Moses Willner Fund / The Art Institute of Chicago 1905.152 / Photo: The Art Institute of Chicago / Art Resource, NY

BOTTOM
CHARLES HAROLD DAVIS (1856–1933)
The Northwest Wind, 1914
oil on canvas
125.7 × 100.3 cm
Walter H. Schulze Memorial Collection / The Art Institute of Chicago / 124.907
Photo: The Art Institute of Chicago / Art Resource, NY

been greatly to his own credit. He specializes in the painting of light."[25]

FitzGerald's Impressionism may have been "self-made," but it was not entirely homemade. In addition to his reading and his contact with informed fellow artists and their works, the young artist travelled at least twice to Chicago before 1921. The first trip saw him staying with relatives between roughly August 16 and October 26, 1910. Family correspondence and a civic promotion pamphlet found in FitzGerald's personal archive, titled *Citadels of Commerce* (c. 1909–10), suggest that he was lured by the prospect of securing a job in commercial art.[26] He returned to Chicago a decade later but stayed only a week, between approximately January 10 and 17, 1920.[27]

Given his tendency to pursue knowledge wherever he could find it, it is safe to assume that FitzGerald visited the Art Institute of Chicago on both occasions. Although Monet, Pissarro, and Sisley were shown in Chicago as early as 1888, the AIC's holdings of major European Impressionist and Post-Impressionist works did not begin taking shape until 1926, with the acquisition of the Helen Birch Bartlett Memorial Collection.[28] However, canvases abounded by American Impressionists such as Twachtman, Hassam, Chase, and Cassatt. In both 1910 and 1920, FitzGerald would have had opportunity to see Edward Redfield's *Centre Bridge*, 1904. The painting was acquired by the AIC in 1905 and placed on permanent display between 1910 and 1920.[29] A second American Impressionist canvas that FitzGerald likely saw during his 1920 trip was *The Northwest Wind*, 1914, by Charles Davis. This work was in the "possession" of the AIC (but not formally acquired until 1924), and although no checklist exists, it was very probably installed in the exhibition *Paul Schulze Collection*

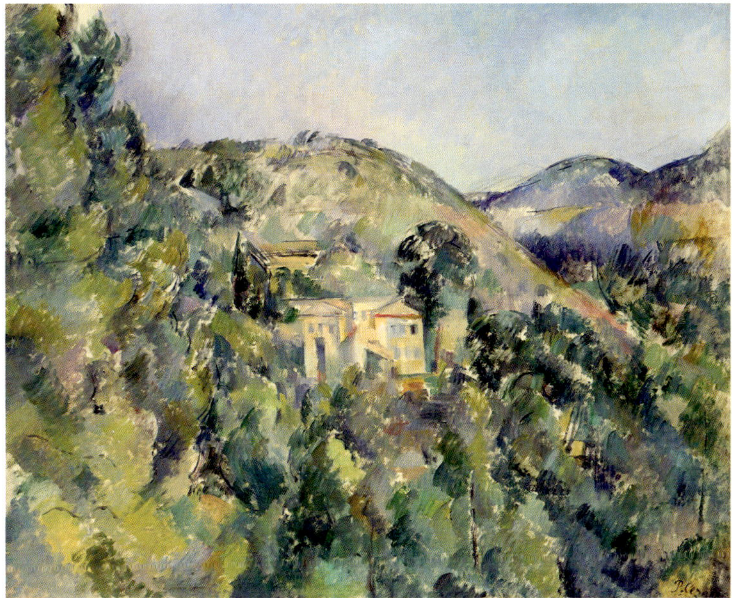

PAUL CÉZANNE
(1839–1906)
View of the Domaine Saint-Joseph, late 1880s
oil on canvas
65.1 × 81.3 cm
Catharine Lorillard Wolfe Collection, Wolfe Fund, 1913
The Metropolitan Museum of Art, New York / 13.66
Photo: Malcolm Varon
Image copyright © The Metropolitan Museum of Art.
Image source: Art Resource, NY

of Paintings, on display between January and March 1920.[30]

The Redfield and Davis paintings are significant for their compositional similarities to a pair of FitzGerald's canvases that would soon follow. Like *The Northwest Wind*, FitzGerald's *Summer Afternoon, The Prairie* (originally know as *The Prairie, Summer*), 1921 (p. ix), is a landscape with an unconventional vertical orientation and a radically lowered horizon, which directs the viewer's attention toward the ephemeral play of summer clouds. A later, post-Art Students League canvas, *Pembina Valley*, 1923 (p. 57), hints at the new, more formal direction his painting would take in the 1920s, yet its stacked arrangement of landscape features and clouds, with a bare tree or two in the foreground, reveals a similar Japonism to that found in Redfield's *Centre Bridge*.

The response to FitzGerald's first solo exhibition at the Winnipeg Art Gallery, in 1921, provided a clear indication that he had achieved a considerable local following. He sold eighteen works, including *Summer Afternoon, The Prairie*, to the WAG for $300. The income provided him with the financial means to begin studying later that year at New York City's Art Students League, a school likely recommended by League alumnus Augustus Tack.[31] The ASL provided FitzGerald with his first formal training and with direct and sustained access to the American Impressionists and Ashcan realists he first encountered in *The Studio* and in the galleries of the Art Institute of Chicago. Of course, he also had direct access to the museums of New York, specifically the Metropolitan Museum of Art's growing Post-Impressionist collection particularly Paul Cézanne's *View of the Domaine Saint-Joseph*, late 1880s, the first and, at the time, lone work by the French modernist to enter a public collection in the United States.[32]

FitzGerald's exposure to modern art was not

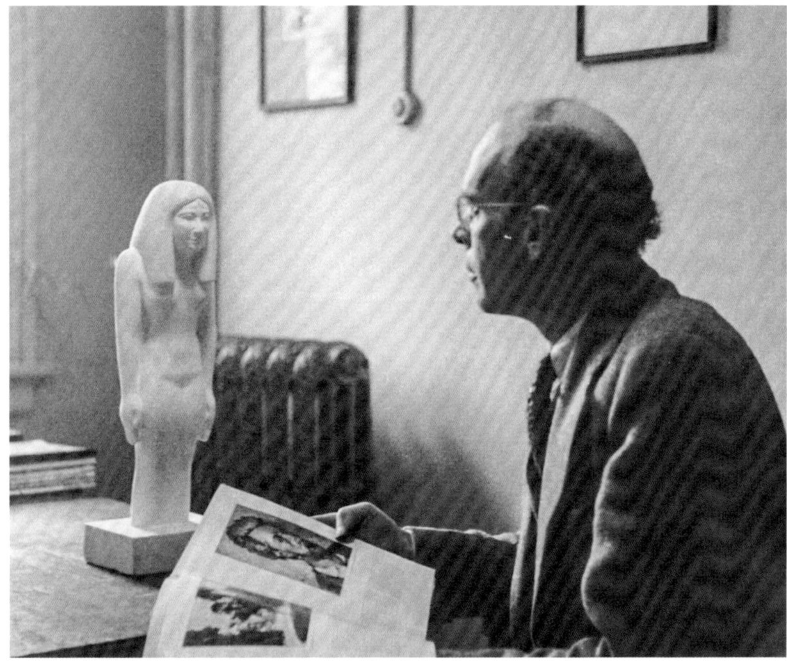

FitzGerald, c. 1939, holding a book open to a reproduction of Cézanne's portrait of Victor Chocquet, c. 1877
Gift of Earl and Patsy Green from the Estate of Patricia Morrison / School of Art Gallery, University of Manitoba, Winnipeg / 1-0316

limited to the Met. He could well have taken in the *Exhibition of Paintings by French Cubists and Post Impressionists* at the Wanamaker Gallery of Modern and Decorative Arts during the first half of December 1921.[33] It featured work by Picasso, Matisse, Georges Braque, and André Derain, among others. That FitzGerald was aware of the Wanamaker program is confirmed by a brochure in the artist's archives for the *Exhibition of Modern American and European Paintings* in March 1922. In addition to canvases by well-known and emerging European and North American modernists—including Diego Rivera, Charles Sheeler, Charles Demuth, and Maurice de Vlaminck—the brochure lists rare examples of Russian Futurist painting by Mikhail Larionov and Natalia Goncharova, the co-founders of Rayonism.[34]

Back in Winnipeg by the summer of 1922, FitzGerald abandoned Impressionism for "an entirely new angle," one that testified to the impact of his encounter with modernism in New York, especially with the work of Cézanne, as one can see by 1925 in paintings such as *Potato Patch, Snowflake* 1925 (facing).[35] By the 1930s, his style had come to incorporate the American Precisionism of Sheeler and Demuth; and by the 1940s, his subtle abstract canvases revealed Rayonist formal principles, which he had discovered in 1921. Clearly, the New York period was a watershed moment that would have an impact on FitzGerald's vision for decades to come.

After his New York sojourn, FitzGerald could claim not only formal training but direct first-hand exposure to the artistic movements that informed his mature career. Yet our attitude to his earlier approach to art making, forged as it was from the fragmented scraps of second-hand information, should be one of deep curiosity rather than dismissal. Perhaps we are better served to see his work as having been catalyzed by external influences throughout, as he honed his own way of seeing. True, his early understanding and application of Impressionism developed through a struggling, "hit and miss method"—by reading Ruskin and a patchwork of art criticism, listening to the hearsay of expat Europeans and Americans, and examining grey-scale reproductions and the Impressionist-inspired canvases of Canadians who had studied abroad. But today, as information on visual culture largely circulates through print and digital media, we are in a position to assess as never before how FitzGerald's path to artistic maturity may have begun earlier than has previously been supposed, setting him on a lifelong path of learning, reflection, and experimentation. ■

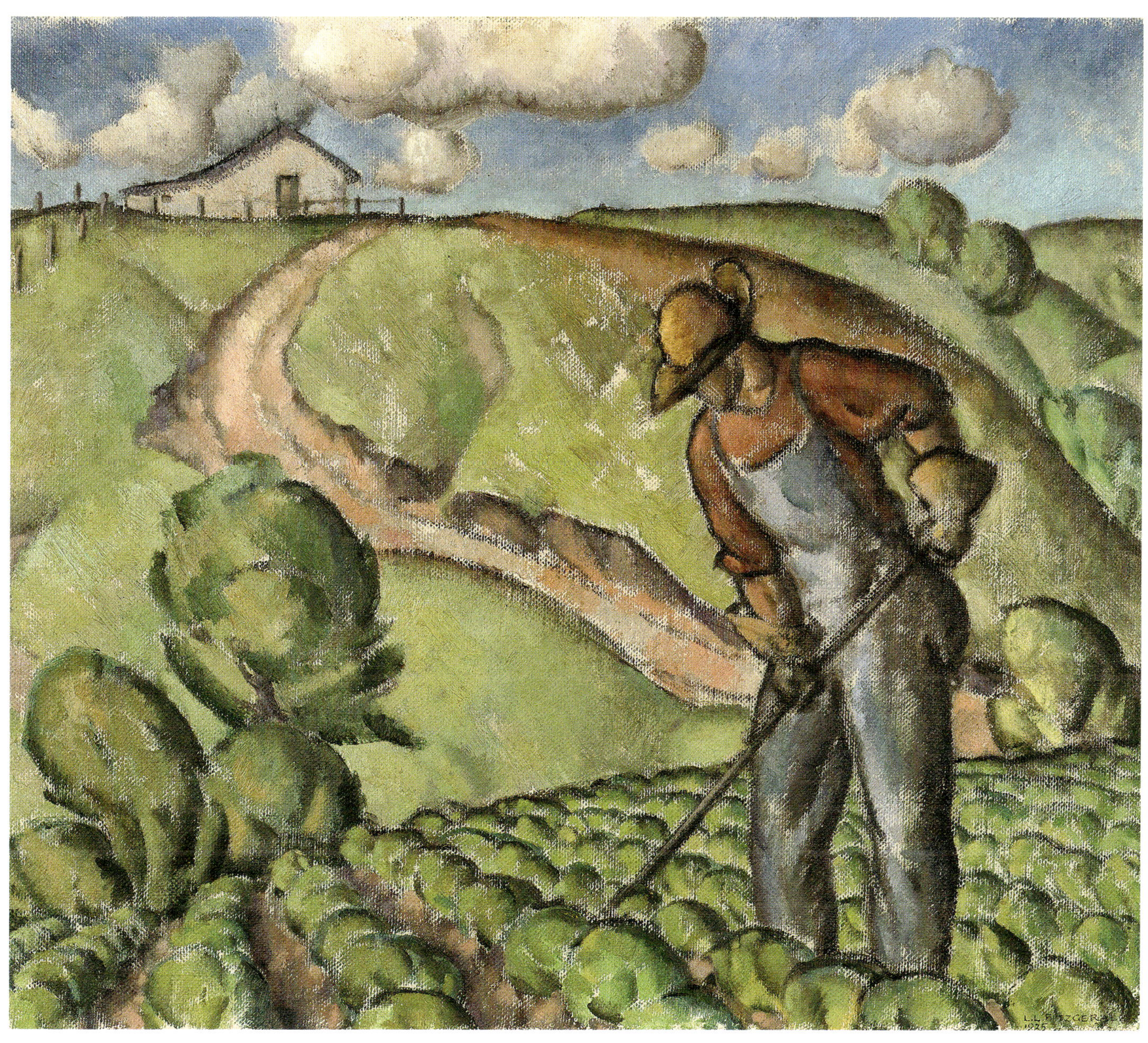

Potato Patch, Snowflake, 1925
oil on canvas on board
43.4 × 52.2 cm

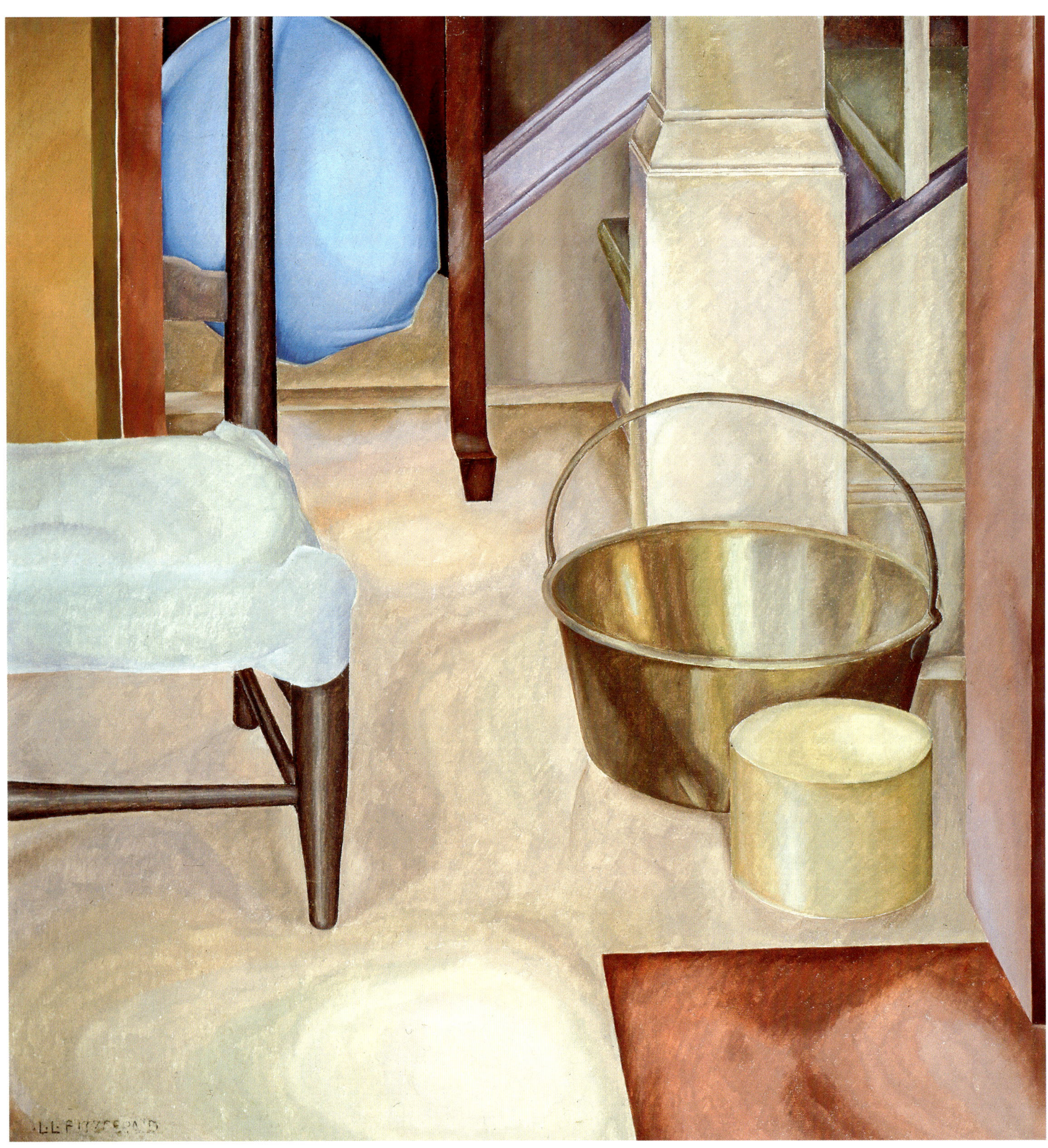

A CANADIAN ARTIST IN AMERICA, 1930
FitzGerald's Travel Diary

MICHAEL PARKE-TAYLOR

"It is indeed a heavy task and means real work and the burning up of much shoe leather."[1] These words, inscribed by Lionel LeMoine FitzGerald in his travel diary, capture the sense of purpose he brought to his month-long excursion to the United States in 1930. The trip was the most extensive travel experience of his professional career, and he made the most of it. In addition to documenting his journey, the diary would also document his aesthetic predilections and ideas about art at a critical moment in his life.

Having taught at the Winnipeg School of Art since 1924, FitzGerald had been appointed principal in the fall of 1929 following the departure of his predecessor, the American artist C. Keith Gebhardt. Despite the harsh economic times following the infamous stock market crash in October 1929, the Winnipeg School of Art still had an enrolment of 296 students in January 1931.[2]

FitzGerald was flourishing as an artist. Having gained a significant reputation among his peers, he was invited by the Group of Seven in 1928 to participate in a solo exhibition in Toronto at the Arts and Letters Club. In 1927 FitzGerald had painted the small but significant *Williamson's Garage* (p. 132), which the Toronto artist Bertram Brooker reproduced in his influential *Yearbook of the Arts in Canada, 1928–1929* and which FitzGerald would see installed in the Grand Central Art Galleries in New York during his 1930 trip.[3] *Pritchard's Fence*, one of the first major pictures of FitzGerald's maturity, was completed in 1928 (p. 137). The following year, he began to paint *Doc Snyder's House*, which would become his best-loved masterpiece when it was finished in 1931 (p. 146). By June 1930, when he embarked on his trip to the United States, the forty-year old FitzGerald was nearing the height of his career. Two years later he was invited to become the final member of the Group of Seven.

It was in the midst of this time of growth and consolidation, in early June 1930, that FitzGerald

Interior with Chair,
c. 1930
oil on canvas
75 × 70 cm

departed from Winnipeg to visit nine major cities in the United States and Eastern Canada. His itinerary included Minneapolis, Chicago, Pittsburgh, Washington, Philadelphia, New York City, Montreal, Ottawa, and Toronto.[4] The twofold purpose of the trip was to investigate the latest developments in art education and to study major works of art in public collections in the United States.

The diary that FitzGerald kept during this trip (now held in the L.L. FitzGerald fonds, University of Manitoba Archives and Special Collections, Winnipeg) chronicles twenty-nine days, starting with his departure for Minneapolis on June 2 and ending in New York on July 1, 1930. His lively pencil entries, written in elegant script, amount to approximately 22,500 words and cover ninety-six journal pages. Composed each evening before FitzGerald went to sleep, the diary entries capture daily events and speak to the artist's extraordinary visual memory and ear for conversation. What makes the timing of FitzGerald's text particularly fortuitous is that it coincides with a key moment in the development of art museums and collections in America. Many of the institutions he visited were either newly opened or had recently installed major collections of Post-Impressionist and early European and American modern art. FitzGerald's diary is thus a valuable document of the way advanced art was received by a Canadian artist in 1930.[5] Moreover, FitzGerald's record of his visits to schools of art in Minneapolis, Chicago, New York City, and Chester Springs, Pennsylvania, underscore what he found noteworthy about current teaching methods and art school facilities in America and what might be adopted at the Winnipeg School of Art. FitzGerald's comments in his diary about the people he met (art educators, museum personnel, artists, dealers, and friends), his account of his conversations, as well as his observations of quotidian life in American big cities against the backdrop of troubled economic times, combine to convey a rich feeling for the period as observed by one of Canada's leading artists.

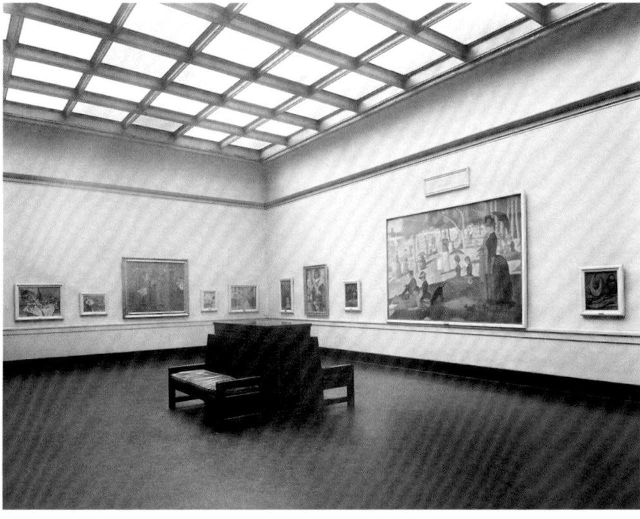

Installation of the Helen Birch Bartlett Memorial Collection, The Art Institute of Chicago, 1926
The Art Institute of Chicago
Photo: The Art Institute of Chicago / Art Resource, NY

At the halfway point of his trip, FitzGerald pondered whether it would have been more effective to travel for a shorter period of time and focus on copying works of art. "Would like to go to Chicago and spend a few weeks making drawings from things in the Museum and Institute and spend practically all the time doing this. It would be a much better way to absorb things and one would have concrete things when finished. A summer doing this would be a fine education for any student if they would stick to it."[6]

Although there are apparently no extant sketches made in museums during his trip, FitzGerald's diary is a treasure trove of commentary on what he saw. More than any other writing by the artist during his life, the diary reveals FitzGerald's reactions to Old Master and modern

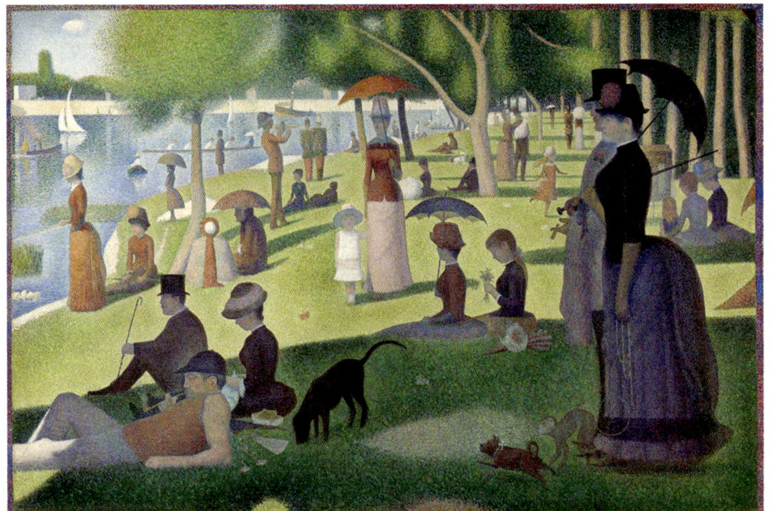

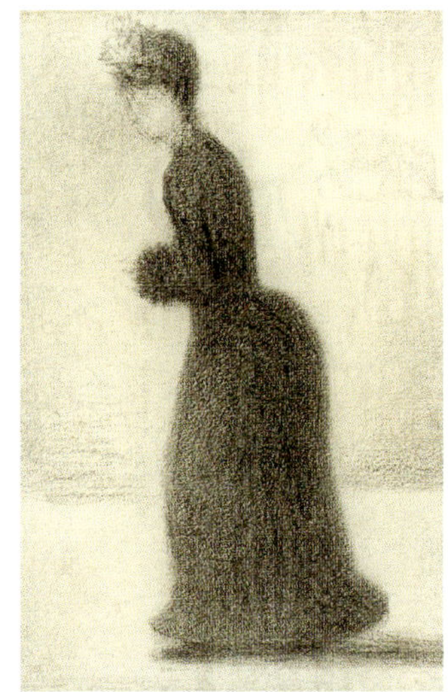

LEFT
GEORGES SEURAT
(1859–1891)
A Sunday on La Grande Jatte—1884, 1884/86
oil on canvas
207.5 × 308.1 cm
Helen Birch Bartlett Memorial Collection / The Art Institute of Chicago / 1926.224
Photo: The Art Institute of Chicago / Art Resource, NY

RIGHT
GEORGES SEURAT
(1859–1891)
Woman with a Muff, 1884–86
black Conté crayon, with erasing, on ivory laid paper, laid down on cream laminate board
313 × 238 mm
Gift of Robert Allerton
The Art Institute of Chicago
1926.716 / Photo: The Art Institute of Chicago
Art Resource, NY

pictures (as well as non-Western art that he saw at the Field Museum in Chicago and the American Museum of Natural History in New York).[7] How he defined the successful components of a great work of art on the trip would inform his teaching back in Winnipeg. What he noted in his diary also set the direction for what he wished to achieve in his own art.

At the Art Institute of Chicago, FitzGerald was taken with Post-Impressionist and modern paintings from the Helen Birch Bartlett Memorial Collection, which had been installed only four years earlier. He mentions specifically looking at paintings by Vincent van Gogh, Paul Gauguin, Henri de Toulouse-Lautrec, Ferdinand Hodler, Amedeo Modigliani, Henri Matisse, André Derain, and André Lhote. FitzGerald was "particularly enthused" by the light in Georges Seurat's Neo-Impressionist *A Sunday on La Grande Jatte—1884*, 1884/86. "There is a real naivety through it all that only emphasizes the real quality and the color is beautiful, the feeling of sunlight extremely fine and the color seems to give the glow that sunlight has. The very remarkable thing is that on such a huge canvas, such a technique would hold together and be so simple in the great masses, all little strokes or spots of broken pigment superimposed."[8] Some years later, FitzGerald modified Seurat's Pointillist technique, notably in *The Little Plant*, 1947 (p. 106), where paint is applied with a palette knife so that the entire surface appears to shimmer like a ridged mosaic. Likewise, in his later career, FitzGerald would adapt Seurat's dot technique, extending it in works in ink, chalk, or watercolour in which form is built up through myriad tiny flecks, strokes, or points (see, for example, *Four Apples on Tablecloth*, 1947, p. 126). Not surprisingly, a "beautiful" drawing of a "lady with the long dress of the period, extremely alive" by Seurat at the Art Institute of Chicago, *Woman with a Muff*, c. 1884, also captured his attention.

FitzGerald mused in his diary on the role of technique in the work of Seurat and other artists in the Birch Bartlett Collection. "The technique is so much a part of all the bigger things that one

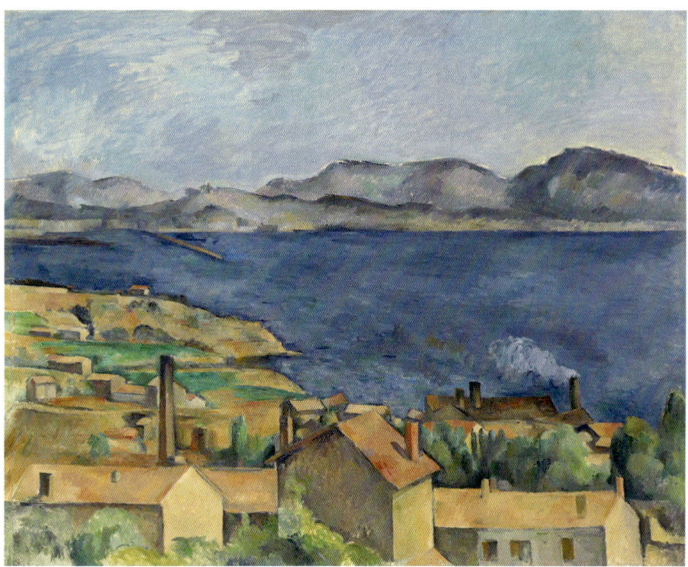

PAUL CÉZANNE
(1839–1906)
The Bay of Marseilles, Seen from L'Estaque,
c. 1885
oil on canvas
80.2 × 100.6 cm
Mr. and Mrs. Martin A. Ryerson Collection, 1933.1116
Photo: The Art Institute of Chicago/Art Resource, NY

only sees it by thinking of it from a painter's angle. It is not on the surface of the better things and is *really* only the means whereby the greater things are achieved."[9] FitzGerald always maintained that technique was subordinate to the idea of the work. "Each of us has something to say in paint about our contact with life, no matter how small it may be and the conclusion arrived at seems always the same, that is to work first and foremost and to be as little conscious of [the] way we are saying it as possible. To be so wrapped up in the thing to be said, that the means are very much in the background."[10]

Of all the artists whose work FitzGerald encountered in museums during his trip, no one's painting fascinated him more than Paul Cézanne's. This keen interest had already been evident in his early career with paintings such as *Rivière-des-Prairies, P.Q.*, 1922, and *Potato Patch, Snowflake*, 1925 (p. 15). Both pictures present a limited range of colours scrubbed onto the canvas so that the bare weave shows through—an unfinished look characteristic of many paintings by Cézanne. These earlier paintings were likely made in response to works by the Post-Impressionist master that FitzGerald had seen at the Metropolitan Museum of Art or the Brooklyn Museum while studying in New York from 1921 to 1922. But like many earlier twentieth-century modernists, FitzGerald continued to grapple with Cézanne's example throughout his career. When he viewed *The Bay of Marseille, Seen from L'Estaque*, c. 1885, at the Art Institute of Chicago during his 1930 trip, he confided, "I hardly like to admit it, I feel again a sense of something not quite complete, but how beautiful in some parts. Strange after looking at it for a long time how it really begins to build itself and become extremely abstract. One forgets almost the houses and trees, mountains, water and sky in the intricacy of the design."[11]

Also during the trip, he considered Cézanne's *Mont Sainte-Victoire*, 1886–87, which he saw at the Phillips Collection in Washington, DC, to be "the most beautiful Cézanne I have yet seen, thoroughly satisfying in every way."[12] Later, when he visited the Metropolitan Museum of Art in New York, he was impressed particularly by three landscapes by Cézanne from the Havemeyer bequest, including *The Gulf of Marseilles Seen from L'Estaque*, c. 1885, which is similar in composition to the Art Institute of Chicago painting. "The outstanding quality in all these big things, which is being more and more impressed on me, is the terrific sense of unity, everything being thought of to keep the eye within the picture and still it remains a thing of apparent ease. And always a great sense of reality, no matter how abstract the thing may be."[13] This relationship between abstraction and representation was to intrigue FitzGerald for the rest of his life.

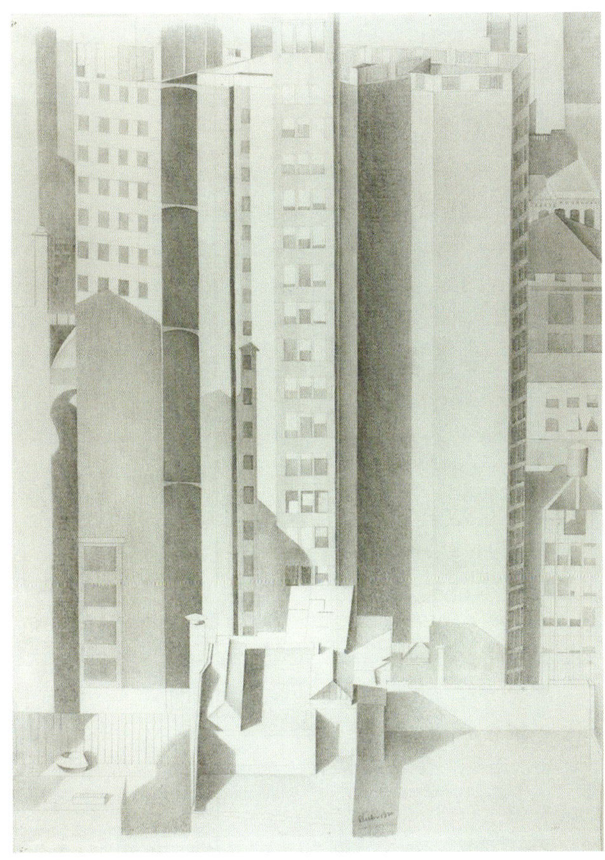

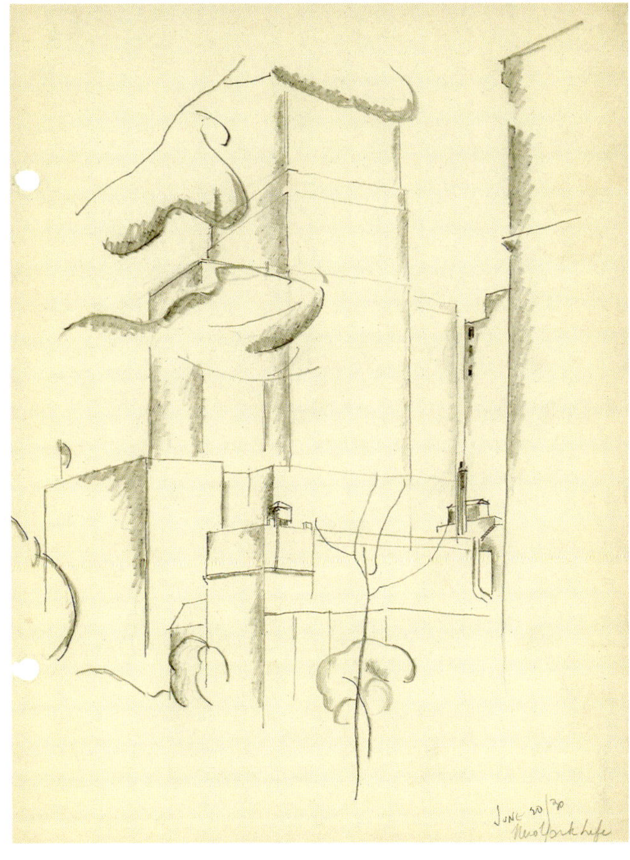

When he reached New York in 1930, he recalled his earlier, student days as he walked the streets, visited old haunts, and noted the ways in which the city had changed. Studying at the Art Students League from December 1921 to the end of March 1922 had been a formative experience, and his encounter with Cézanne at that time was only part of his self-described "sudden jolt into everything."[14] FitzGerald had also seen the work of the American Precisionists during his student days, and eight years later, in 1930, he was still engaged with this school of painting, recording that Charles Sheeler's drawing *New York*, 1920, at the Art Institute of Chicago, attracted his attention as "a pencil drawing of some low buildings seen against some skyscrapers, a very powerful extremely careful rendering."[15] As Sandra Shaul has suggested, he may have "emulated it (consciously or unconsciously)" when in New York a few days later sketching the New York Life Building with his architect friend Milton Osborne.[16] "Good fun trying the big building with the smaller ones in front with some overhanging branches directly in the foreground."[17] FitzGerald's fascination with big-city architecture was expressed once again during the trip

LEFT
CHARLES SHEELER
(1883–1965)
New York, 1920
graphite on cream Japanese vellum
505 × 330 mm
Friends of American Art Collection / The Art Institute of Chicago / 1922.5552
Photo: The Art Institute of Chicago / Art Resource, NY

RIGHT
New York Life Building,
June 20, 1930
pencil on paper
20 × 20.5 cm

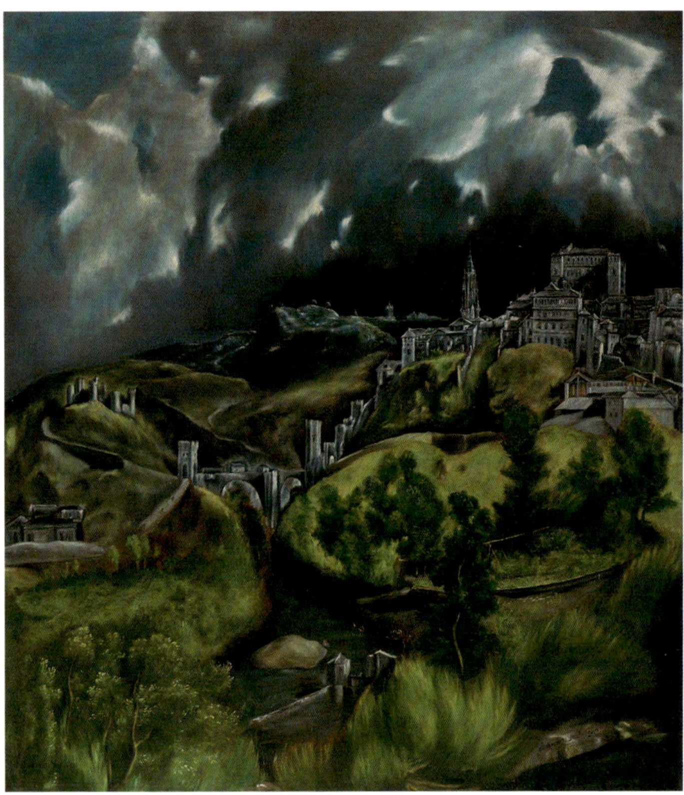

EL GRECO
(c. 1541–1614)
View of Toledo,
c. 1599–1600
oil on canvas
121.3 × 108.6 cm
H.O. Havemeyer Collection, Bequest of Mrs. H.O. Havemeyer, 1929 / The Metropolitan Museum of Art, New York 29.100.6 / Image copyright © The Metropolitan Museum of Art Image source: Art Resource, NY

when he visited the Brooklyn Museum, where he noted a number of paintings of skyscrapers by the American artist Bertram Hartman.[18]

During the course of his 1930 trip, FitzGerald commented in his diary on new architectural and engineering developments he witnessed. In New York he mentions visiting the newly completed Art Deco lobby of the Chrysler Building, seeing the almost complete neo-Gothic architecture of Riverside Church, as well as the George Washington Bridge under construction. A few weeks earlier, in Pittsburgh, he had been eager to visit Kaufmann's department store to see the recently installed set of ten mural panels depicting *The History of Commerce*, c. 1927–29, by Boardman Robinson, his former teacher at the Art Students League. Given that mural painting was one of the subjects he supervised at the Winnipeg School of Art, FitzGerald was particularly attentive to the integration of Robinson's paintings in their newly remodelled Art Deco setting by the architect Benno Janssen. Robinson's panel *Trade and Commerce in the United States*, conceived in the manner of the famous American muralist Thomas Hart Benton, reflects the new America that FitzGerald experienced during his trip, including the zeppelin that floats in the sky in the upper right of the composition. FitzGerald observed the zeppelin USS *Los Angeles* flying over Manhattan on June 23.[19]

Throughout his 1930 trip, FitzGerald continually affirmed his belief that artists from all eras—whether Old Master or modern—have confronted similar formal problems.[20] He often mentioned a sense of "unity" and "oneness" in a picture as the source of its success. Examining El Greco's *View of Toledo*, c. 1599–1600, at the Metropolitan Museum of Art, for example, he thought of Cézanne: "One feels very much the kinship with

Cézanne, that same great sense of unity and some great reality and a peculiar mental attitude seems to pervade both."[21]

FitzGerald considered Pierre-Auguste Renoir's *Luncheon of the Boating Party*, between 1880 and 1881, at the Phillips Collection, Washington, DC, "the most glorious thing of his I have yet seen," describing its "beautiful colour" and "wonderful abstract design" as the formal elements that "left the feeling that a story or incident as subject matter cannot destroy the Art in it."[22] After FitzGerald visited the Philadelphia Museum of Art, he described another multi-figure narrative painting he referred to as "Village Wedding," which he believed to be by Pieter Bruegel the Elder.[23] This picture may have been *Wedding Dance in the Open Air*, c. 1600, catalogued as Pieter Brueghel the Younger.[24] He remarked that "never once does the eye get out of the picture," which is something he notes frequently when judging the merits of a composition.[25] It is a feature that contributes to "the essential oneness" of a work: "In this thing of Breughel I feel a certain kinship to the large painting of Renoir's in the Phillips Gallery. The same free spirit, many ways similar in composition, the one light and delicate . . . and the other more ponderous and . . . at the same time a fine feeling for design underlying both of them."[26]

Unexpected comparisons between artists of different eras enliven FitzGerald's diary. At the Philadelphia Museum of Art, he was drawn to another Old Master picture, *Rest on the Flight into Egypt* by the Workshop of Joachim Patinir. Without specifying exactly what he meant, FitzGerald saw a parallel between the formal elements of this painting and those found in the art of his own time. Yet it reminded him most of a nineteenth-century painting he had just seen in

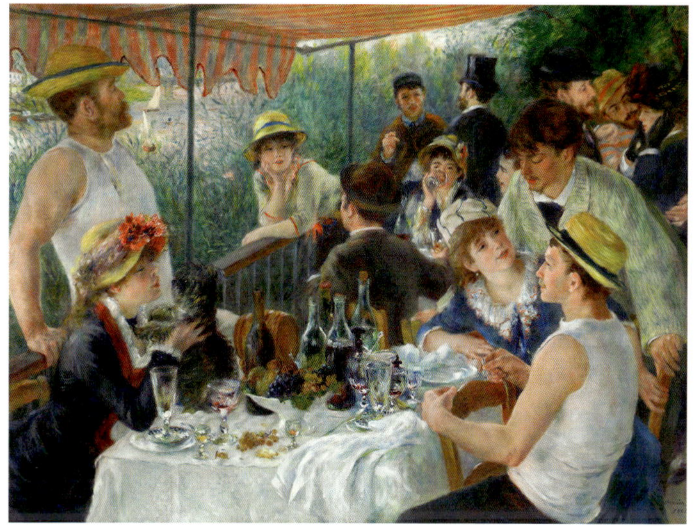

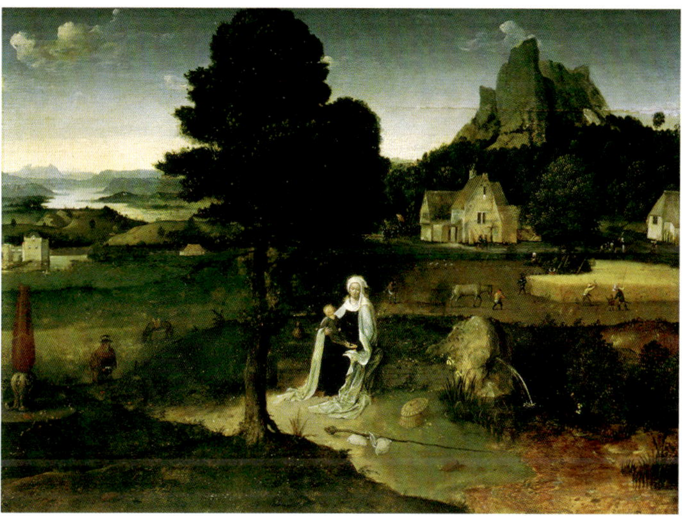

TOP
PIERRE-AUGUSTE RENOIR (1841–1919)
Luncheon of the Boating Party, between 1880 and 1881
oil on canvas
130.2 × 175.6 cm
Acquired 1923 / The Phillips Collection, Washington, DC

BOTTOM
WORKSHOP OF JOACHIM PATINIR
Rest on the Flight into Egypt, early 16th century
oil on panel
46.3 × 60.8 cm
John G. Johnson Collection, 1917 / Philadelphia Museum of Art / Cat. 377

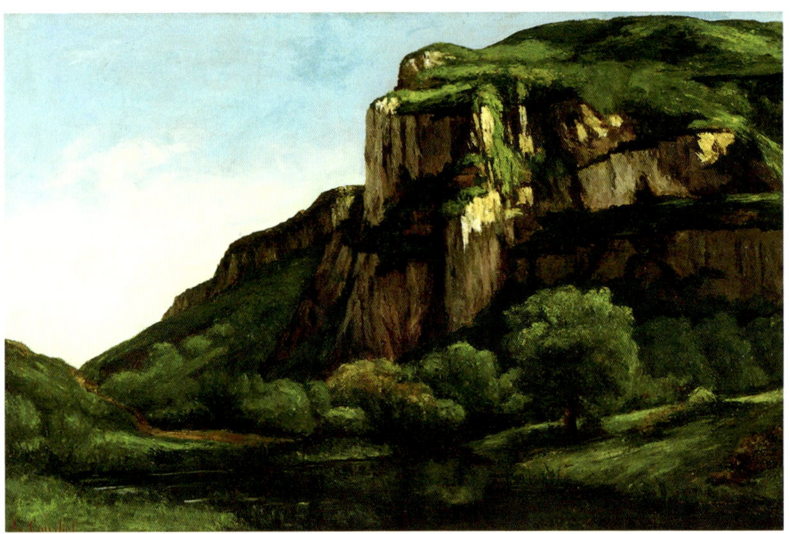

ABOVE
GUSTAVE COURBET
(1819–1877)
Rocks at Mouthier,
c. 1855
oil on canvas
75.57 × 116.84 cm
Acquired 1925 / The Phillips Collection, Washington, DC

OPPOSITE
Red Barn, c. 1934
oil on canvas
43.2 × 35.8 cm

the Phillips Collection, Gustave Courbet's *Rocks at Mouthier*, c. 1855. "In the upper right hand corner is a part [that] if separated from the rest would be almost identical with Phillips' large mountain piece of Courbet's. The sky is almost identical and the forms very similar. This is a fine picture, the sky being extremely beautiful and something in the whole picture very akin to the present day outlook."[27]

Perhaps the most important conversation about "the present day outlook" that FitzGerald recorded on his trip was with the artist Lucile Blanch when he met her in Woodstock, New York.[28] Here he revealed how rooted he remained in the writings of the nineteenth-century British critic and artist John Ruskin—particularly *The Elements of Drawing* (1857)—who advocated for the empirical observation of nature. "Agreed on the feeling that purely abstract had a tendency to lose contact with the living thing which was the most important and that the move today is rather a swing towards an inspiration from nature. An eternal contact with humanity and nature and a greater sense of unity. This has been very strongly impressed on me during this trip, the sense of unifying all the elements in a picture to the making of a creation. The picture a living thing, one great thought made up of many details but all subordinated to the whole."[29] This quotation remains the most important summation of FitzGerald's aesthetic philosophy.[30]

At the end of his stay in New York, on June 30, FitzGerald wrote a fitting conclusion that offers his perspective on the experience of looking at great art in great museums. "Went over to the Metropolitan for a final review of some of the things just to try and find a little more wherein lay the greatness of Cézanne and Courbet etc. Enjoyed them all over again and got a little more intimate with some of [the] things. Finally I feel that each one of us must go on with our ideas as they present themselves and try and work out our salvation that way as one feels all the big men did. It is a great inspiration seeing these things and how they are developed but only an inspiration, because they went right on as they felt."[31]

FitzGerald always maintained that it is ultimately the responsibility of artists to find their own unique self-expression. Ultimately his trip confirmed the direction of his artistic philosophy—that it is from a personal journey of hard work and discovery, combining the study of major works of art with an even greater devotion to the study of nature, that the true artist is formed.[32] ■

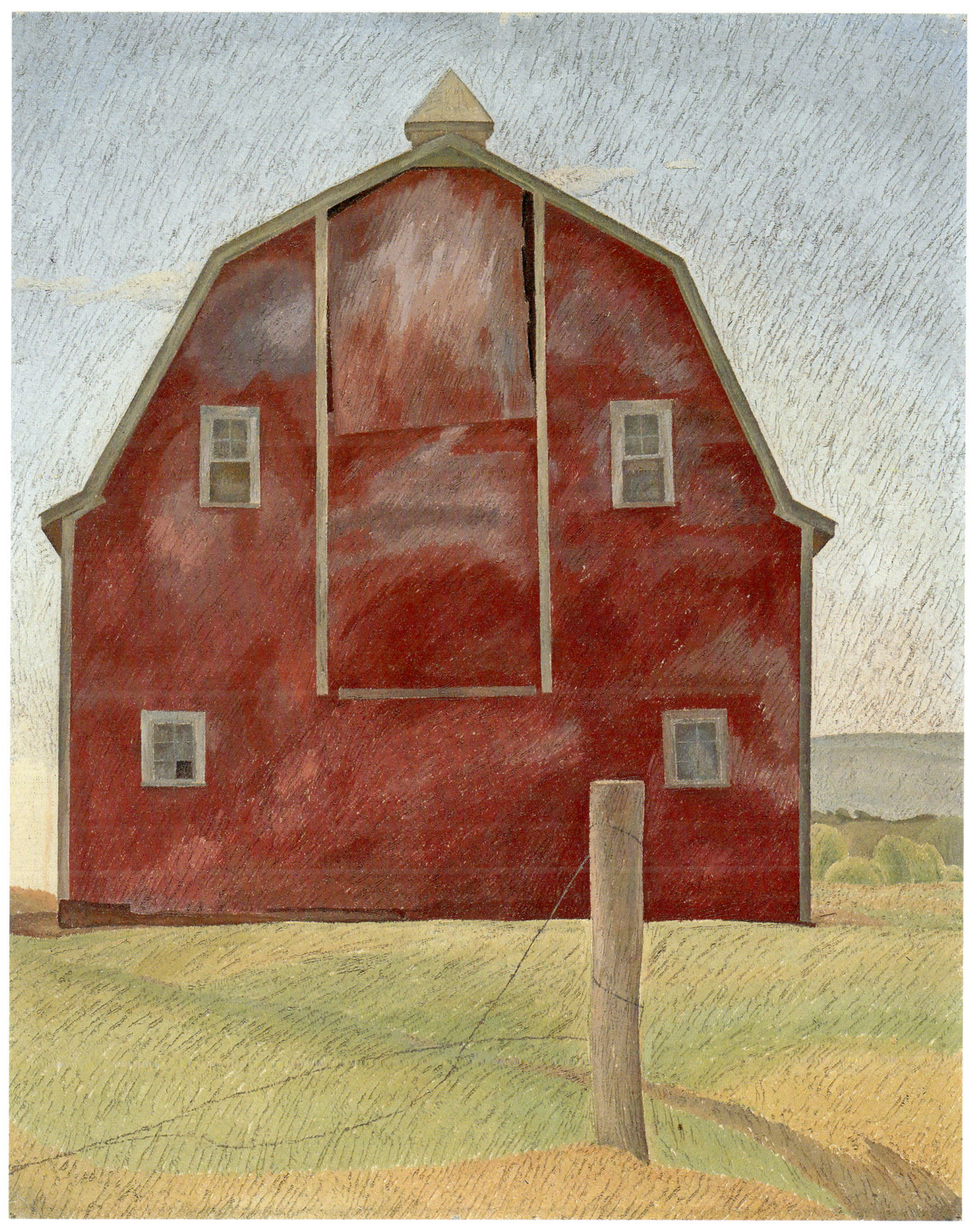

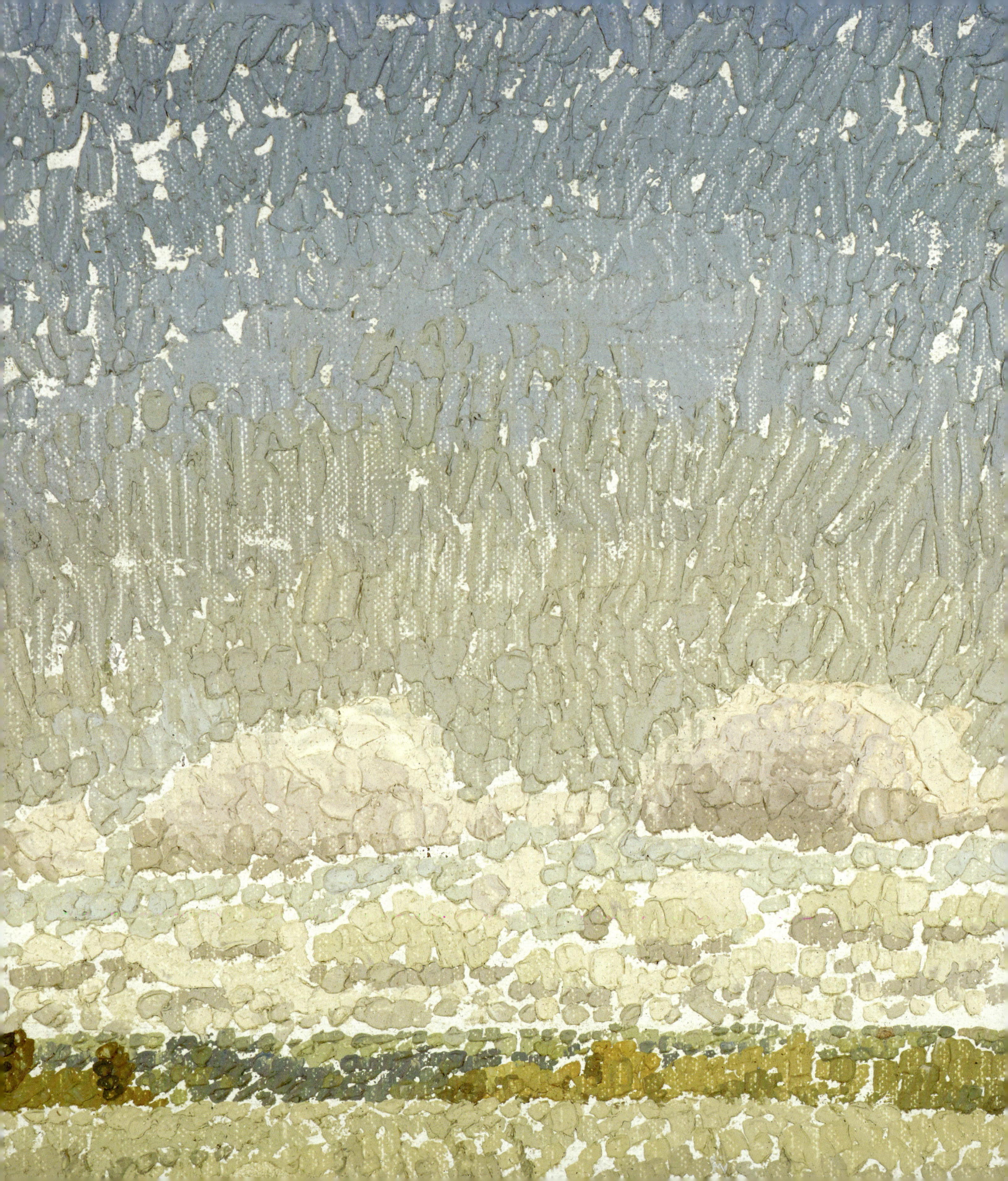

ON THE PRAIRIE

Throughout his life, FitzGerald would speak of his connection to the landscape of Manitoba and his rich memory of summers spent on his grandmother's farm in Snowflake, Manitoba, near the United States border. His early adherence to the ideas of the British artist and art critic John Ruskin (1819–1900), whose *Elements of Drawing* FitzGerald first read in his teens, affirmed his interest in the close observation of nature—a focus that would be central to his art practice throughout his career. Whether he was drawing a blade of grass, a swaying field of grain, a solitary barn punctuating the horizon, or the wide sky and clouds breathing with light and air, FitzGerald is cherished for his devotion to the Manitoba landscape and for his singular expression of his spiritual ties to home.

PRAIRIE LANDSCAPE

ROBERT HOULE

This drawing, *Prairie Landscape*, brings me back to my childhood. I have always been fascinated by the sky. I grew up in Kaa-wii-kwe-tawang-kak, Sandy Bay, a reserve on the western shore of Lake Manitoba. When a storm would be coming, with its great clouds, it wouldn't arrive for a couple of hours, maybe three hours, and it was beautiful to see that—the immensity of the sky and your own personal scale. There's a spiritual aspect to that abundance of light and that abundance of space. If you glance down to the horizon line in this drawing, it gives you some notion of that contrast, of man in nature—that little grain elevator, these barns. It looks like the kind of barns the Hutterites had.

I went to Sandy Bay Residential School up until Grade 8. High school was in Winnipeg. This drawing also reminds me of travelling on the bus between Winnipeg and my reserve, past Portage la Prairie on the Number 1 Highway, looking out the window. In winter you don't see that horizon at all because of the snow and the greyness of the sky, so this drawing must be summertime.

In my Saulteaux culture we are given spiritual names when we are children. They are all names related to the sky in our Anishnabemowin language. My mother would call the shaman to the house to give us names. We would all sit on the floor. There would be special food. Mum would close all the curtains because we were forbidden to do our rituals—they were seen as anti-Catholic. The shaman would come, and he would go through his ritual and he would travel probably through all of those skies up there with his rattle. There would be a point where he would laugh, talking to someone, responding—these were either storytellers or ancestors or some other spiritual creatures. One of them would finally say, "*Neen suh gah meenah neewesoowin*"—I will give this person my name. The shaman would repeat that name, and we would know right away. The child would be picked up, named, and then passed around.

Ozhahwushquah Penaise Dezhenekango. I am known as Blue Thunder, and if you wish to know me you must seek me in the clouds.

Prairie Landscape, 1935
graphite on paper
sheet: 30.7 × 23 cm

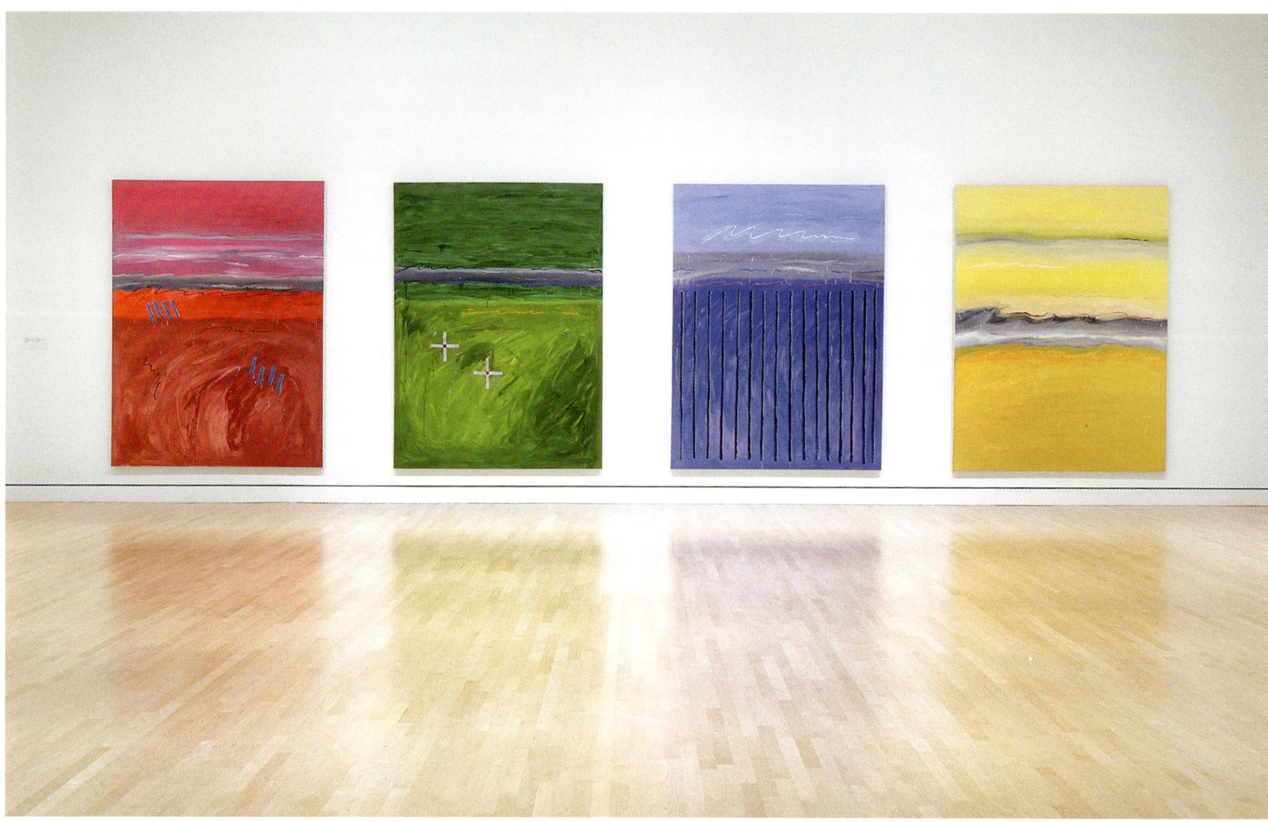

You never knew why the name was given to you. It's only now that I'm over sixty that I introduce myself by my spirit name, because we were discouraged from sharing that. It's not so much being possessive as trying to avoid ridicule. At my age now, I find that I am more confident. I've lived long enough, been through enough. I never realized that people would enjoy my name.

My late sister, her name was *Akwahsimookwe*, Bright Lightning Woman. My other sister had the name *Kihshi Pahtohnohkii Penaisekwe*, Circling Thunderbird Woman. She was the leader of the pack, the first one. Then there's my late brother, *Tetebesa Penaise*, Rolling Thunder. My mother's name was *Nahgwáyaub Ikwe*, Rainbow Woman. She's the woman who shows off the rim of her dress, with all the colours. She's celebrating because she has calmed the young thunderbirds.

If there was a storm coming, I remember my mum would put tobacco out, or she would ask us to put it near a tree, especially in the cracks of the bark, to appease the Thunderers. They are younger then, in the spring, and when they come, they frighten people down below. If a storm was happening and this had not been done, my mother would put a black mark on our foreheads so we wouldn't be harmed. Or she would recite our names, because these names were given to us for protection. I would often forget what my siblings' names were until there was such an occasion.

On the prairie you can see a tornado coming from two or three hours away too. It is terrifying. Also hail. The clouds are very black or dark grey, and you can see lightning going back and forth. If the storm was far away, you could put your head on the ground and you could hear the drums. You could pick up the vibration. We used to entertain ourselves that way. That was the only toy we had. In this drawing, though, the storm is over. The sky is clearing.

The first work that I made about the sky was in 1989, a series of paintings called *Muhnedobe uhyahyuk (Where the gods are present)*, which takes its name from an island up in the north end of Lake Manitoba, Manitou Island. When these paintings were shown in a gallery for the first time, the title was changed and Christianized a bit in translation to read *The Place Where God Lives*. But the origin of the word *Manitoba* is in the title I gave the series.

In August 1988, my father and I went to Manitou Island with Shirley Madill from the Winnipeg Art Gallery. We went to record the sound of the waves drumming on the beach. It's where all our altars to our ancestors are. We have been going there forever to ask for interventions, especially for young couples courting.

After my mother died, I never really returned to live to Manitoba full-time. When I went away to university at McGill, I would return home from Montreal and my parents would pick me up at the airport in Winnipeg. There would be this long drive. About a half hour in, that would be the time my mother would say, "*Ahneen uhpee dush kewaken?*" When are you going to come home? And it would always hurt my heart to say to her, "I don't know . . . I don't think so." ■

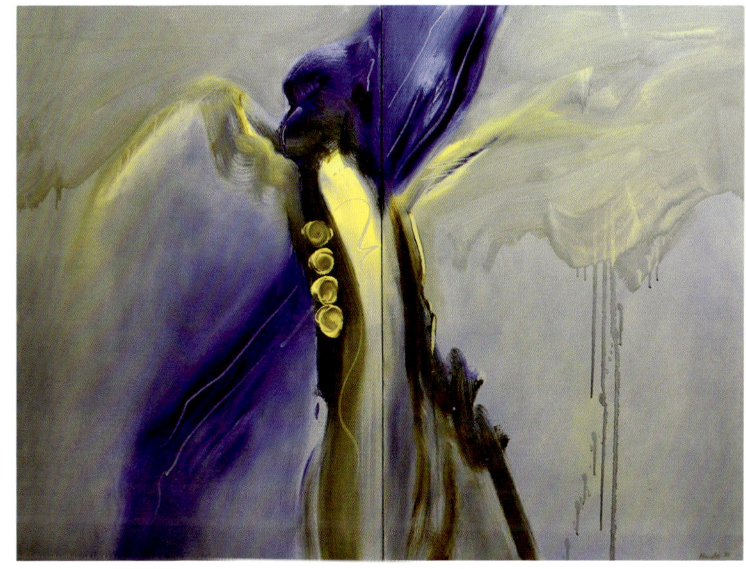

OPPOSITE
ROBERT HOULE
(b. 1947)
Muhnedobe uhyahyuk (Where the gods are present), 1989
oil on canvas
244 × 182.4 × 5 cm each
Purchased 1992 / National Gallery of Canada, Ottawa 36168.1-4 / Photo: NGC

ABOVE
ROBERT HOULE
(b. 1947)
Blue Thunder, 2011
oil on canvas
two panels, each
91.44 × 60.96 cm
Collection of Glen and Marion Knott / Image courtesy of Galerie Nicolas Robert

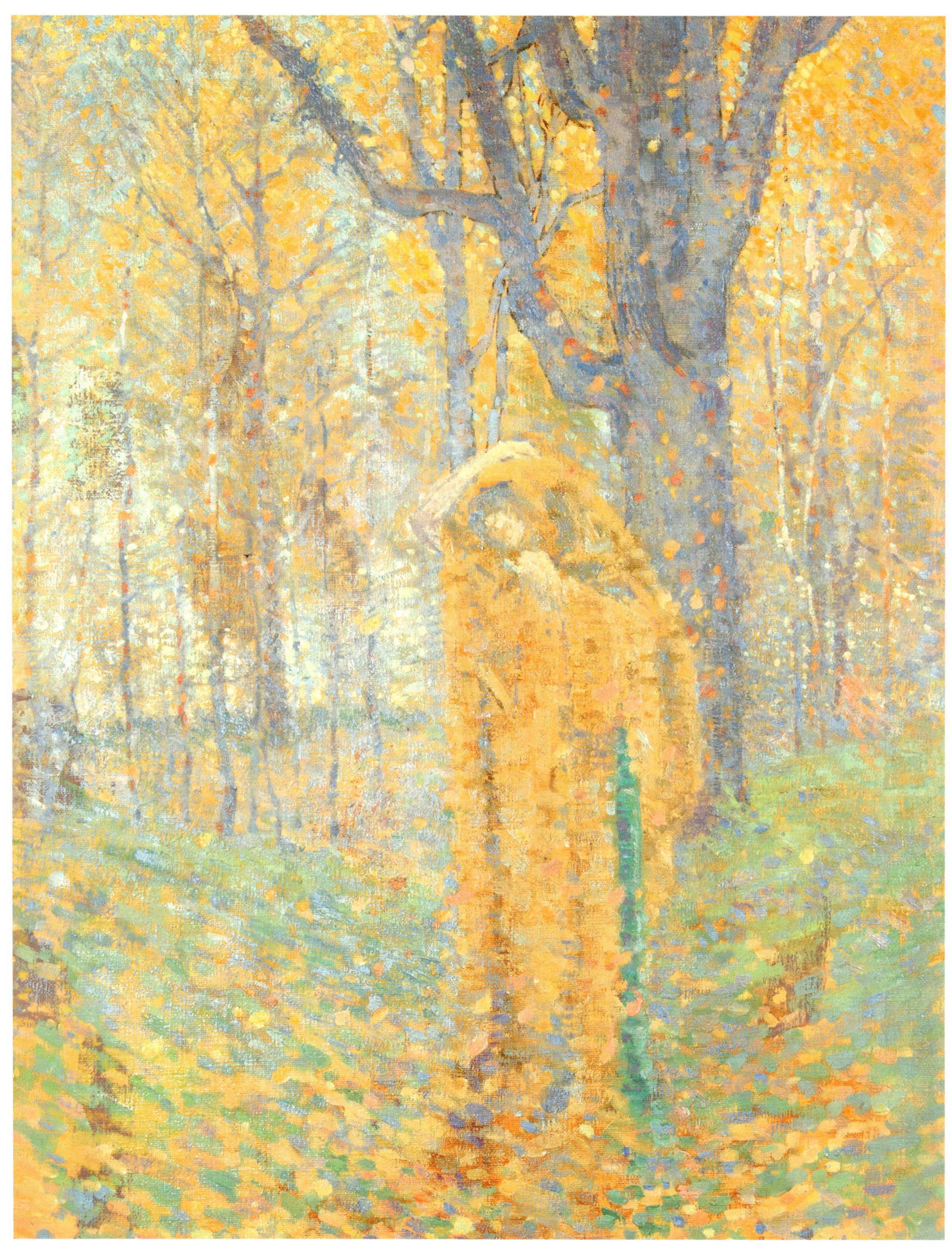

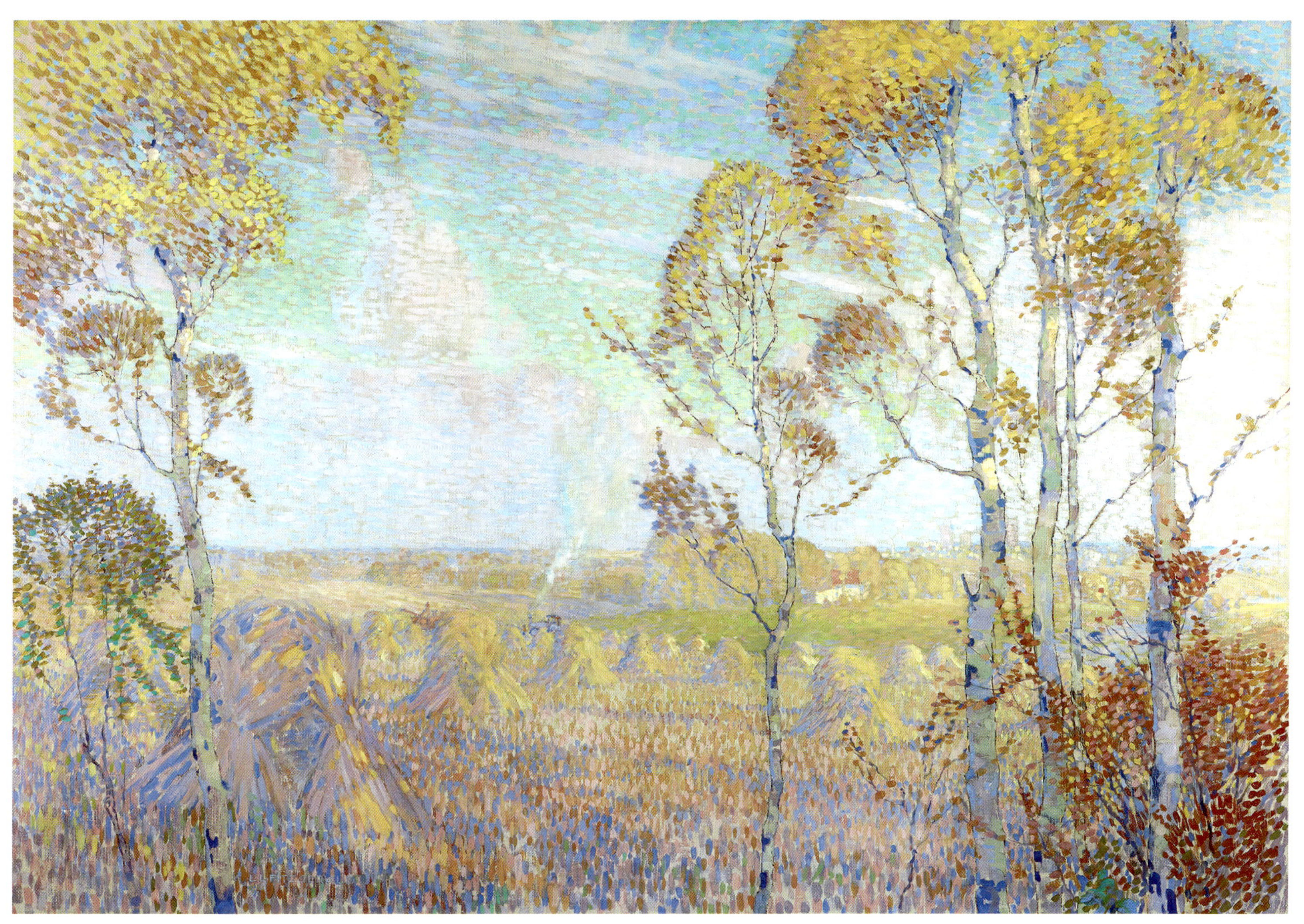

OPPOSITE
Figure in the Woods, 1920
oil on canvas
91.4 × 61 cm

ABOVE
Untitled, n.d.
oil on canvas
90.5 × 130.5 cm;
framed: 102.2 × 142.2 × 5.7 cm

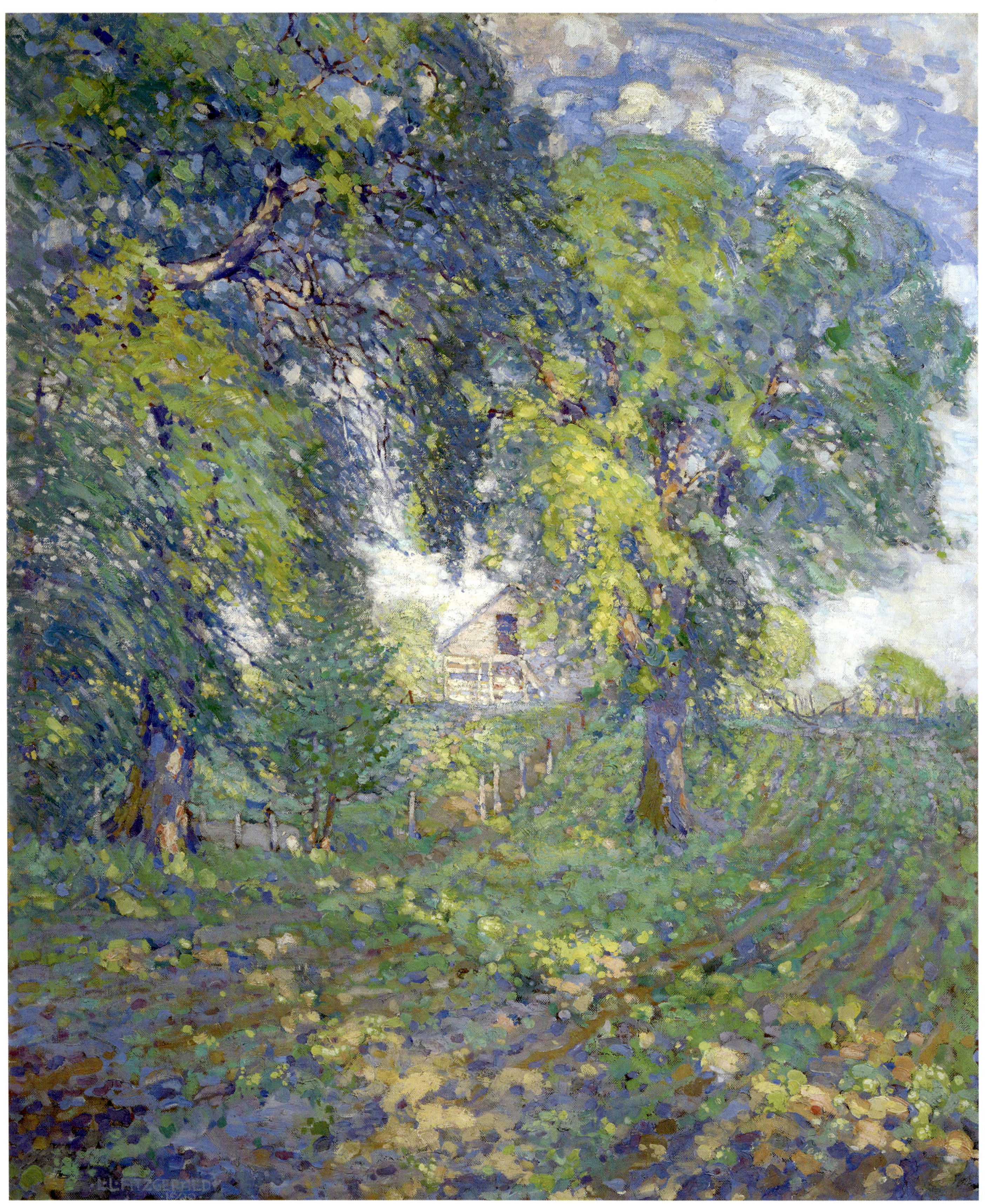

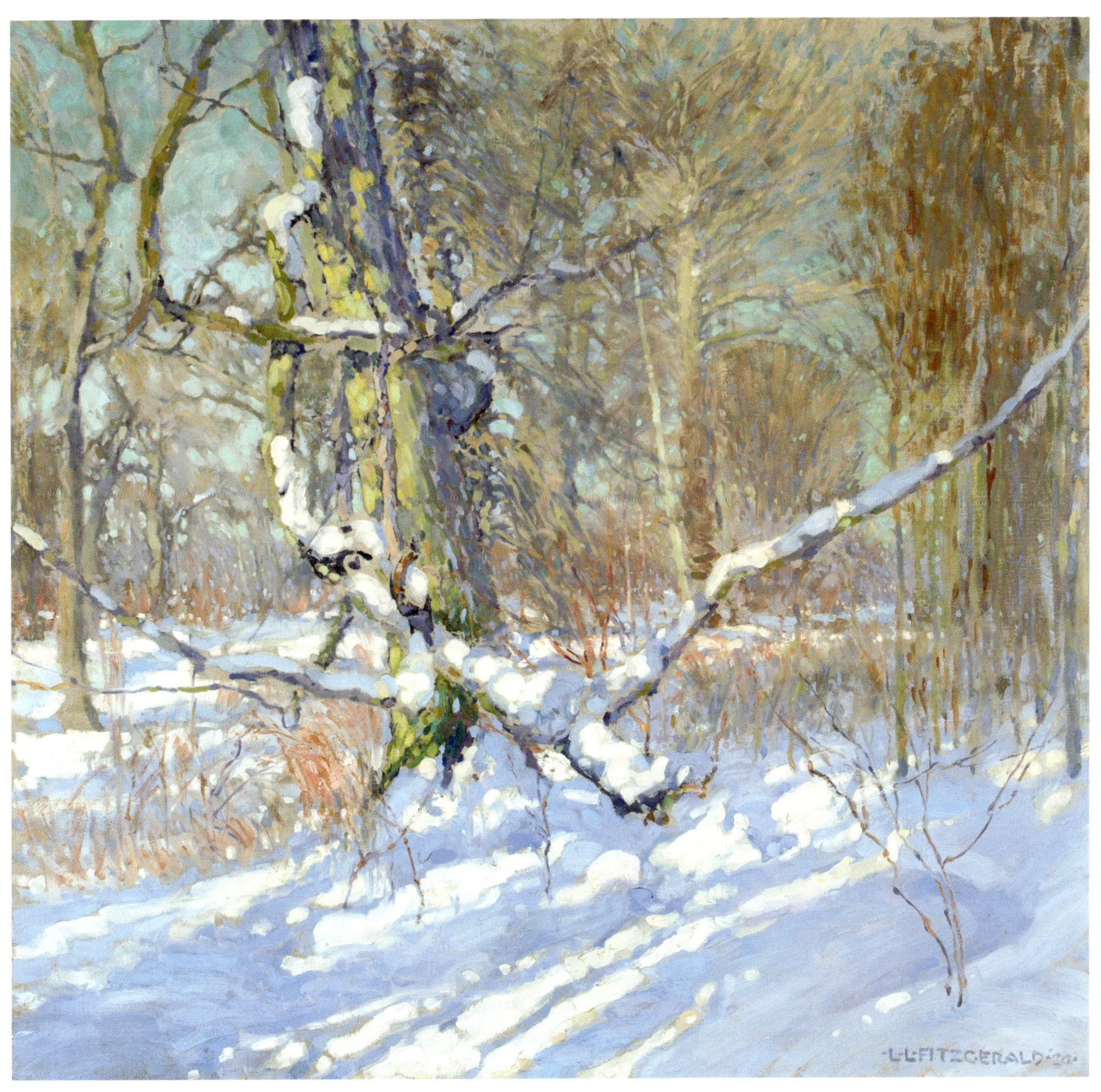

OPPOSITE
Summer, East Kildonan, 1920
oil on canvas
127.6 × 107.3 cm;
framed: 148.6 ×
128.3 × 10.2 cm

ABOVE
Broken Tree, Kildonan Park, 1920
oil on canvas
83.8 × 88.9 cm

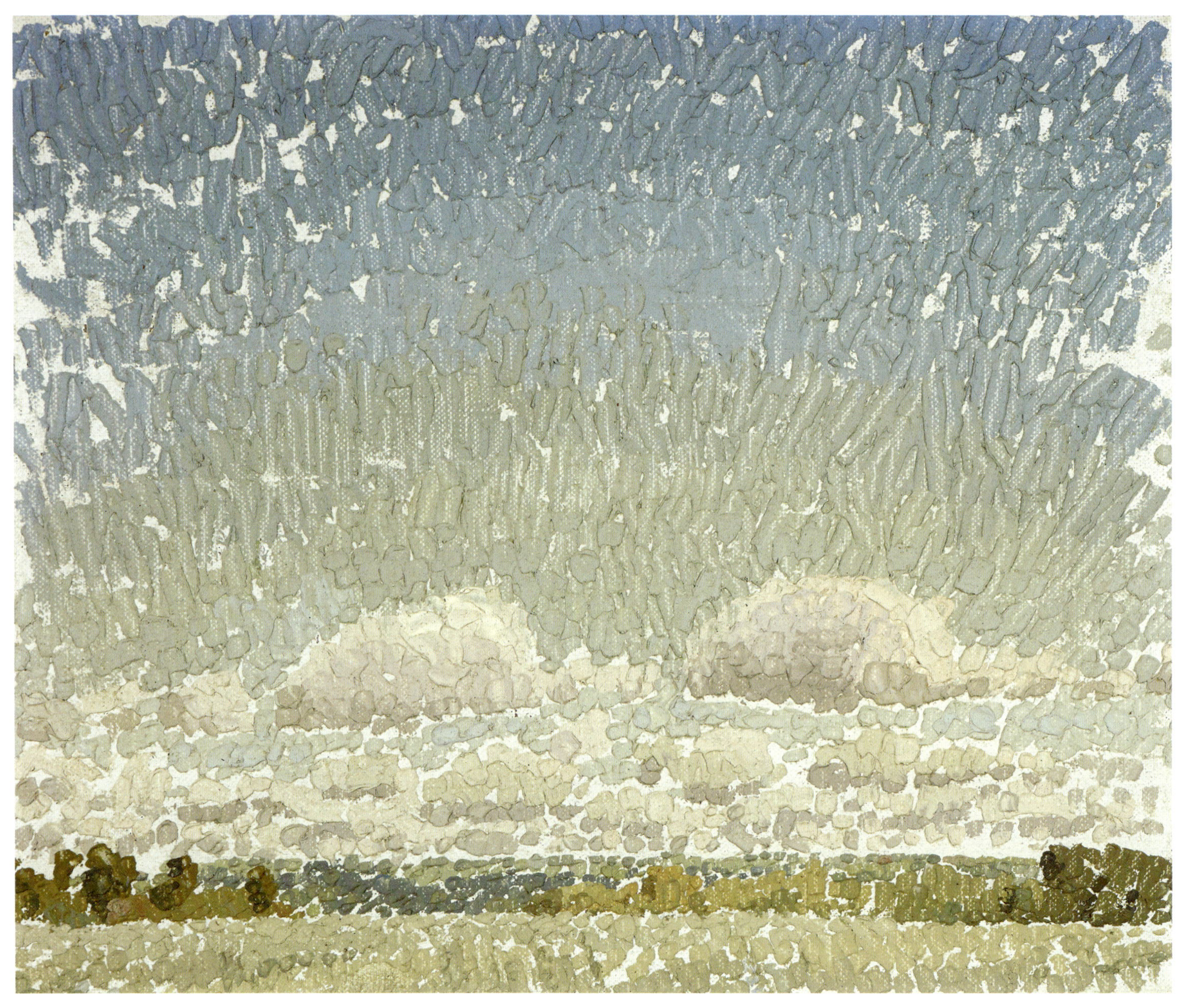

Prairie, c. 1921
oil on canvas, laid down on paperboard
18.2 × 22.2 cm

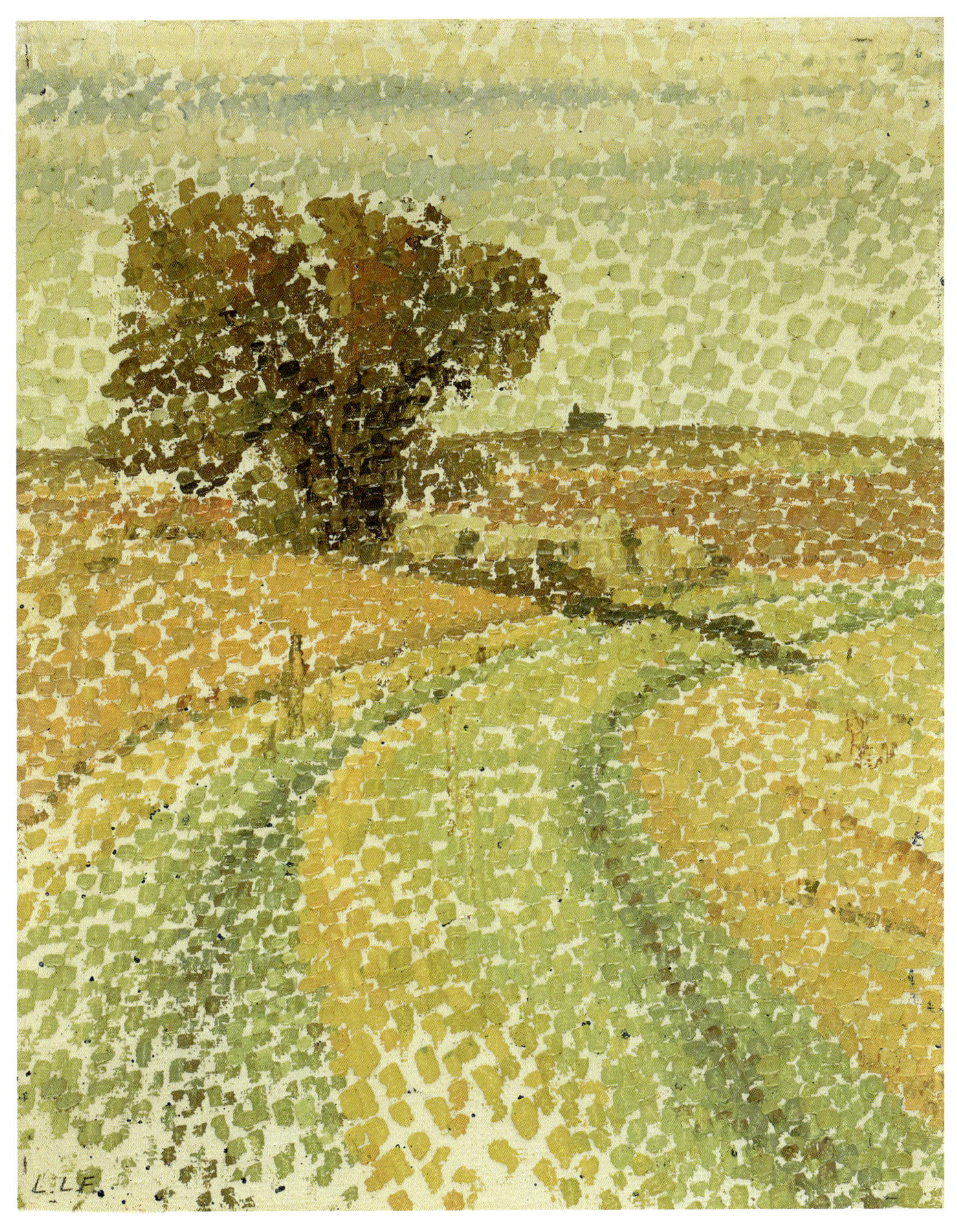

Road to Snowflake, 1923
oil on panel
19.1 × 15.9 cm

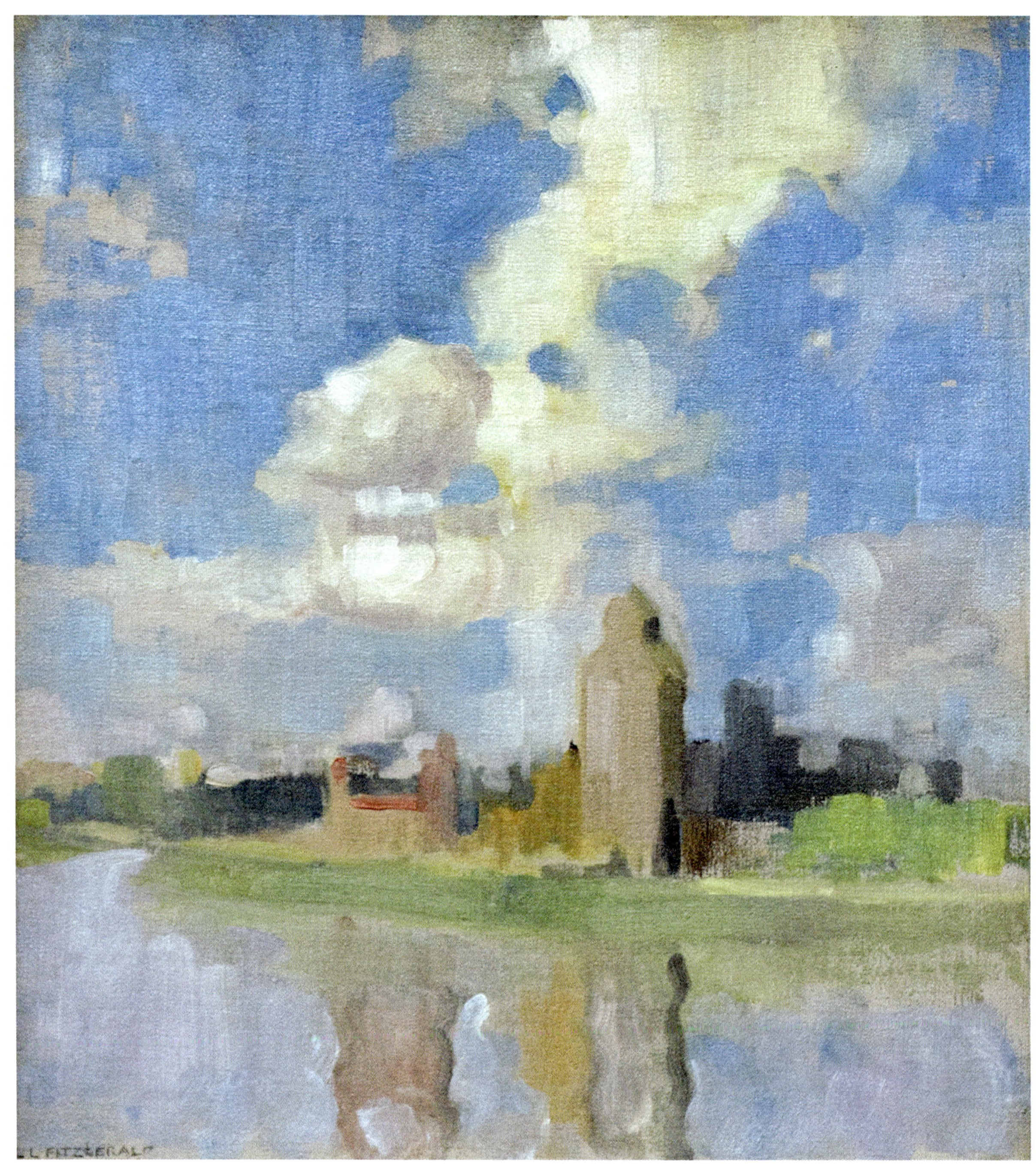

Grain Silos, Saskatchewan, n.d.
oil on canvas, laid down on board
30.5 × 27.9 cm

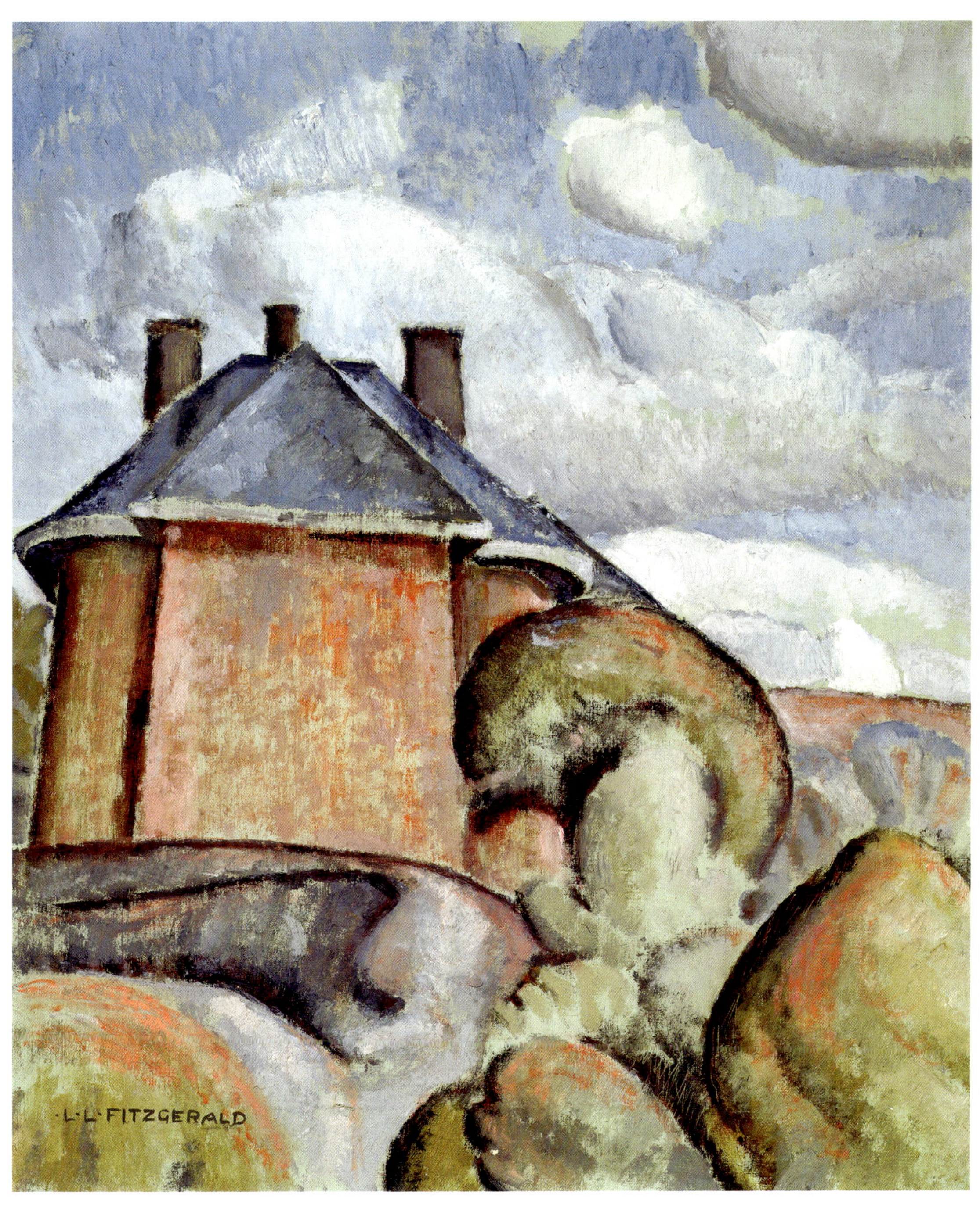

The Red House,
c. 1925
oil on canvas
50.8 × 41.9 cm

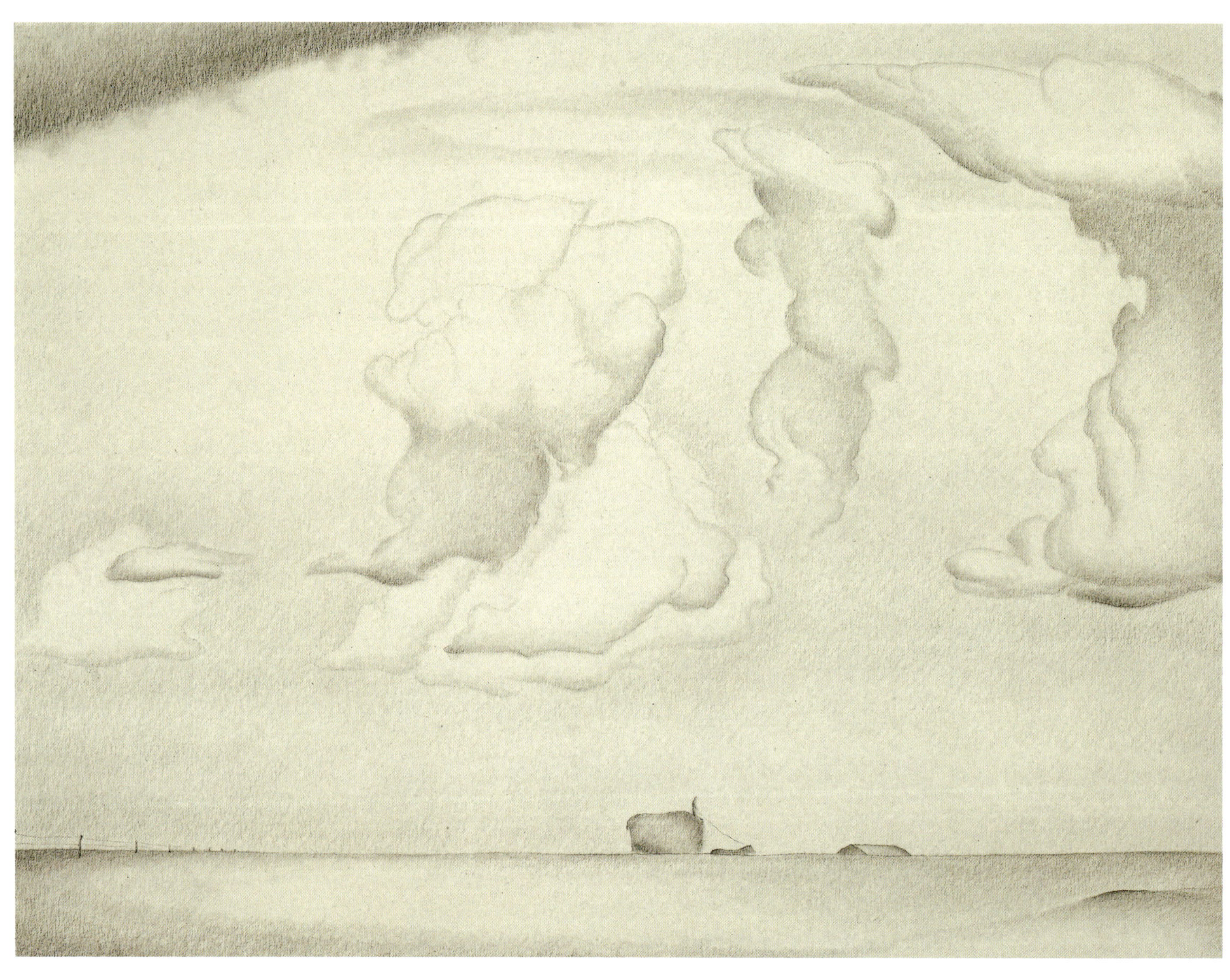

Storm on Prairies, 1935
graphite on paper
22.1 × 29.4 cm

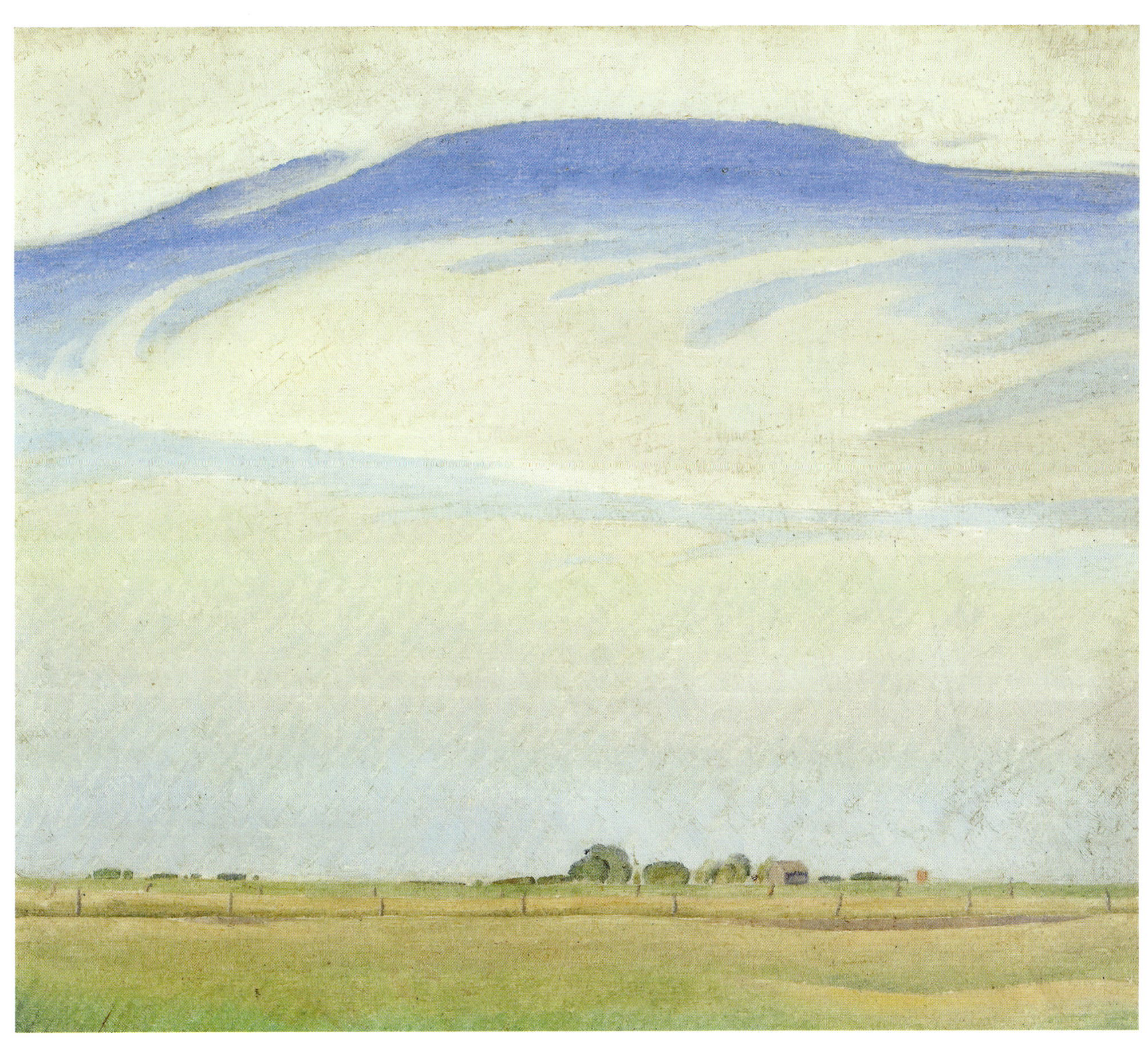

The Prairie, 1929
oil on canvas
28.7 × 33.6 cm

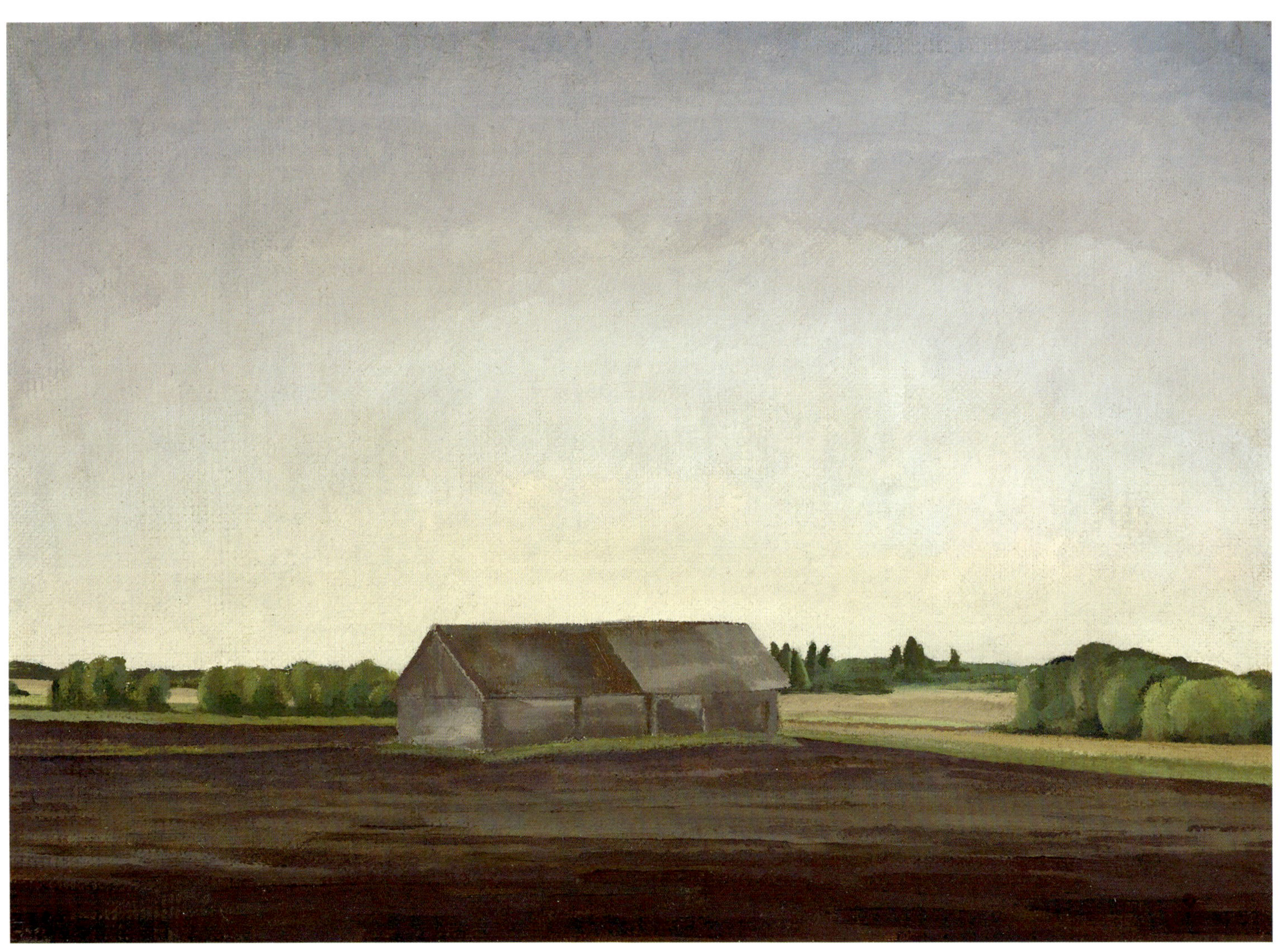

Landscape
with Barn, n.d.
oil on canvas
25.4 × 36.2 cm

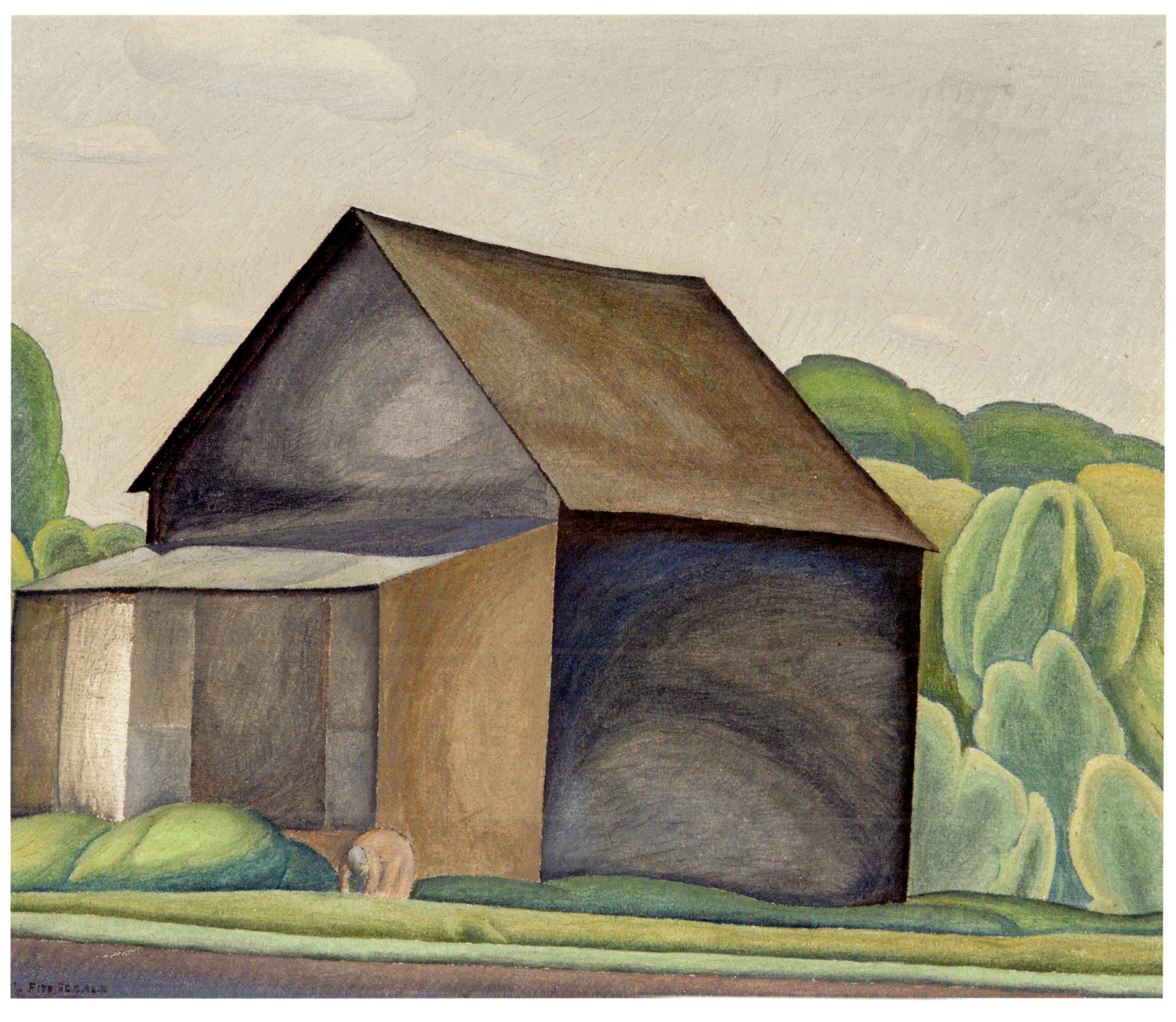

The Barn, c. 1930
oil on board
29.7 × 36.4 cm

Lake Winnipeg, 1929
oil on canvas
29.8 × 36.2 cm

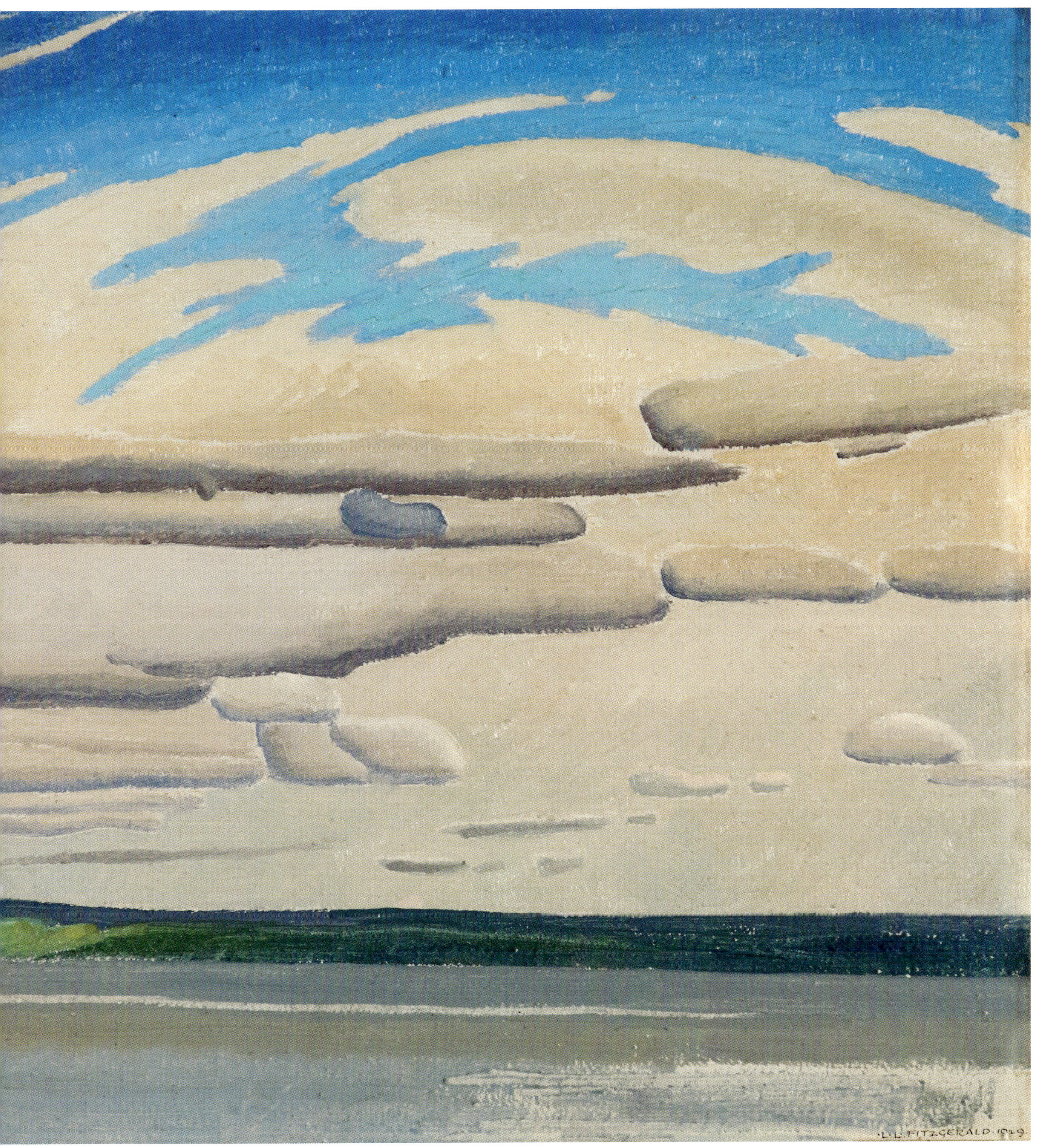
·L·L·FITZGERALD·1949·

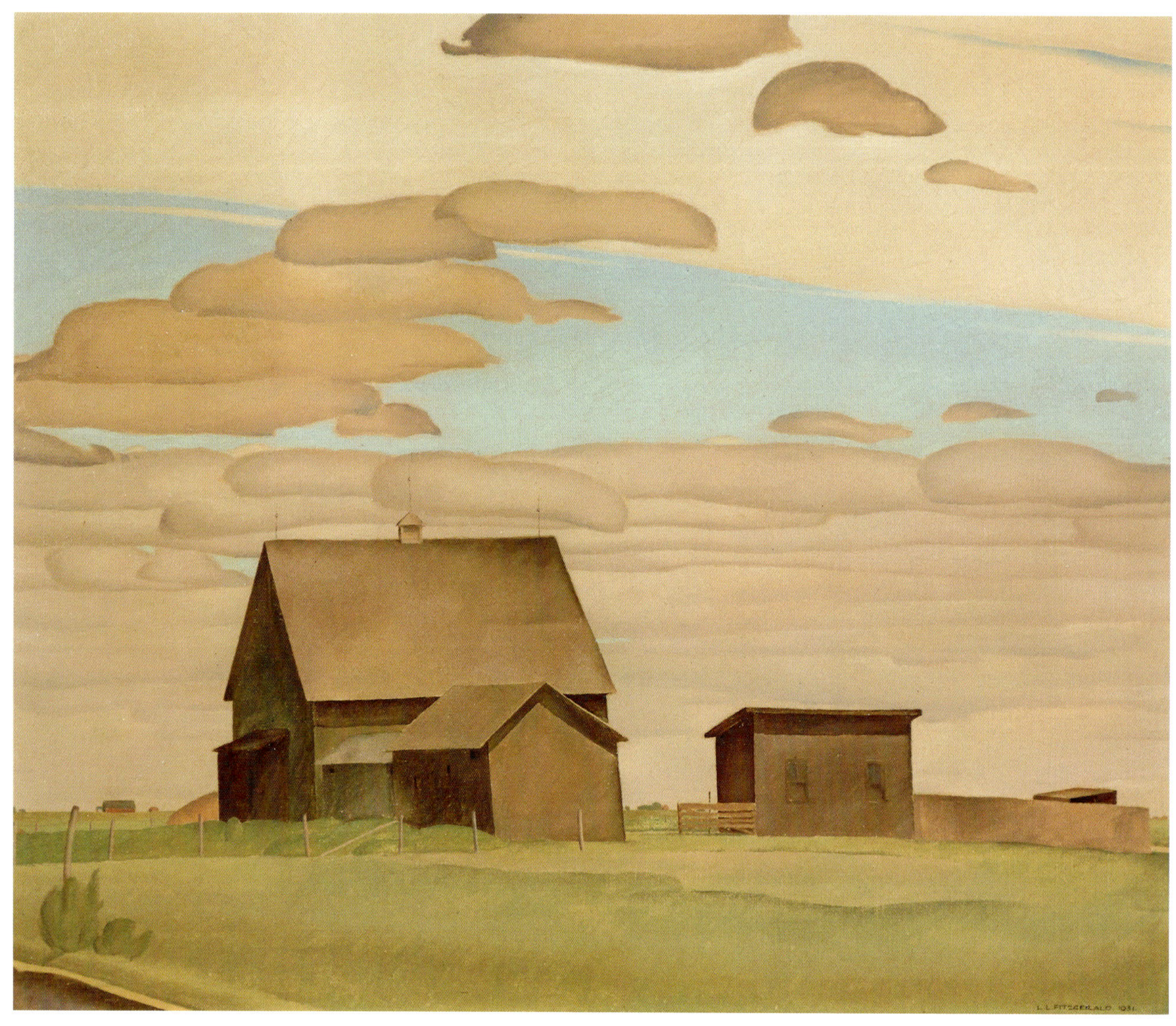

Prairie Farm, 1931
oil
35.9 × 43.2 cm

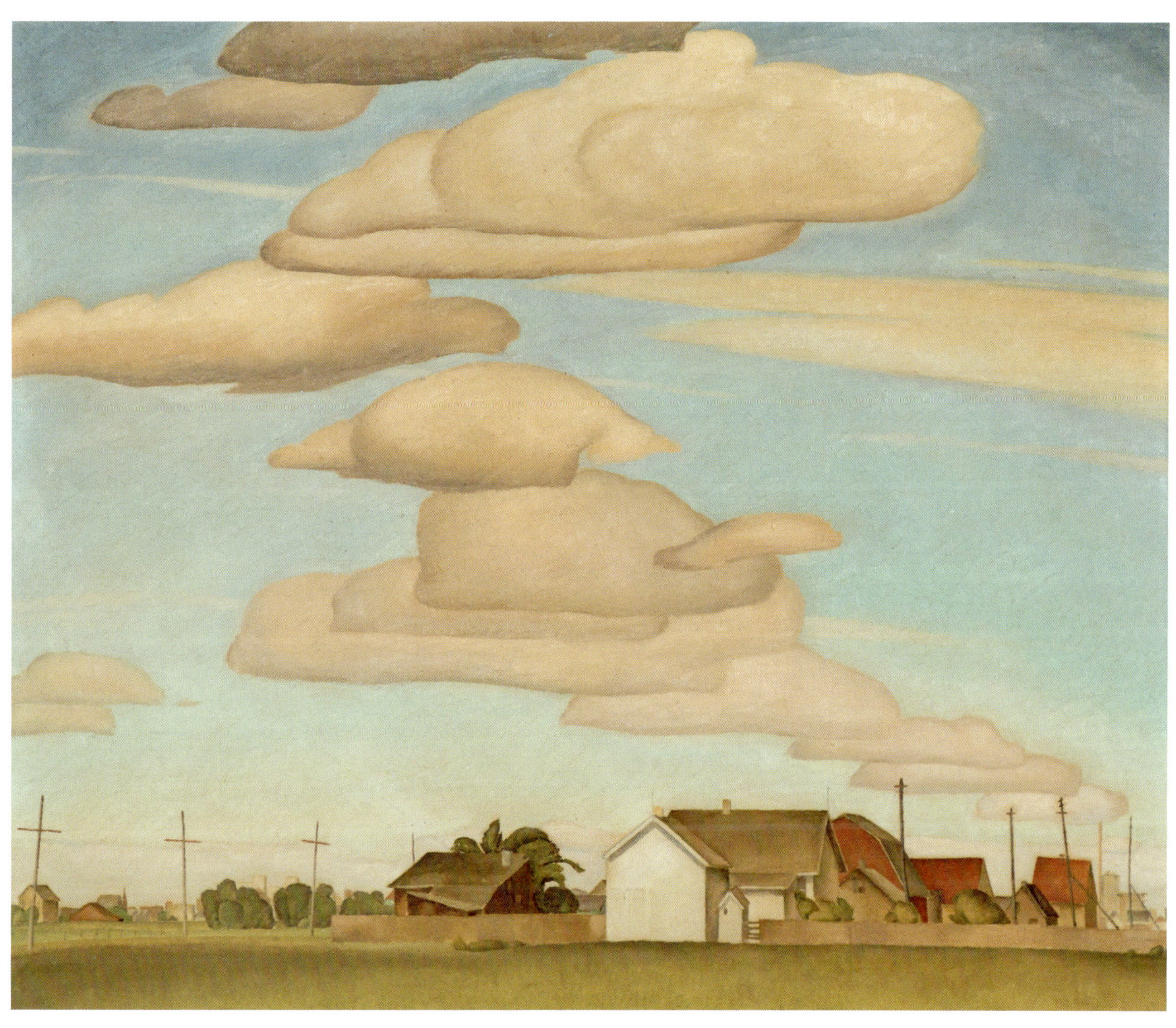

Prairie Town, 1931
oil
35.9 × 43.5 cm

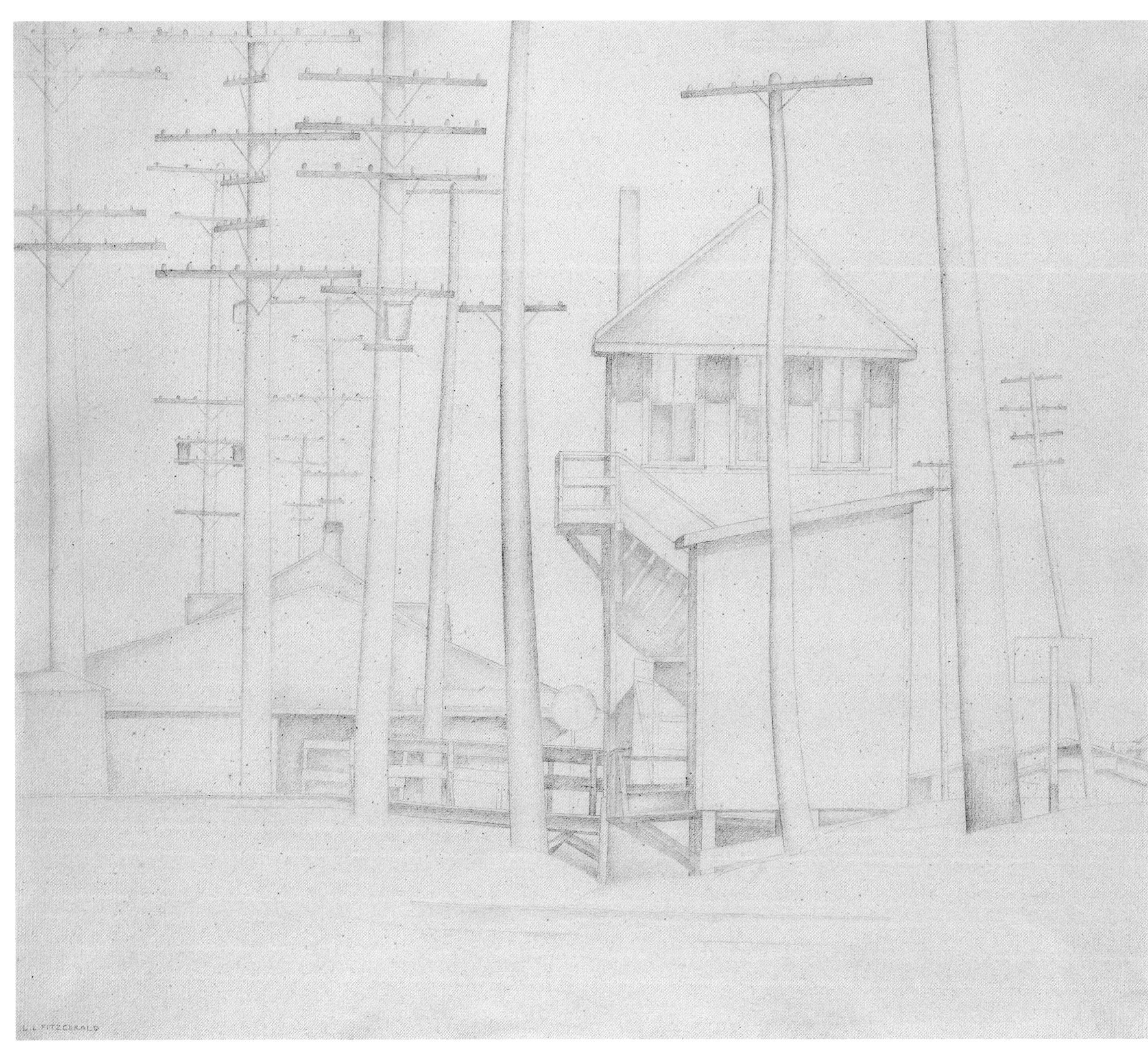

Railway Station, c. 1930–31
graphite on paper
sheet: 31.4 x 35.8 cm

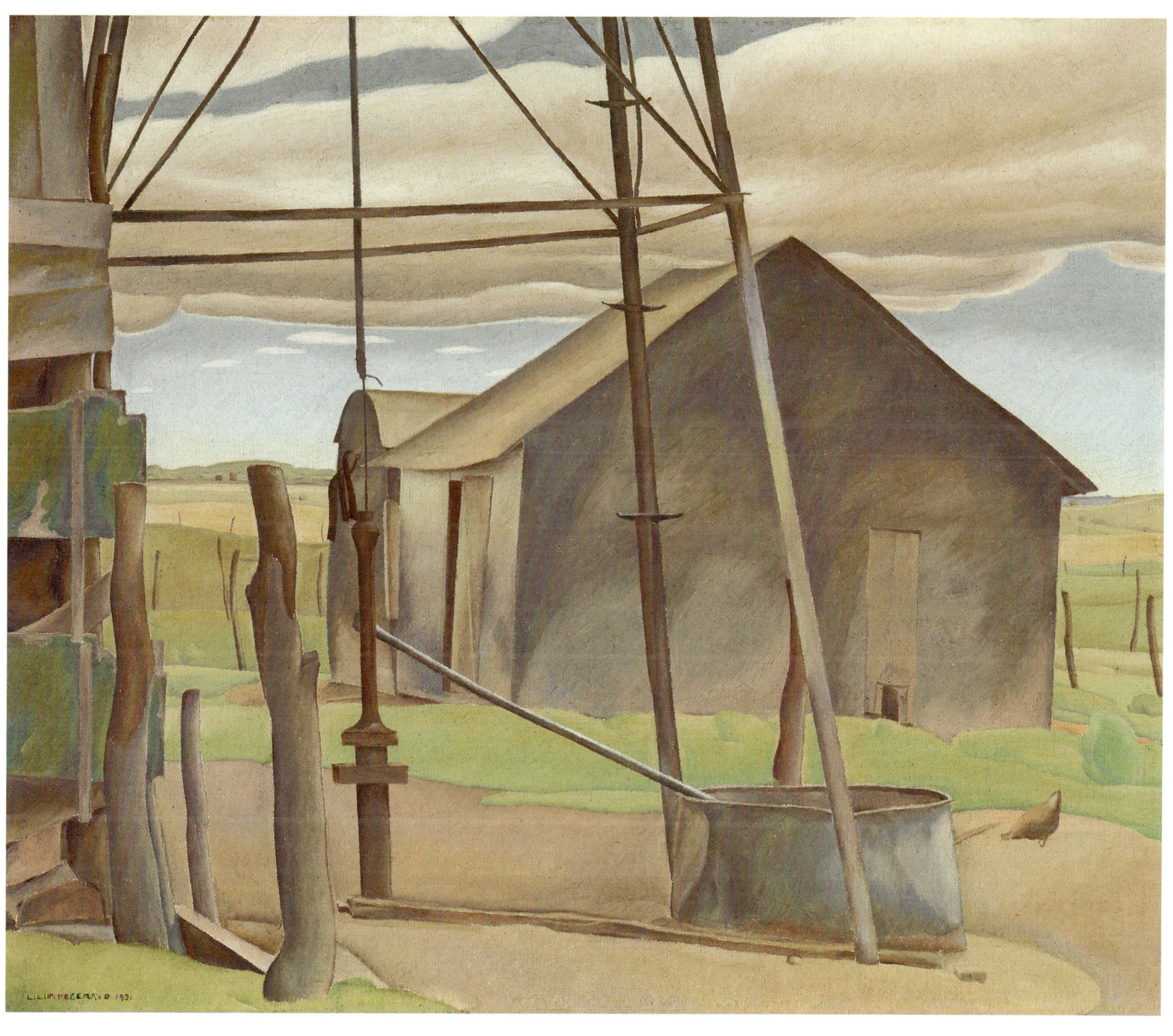

Farmyard, 1931
oil on canvas
34.9 × 42.6 cm

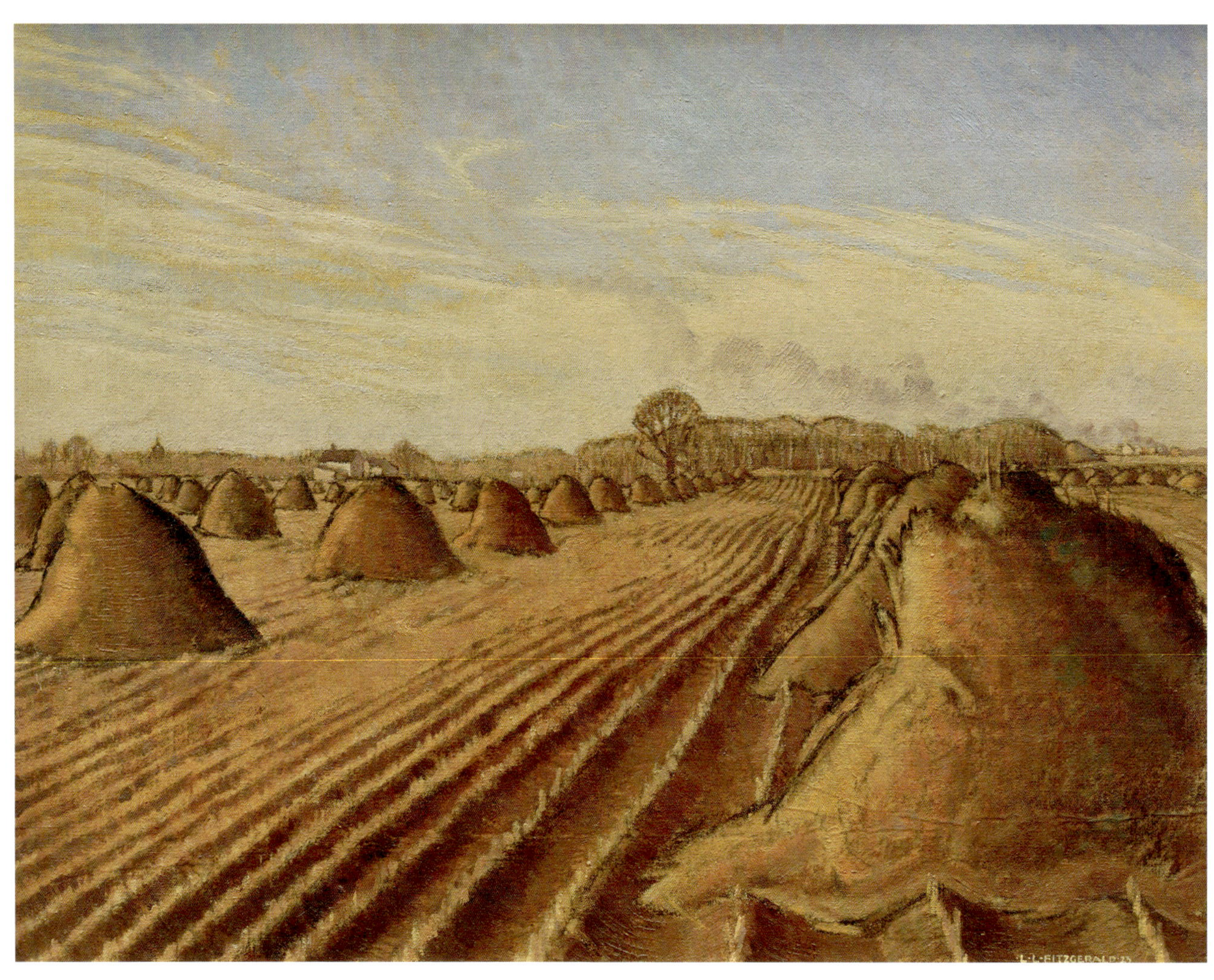

Stooks near Snowflake, Manitoba, 1923
oil on canvas
38.1 × 48.3 cm

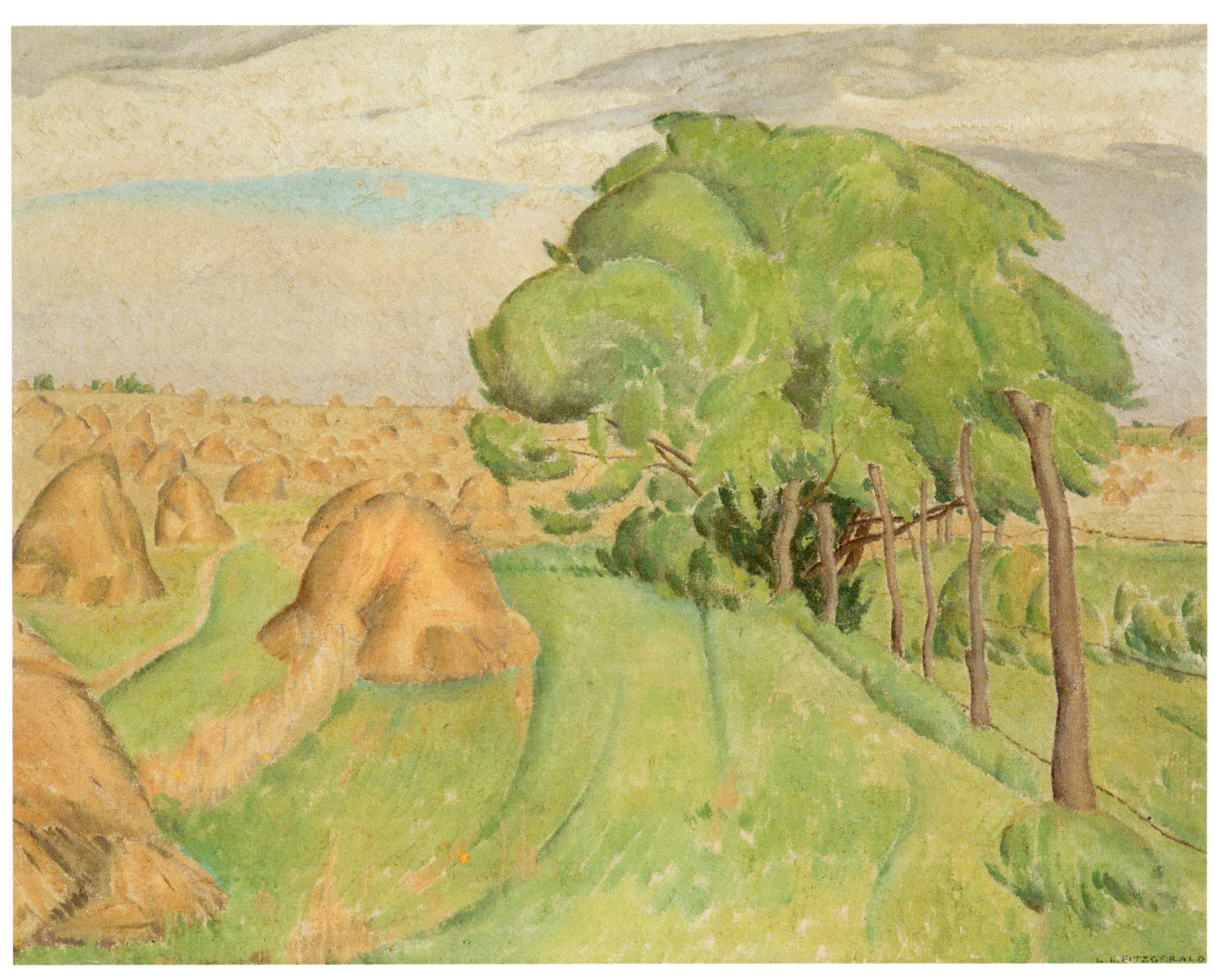

Stooks and Trees, 1930
oil on canvas
29 × 37.7 cm

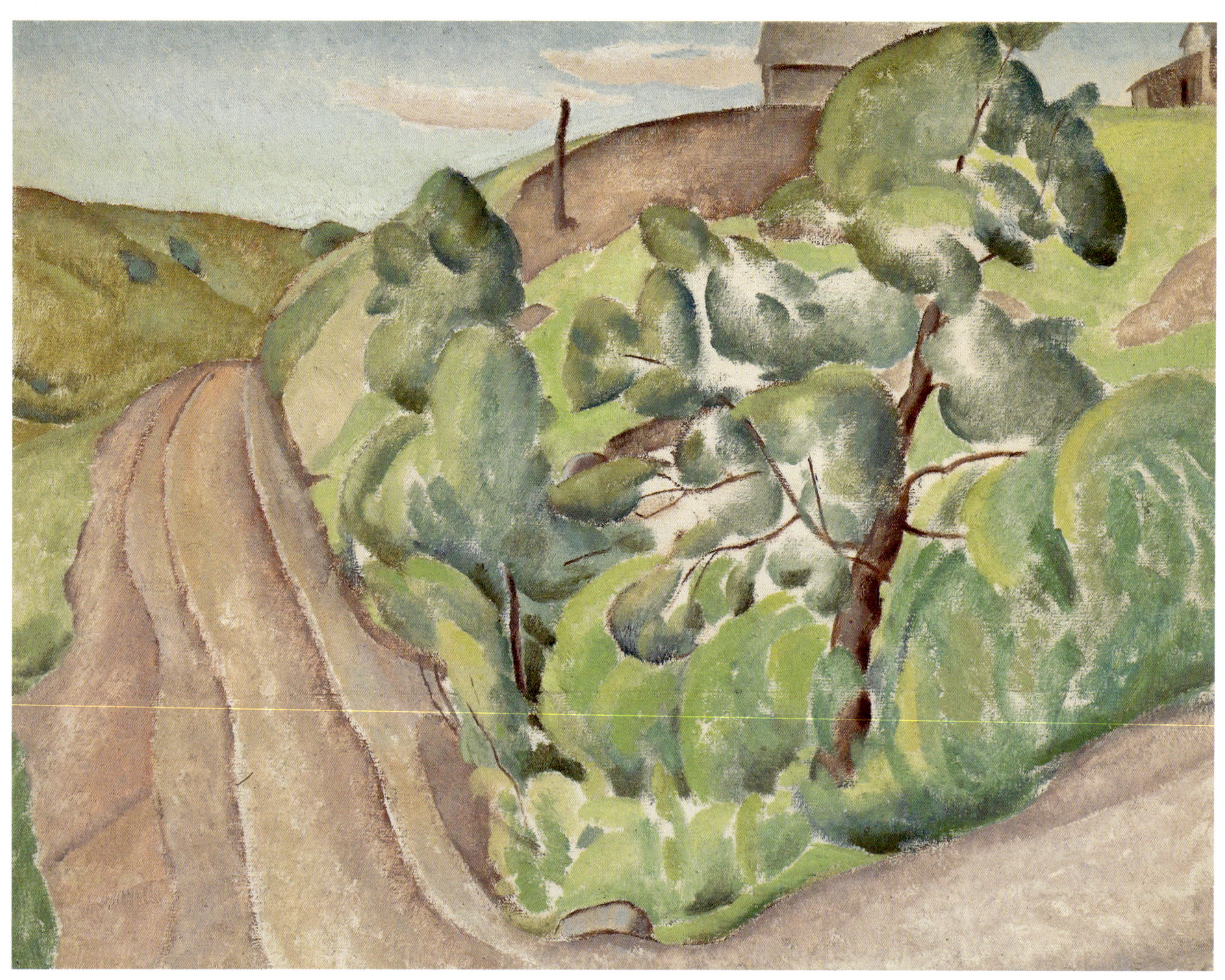

Road in the Country, 1927
oil on canvas
30 × 38 cm

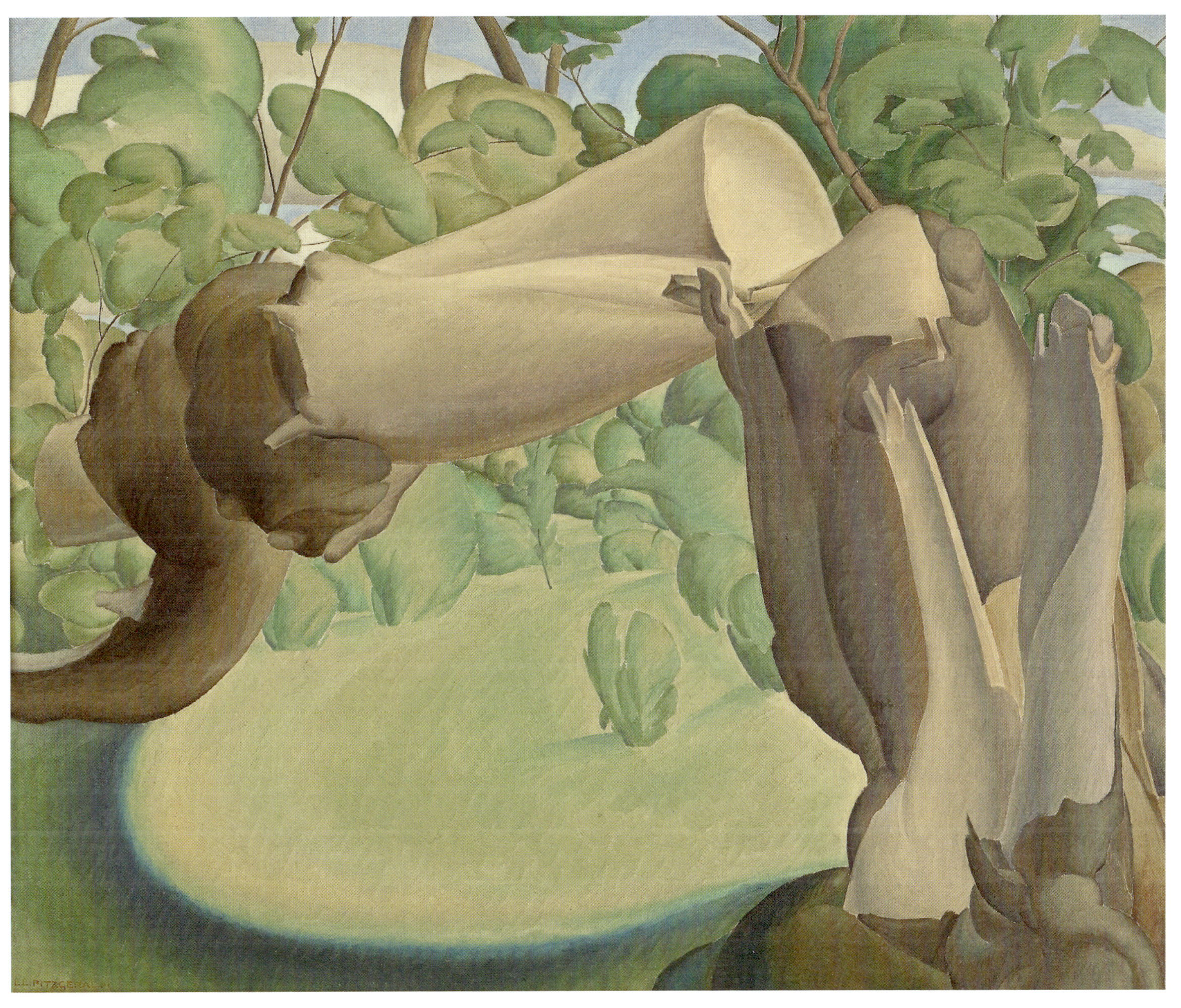

Broken Tree in Landscape, 1931
oil on canvas
35.5 × 42.8 cm

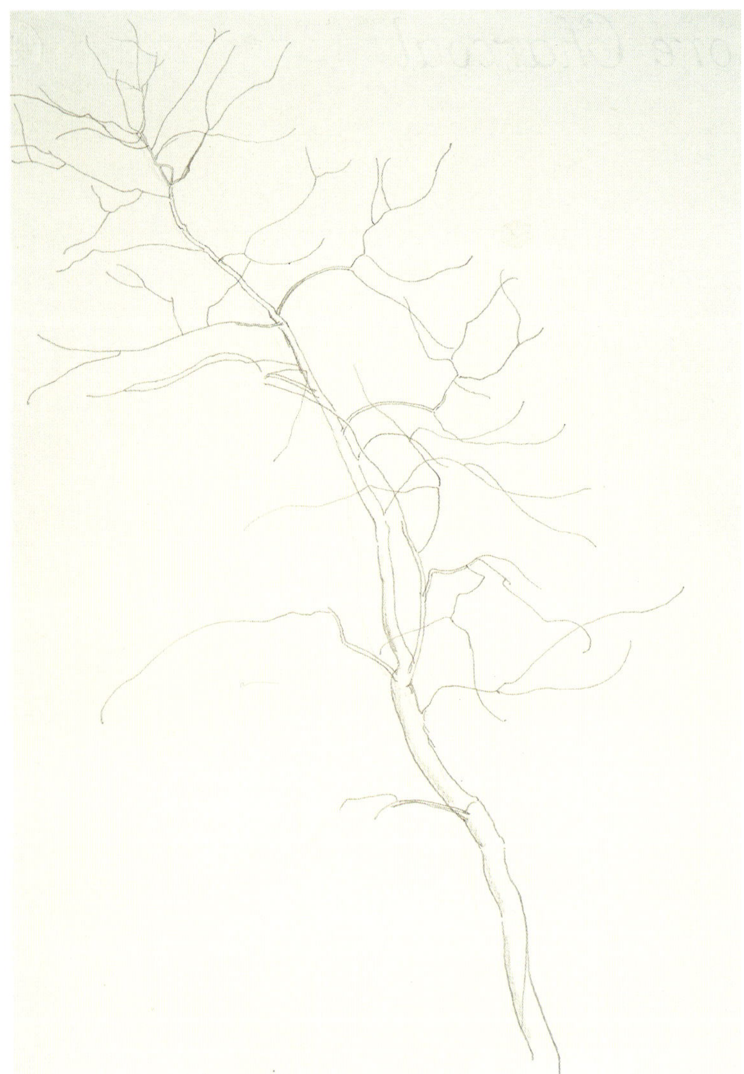

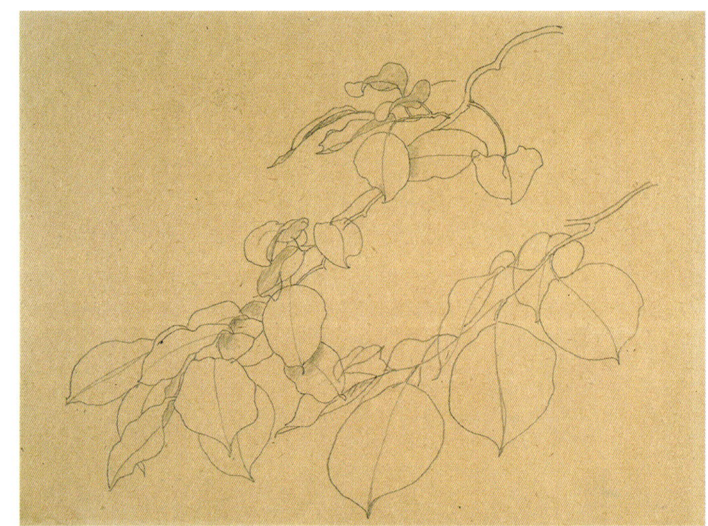

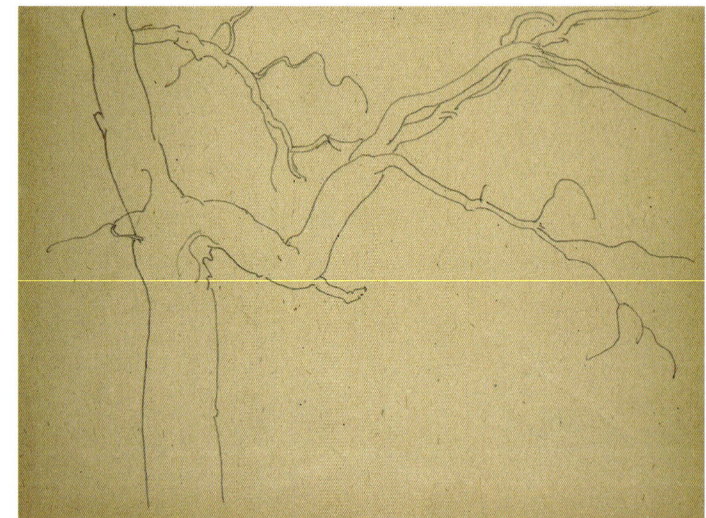

ABOVE
Tree, n.d.
graphite on paper
31.6 × 24 cm

TOP RIGHT
Two Branches with Leaves, n.d.
graphite on paper
22.2 × 29.8 cm

BOTTOM RIGHT
Untitled (Trees), n.d.
graphite on paper
22.3 × 29.8 cm

OPPOSITE
Dead Trees, c. 1930
oil on canvas
50.5 × 55.5 cm;
framed: 53.7 × 58.6 cm

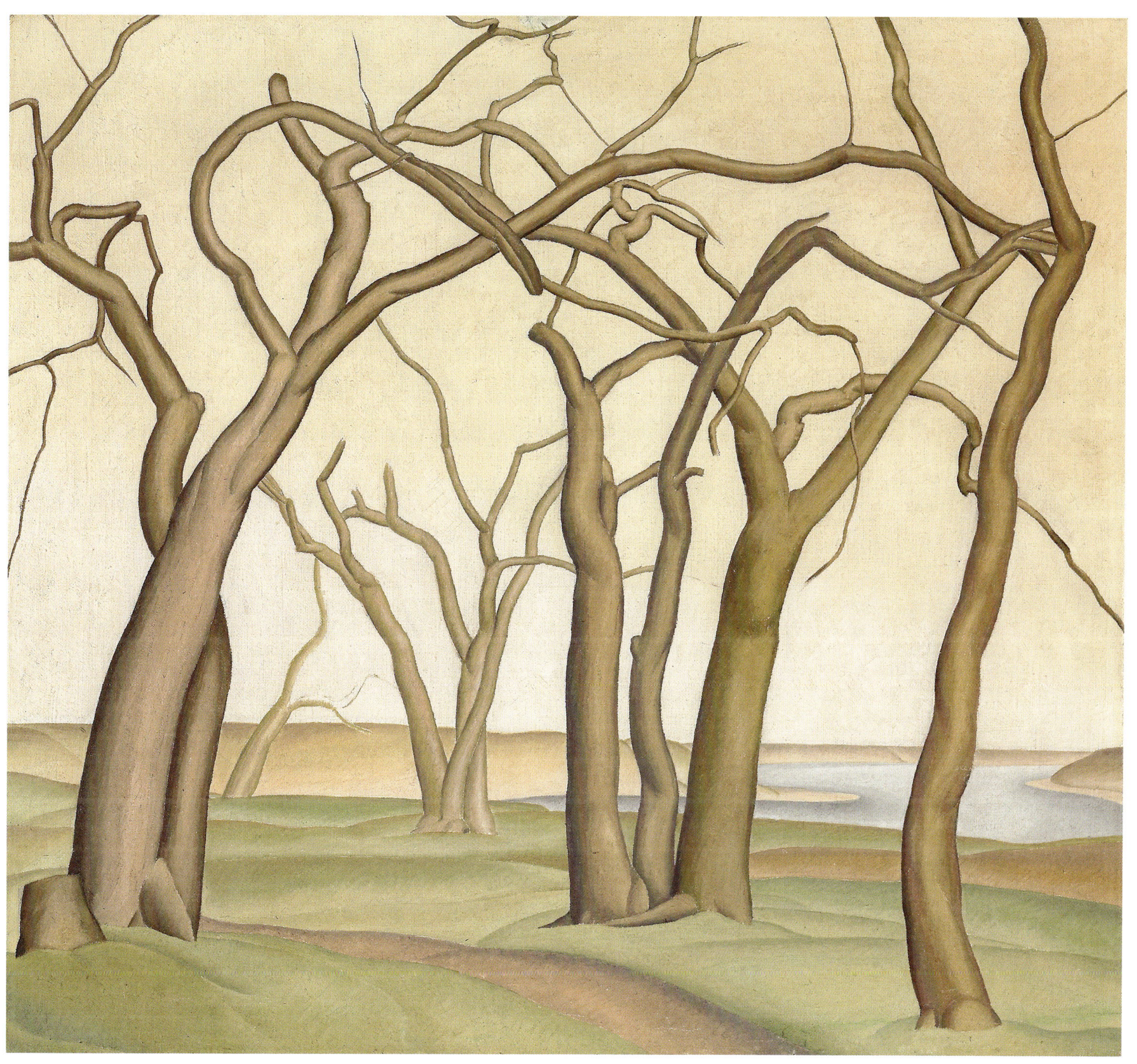

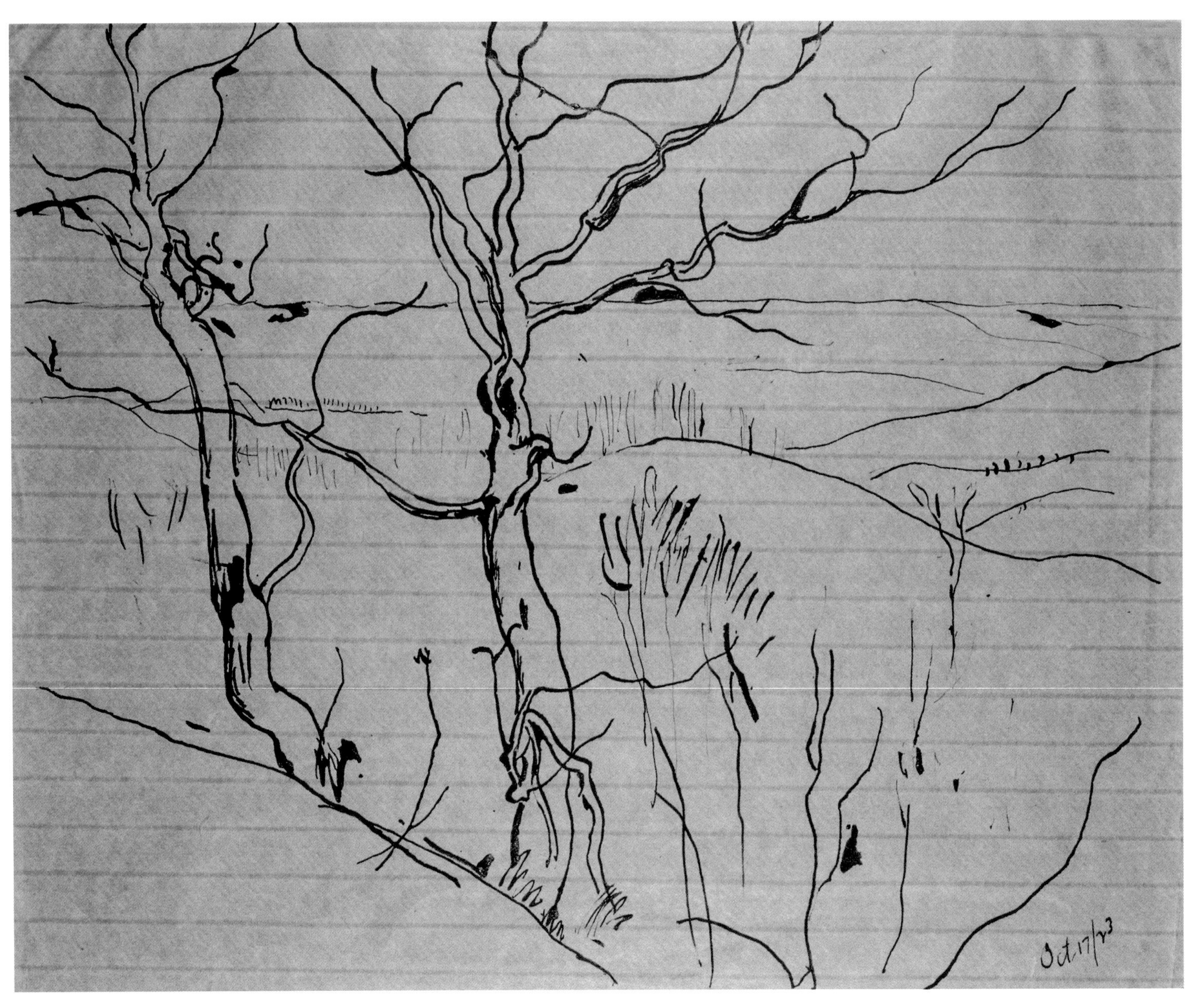

Untitled (Landscape), 1923
ink on paper
30.4 × 37 cm

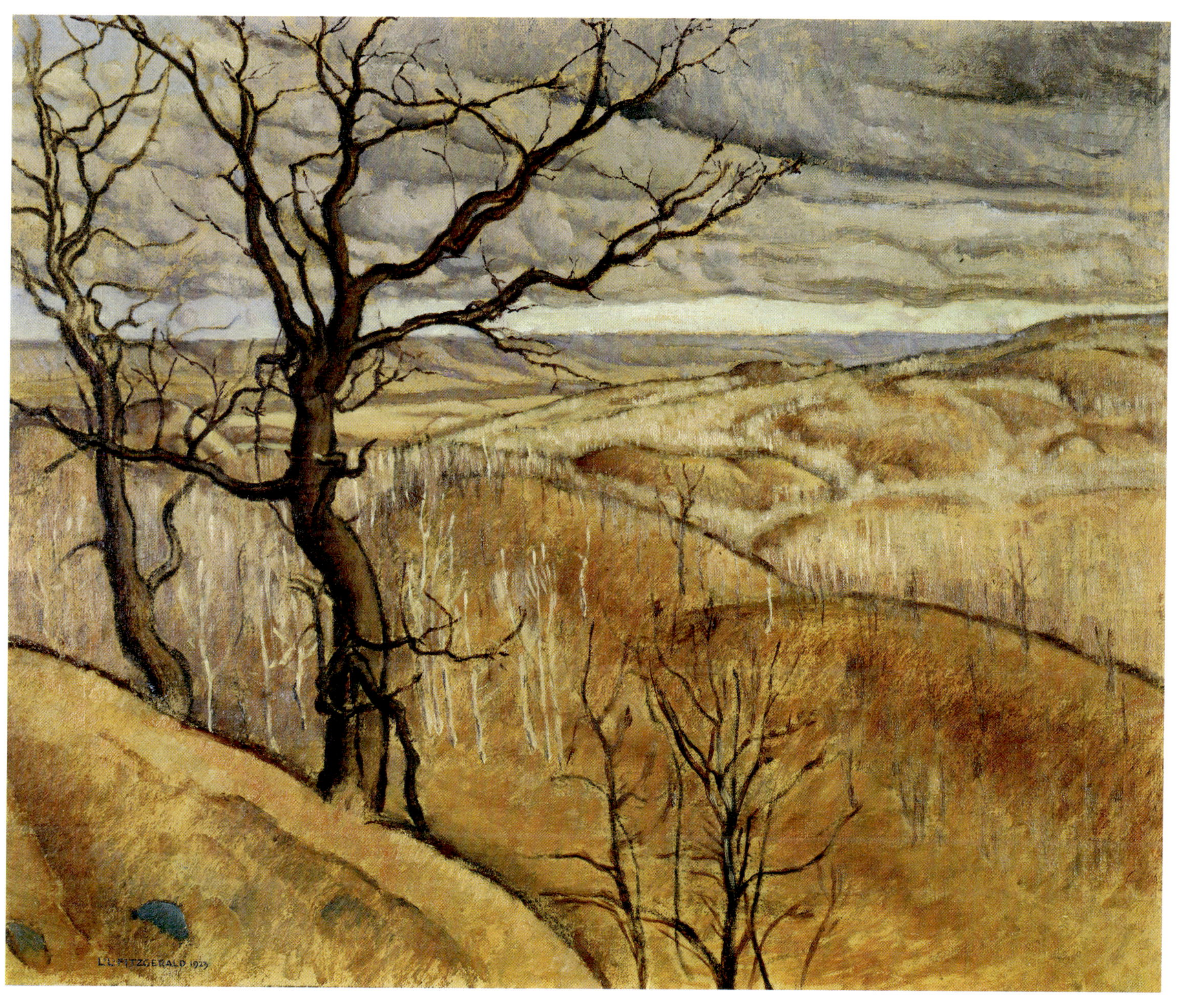

Pembina Valley, 1923
oil on canvas
46 × 56 cm

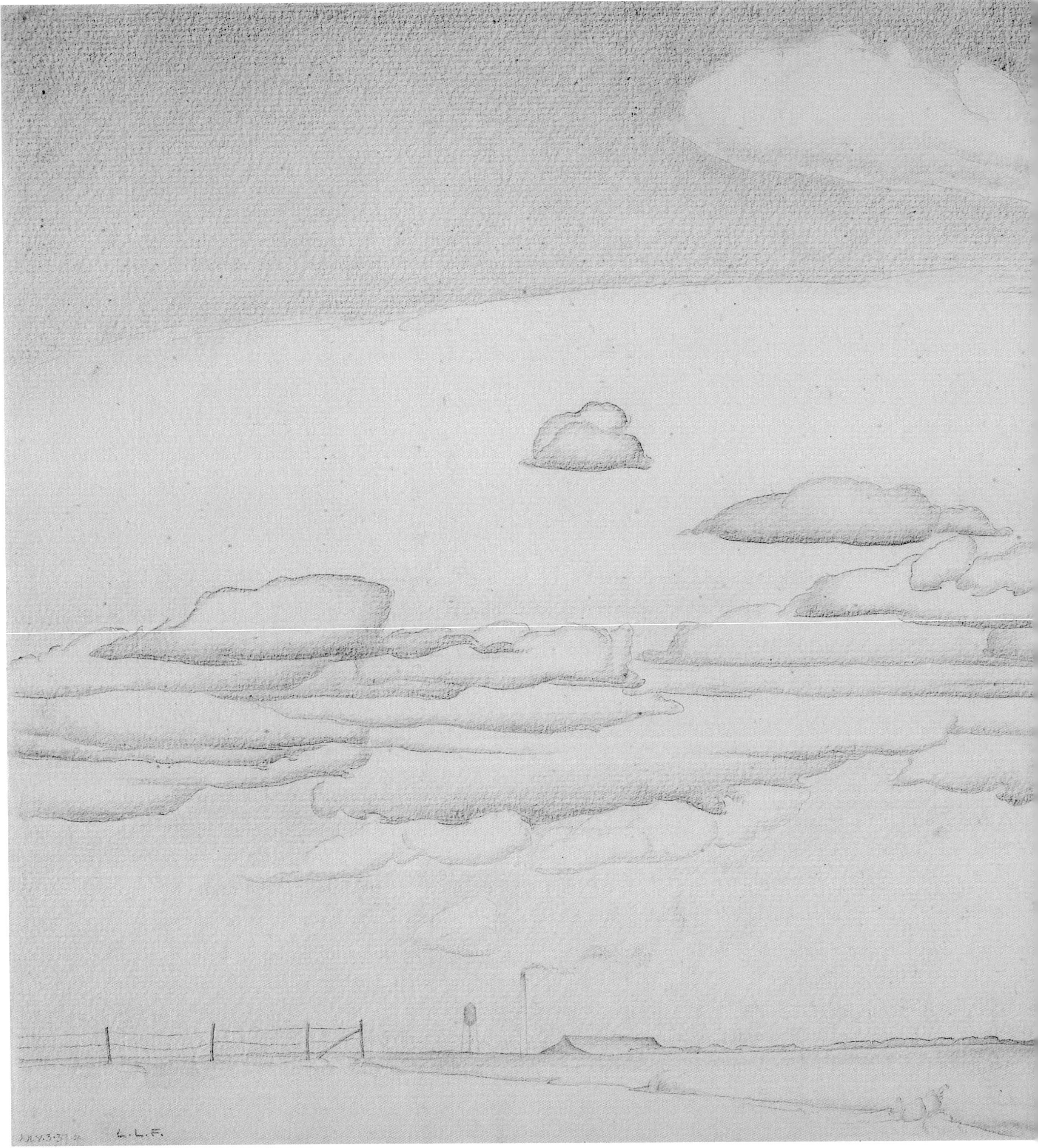

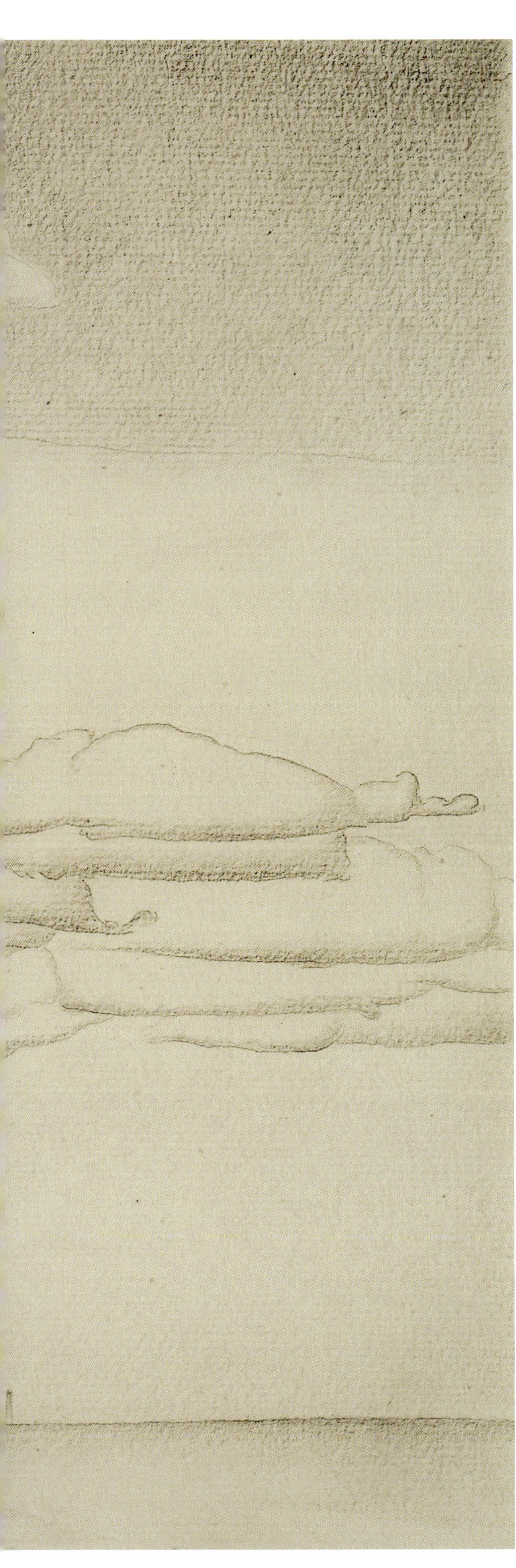

Landscape with Clouds, 1937
graphite on laid paper
24 × 32 cm

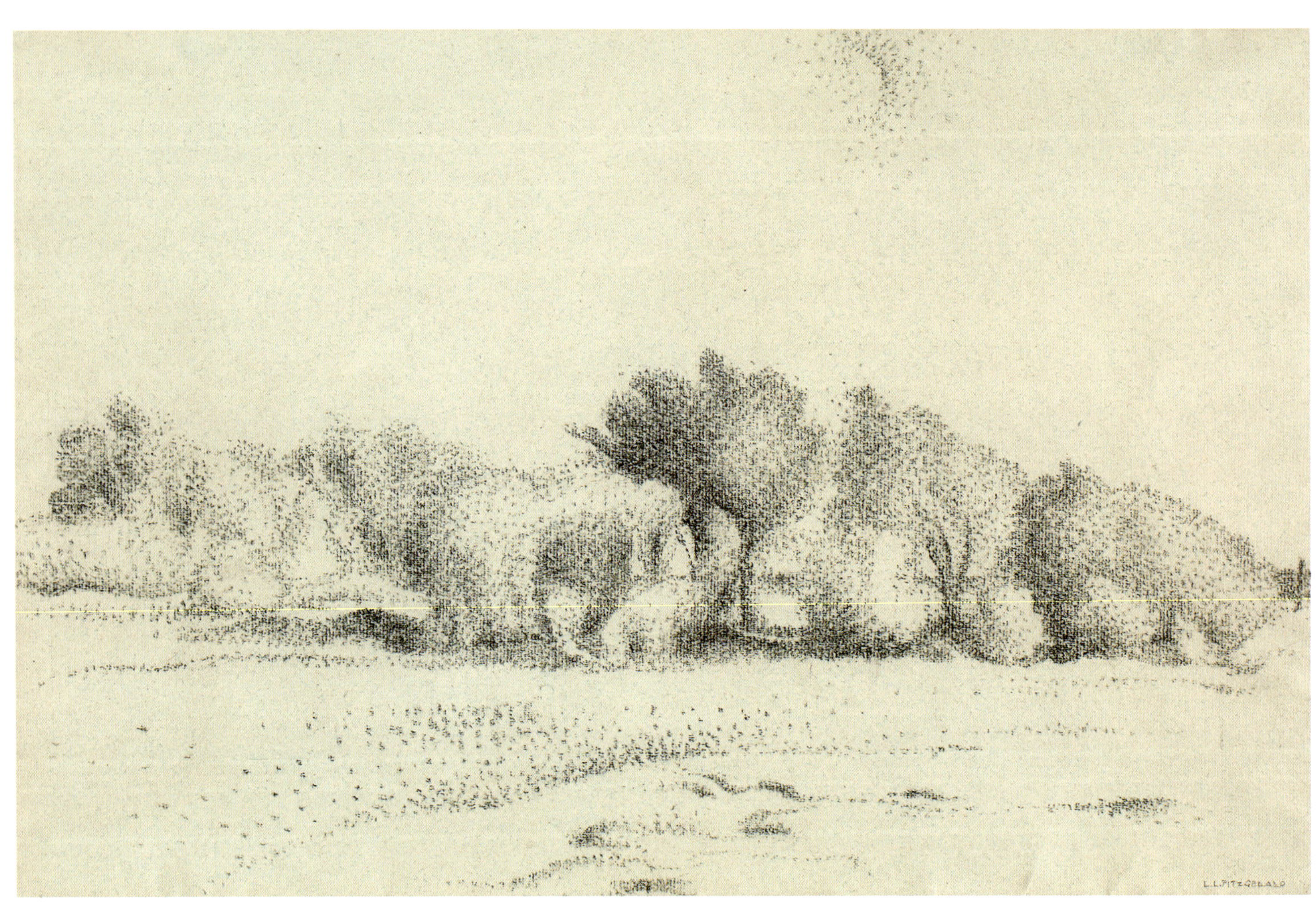

Snowflake, 1949
charcoal on laid paper
31.4 × 47.6 cm

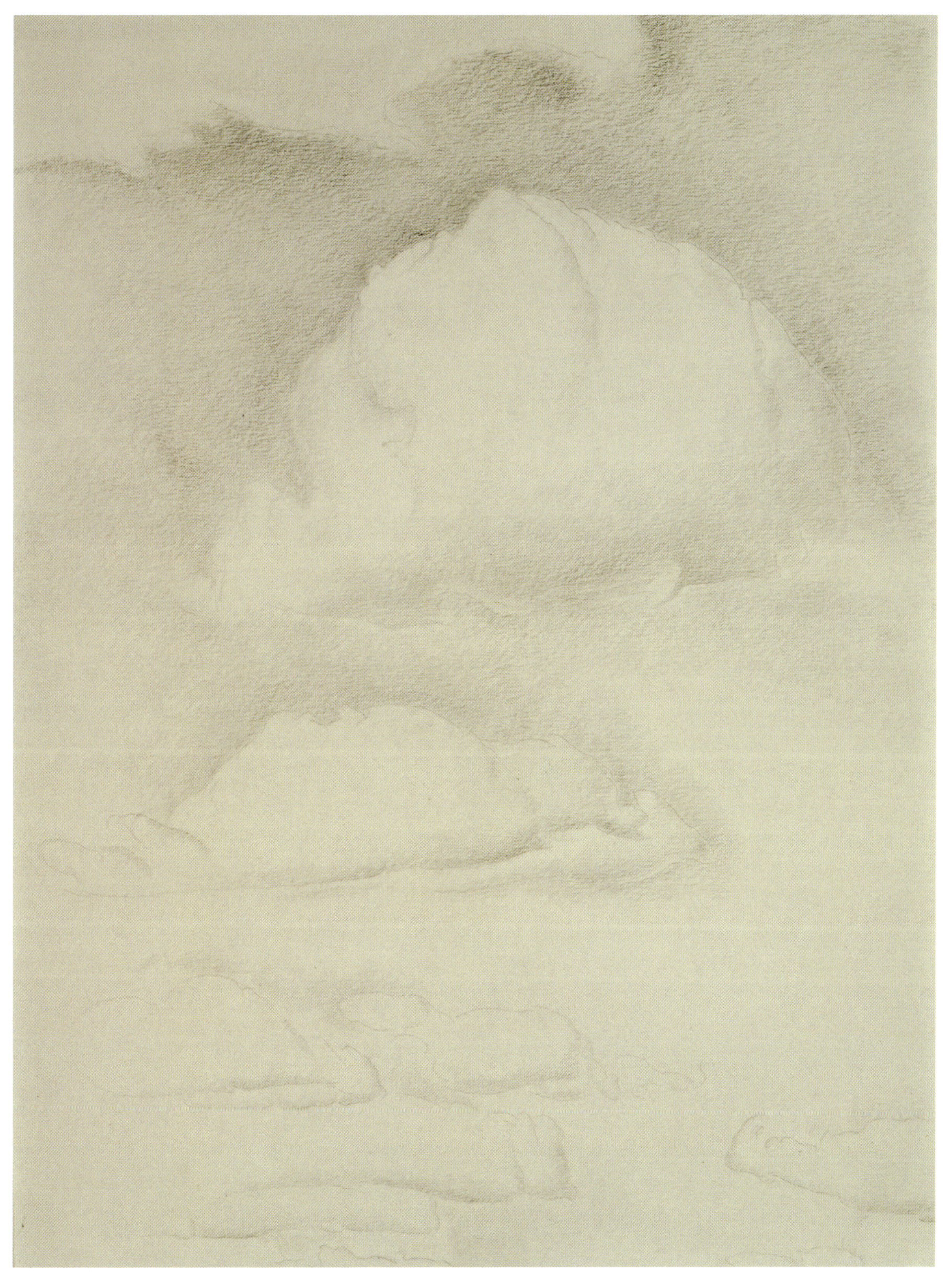

Clouds, 1931
graphite on paper
30.5 × 22.9 cm

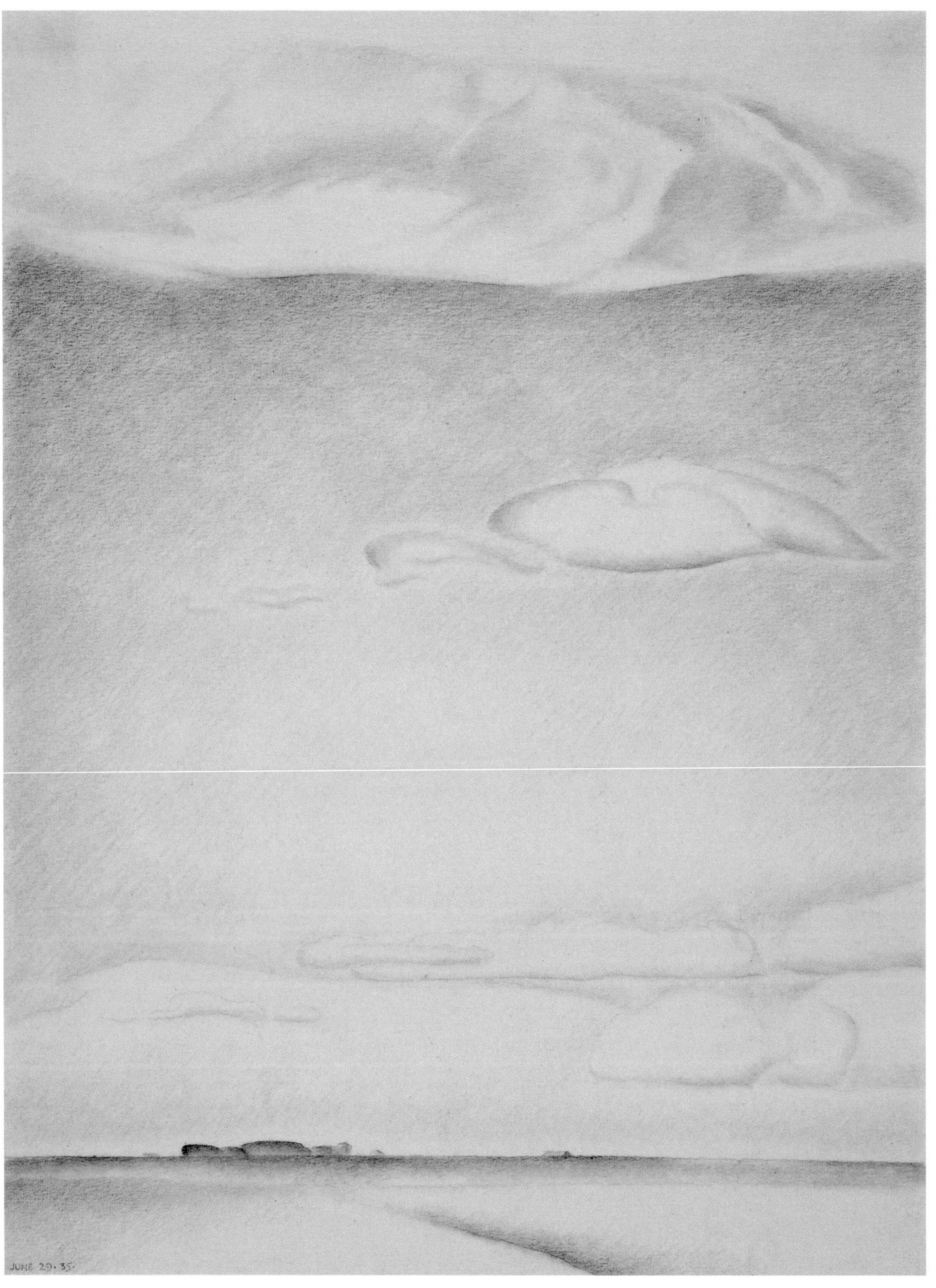

Prairie Sky,
June 29, 1935
graphite on
wove paper
30.5 × 22.9 cm

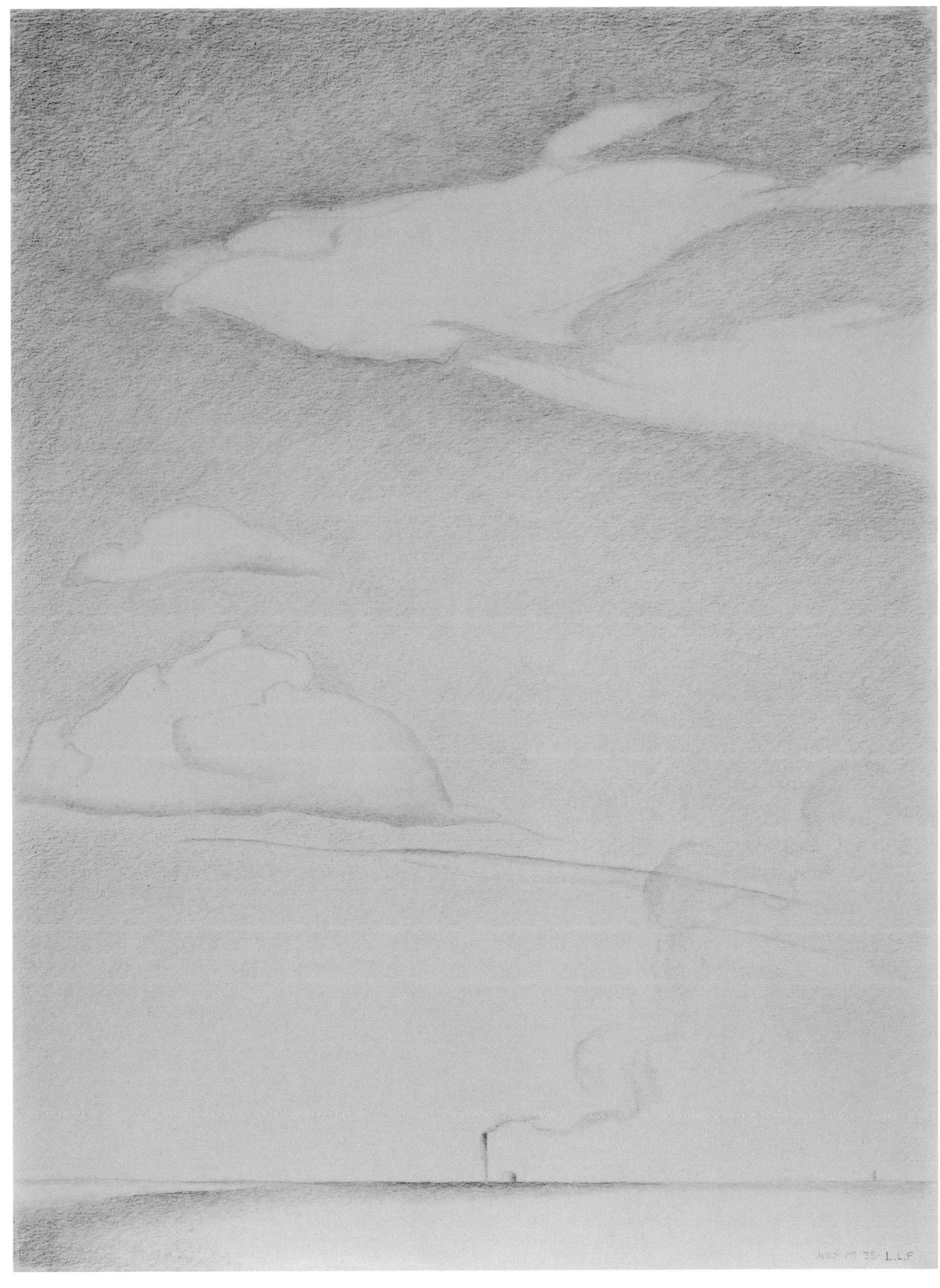

Smokestack and Clouds, 1935
graphite on paper
30.5 × 22.9 cm

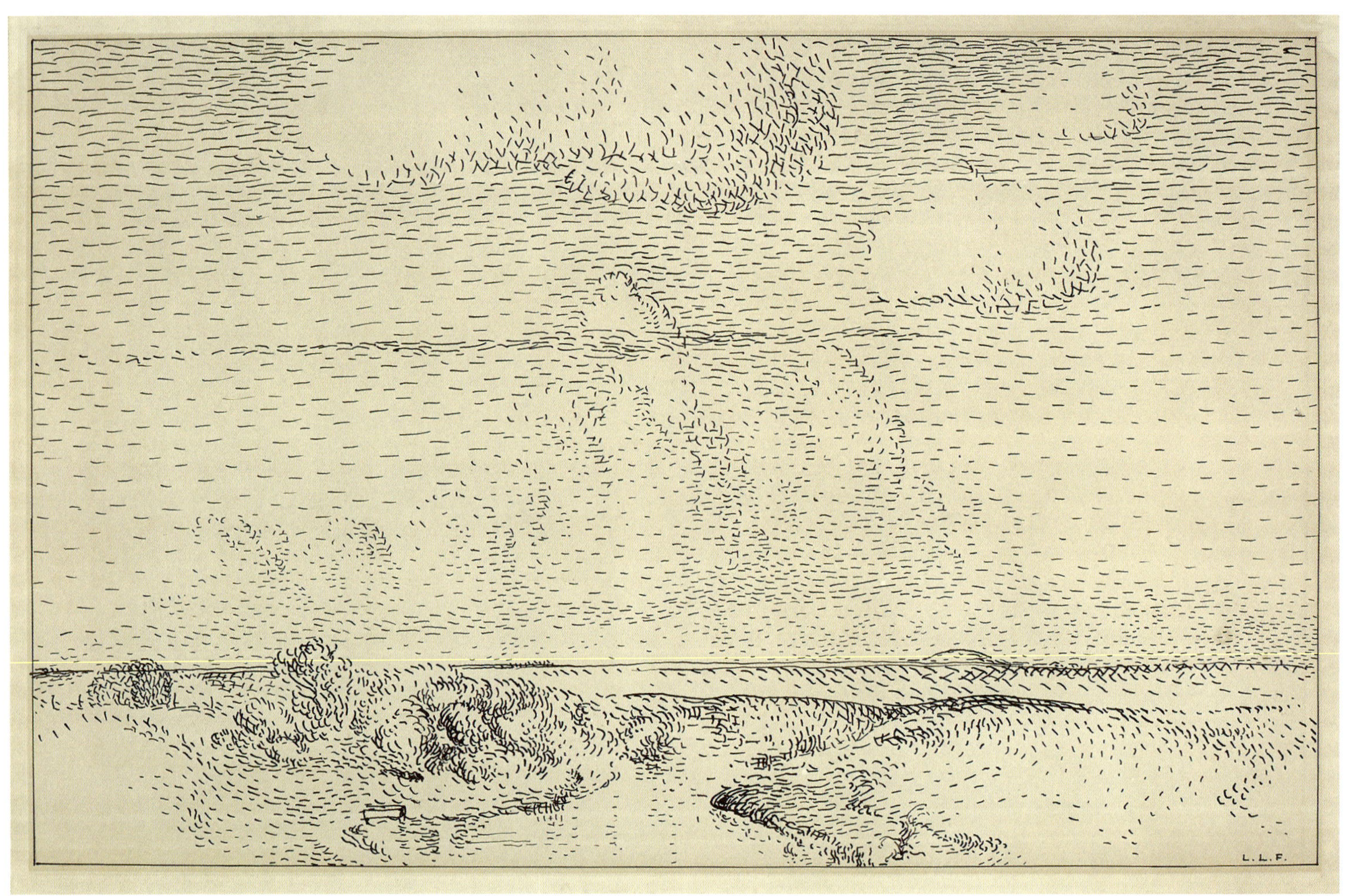

Landscape with River, 1955
ink on paper
sheet: 27.9 × 42.9 cm;
image: 25.5 × 41.8 cm

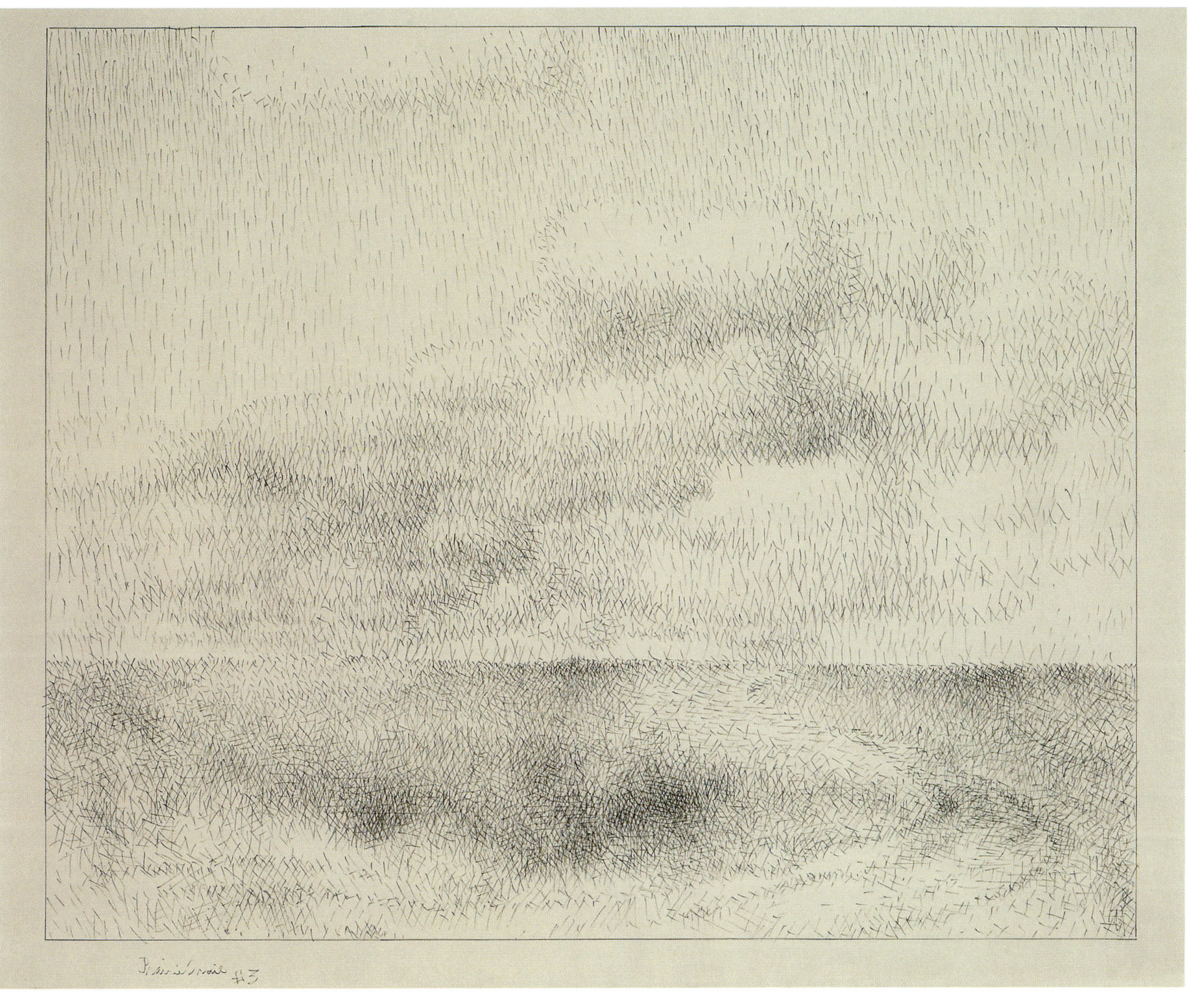

Prairie Trail No. 3,
July 17, 1956
pen and black ink on
laid paper
45.2 × 56.7 cm

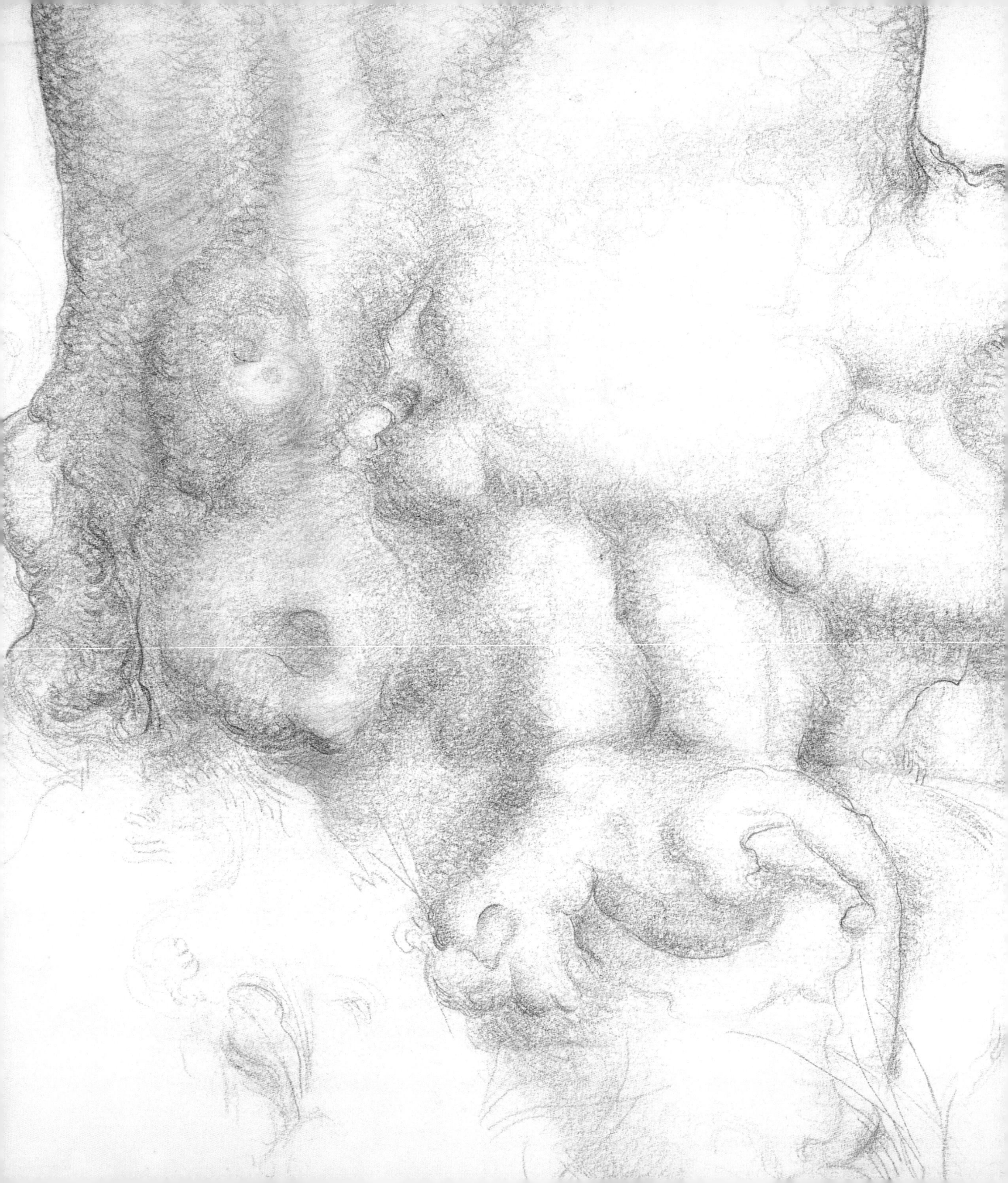

THE LIFE FORCE

Like many of his contemporaries on the Canadian art scene, such as his fellow members of the Group of Seven, FitzGerald had a deep connection to the rendering of landscape, but he was also intrigued by the human figure and the vitality of the body. His depictions of trees and plants often evoke the sleek and satiny contours of a nude, most vividly perhaps in his many exquisite drawings of tree trunks. While the Group of Seven made art that heralded the vitality of an emerging nation—raw and wild and often magnificent in scale—FitzGerald was undertaking an altogether more intimate project, documenting the elements of nature to be found in his own neighbourhood and nearby parks, or the nude subjects who were engaged to model at the Winnipeg School of Art, which he led from 1929 to 1949.

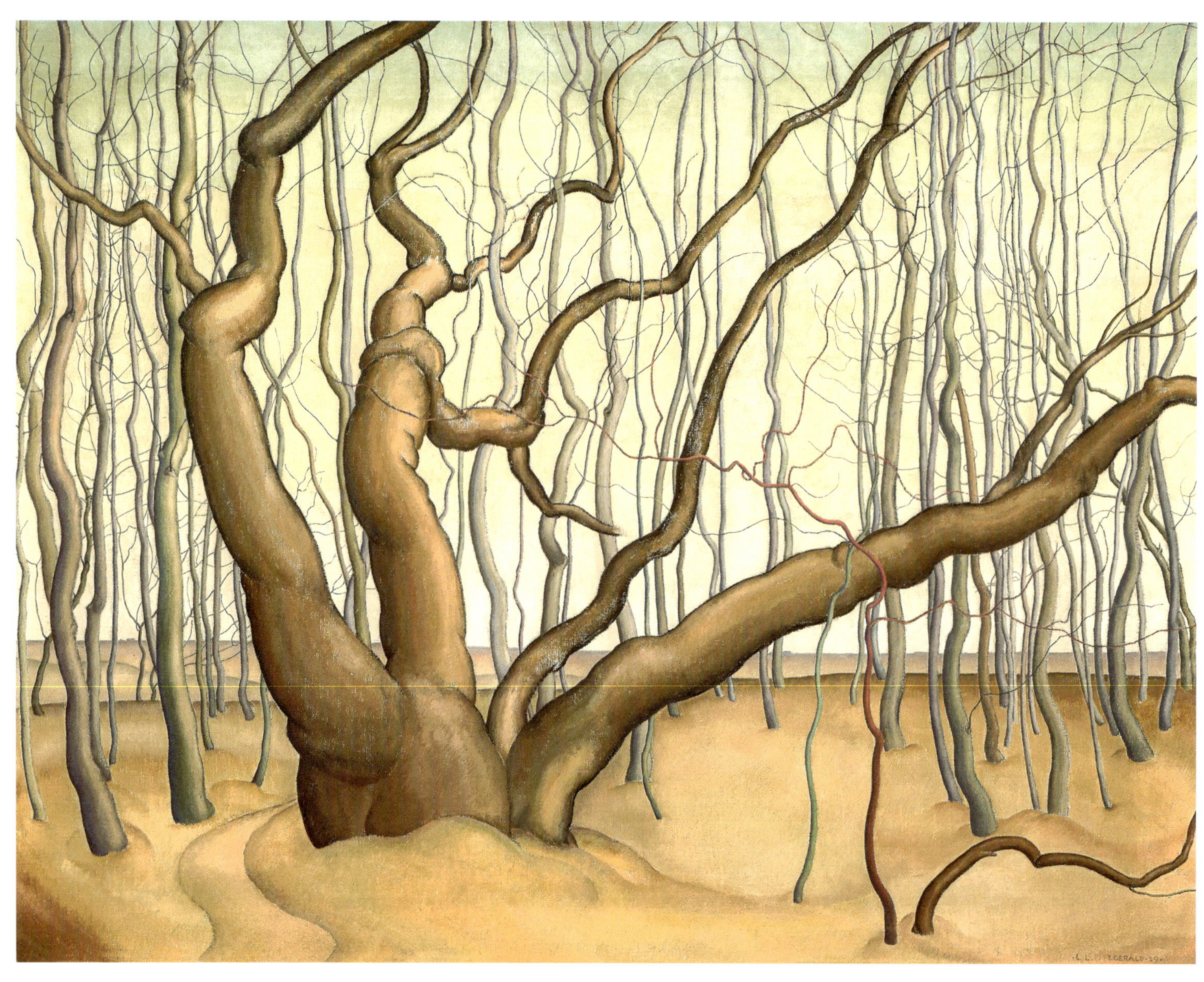

Poplar Woods
(Poplars), 1929
oil on canvas
71.8 × 91.5 cm

SOMETHING FROM UNDER THE SKIN

WANDA KOOP

When I was a child, I took Saturday morning art classes at the Winnipeg Art Gallery, which in those days was in what is now the Manitoba Archives Building. I started when I was seven, and I went until I was fourteen. I had been chosen by my school to attend, and I loved it. I counted the sleeps until I could go again. I didn't do well in school, so this was everything for me.

I went for three years and then they decided it was another child's turn. I thought I was going to die. I went on my own on the bus to the art gallery on a Saturday. I knew that the director, Ferdinand Eckhardt, would often work on the weekends; I had seen him in his office. So I went to his office and the door was open a crack, and I knocked and in his booming voice he said, "Come in. Can I help you?" I was trembling from top to bottom. He said, "Tell me, what do you want?" I said, "I need art classes," and he said, "Oh, well, let's see what we can do about that, then." And he took my hand and he put me in an art class. And we repeated that every year until I was fourteen.

So I grew up at the WAG surrounded by the LeMoine FitzGerald paintings and the Renaissance works in the Lord Gort collection and Christiane Pflug and all the rest. I can remember sitting on the floor in front of FitzGerald's painting *Poplar Woods* during our classes. It stimulated something inside me. I remember thinking that it wasn't quite about trees. Other than that, I don't think I could verbalize what I was feeling. Now, as an adult, I can see the metaphor. It is totally erotic.

At that time I also used to read Greek mythology, with great difficulty, because I am dyslexic. I remember loving those stories. There was something of this same feeling in them. I also had a tiny fifty-cent book on Delacroix, from a series published by Abrams—I had saved my money and I bought it. I wore that book threadbare in my back pocket; I took it to school and everywhere. In the winter of 2018, I went to see the Delacroix show in New York, and I burst out laughing. As a kid, you don't know what you're tapping into—that sense of the bodies being so visceral, all the muscles twisting. I see that here. Looking at this painting now I also think about the craziness of a Bruegel, in the way the picture is painted, with all the attention to the details. It's like photorealism on acid. It's not really realistic but it makes you think that it is.

I grew up in a very repressed religious environment. At one point I wanted to be a dancer but I was not allowed to dance. There was a conflict in me about whether to become a dancer or an artist. But what I found so wonderful about making art was that no one really had to know what was happening inside me. I could use images and I could create my own iconography to express what I was feeling. People could perhaps look at my work and see recognizable subject matter, but from very early on I understood metaphor—that I could be subversive in a certain way.

This is what I feel about this work. FitzGerald was living in a time when perhaps he couldn't be truly who he needed to be. If you look at those wispy trees in behind, they're like blood vessels, almost like varicose veins—blue and green. These are human forms. It's really a figurative work—it's not a picture of trees. It's a painting that's expressing something about an internal state. Yet it alludes to everything that we need it to allude to; we can recognize it as trees and the ground. FitzGerald creates that safe place for the viewer. Of course, I can't be sure he was thinking all these things when he made this, but as somebody who reads things visually, I've always read this painting as saying something from under the skin.

I can also see here that he is a very anxious man, a very precise person. This painting is like a lament. There's a kind of grasping for something that's not ever going to happen. How old was he when he painted this? About forty, I think. He was probably just starting to think that he was getting old. He was headed there. It reminds me of some work that my ex-husband, William Eakin, made when his father was dying. William went to visit a horticultural society garden—it was at the end of the growing season, and he photographed all the vegetation that was dying. It feels like this. There is the same kind of sadness there.

There is one branch at the centre of this painting that just sort of fades away and attaches to the white ground in the background. That's the key to the whole painting for me, right there. It's smack in the middle of the composition; it's the first thing I see, and it's his way of saying, "This is a painting. This whole thing is an abstraction." ■

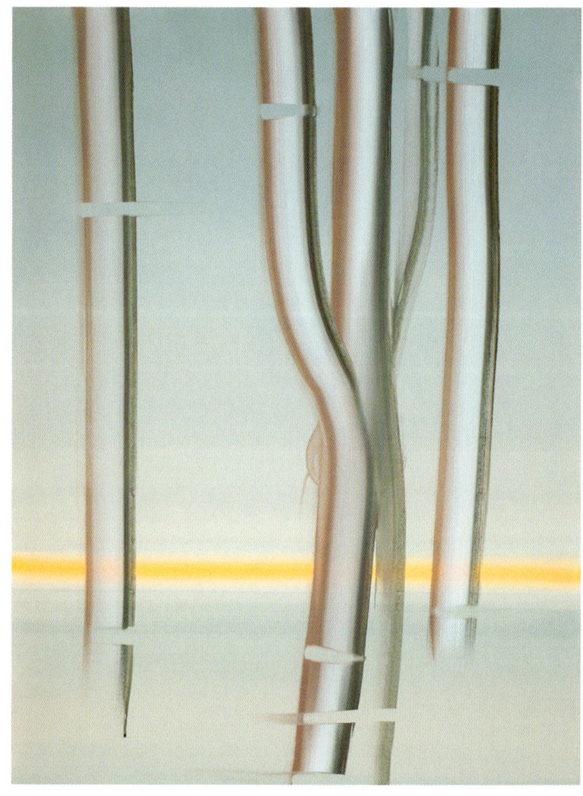

WANDA KOOP
(b. 1951)
Note from Scandinavia, 2019
acrylic on canvas
101.6 × 76.2 cm
Courtesy of the artist

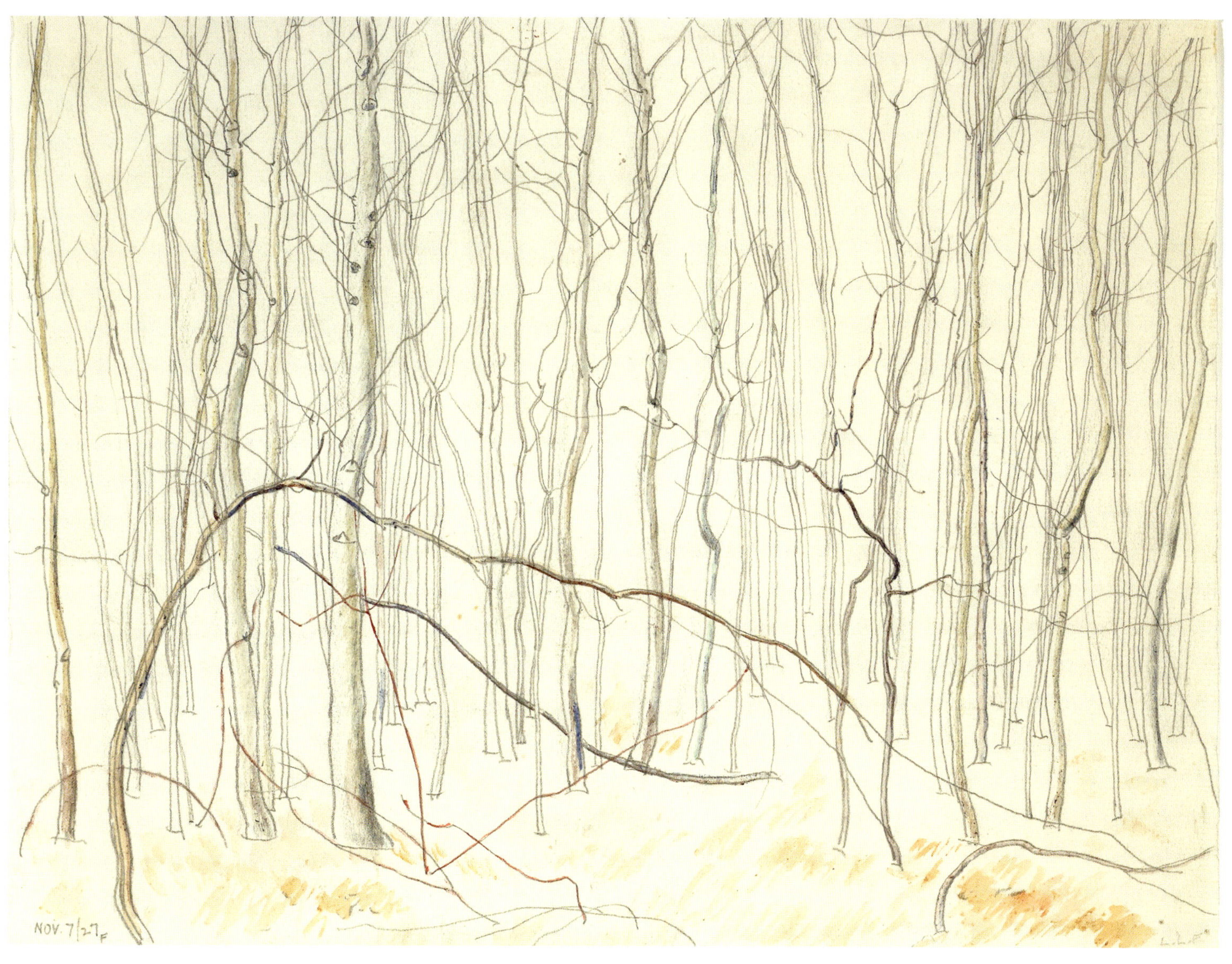

Sketch for "Poplar Woods," 1927
graphite, ink on paper
23.7 × 31.8 cm

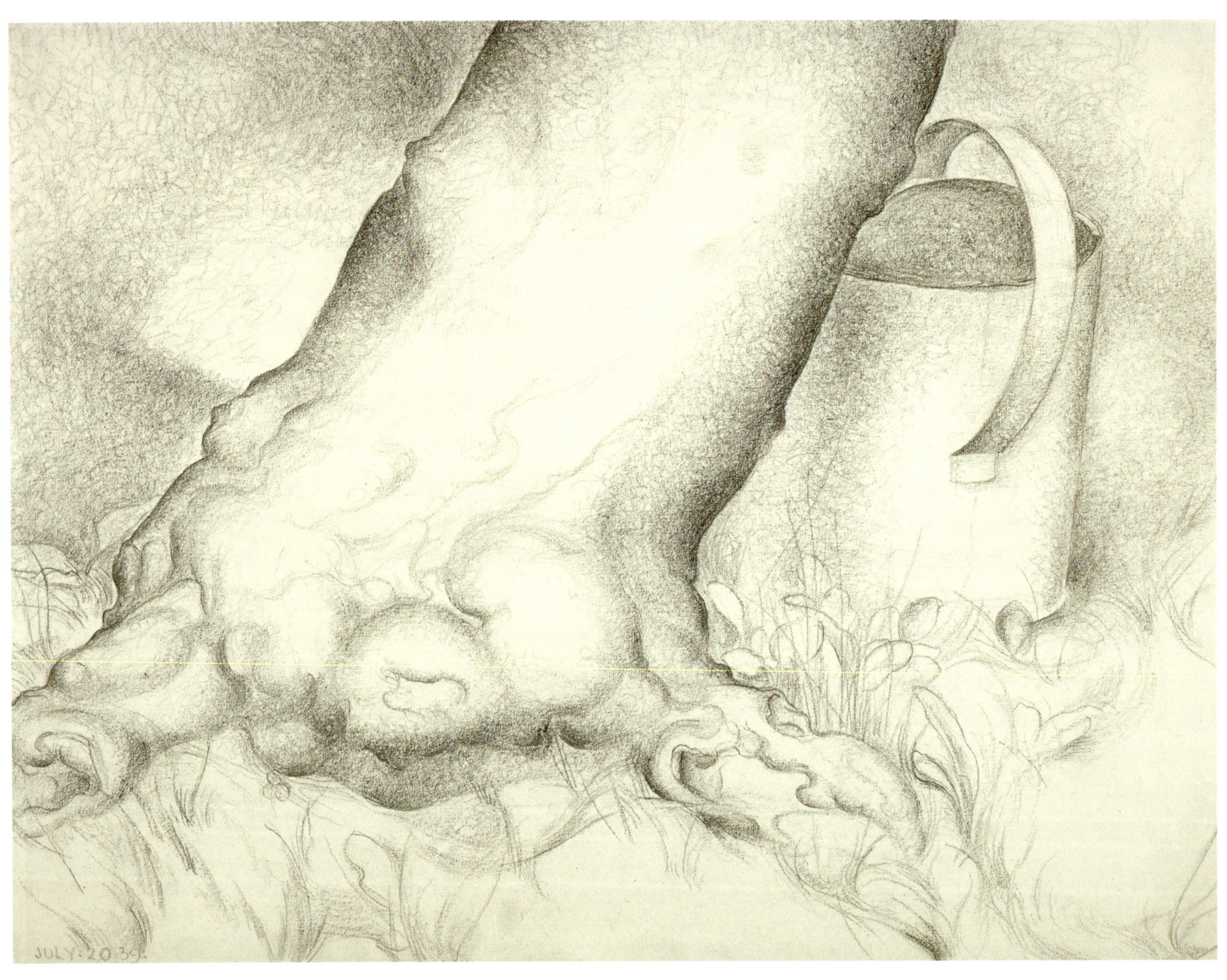

Tree Trunk, 1939
graphite on paper
28.3 x 37.1 cm

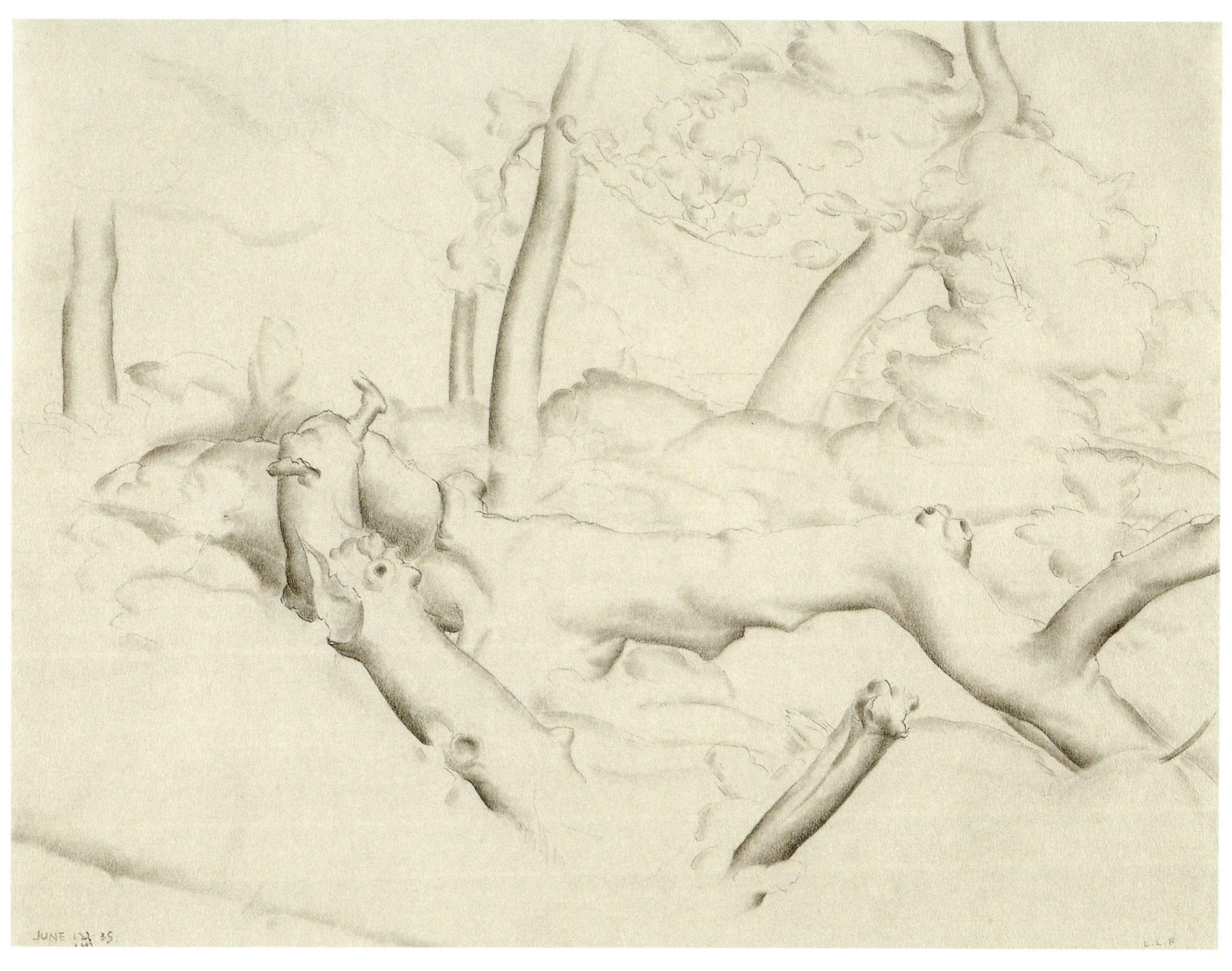

Trees and Stumps,
June 12, 1935
graphite on wove paper
22.9 × 30.2 cm

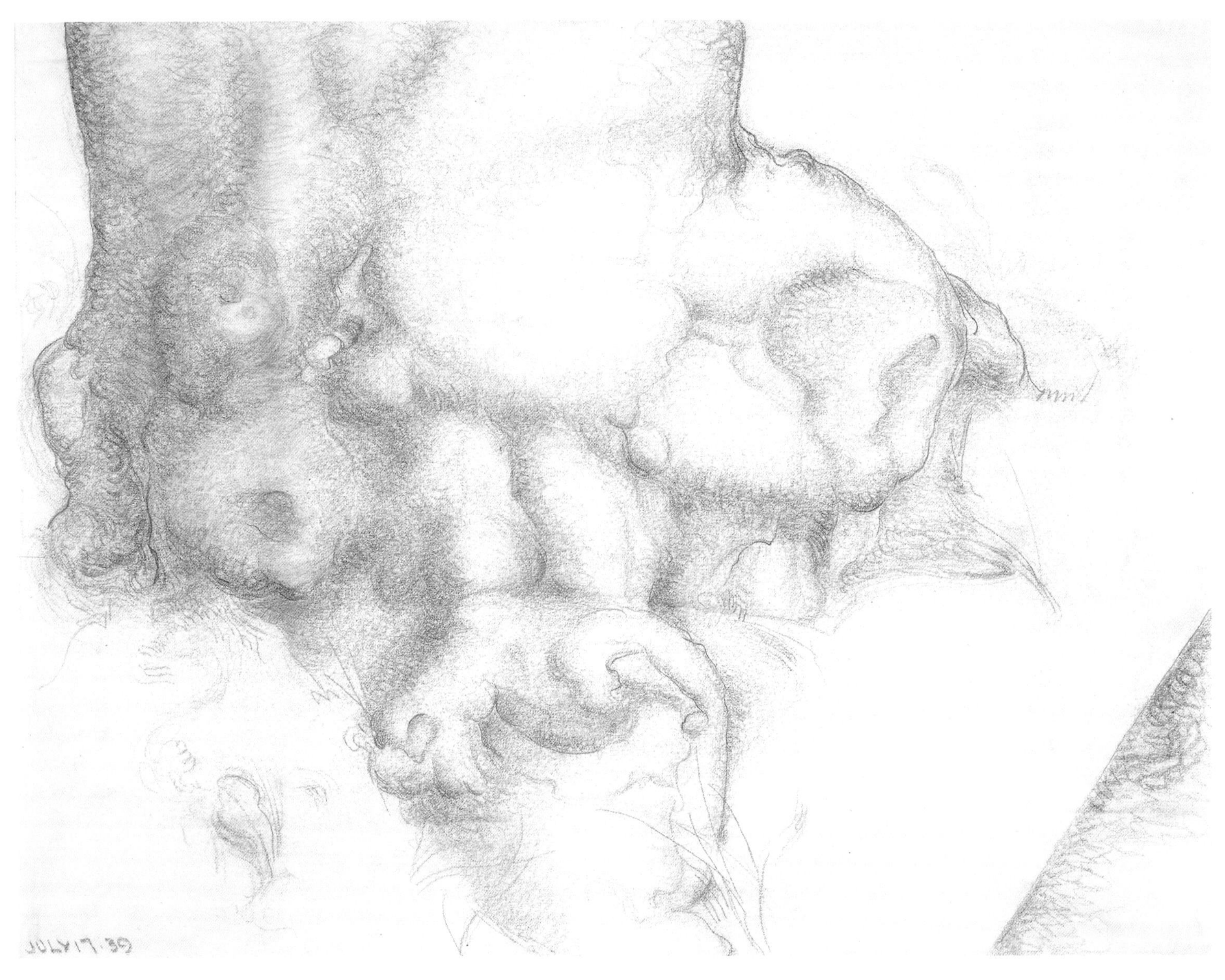

Tree Roots, 1939
graphite on paper
27.6 × 38.1 cm

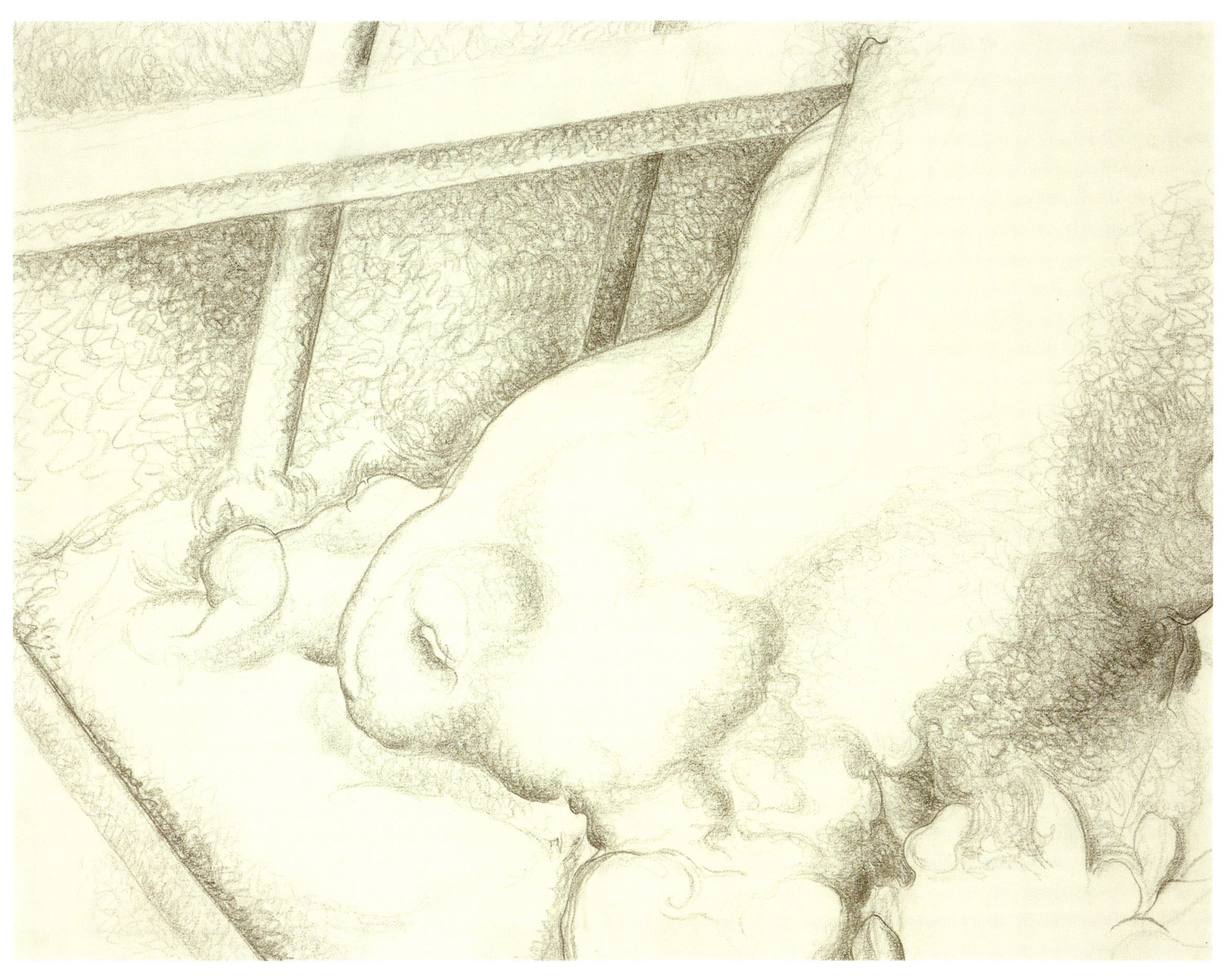

Untitled, n.d.
graphite on paper
29.1 × 38.1 cm

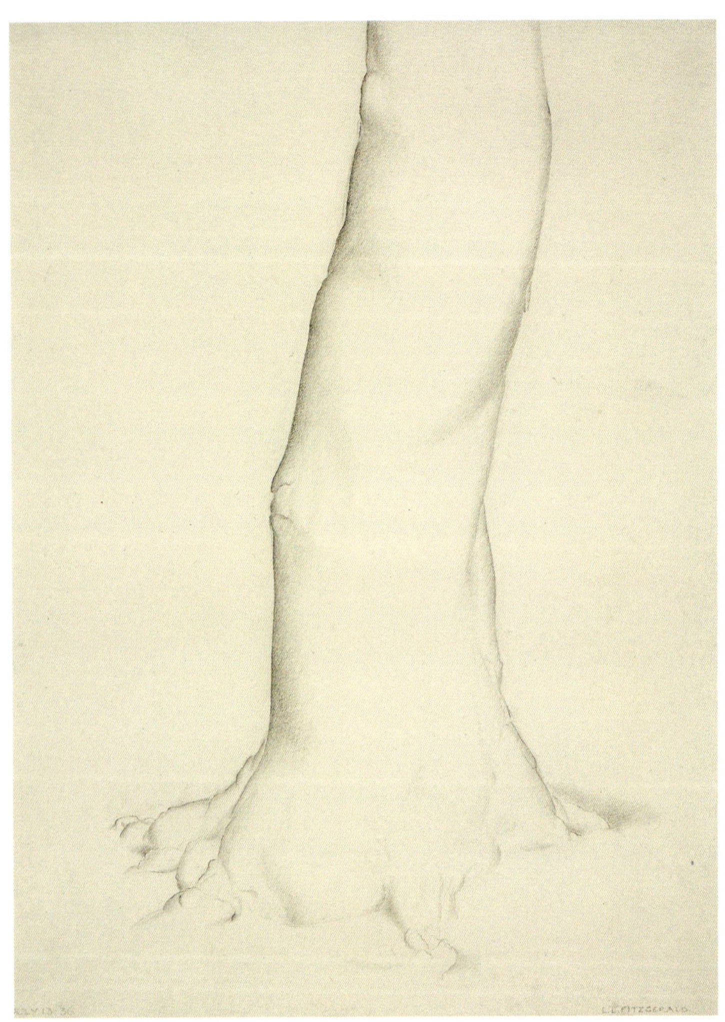

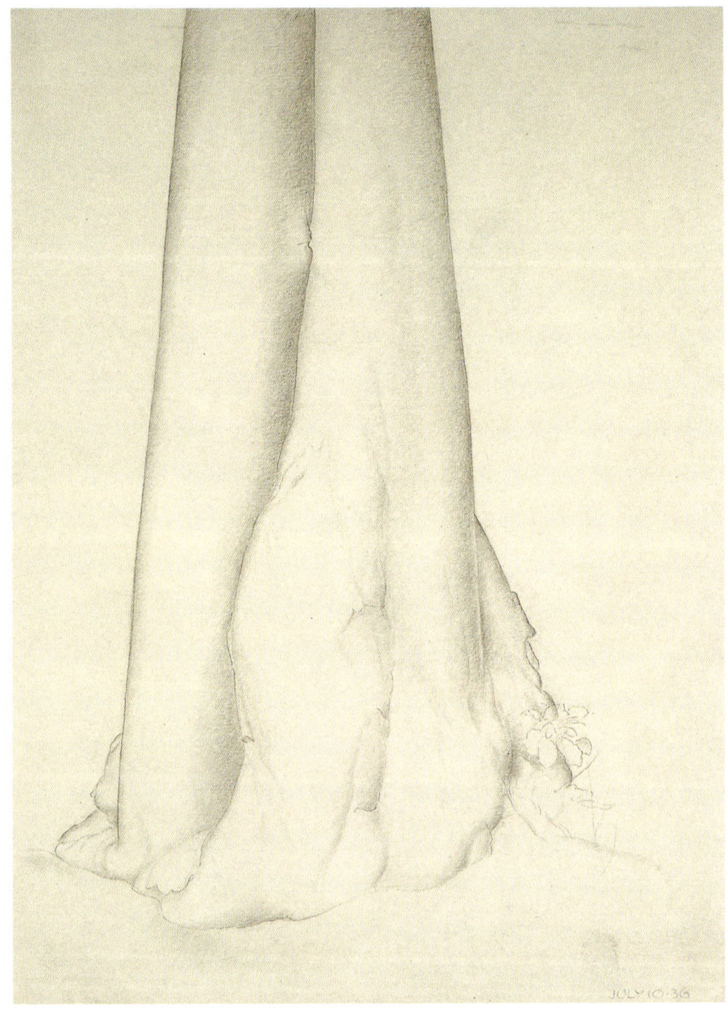

Tree Trunk, 1936
graphite on wove paper
30.4 × 22.8 cm

Tree Trunk with Flower, July 10, 1936
graphite on wove paper
30.3 × 22.8 cm

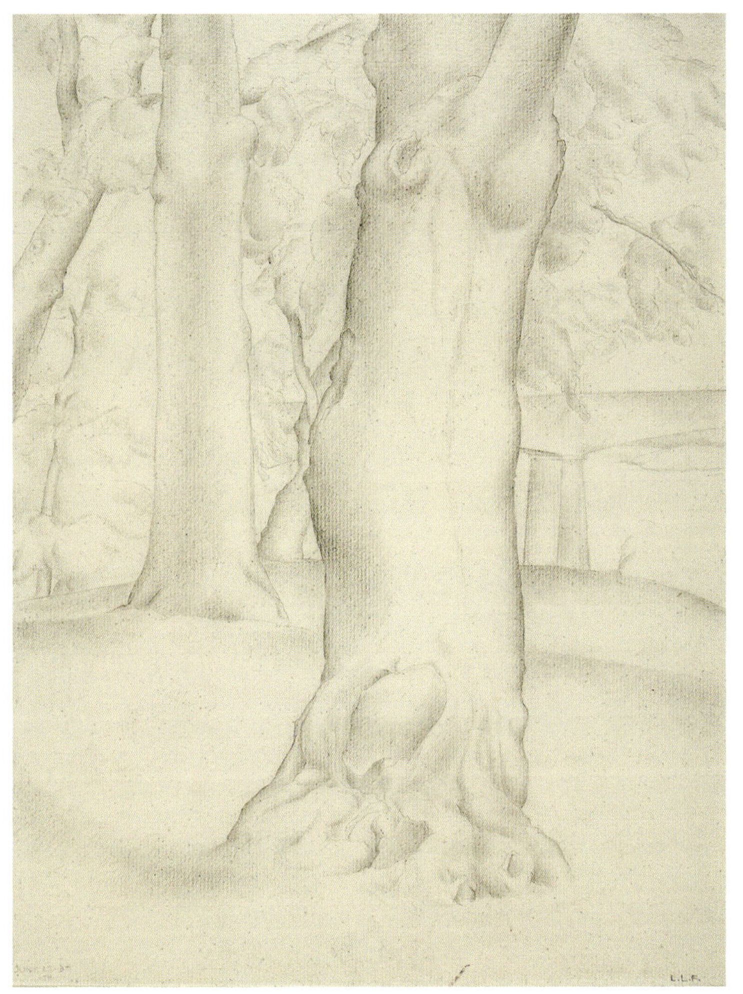

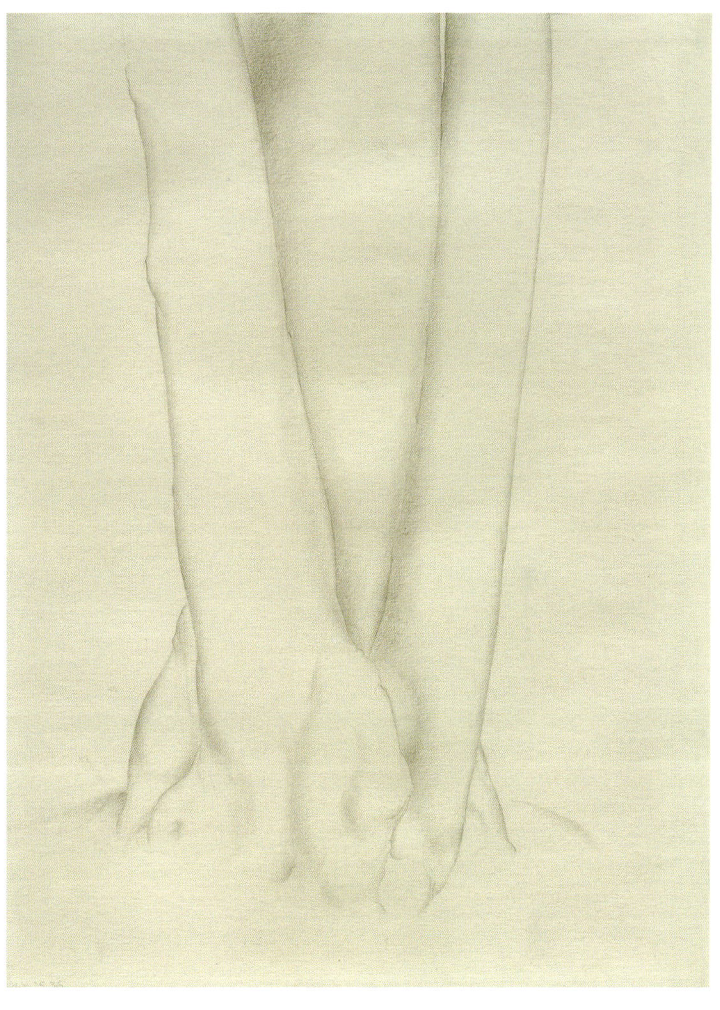

Large Trees and Bridge, June 17, 1937
graphite on laid paper
31.5 × 24 cm

Tree Trunk Study, 1937
graphite on paper
29.4 × 22 cm

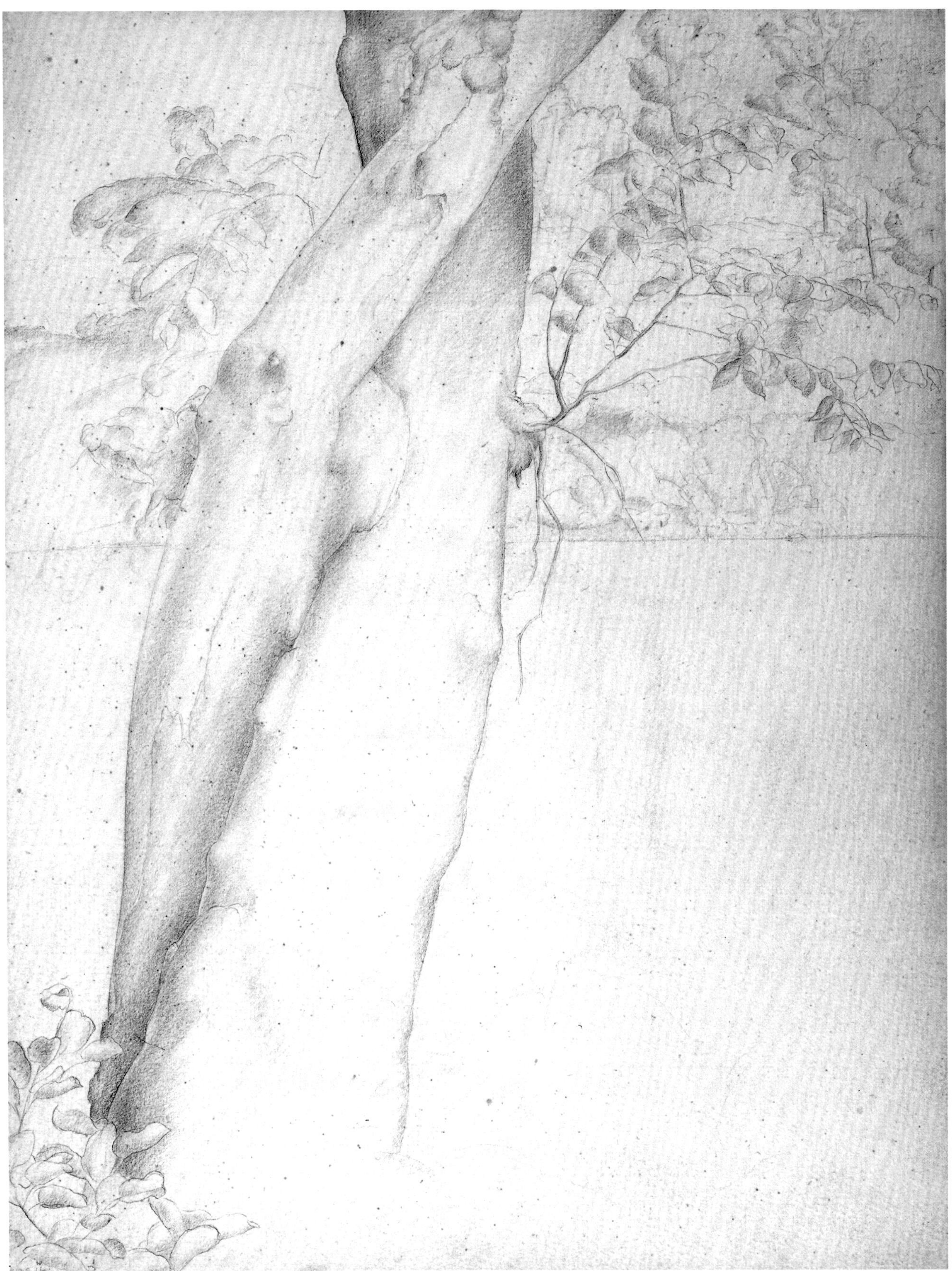

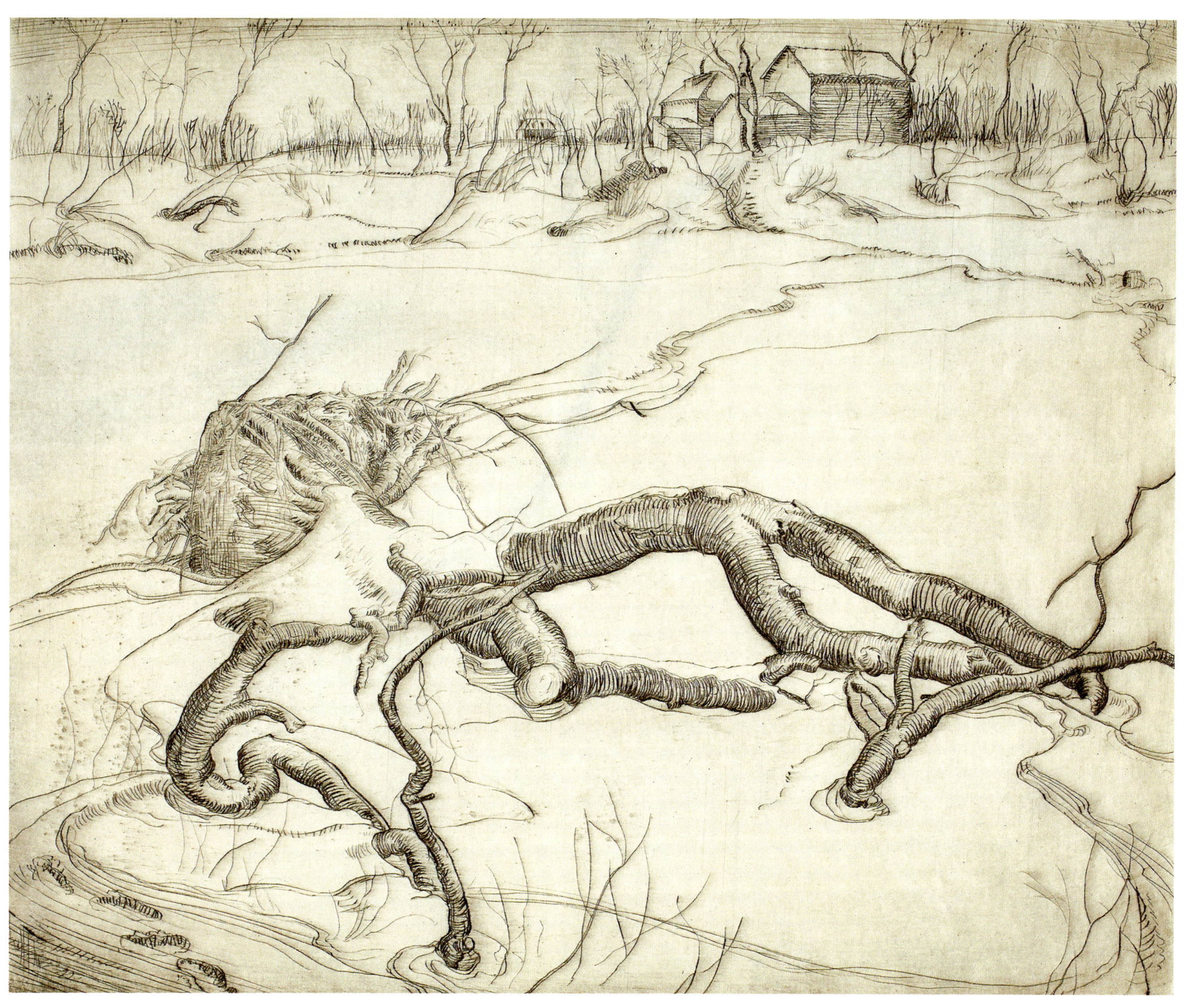

OPPOSITE
Trees, n.d.
graphite on paper
31 × 24 cm

ABOVE
Fallen Tree (Uprooted Tree), c. 1926
drypoint on paper
sheet (irregular):
24.4 × 31.6 cm

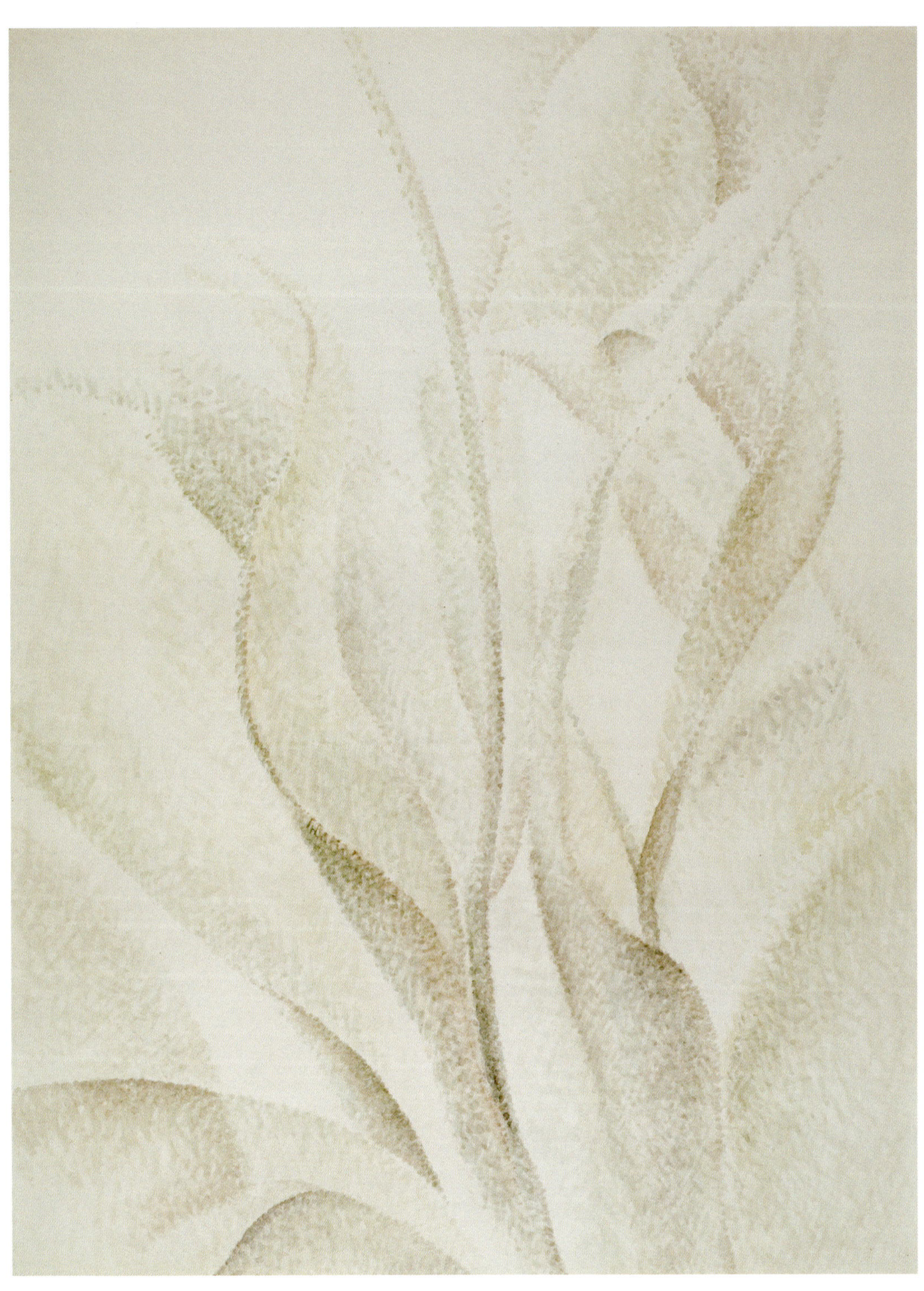

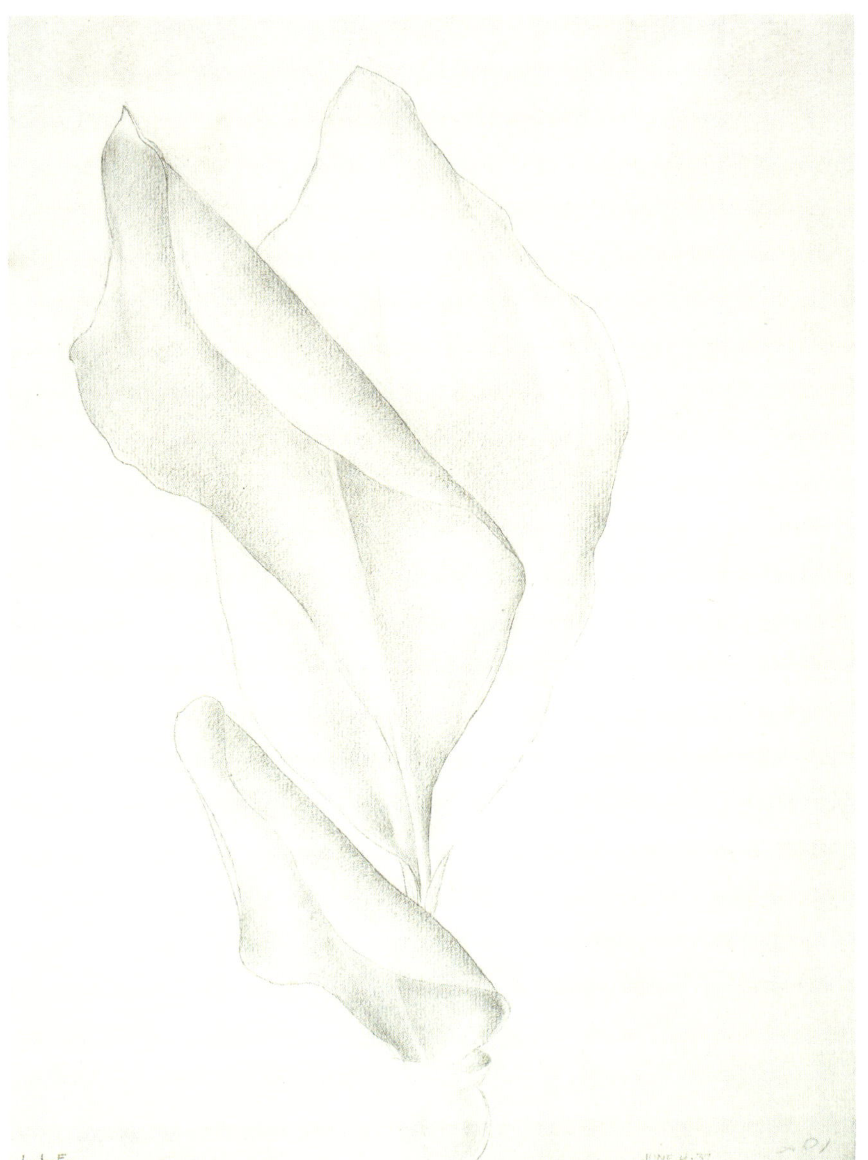

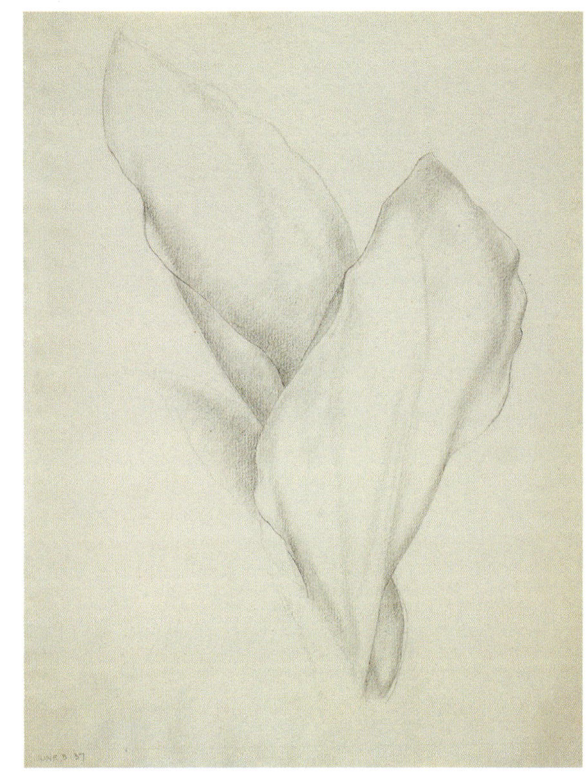

LEFT
Leaves, 1937
graphite on paper
31.7 × 24 cm

RIGHT
Two Leaves,
June 3, 1937
graphite on laid paper
30.8 × 23.5 cm

OPPOSITE
Tulip Leaves,
c. 1947
watercolour on
wove paper
61 × 45.8 cm

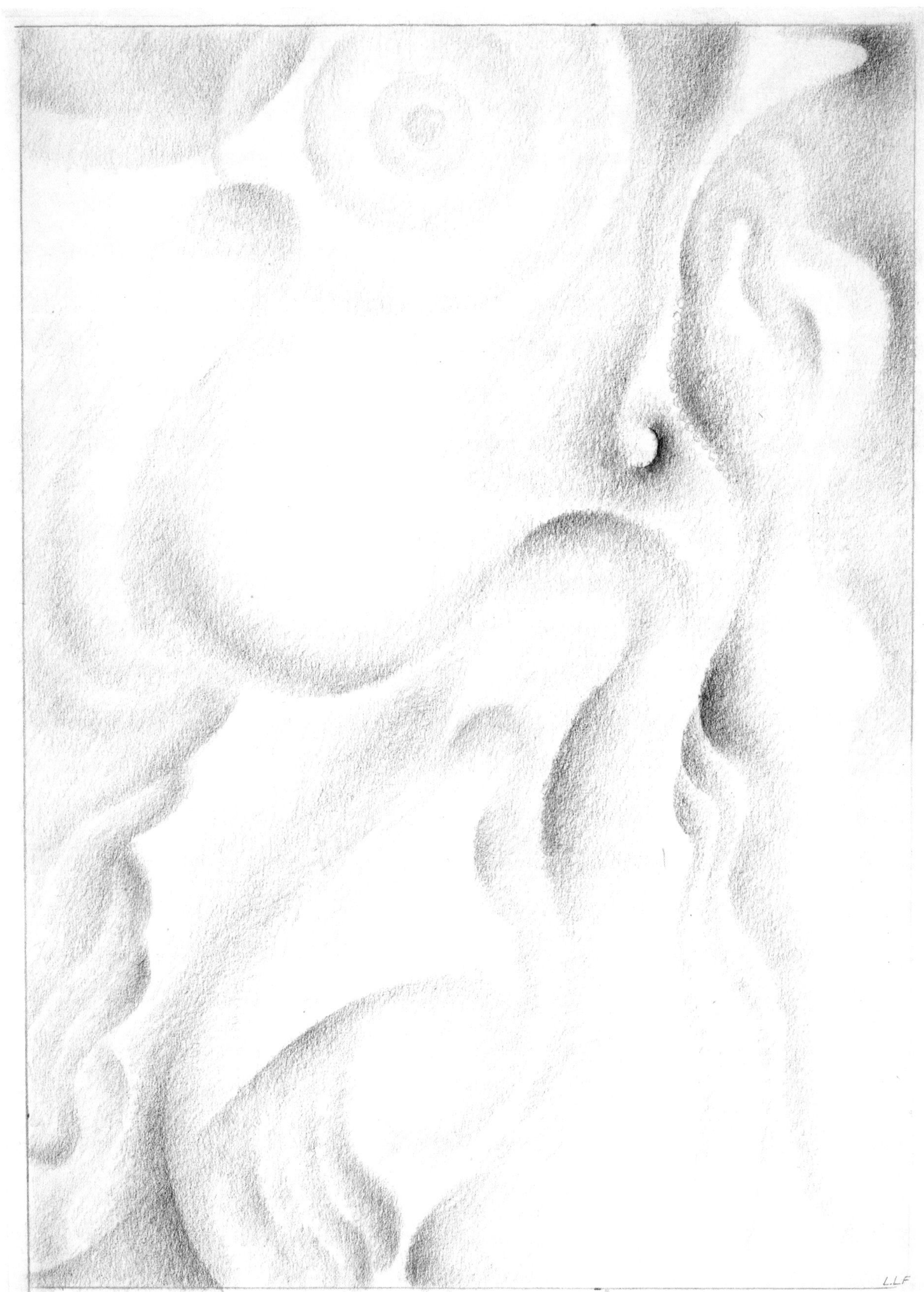
L.L.F

FEELINGS OF VOLUPTUOUSNESS

FitzGerald's Erotic Biocentrism

OLIVER A.I. BOTAR

The feelings with which the artist infects others may be most various . . . feelings of love for native land, self devotion and submission to fate or God expressed in a drama, raptures of lovers described in a novel, feelings of voluptuousness expressed in a picture . . .

LEO TOLSTOY, *What Is Art*, 1897

For some years now, I have lived with a drawing by FitzGerald (facing). I acquired it in 2009 because it is beautiful, because it was within my means, and because it is an example of Biomorphic Abstraction, an artistic style I had explored in my PhD dissertation.[1] I recognized the drawing as one of FitzGerald's rare sexually explicit works. This was an aspect of his art that I knew of only because I had visited the Eckhardt-Gramatté Foundation in Winnipeg soon after my defence. There I had seen a drawing acquired by Ferdinand Eckhardt, director of the Winnipeg Art Gallery from 1953 to 1974. It struck me, a newcomer to FitzGerald's work, as being overtly sexual in nature.[2] Many of FitzGerald's erotic works (though not the most explicit ones) were acquired by Eckhardt for the WAG and exhibited in 1963.[3] Included in that show was an extraordinary series of self-portraits in which FitzGerald renders himself in an anguished psychosexual state, as suggested by his pained expression and the profusion of female bodies that hover around him (pp. 90–93). These drawings date from about 1945, during a time of emotional crisis attributable to his faltering relationship with his lover, the artist and poet Irene Heywood.[4]

Composed of delicate, cloud-like swirls of curls and minuscule hair-like marks, my FitzGerald drawing seems to come from a happier moment in his life. It is marked with his cryptic monogram but it is neither titled nor dated. A similar Eckhardt-Gramatté work, bearing the title *Conception*, is dated May 31, 1956, just weeks prior to FitzGerald's death (p. 85).[5] That drawing is rendered in the robust crosshatch

Abstract, n.d.
graphite on paper
framed: 49 × 39 cm

mode FitzGerald employed from the late 1940s onward, while the technique used in mine more closely resembles his drawings of the early to mid-1940s. Both depict abstracted amalgams of delicately labyrinthine, even surreal, erogenous zones.[6] They are explicit without being pornographic. The breast, nipple, vulva, navel or anus, clitoris, testicle, and phallus forms are freely combined to suggest both generalized voluptuousness and the specifics of the sex act.

The drawings provide a window onto an aspect of FitzGerald's life that he was at pains to conceal. Despite his marriage, FitzGerald and his former student Heywood carried on a secret correspondence after she left the Winnipeg School of Art in 1934. Although not all the letters survive, a remarkable series sent to Heywood dated 1942 to 1944, each with FitzGerald's monogram, does. In one he writes, with stirring tenderness:

> this morning I . . . became aware of a lovely rigidity . . . I let myself drift into half sleep—I thought of how nice it would be to give you this—a rare gift for yours of red gold—a filling to satisfy every minute area of its softness—and then to spray the whole interior and mingle it with your delicate juices—perhaps you were still in bed as it was quite some time before the dawn—and perhaps we dwelt together for a few exquisite moments closer than we realize in the fullness of the day . . . awaking before the sun has appeared with the freshness of long sleep pulsing through the body . . . the ease of moving out into space in a waking dream through closed eyes—a longing to touch your lovely flesh to move over and rest on you—to touch your lips and then to penetrate the soft folds of your other opening and lie entranced in beautiful intimacy.[7]

Apart from the letter's poetic candour, what is striking is how it discursively recapitulates the two drawings under discussion, as well as another group depicting hovering, entwined couples.[8] Though he might have intended them as dreamlike, even surreal heterosexual phantasmagoria, they now read as pansexual. They, and the letters to Heywood, are among the most explicit works of Canadian erotica and deserve further consideration for that reason alone, taking into account the current intensified discussion around sexual objectification and agency.

Highly unusual within the Canadian context of the time, these works reflect what I would contend was FitzGerald's biocentric world view.[9] Biocentrism developed in Central Europe in the early twentieth century. A tendency rather than a movement, it revived aspects of Nature Romanticism (Goethe, Blake, American transcendentalism) recharged by ideas arising from the emergence of biology, and theories of evolution in particular, as a science.[10] It was a confluence of several related intellectual currents: vitalism theorized that life cannot be accounted for by purely mechanical means, that a "life force," what Bergson called the *élan vital*, is necessary to account for the phenomenon of living beings. Holism contended that "the whole is greater than the sum of its parts," thereby opposing a mechanistic, reductive view of the world. Monism promoted the essential unity of all things, including matter and spirit, body and soul. The Life Reform Movement, meanwhile, proposed a rethinking of the way we might live in light of these ideas, promoting vegetarianism, sexual freedom, educational reform, clothing reform, "free body culture" (including nudism and gymnastics), and a return to nature.[11] Biocentrism was a reaction to what were seen as the negative effects of exaggerated rationalism, industrialization, urbanization, and technological proliferation during the nineteenth century, which resulted in the destruction of a more natural way of life, as well as nature itself. It emphasized the centrality of "nature," and "life" rather than "culture"; the self-directedness, flux, and unity of all life (Nietzsche's *All-Leben*); and a valorization of what the German philosopher Max Scheler referred to as "vital mysticism" and its "cosmic-vital feeling of unity"—often the result of an epiphanic experience.[12] In a sense, the better-known occultist revival (including Theosophy) was biocentrism's philosophical sibling, in that both posited a unity of nature. But while Theosophy was dualistic in its view of matter and spirit as separate realms, those espousing a biocentric world view professed a belief in the inextricable unity of body and soul.[13] Leading modern artists from Jean Arp, Arthur Dove, Max Ernst, Antonio Gaudí, and Wassily Kandinsky to Paul Klee, Franz Marc, Joan Miró, László Moholy-Nagy, and Georgia O'Keeffe were all biocentric in outlook.[14]

This framework can be applied to some Canadian artists whose world views have proved difficult to classify, among them Emily Carr, Bertram Brooker, and FitzGerald. Because their mutual friend Lawren Harris was a Theosophist, their nature-centric attitudes have been attributed to Theosophy. But even though Theosophical doctrine coincides with some of their positions, these three at least distanced themselves from it. Carr was a Christian pantheist, ultimately rejecting Harris's Theosophical beliefs, and Brooker was a Bergsonian vitalist and a holist who professed Christianity.[15] FitzGerald was not conventionally religious; rather, he espoused nature-centric, holist, and vitalist ideas, without, of course, labelling them as such. Both Brooker and FitzGerald

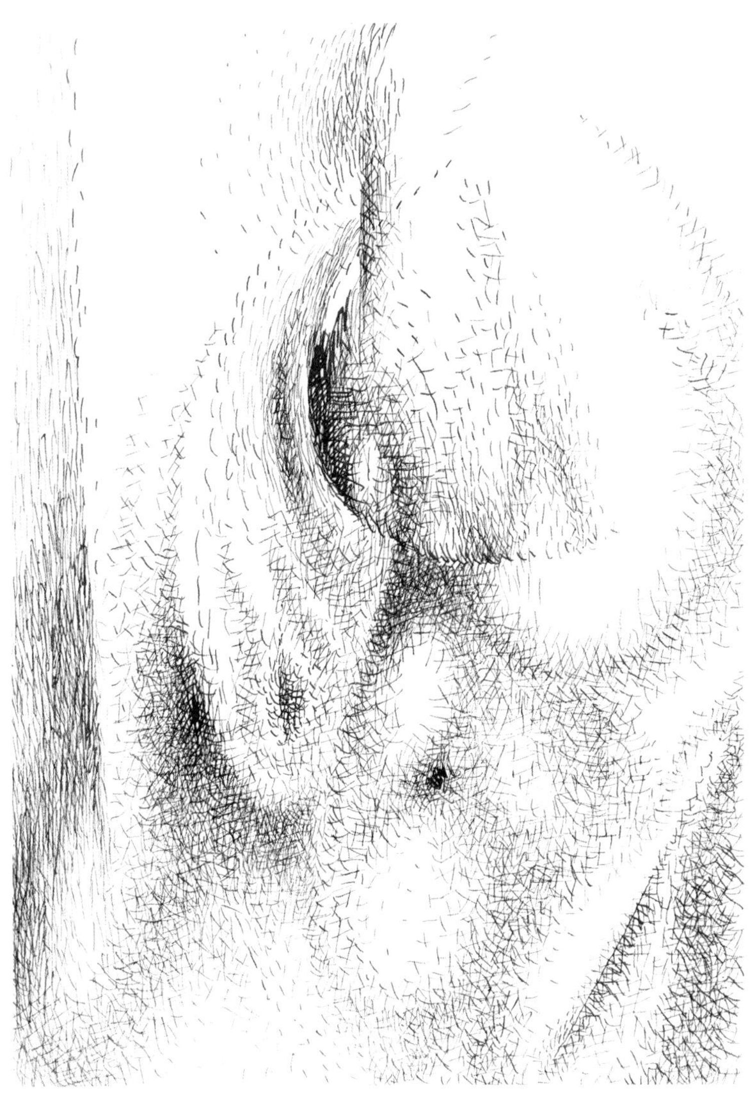

Conception,
May 31, 1956
ink on paper
23 × 16.1 cm

recounted experiences of Scheler's cosmic-vital unity. Phyllis Brooker Smith describes her father's experience: "Everything in the universe is one, united, it was like knowing the answer to everything at once."[16] FitzGerald wrote to Heywood, describing a train trip through the Rockies, that "the impact of the sight of it was almost too much.... I had an uncontrollable desire to weep. There is no description that I could give you that would be any more illuminating.... Each one of us experience this same terrifically overpowering sensation on rare occasions."[17] By my definition, both artists were biocentric.[18]

In FitzGerald's letters to Heywood, erotic and biocentric passages commingle in breathless abandon: "I enfold you... and you entwine me and draw me into you and absorb me and I enter you and absorb you and motion is one and we dwell in a oneness of ethereal light or silent calmness surrounds us and a radiation passes through our oneness of warmth and understanding and we dwell suspended in a passing into and out of each of a living current and time is not..."[19] In fact, FitzGerald identifies making love with making art, and the mutuality of sexual union with the cosmic-vital feeling of unity: "art is an indissoluble oneness... [and, along with humans] it comes from a common source—and that is life—living... the joining of flesh is art... I think it is—in its most expressive form... [the] greatest art—I believe this, now, unashamed to myself—I am sad that [I thought] otherwise for a long time."[20]

His regret is unsurprising, since for FitzGerald's generation the sex drive and even seminal fluid were often *identified* with the life force, something to be conserved rather than expended unnecessarily. This was the message in North American sex manuals of the time that discouraged masturbation, excessive sex within marriage, and even marital sexual relations over forty-five.[21] While Heywood in her later years described having initiated their sexual relationship in order to overcome an earlier rape trauma,[22] for FitzGerald this consummation seems to have induced an awakening to the full potential of his sexuality. For both it appears to have engendered healing. FitzGerald no longer feared the emission of his "life force." Rather, he now wished to "spray" it and "mingle it with [his lover's] delicate juices." For him, that ecstasy induced a new bodily self-awareness, as he writes to her in a letter about his first summer working on Bowen Island: "For two months I swam in the sea each day and painted the water and rocks and mountains and sky.... I went as close to naked as I could... my... whole body took on an elasticity and new strength that still amazes me."[23] Unclothed immersion in nature, "free body culture," was a defining aspect of the Life Reform Movement.[24] FitzGerald's experience of this was transformative, and it affected his art. At this point he shifted toward abstraction.[25] It is also when he began making erotica.

The drawing on my wall reminds me each time I look at it of the erotic as life affirming. It is a late materialization of FitzGerald's early insight (borrowed from Tolstoy) that artists can induce in others "feelings of voluptuousness expressed in a picture." ■

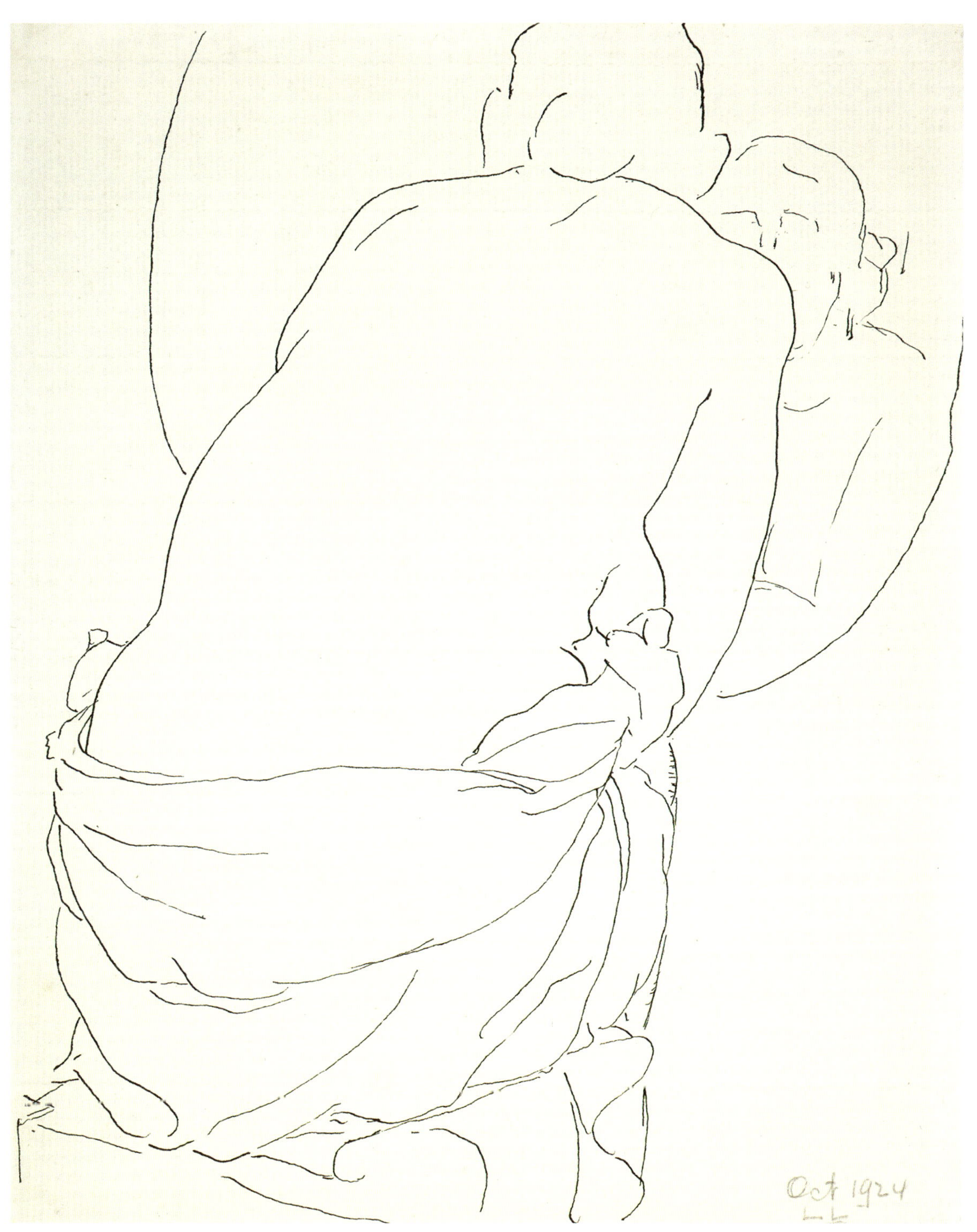

Untitled (Figure Crouching before Mirror), 1924
ink on paper
23.1 × 18.6 cm

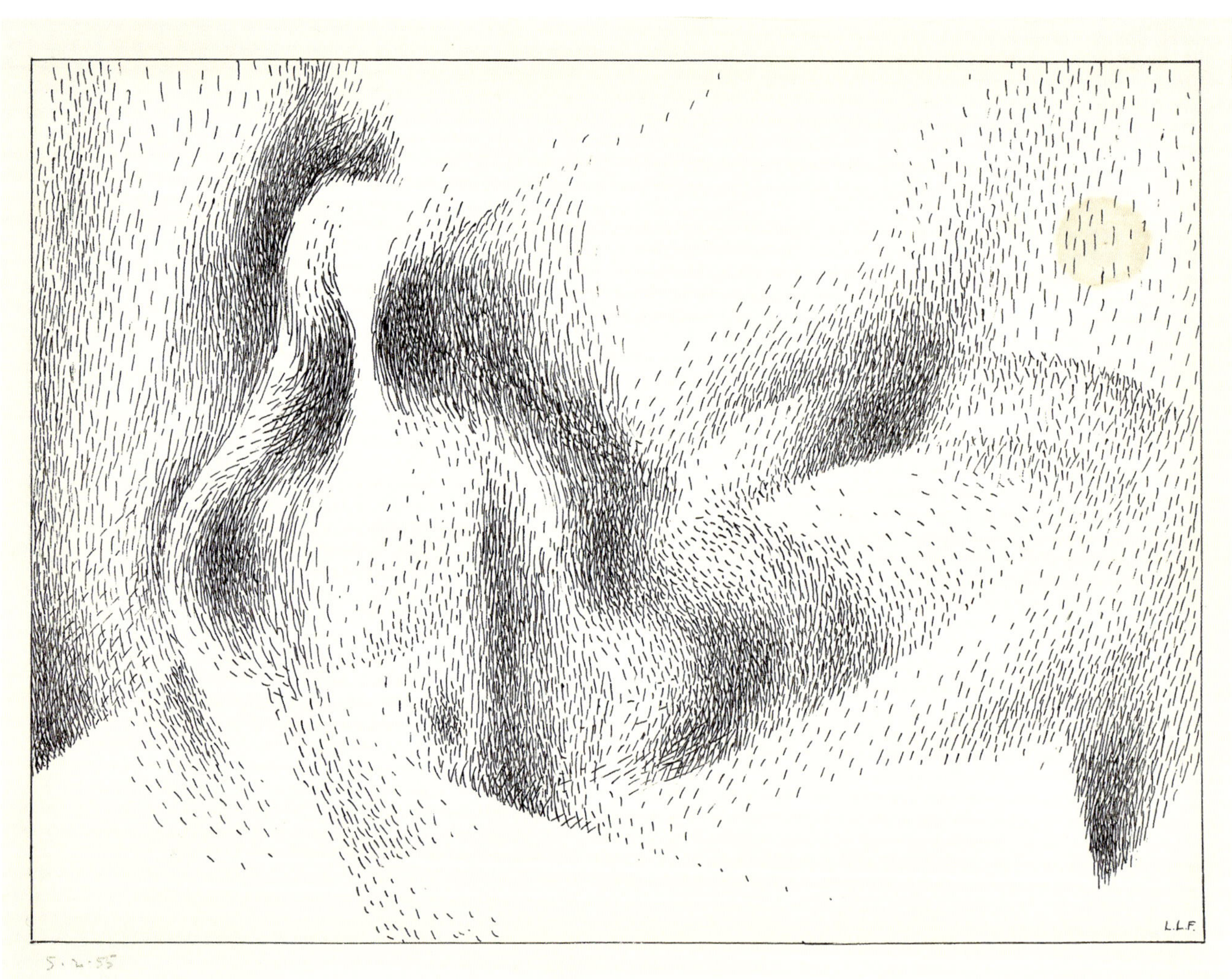

Untitled, 1955
pen and ink on paper
sheet: 23× 30 cm

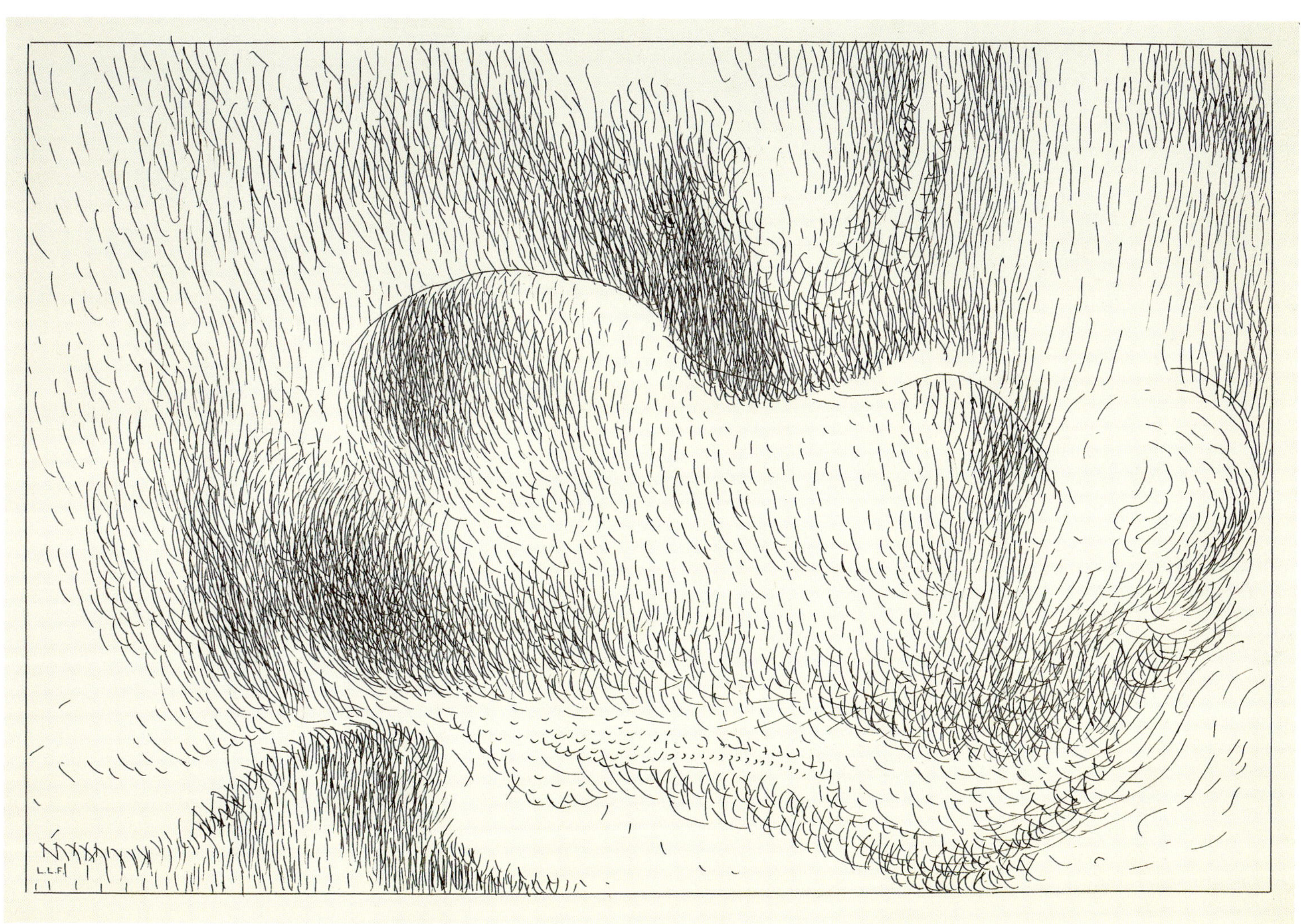

Reclining Nude, n.d.
pen and ink on paper
sheet: 26.8 x 39.5 cm

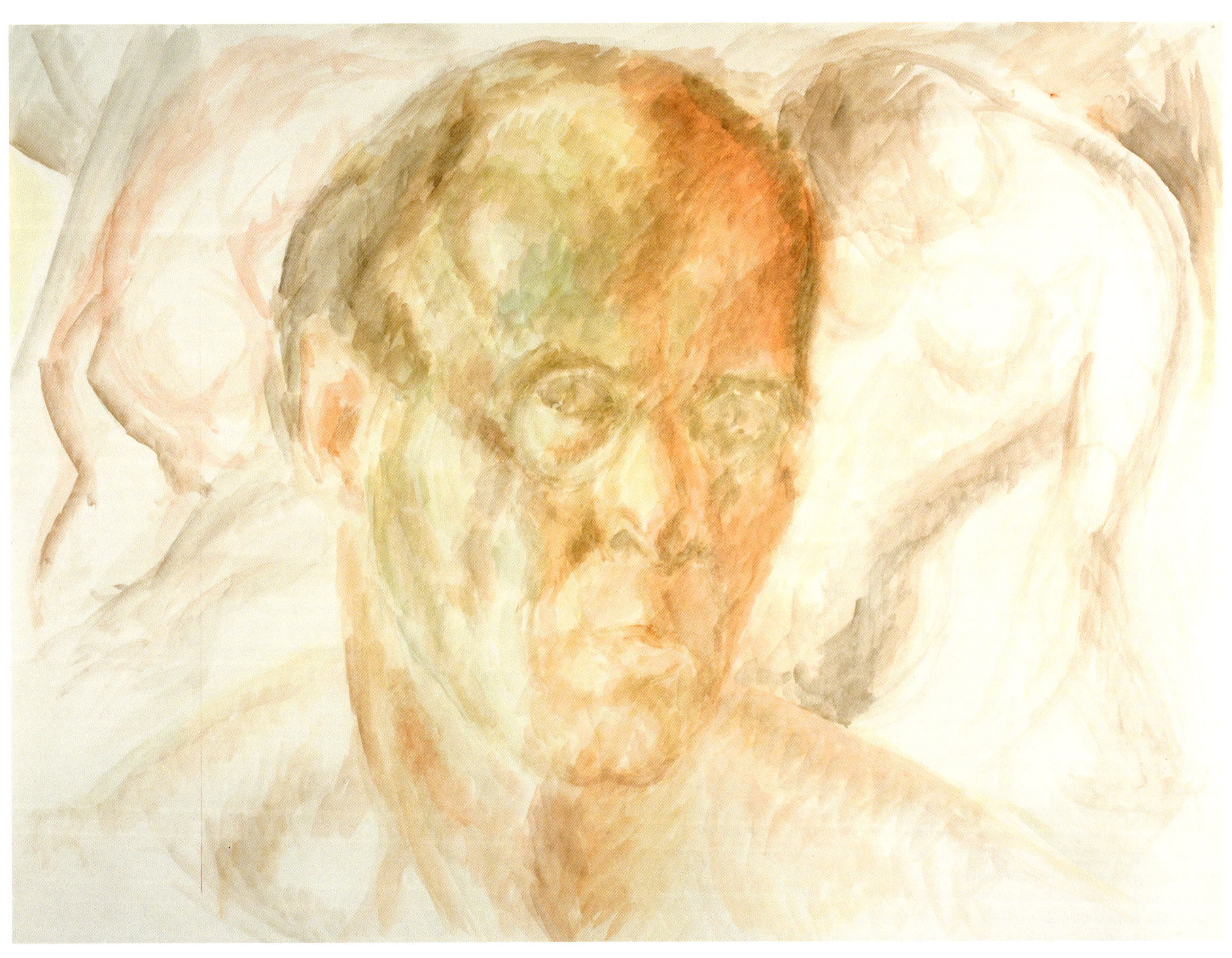

Self-Portrait (3 Nudes), c. 1945
watercolour on paper
45.7 × 60.9 cm

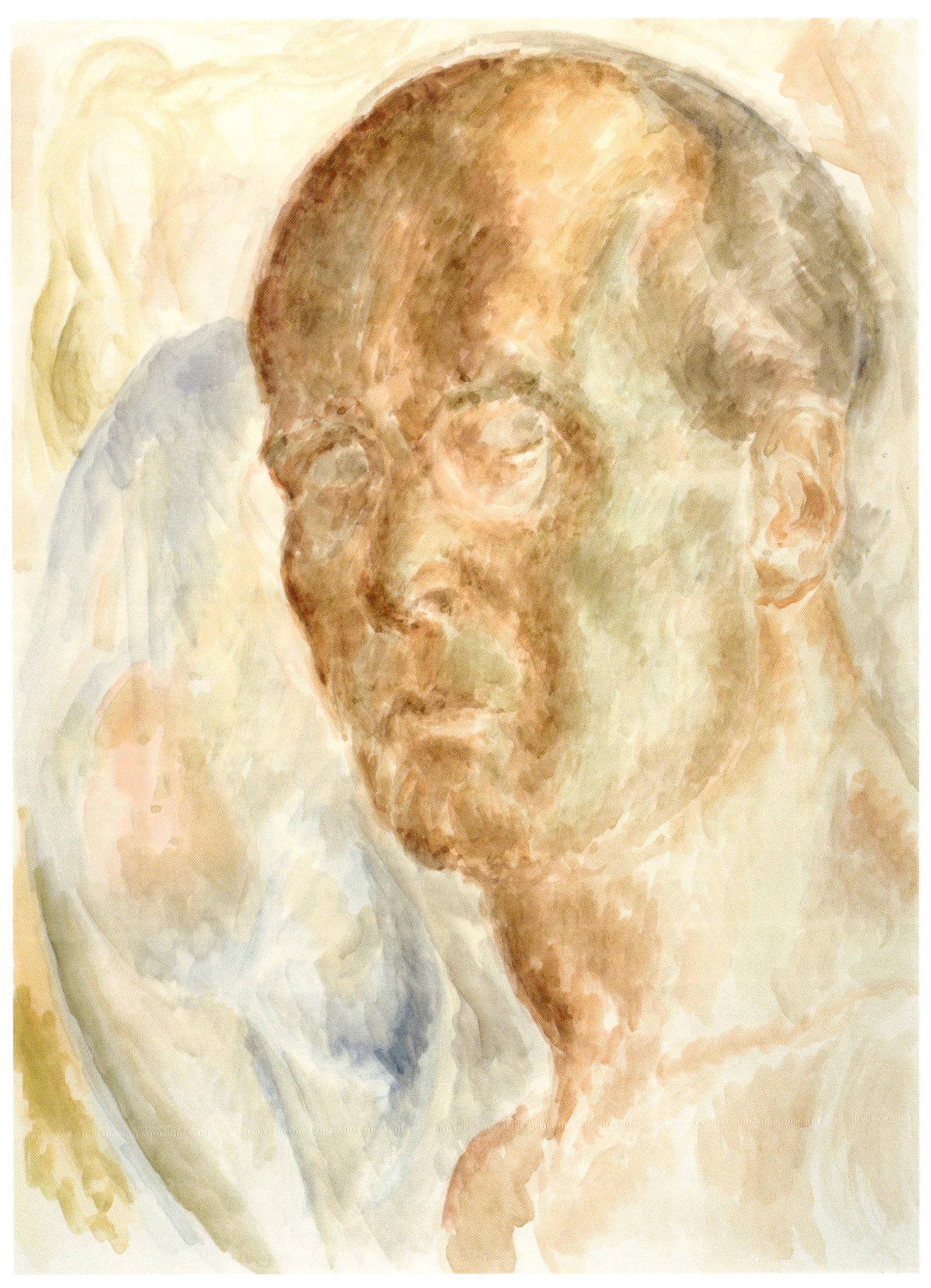

Self-Portrait (with Nude in Upper Left Corner), c. 1945
watercolour on paper
60.9 × 45.7 cm

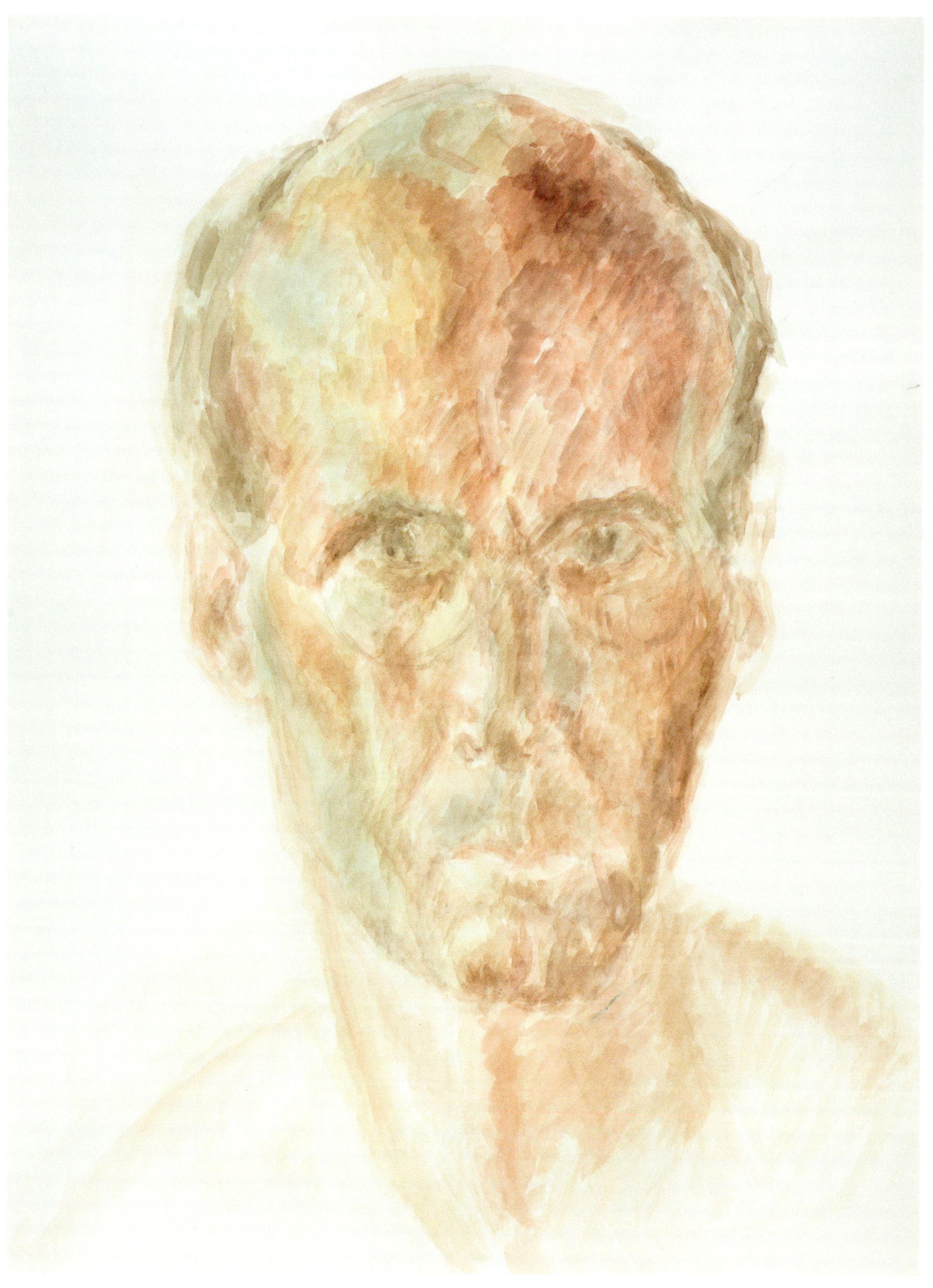

Self-Portrait, c. 1945
watercolour on paper
60.9 × 45.7 cm

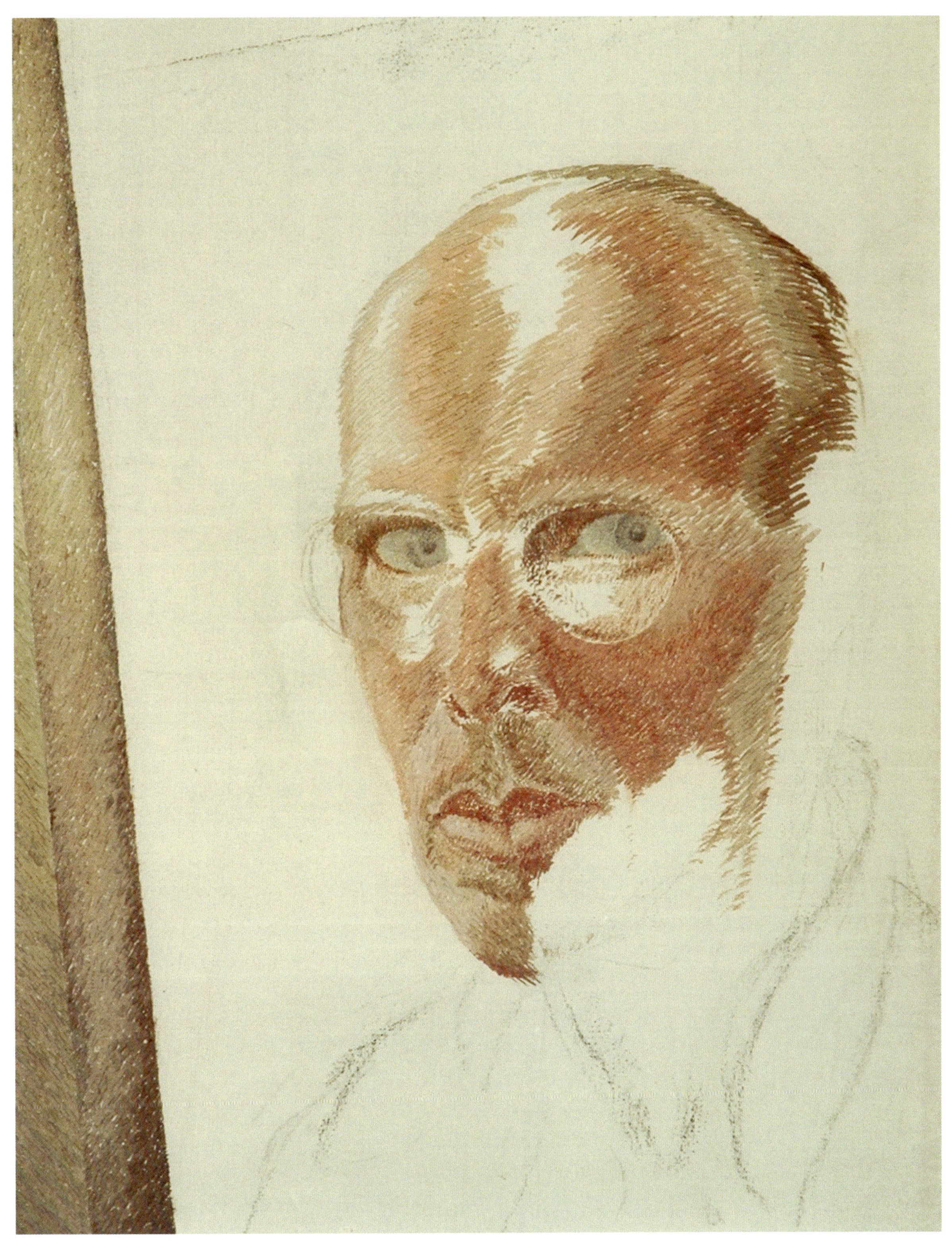

Self-Portrait (Unfinished), c. 1945
oil on canvas
54.5 × 44.5 cm

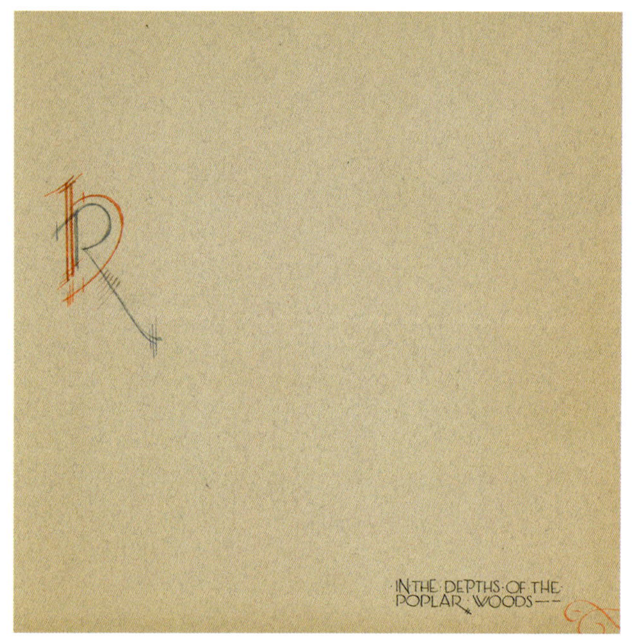

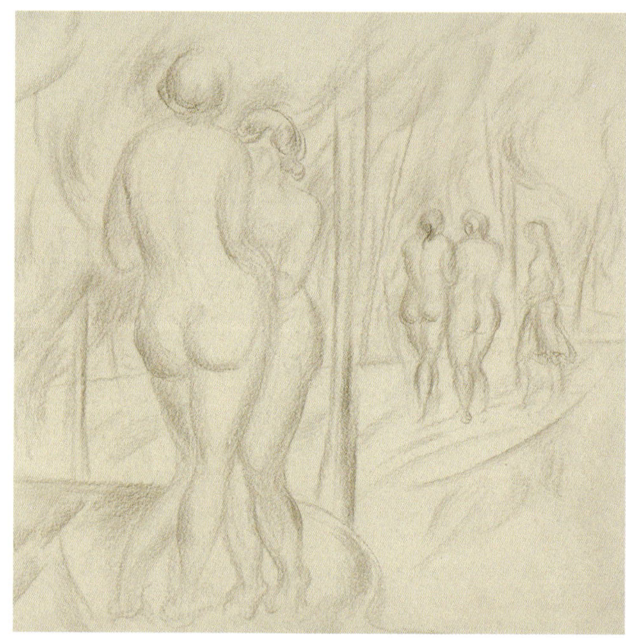

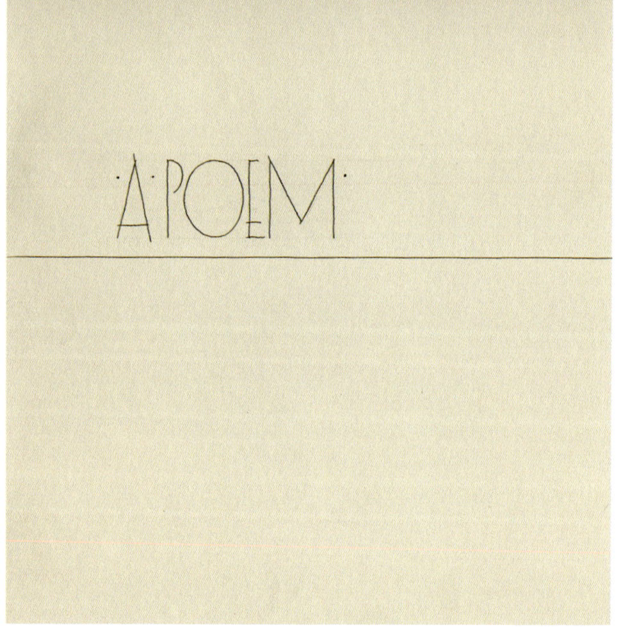

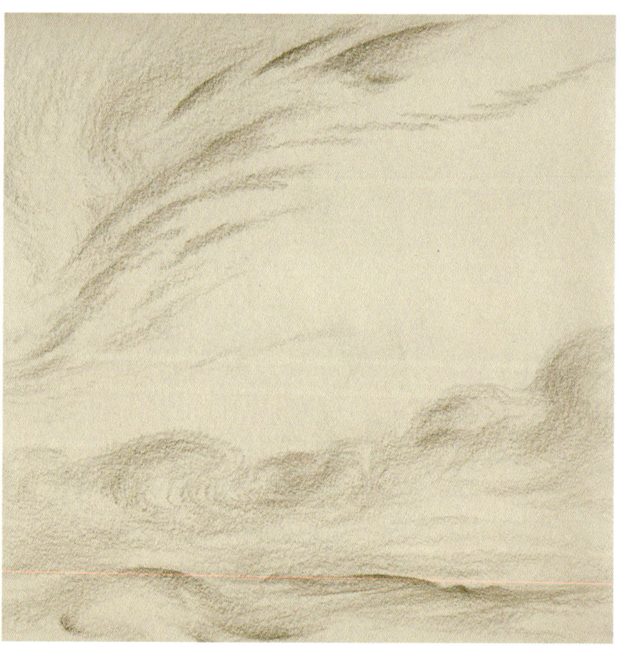

Into the Poplar Woods, n.d.
hand-lettered folder with
title page and six drawings
in graphite on paper

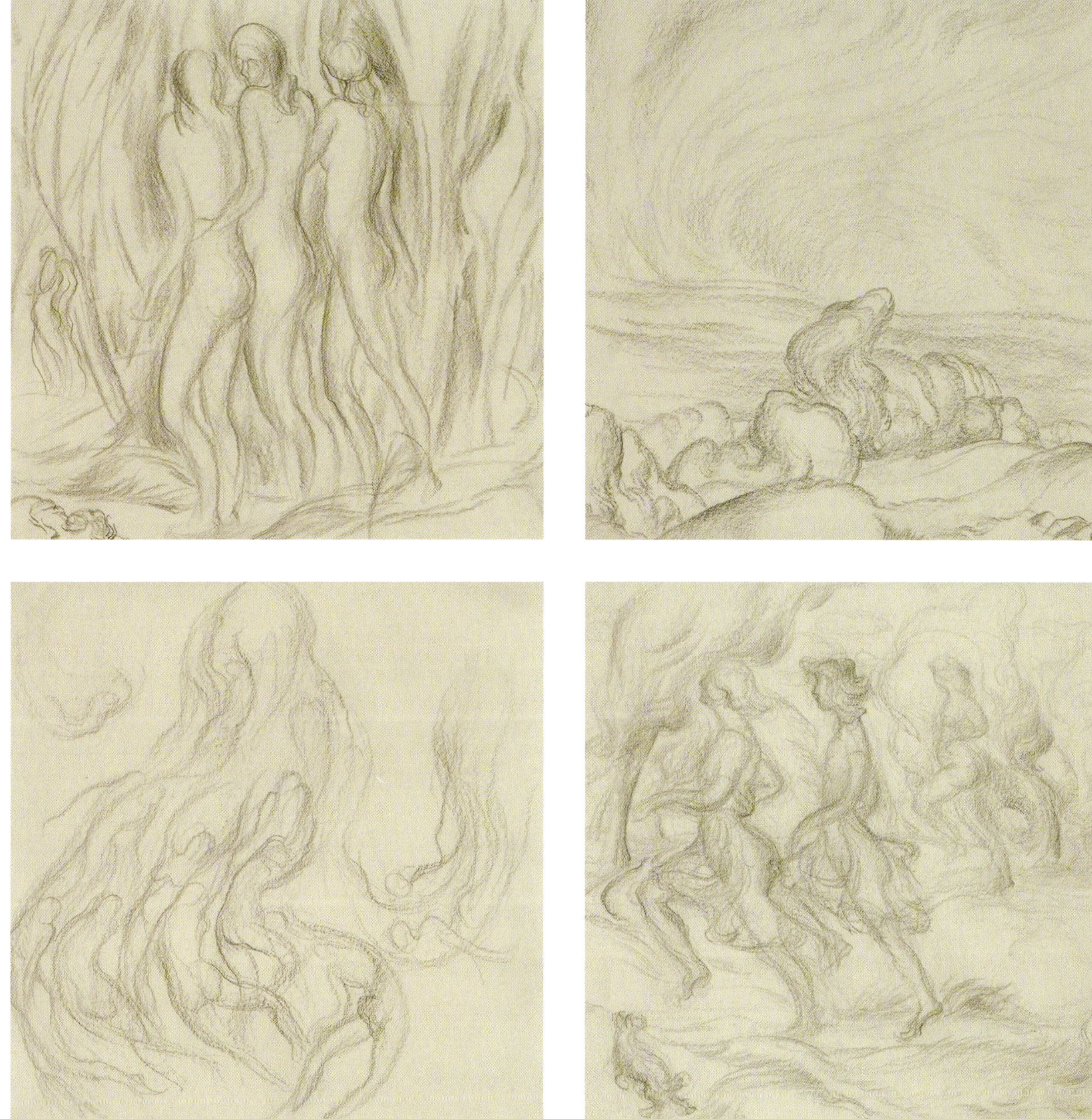

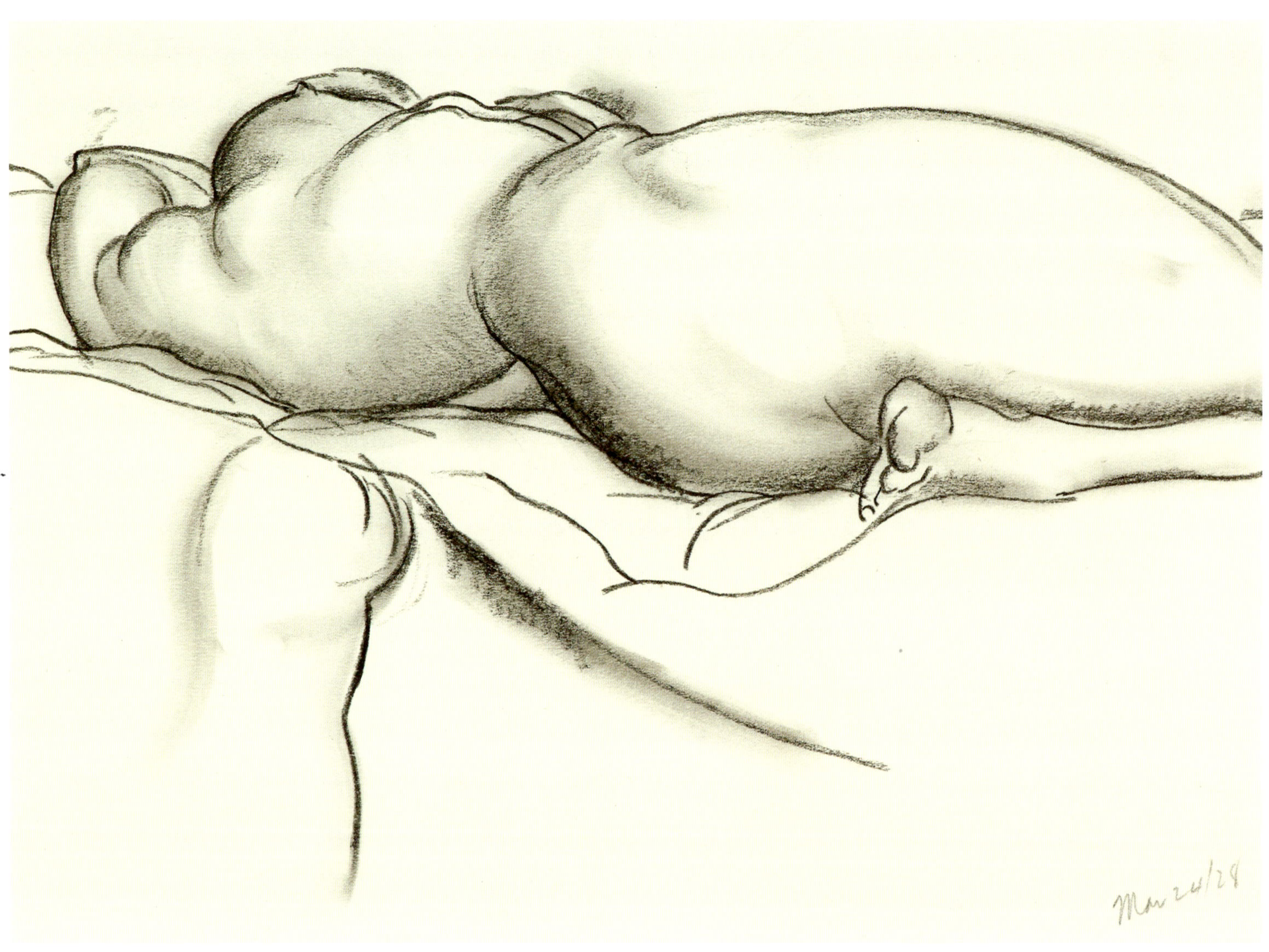

Nude Reclining on Bed, 1928
chalk on paper
22.9 × 30.5 cm

FITZGERALD AND THE MORPHOLOGY OF DESIRE

ROBERT ENRIGHT

Lionel LeMoine FitzGerald made four states of a drypoint called *Recumbent Daphne*, c. 1926 (pp. 98, 99), now in the collection of the National Gallery of Canada. The small prints show a naked woman lying curled on her right side in a grove with a pool in the foreground and a distant landscape in the background. These are my topographical guesses, to some extent, because the components of the image are not clearly defined. What is clear, though, is that as the series of prints continues, the lines on the woman's body become darker and more numerous, so much so that by the fourth state she is almost entirely covered by black marks. If you know the mythological story of Daphne, you would surmise that she is in the process of changing into a laurel tree.

As Ovid tells us in Book 1 of the *Metamorphoses*, Daphne is a beautiful water naiad who "takes delight in the depths of the woods" and is committed to remaining a virgin. She is pursued so relentlessly by Apollo that she begs her father, a river god, to destroy her beauty so she will no longer be the object of Apollo's obsession. Instead, her father transforms her into a laurel. The lines from Ovid have a poignant and almost narcotic simplicity: "she feels / a heavy numbness move across her limbs, / her soft breasts are enclosed by slender bark, / her hair is changed to leaves, her arms to branches, / her feet, so swift a moment before, stick fast / in sluggish roots, a covering of foliage / spreads across her face. All that remains of her / is her shining beauty." That remaining beauty is enough for Apollo, whose rapture continues even after her metamorphosis. "He clasped the branches as if they were parts of human arms," the poem tells us, "and kissed the wood." Earlier, his appreciation of Daphne's beauty had led him to praise her hands, arms, and her partially covered shoulder, but now he imagines "those parts which lie concealed are even lovelier."

We may not know what specifically attracted FitzGerald to this narrative of a god, a nymph, and obsessive desire, but the story has elements that turn up in altered ways in his own practice;

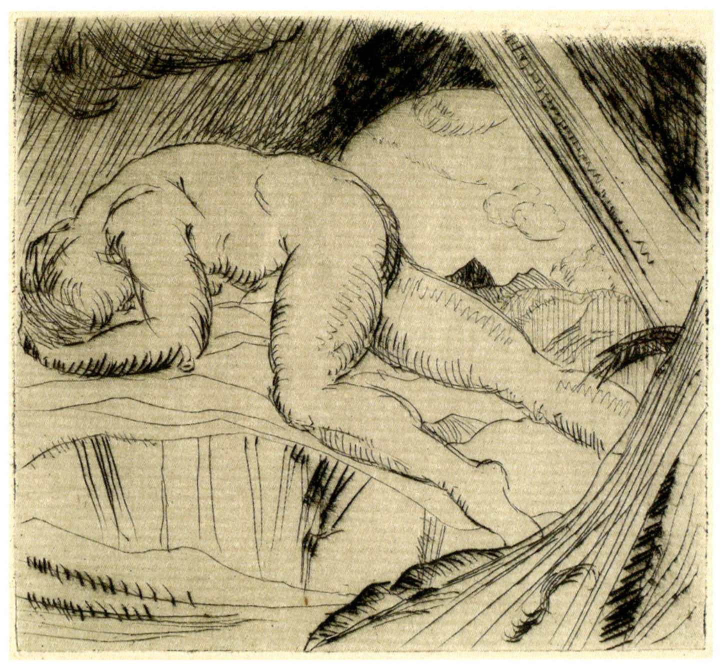

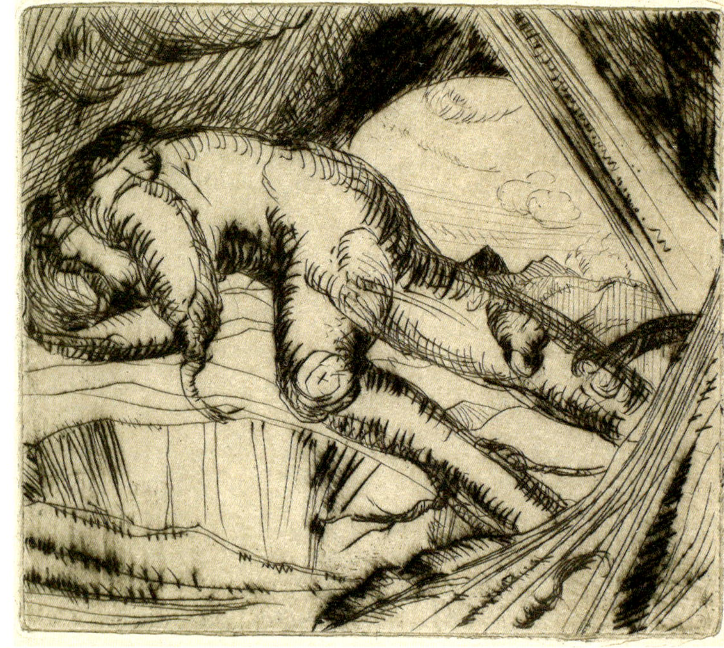

Recumbent Daphne,
c. 1926
drypoint on buff laid paper
11.5 × 13 cm;
plate: 7.4 × 8.3 cm

Recumbent Daphne,
c. 1926
drypoint on buff laid paper
15.5 × 23.3 cm;
plate: 7.4 × 8.3 cm

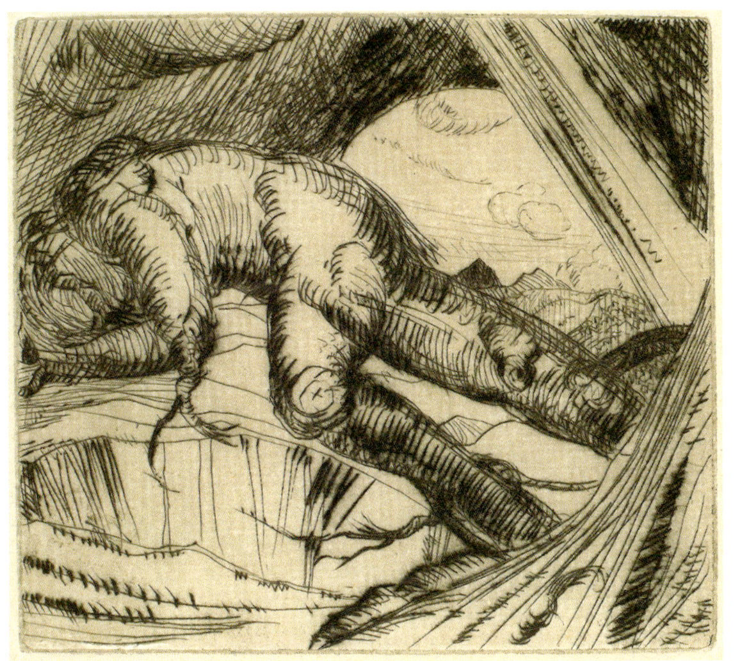

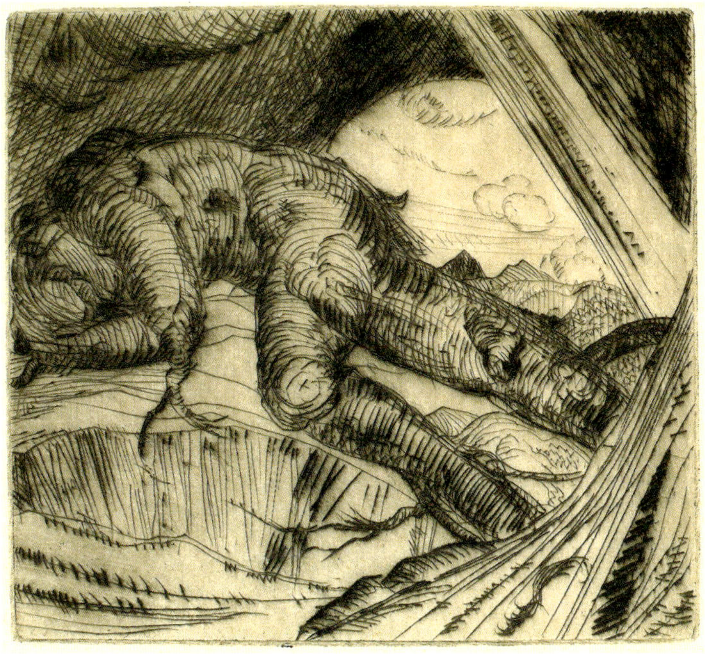

Recumbent Daphne,
c. 1926
drypoint on wove paper
12 × 15.5 cm;
plate: 7.4 × 8.3 cm

Recumbent Daphne,
c. 1926
drypoint on wove paper
12.1 × 15.5 cm;
plate: 7.4 × 8.3 cm

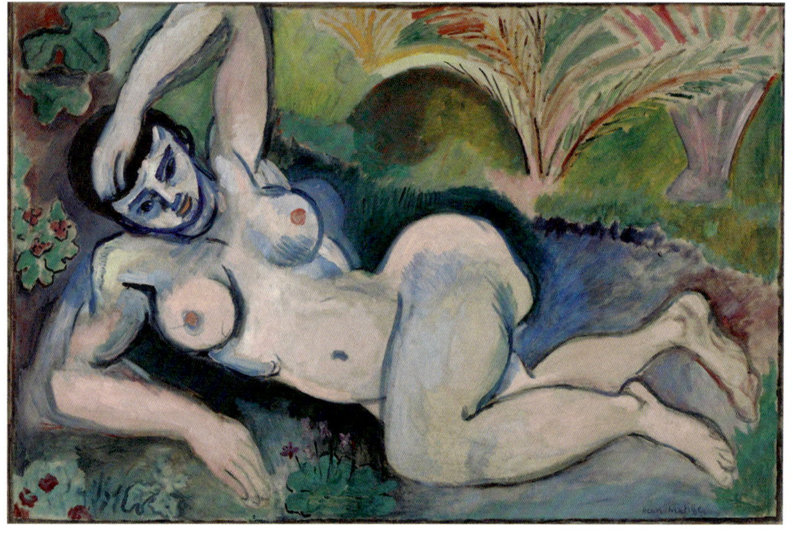

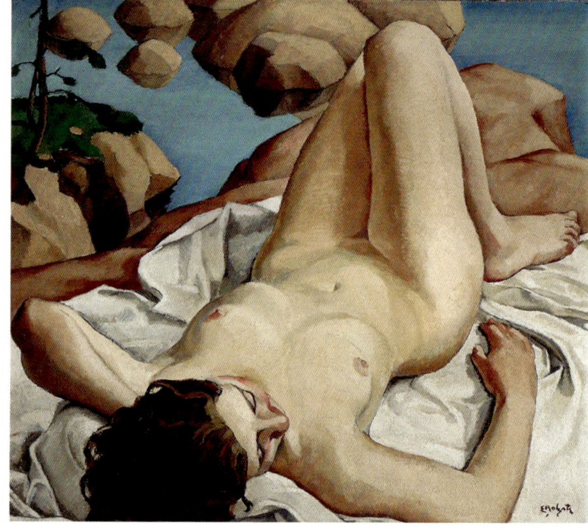

LEFT
HENRI MATISSE
(1869–1954)
Blue Nude, 1907
oil on canvas
92.1 × 140.3 cm
The Cone Collection, formed by Dr. Claribel Cone and Miss Etta Cone of Baltimore, Maryland
The Baltimore Museum of Art BMA 1950.228 / Photo: Mitro Hood / © Succession H. Matisse / SOCAN (2019)

RIGHT
EDWIN HEADLEY HOLGATE
(1892–1977)
Nude in the Open, 1930
oil on canvas
overall: 64.8 × 73.6 cm
Gift from Friends of Canadian Art Fund, 1930 / Art Gallery of Ontario, Toronto / 1326

the connection between the natural and the human, the landscape as a place where transformation occurs, and the imaginative projection of desire. For FitzGerald the landscape was a generative space in which he gave his imagination permission to investigate and picture things he was otherwise reluctant to reveal. At the same time, landscape could function as a terrain where things could be concealed and where they could undergo subtle and ambiguous changes in form.

The conjunction of the nude and the natural world is not unprecedented in Canadian visual art among FitzGerald's contemporaries. A number of artists took the nude out into nature in an attempt to delineate an accommodating relationship between body and space; these encounters were often reimagined through an already established history of representation. Paintings such as Henri Matisse's *Blue Nude*, 1907, and *The Dream* by Henri Rousseau, 1910, provide evidence that the relationship between the nude and the landscape can in modern painting be exhilarating. Rousseau's nude stretches out on a divan that is improbably located in a lushly stylized jungle, while Matisse's angular nude fairly vibrates with sensual energy in a landscape of fronds and feverish brush strokes.

The reason these bodies seem to so convincingly occupy their exotic landscapes is that neither artist was considering a nude in a landscape as two discrete parts. The painting made them a whole. In Canadian art, however, the ground is typically too prominent, our painters tending to regard it as a subject equal in importance to the figural component of the composition. They don't invest in painting as an end in itself; they invest only in what the painting is about.

What becomes most apparent, then, is the strain visible in the attempts to add the nude to the Canadian landscape. Artists as different as Edwin Holgate, Kathleen Munn, Prudence Heward, Charles Comfort, and Marc-Aurèle de Foy Suzor-Coté have all made work in which a languorous female body is presented in various kinds of landscape. In *Nude in the Open*, 1930, Holgate tries to form an equivalence between the nude woman and the summer landscape in which she reclines. To suggest this, he renders the woman's thighs and arms in the same tan and brown tones as the surrounding rocks. Unfortunately, the effect of this shared palette is not to soften her flesh but to make it seem like stone. The white cloth under her appears more like marble than fabric, so much so that the overall feeling of the painted woman is sculptural.

Invariably, the sensuous pleasure offered by the nude in the Canadian landscape is only visual, not latently tactile. Kathleen Munn tries Cubist forms and some kind of tonal and compositional all-overness as stylistic ways to bring the nude into nature. The most successful is her *Two Nude Women Reclining under Trees*, 1930, in which she places her women in a swirling landscape where human skin and natural textures are tonally indistinguishable. Here, figure becomes ground in a successful merging. Prudence Heward's *Dark Girl*, 1935, sets the black Other in a compressed jungle of exotic voyeurism, but her model looks forlorn and holds her arms in a way that is less about display than enclosure and self-protection. In Heward's *Girl under a Tree*, 1931, however, the nude is unapologetically available to both eye and hand. The painting is singular in its sense of complicit desire and comes closer than any Canadian painting to the erotic charge that Rousseau and Matisse were able to generate.

FitzGerald imagines the nude in the landscape, but for the most part he does so without picturing the body at all. He is thus our most psychologically reticent and evasively complicated practitioner of the genre. Though we may recognize that what we are looking at could be a nude man or woman or a tree trunk, FitzGerald's tendency is to deliberately render these subjects in ways that confuse clear identification. The result is

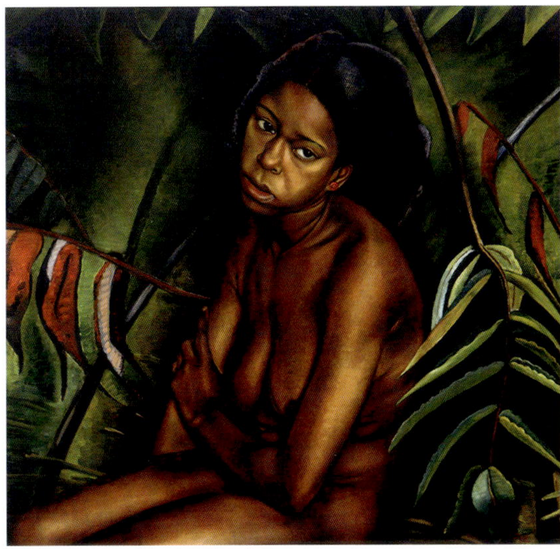

PRUDENCE HEWARD
(1896–1947)
Dark Girl, 1935
oil on canvas
92 × 102 cm
The Hart House Collection, Purchased by the Art Committee with income from the Harold and Murray Wrong Memorial Trust Fund, 1936
Art Museum at the University of Toronto / HH1936.001

that we begin to entertain more fluid perceptual associations.

FitzGerald's predisposition to see the natural and the human through the same perceptual lens is not so unusual. Humans and trees have a traceable morphological connection; we commonly talk about branches and limbs and bodies and trunks, insides and surfaces, bark and skin. FitzGerald, like Ovid, understood that common morphology, and in rendering the human and the natural his inclination was to let one drift toward the other. He was resolute about which of the two categories had the most potential for expressing what he called "the endlessness of the living force." In a letter to Bertram Brooker in 1937 he wrote, "The seeing of a tree, a cloud, an earth form always gives me a greater feeling of life than the human body. I *really* sense the life in the former and only occasionally in the latter."[1] His work bears out this preference. FitzGerald seldom painted or drew a nude that is as sensuous as his lithe and silken trees; no female body received the close attention and delicate, even exquisite, touch evident in his drawings of trees and undulating topographies. He eroticizes the mark but not the body.

FitzGerald's perception of the shared forms of the human body and those found in nature led him to a preoccupation with metamorphosis and transformation. Drawing was his most adaptable medium for exploring this suggestive drift. In the drawing *Reclining Nude*, n.d. (p. 89), the woman rests in an ambiguous space that could be a bed or a landscape. Her body and the space she occupies are drawn in the same way. She is curled up on her side with neither her legs nor her arms visible; her head is bent slightly forward and leaning to the left. Along with a pair of other darkened areas above and below her body, her buttocks are the most noticeable area of the composition, their lush form emphasized by a density of black pigment. But if you cover her head with your hand, the drawing isn't any different from any number of FitzGerald's graphite-and-ink abstractions of plants or landscapes, where he is concentrating on the careful modulation of tones.

Similarly, in *Nude Reclining on Bed*, 1928 (p. 96), you are confronted with a disorienting perspective: the placement of the woman's body slightly above the viewer's eye level creates an exaggerated sense of mass in the lower body. Then you see that FitzGerald has added shapes below and adjacent to her breast that are concentrated mounds of something, but not muscle. The longer you look at the drawing, the stranger it becomes: the curl of the foot and toes tucked underneath the body, the dark lines defining the rib cage and the upraised arm that extends toward the top of the page begin to seem as much like shapes and contours in a landscape, or a fallen tree in the forest, as they do recognizable parts of a reclining body.

In *Organic Forms*, 1942 (p. 174), a crayon drawing of a rock with seaweed on it amid a swirling tide (or a valley and mountaintop rising through the fog), it is easy to see the suggestive tracing of a woman lying on her stomach in the foreground. There are very few angles of trees and bodies in FitzGerald's drawings, and when they do occur they are softened, the diffuse lines and shapes opening to a range of morphological conjecture. Exactly this kind of double read occurs as well in *Tree Trunk*, 1939 (p. 72), where the amorphous drawing of the tree seems to slide toward the bottom left of the composition, as if it were giving over to age and gravity. A small protrusion on the trunk's upper left reads as a nipple. Other small marks suggest an eye or a navel. FitzGerald encourages a way of seeing in which everything, even in the abstract drawings, is in some process of reconfiguration.

It seems clear that FitzGerald, whether consciously or unconsciously, often had the body on his mind. The numerous watercolour self-portraits he made around 1945 (pp. 90–93), some with arrangements of nude women swirling about his head, are fascinating pictures of the intimate workings of his imagination. In all of them, though, the women seem to be slipping away as much as they are present. That frustration, coupled with our intrusion, seems to enrage him. We have stumbled on some intimate moment. He and his women are naked, and his angry outward gaze sends us back to the landscapes he has drawn and painted, with their confusion of forms. He wants us to engage with that world, but he also seems to suggest that we are not welcome in the most private chamber of his imagination. ■

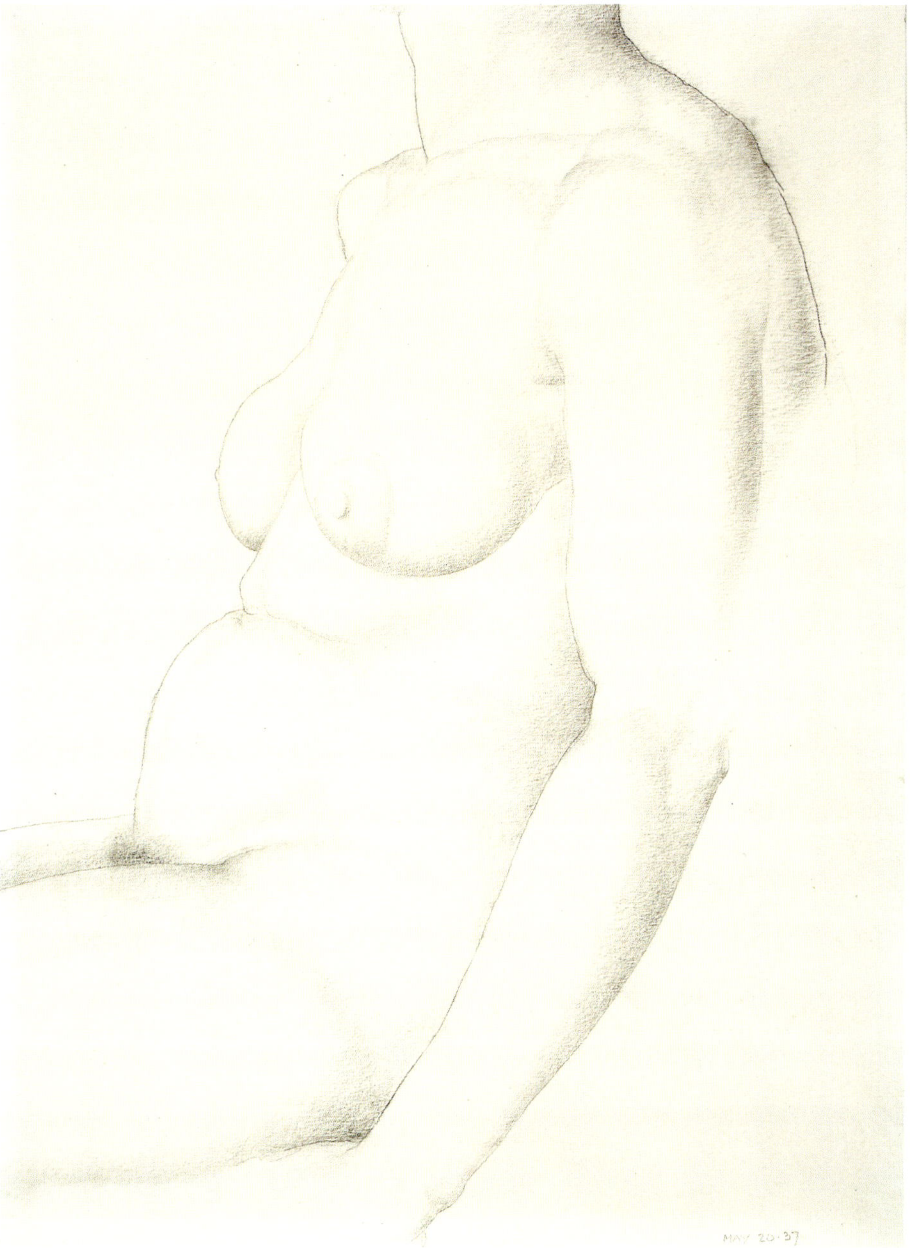

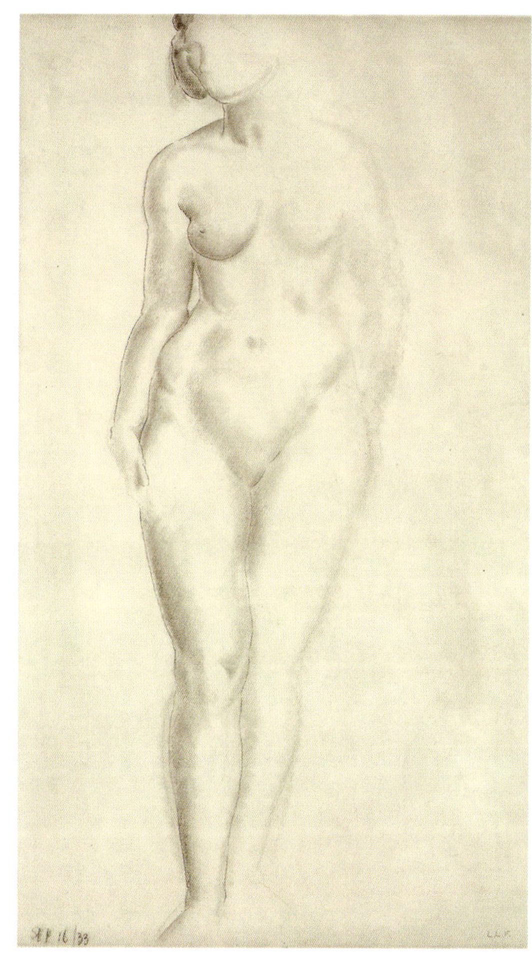

LEFT
Seated Nude Torso, 1937
graphite on paper
30.5 × 22.8 cm

RIGHT
Slavic Nude, 1933
graphite on paper
48.3 × 27.9 cm

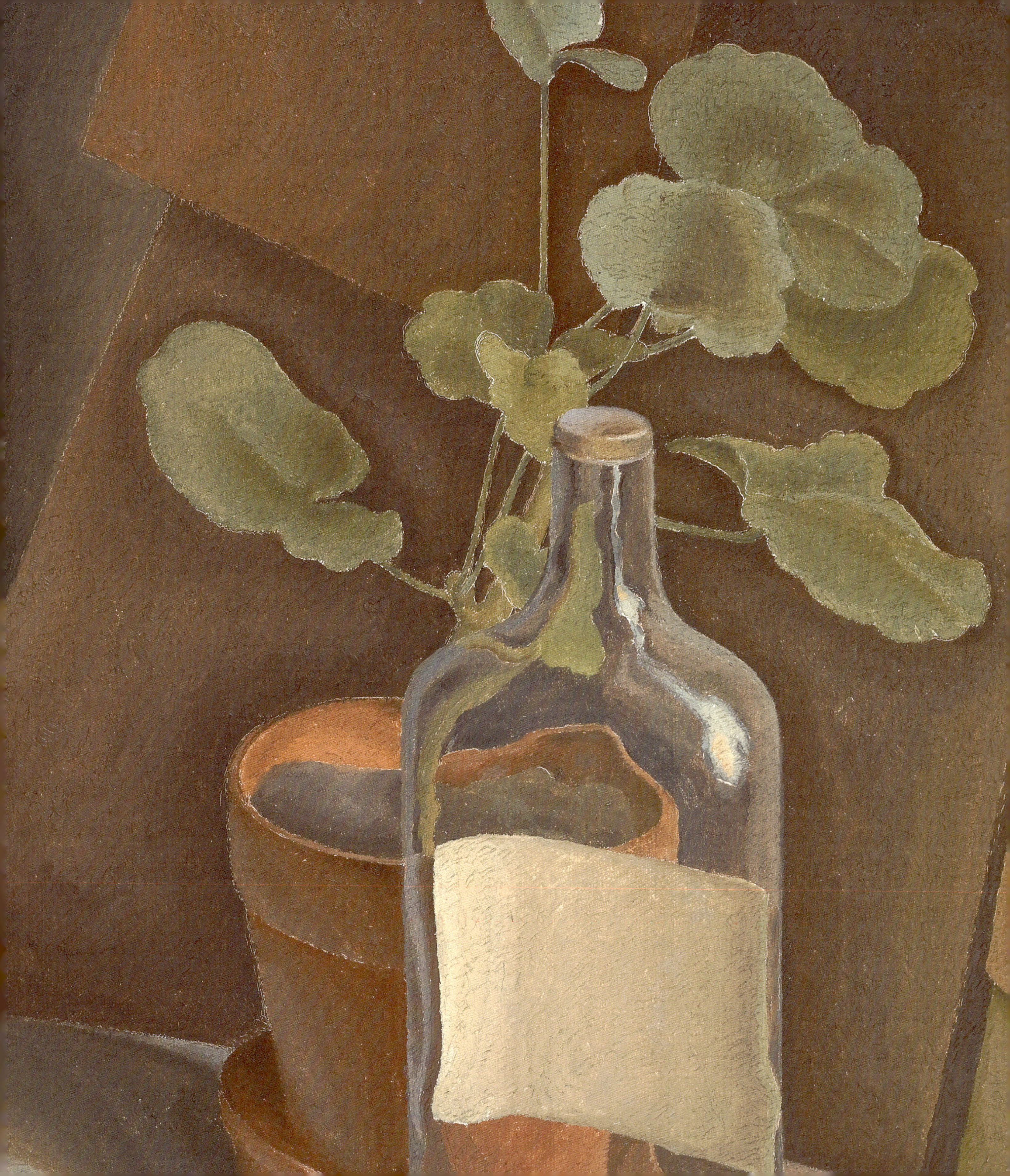

STILL LIFE AND WINDOWSILLS

The tradition of still life has a long history, with artists from Chardin to O'Keeffe elevating it to a genre that evokes the fleeting nature of life and the passage of time. FitzGerald follows in those painters' footsteps in still-life compositions that seem to radiate light. Often he positioned objects on windowsills to examine more closely the play of light on surfaces and architectural forms. The drawings and paintings of Seurat, seen by FitzGerald during his tour of the major museums in the eastern United States during the summer of 1930, would have an indelible effect on this technique, as he experimented with breaking down form into a flurry of tiny flecks. Other still-life works by the artist explore a kind of Precisionist exactitude, with smoothly modelled surfaces seemingly caressed by the fall of light. All celebrate the exquisite pleasure of seeing and recording moments of distilled experience.

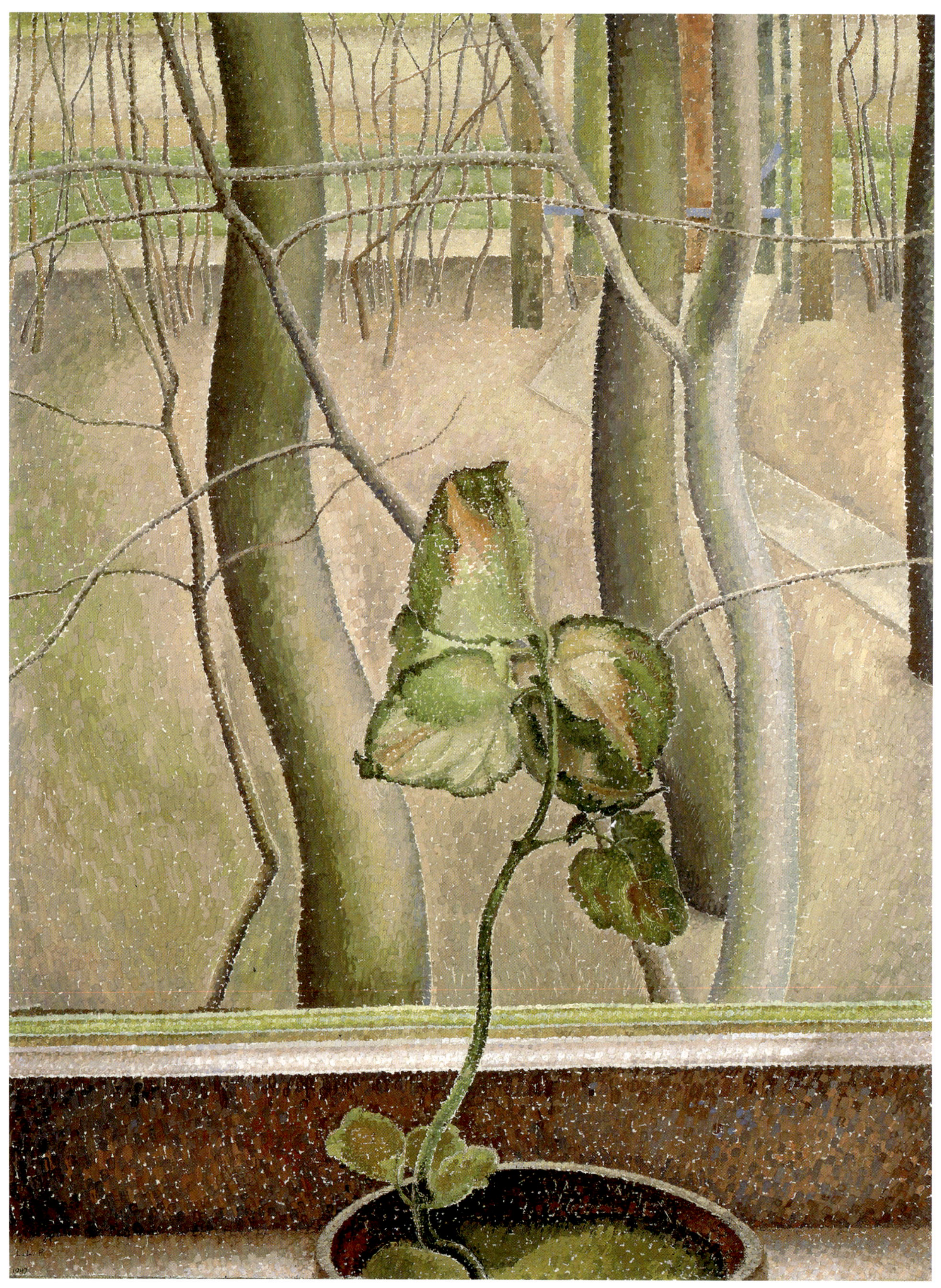

THE LITTLE PLANT

IAN A.C. DEJARDIN

The Little Plant is the outstanding masterpiece of the McMichael's holdings of the work of Lionel LeMoine FitzGerald. That the McMichael has thirty-three works by the artist, including paintings, drawings, and prints, is largely due to the fact that, in 1932, he was invited to join the Group of Seven, becoming the tenth artist to be a member of that exclusive body with which the McMichael is particularly associated. At first sight he seems an unlikely choice. Previous late invitees A.J. Casson and Edwin Holgate—excellent artists both—had more obviously strong stylistic affiliations with the original members of the Group.

It may well be that FitzGerald's appointment signalled a change of direction for the Group, a recognition of the need to spread their net beyond their Ontario/Quebec base, and an attempt to move on from the by then well-established tropes of forest, mountain, and lake. But in fact there were powerful links. What the Group of Seven was to Algoma and Southern Ontario, what A.Y. Jackson was to the rolling hills and rural communities of Quebec, FitzGerald just as surely was to the prairie landscape of Manitoba. He was as obsessed with trees as any of them, albeit the urban elm forest of Winnipeg. And his fascination with the visual opportunities afforded by Winnipeg's backyards and laneways chimed with Lawren Harris's early street scenes of Toronto. He and Harris were kindred spirits, too, in their paring back of detail to concentrate on form. Harris's monumental and formally simplified icebergs and mountains, like FitzGerald's neighbourhood houses and sinuous trees, were symphonies of "found" geometry pointing toward the artists' future interest in pure abstraction; they had both been finding abstract form within figurative subject matter for years.

The Little Plant, 1947
oil on canvas
60.5 x 45.7 cm

The Little Plant dates from 1947, fourteen years after the Group of Seven had dissolved in January 1933, just a few short months after FitzGerald joined. The deciding factor in that dissolution was the death, late in November 1932, of J.E.H. MacDonald. Whatever development in the Group's direction that had been signalled by FitzGerald's joining was transferred to the Canadian Group of Painters, a much larger and more inclusive body of artists.

The painting demonstrates one of FitzGerald's favourite themes, the view framed by a window, the windowsill representing a formal dividing line between inside and outside. Such windowsills were often his preferred location for still lifes, and outside the window the graceful elms strike another favourite note. There is an element of quiet humour here as well: the little geranium, looking sun starved, pot bound, and feeble, is contrasted with the thriving trees outside, its leaves turned, as if wistfully, outward.

The hallmarks of FitzGerald's mature style are all here: the simplified geometry of the composition, based on horizontals and verticals, the subtle and subdued palette of fawns, greys, pinks, and sage greens, against which the brighter green of the little plant pops nicely. His interest in painting the trees outside the window is not in detail—he never tries to evoke the tactile quality of bark, for instance—but in pure form. The backdrop against which the trees provide the vertical interest is vague, out of focus, a series of horizontal planes subtly differentiated in colour to suggest a receding landscape. The little plant itself is centrally placed, bracketed compositionally by the two nearest trees. A path strikes an angular note to the right, to balance the pronounced horizontal of the sill and another landscape element—a road, perhaps—beyond the trees. Where road and path join is marked by a small grace note of blue against terracotta. All is formal, controlled, and subtle.

FitzGerald's technique seems to be derived from the Post-Impressionism of a much earlier era—that of Seurat and Signac—a Pointillism of dry dabs of pigment that sets up a movement and vibration across the surface of the work. Seurat's influence, incidentally, is visible, too, in many of FitzGerald's most delicate drawings, created out of a miasma of tiny flicks of the pencil. Draftsmanship is ultimately the foundation stone of FitzGerald's virtuosity; he drew all the time, no doubt as a crucial element of his day job, which was teaching art, but with an obsessive quality that led him to record a whole train trip in the series of stops made along the route. The exquisite balance seen in *The Little Plant* is the product of a seemingly effortless control of line and rhythm—the very features that would inform FitzGerald's abstracts in the years to come. ■

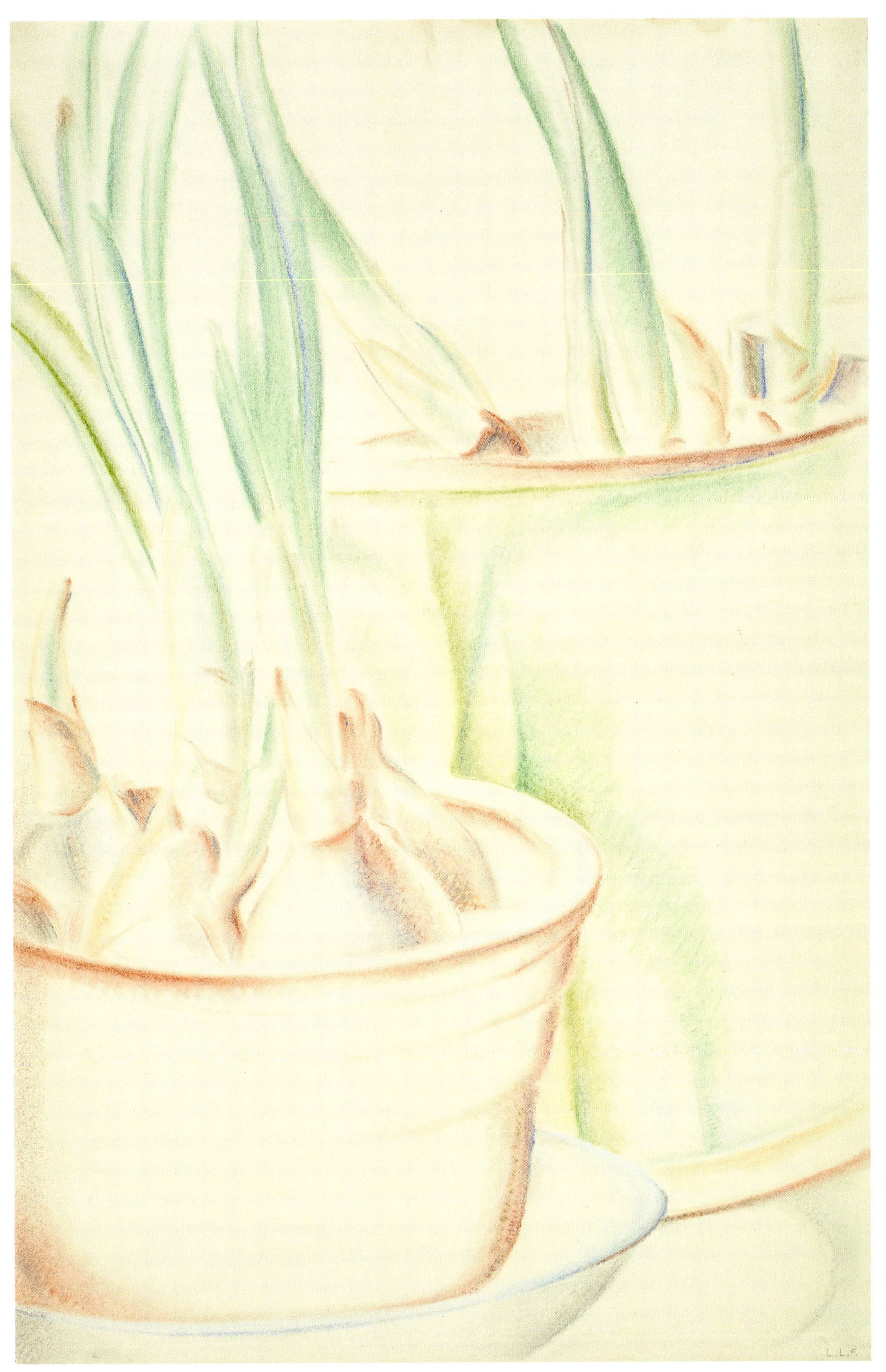

Still Life with Bulbs, 1938
pastel on paper
sheet: 46 x 30.6 cm

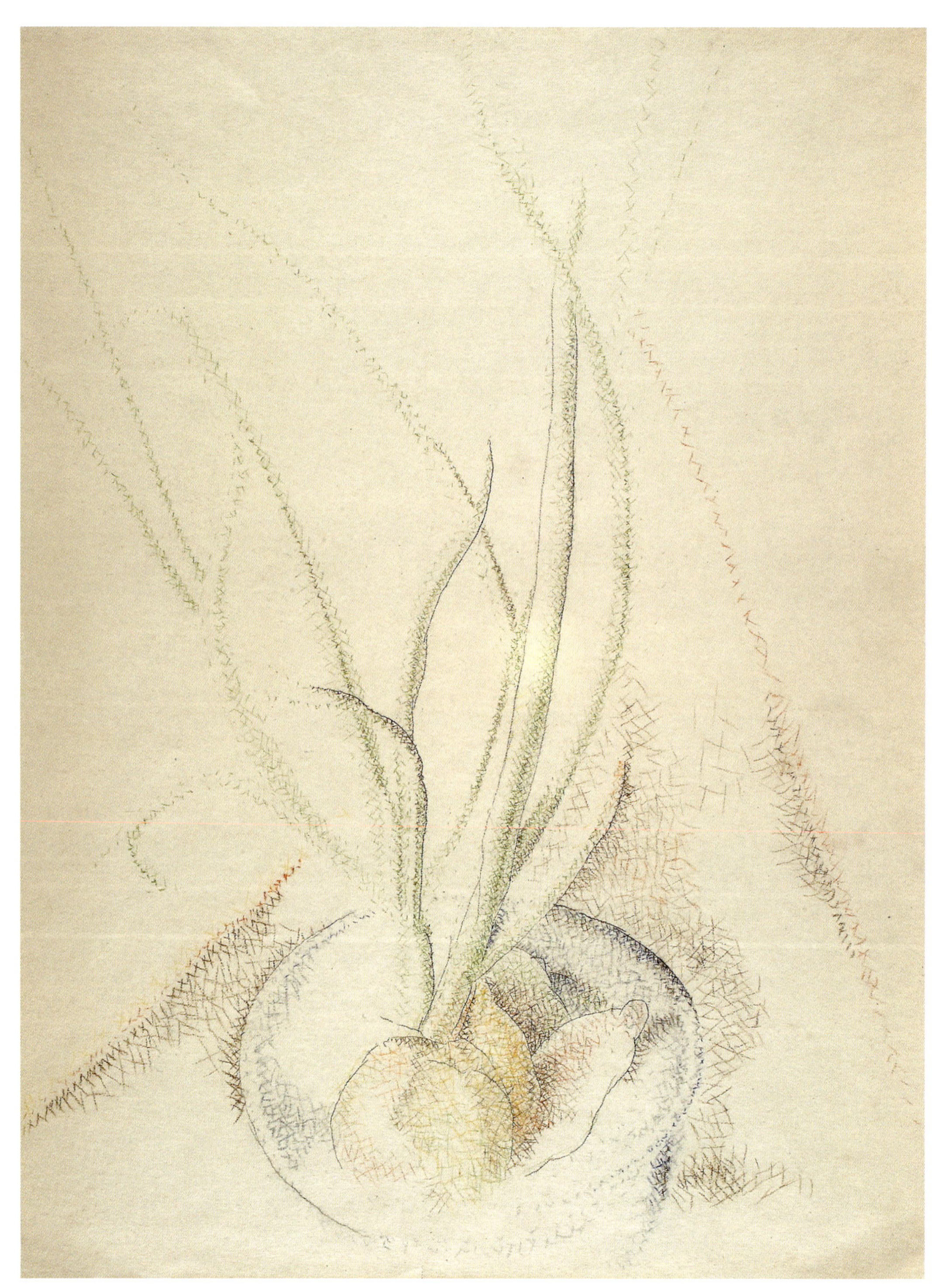

Spring Bulbs, 1944
coloured chalk on
wove paper
60.9 × 45.8 cm

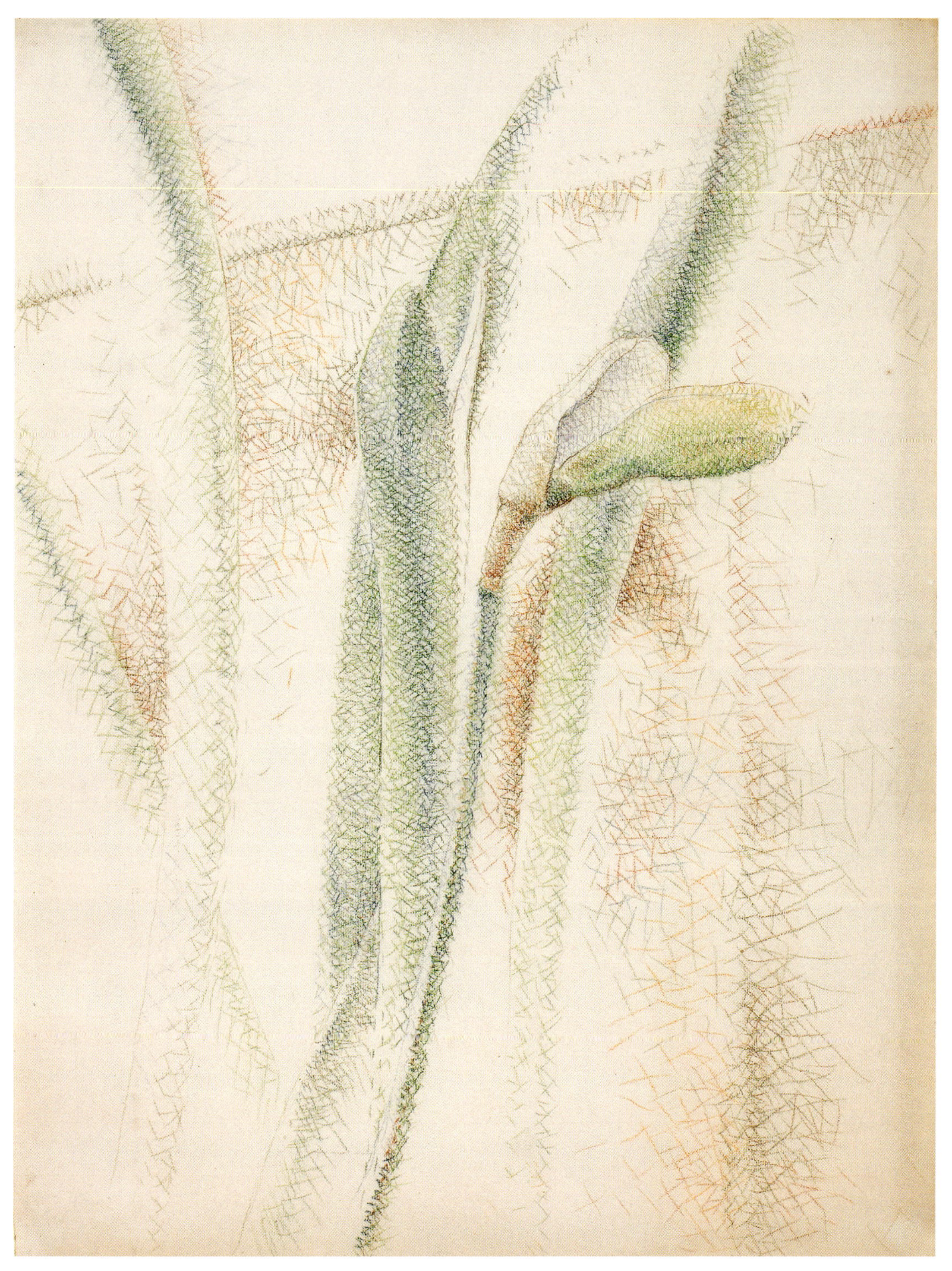

Daffodil, c. 1940
coloured chalk on paper
63 × 48 cm

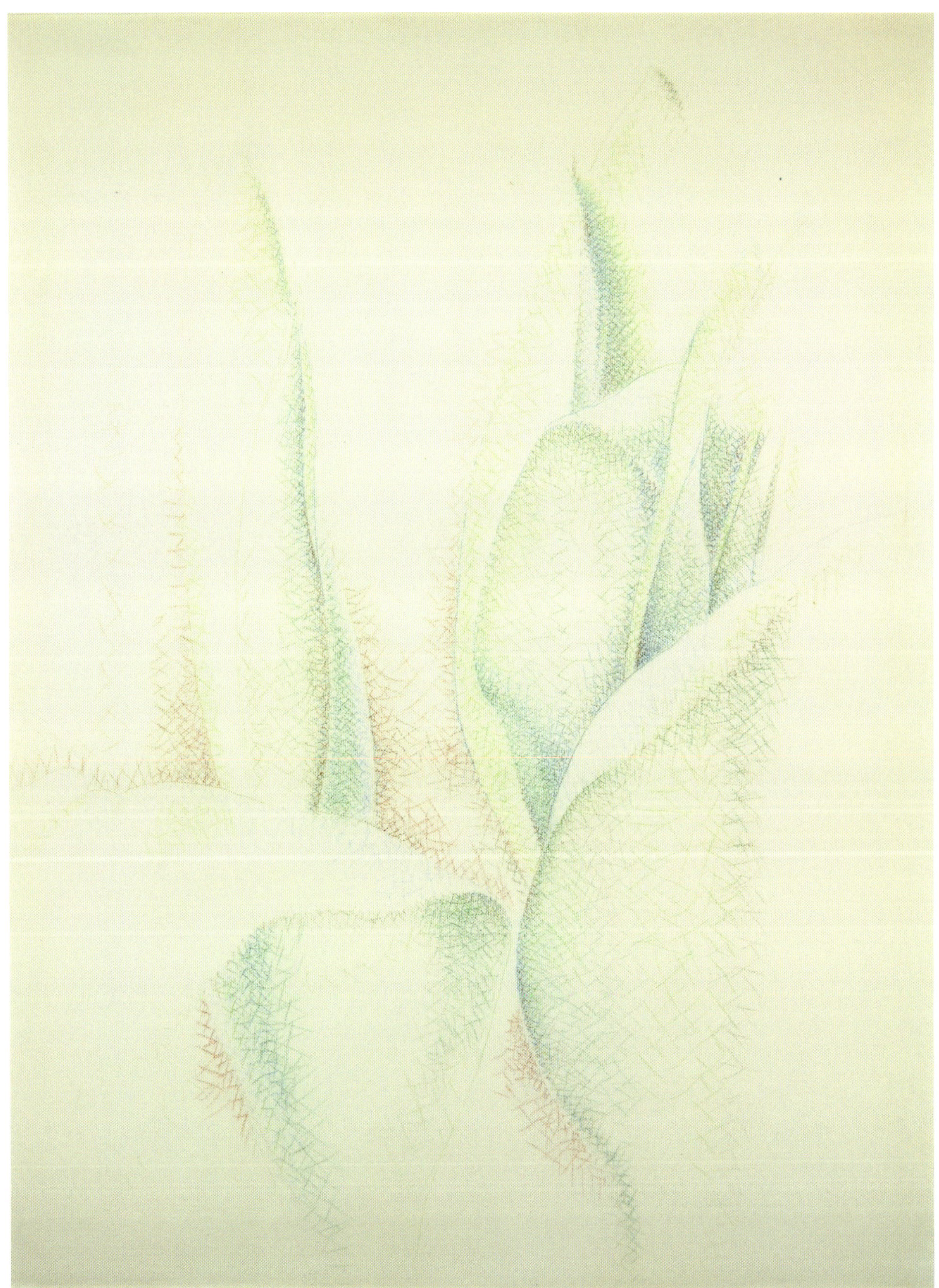

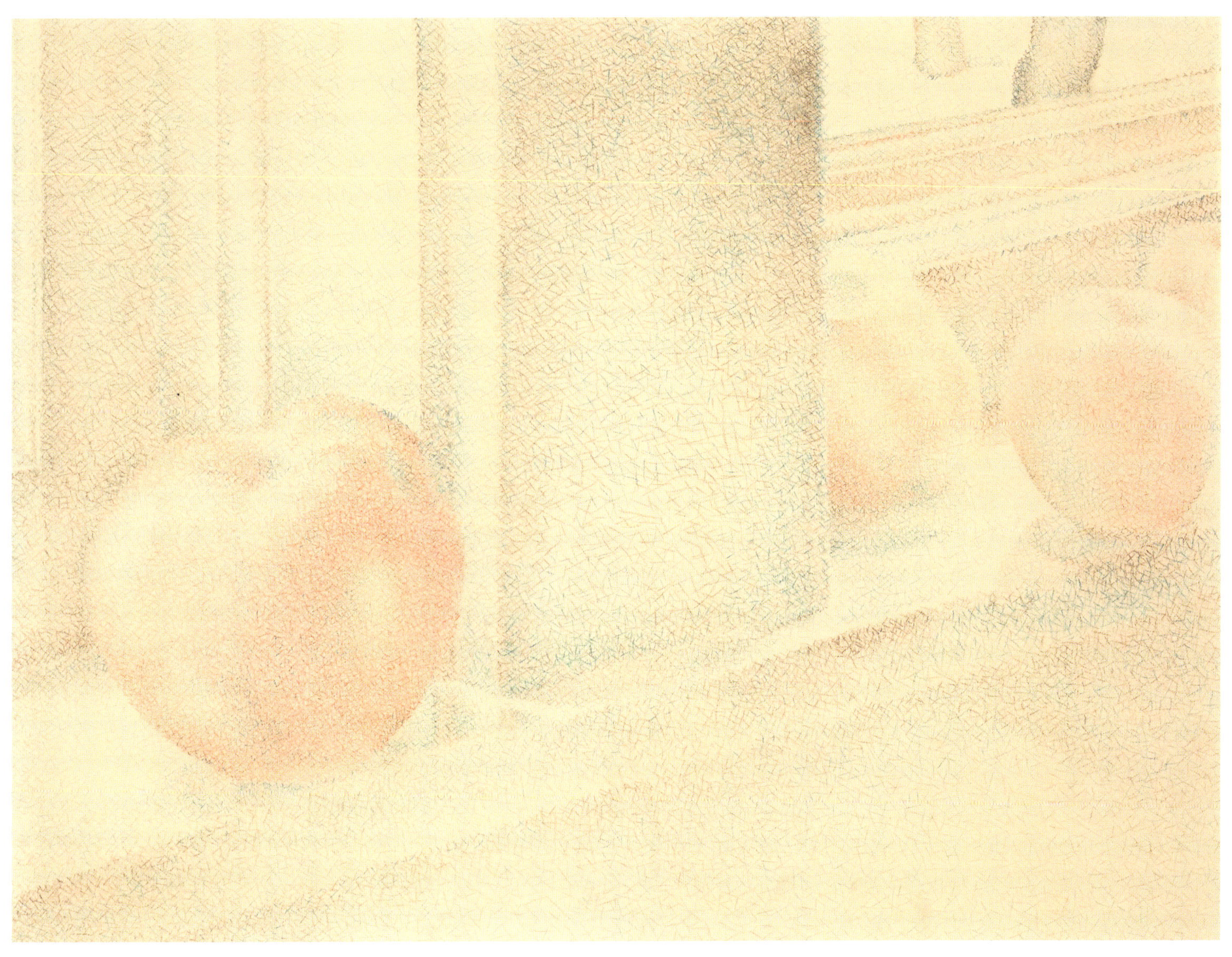

OPPOSITE
Leaves, n.d.
chalk on paper
63 × 48.2 cm

ABOVE
Four Apples on a Window Sill, c. 1943
coloured chalk on paper
46 × 61 cm

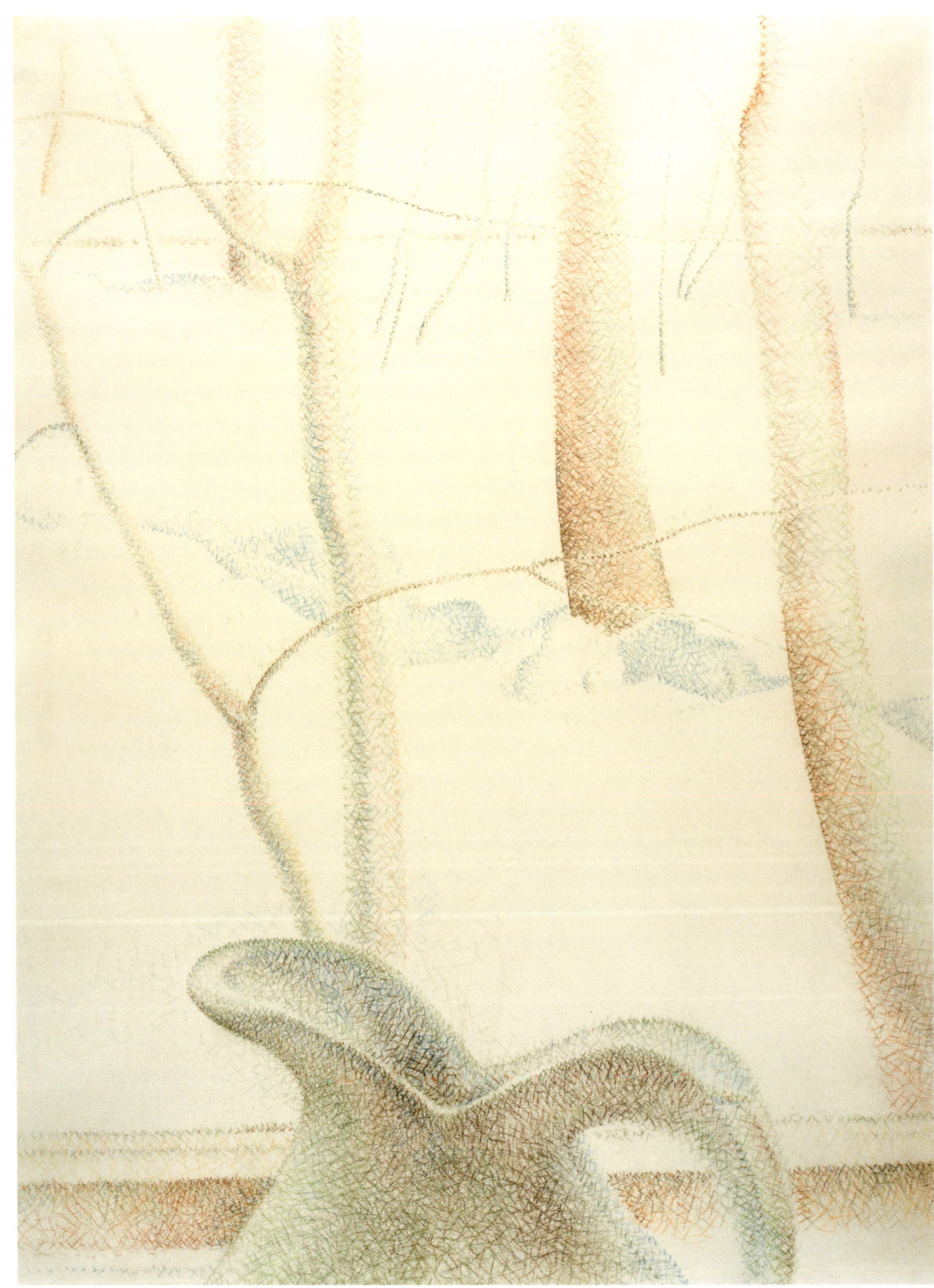

Jug on the Window Sill, 1943
chalk on paper
60.8 × 45.7 cm

OPPOSITE
From an Upstairs Window, Winter, c. 1950–51
oil on canvas
61 × 45.7 cm

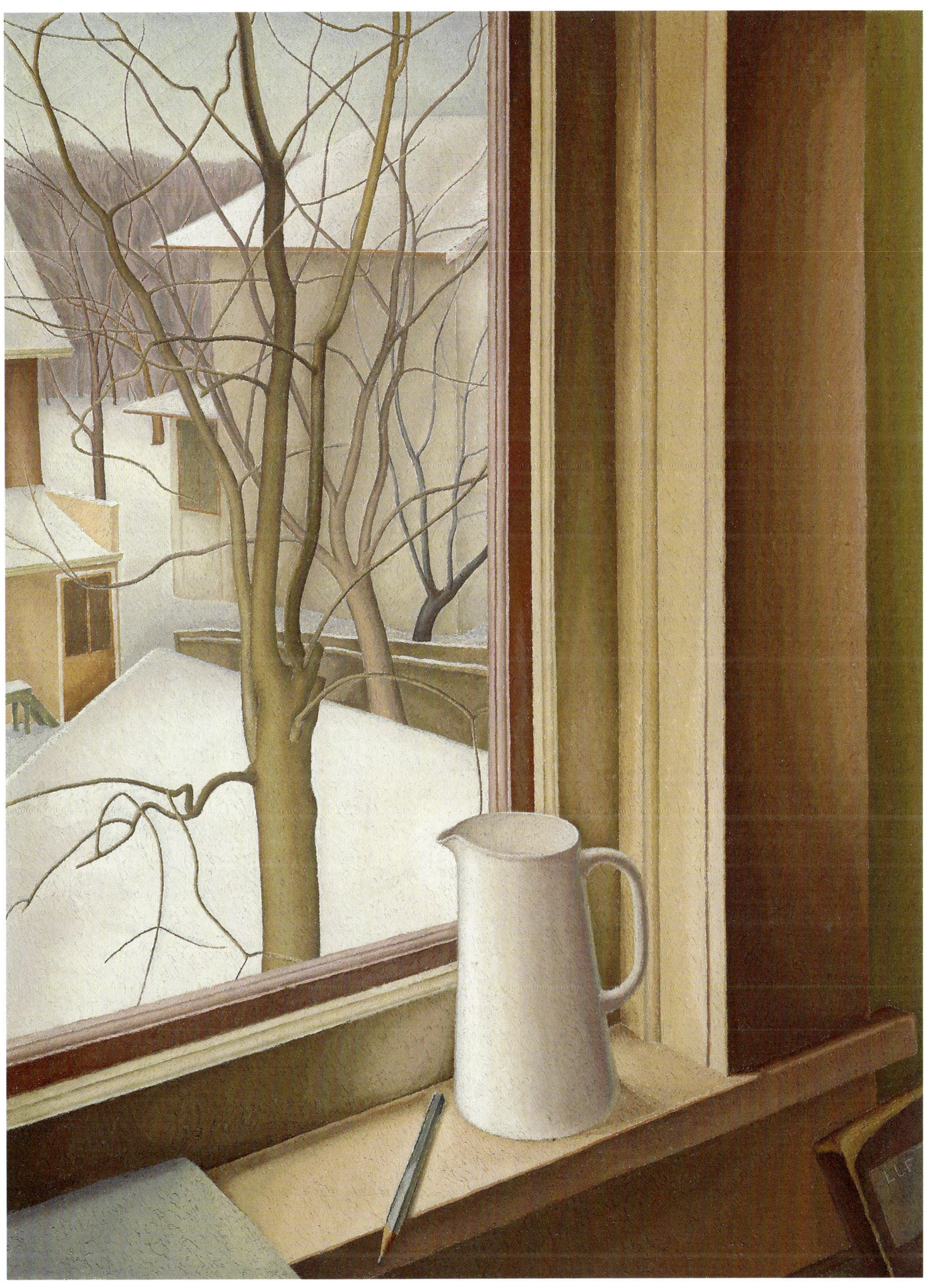

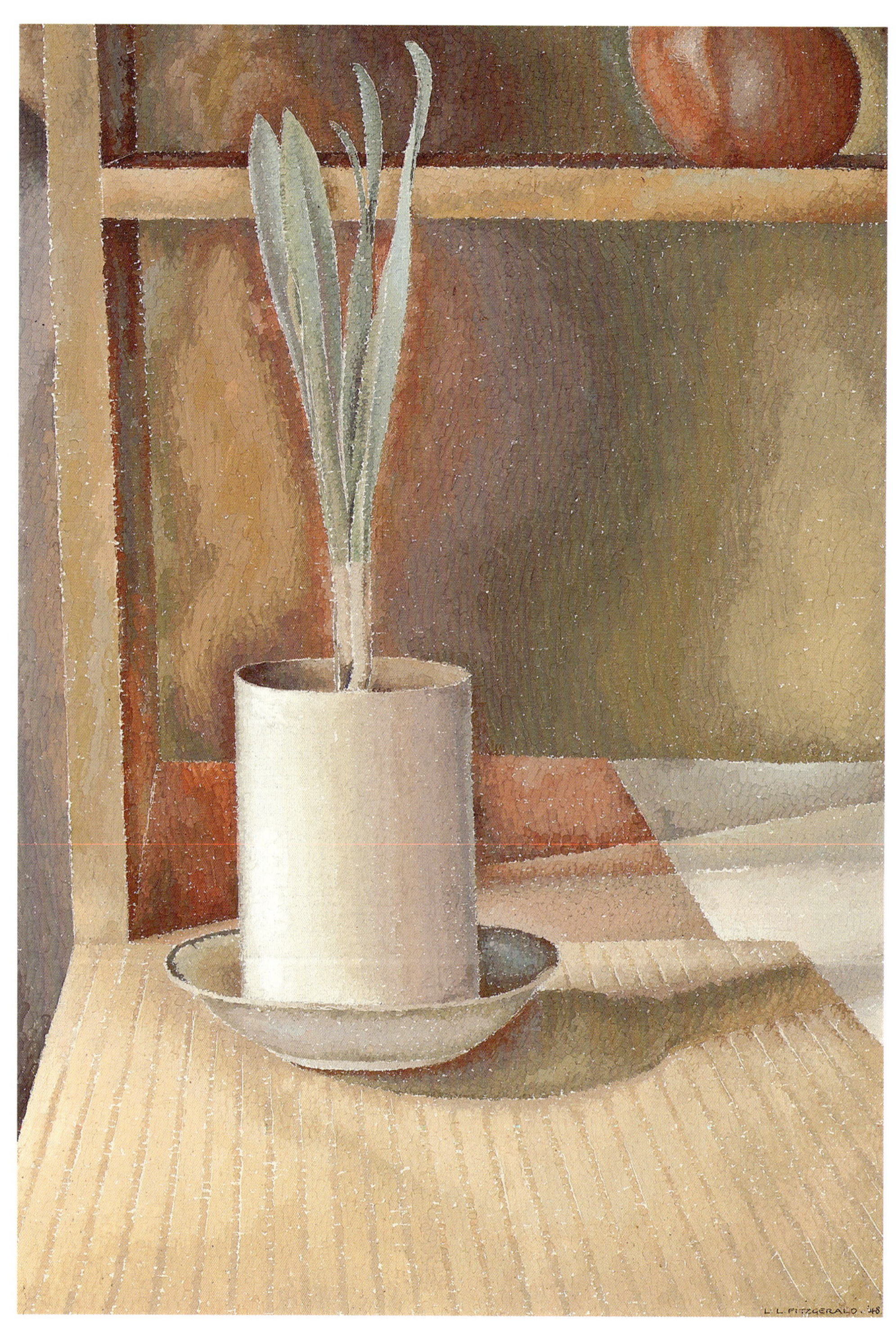

Still Life with Plant, 1948
oil on canvas, laid down on board
47.9 × 35.6 cm

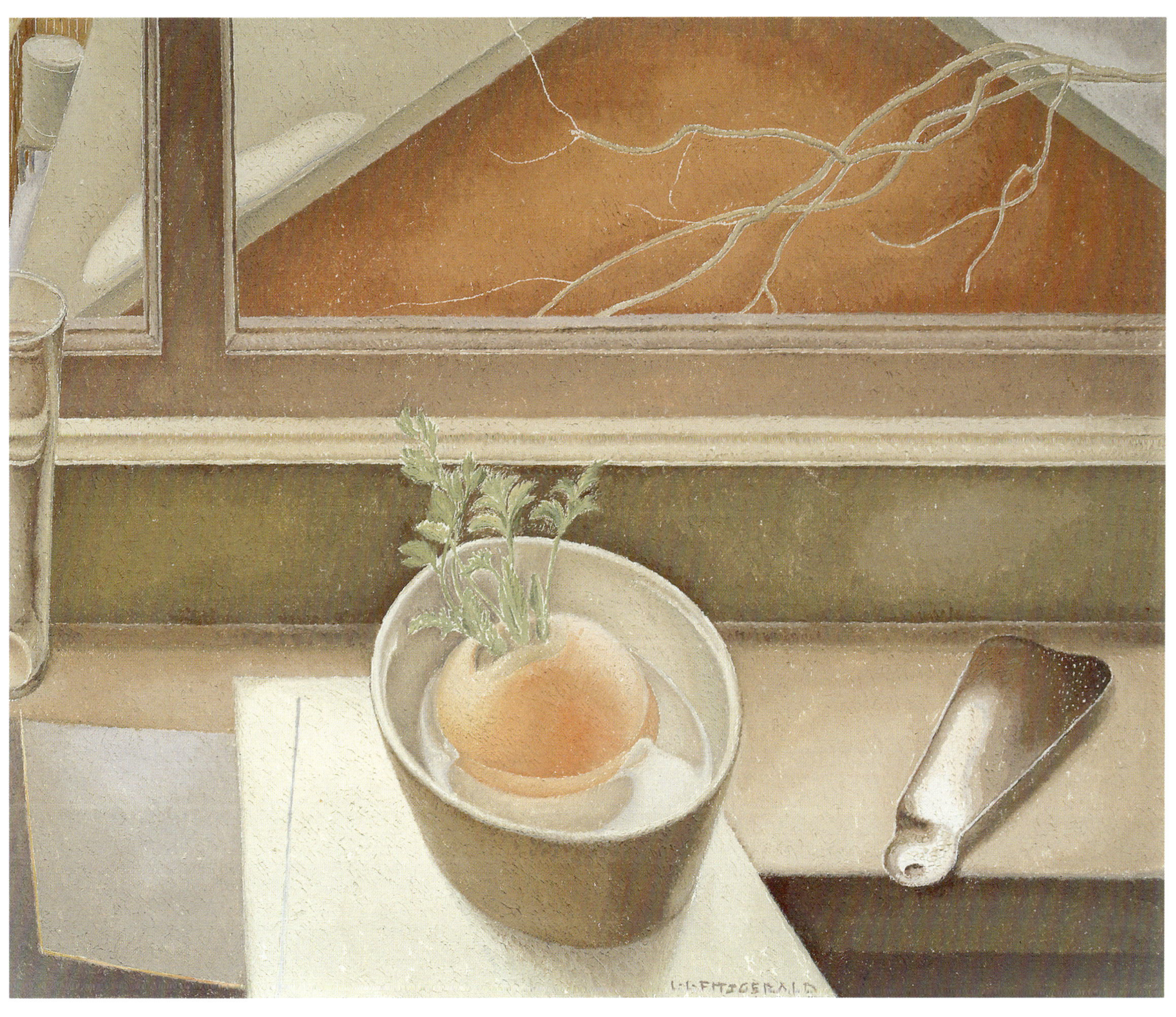

Still Life from Window, 1952
oil on canvas
36.3 × 44.2 cm

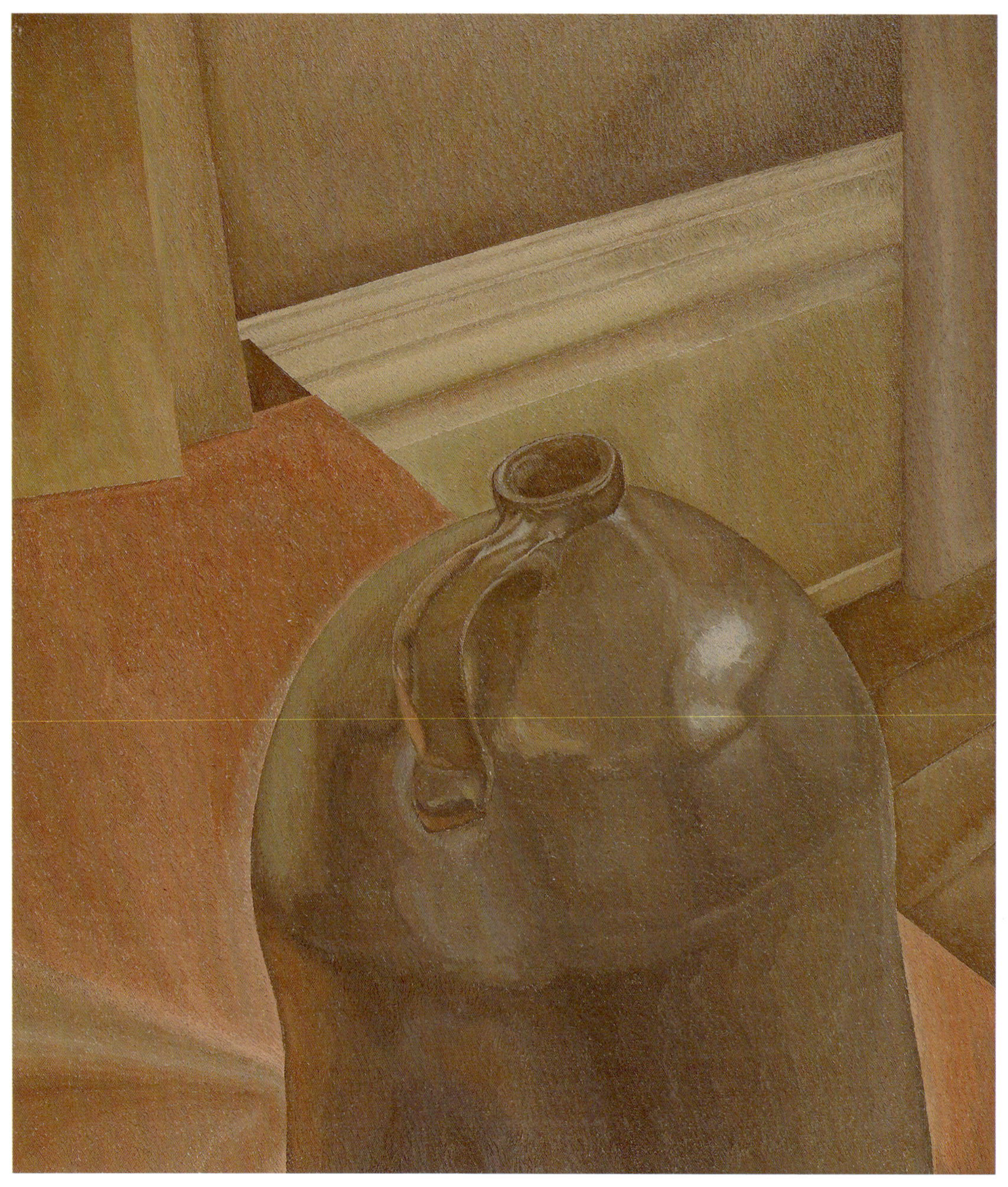

ABOVE
The Jar, 1938
oil on canvas
61.3 × 53.9 cm

OPPOSITE
Still Life with Jars, 1924
oil on canvas
76.5 × 61 cm

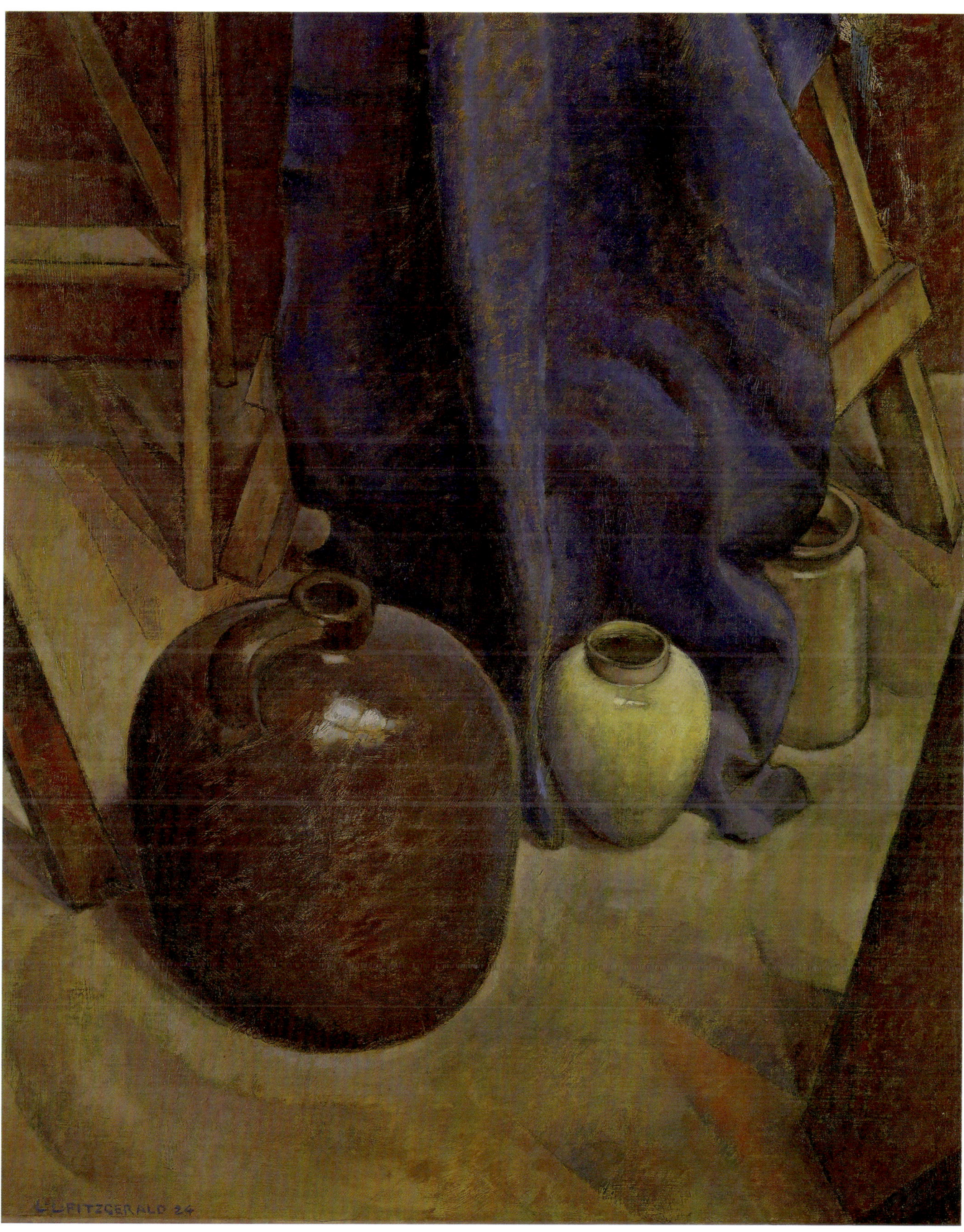
L.L. FITZGERALD 24

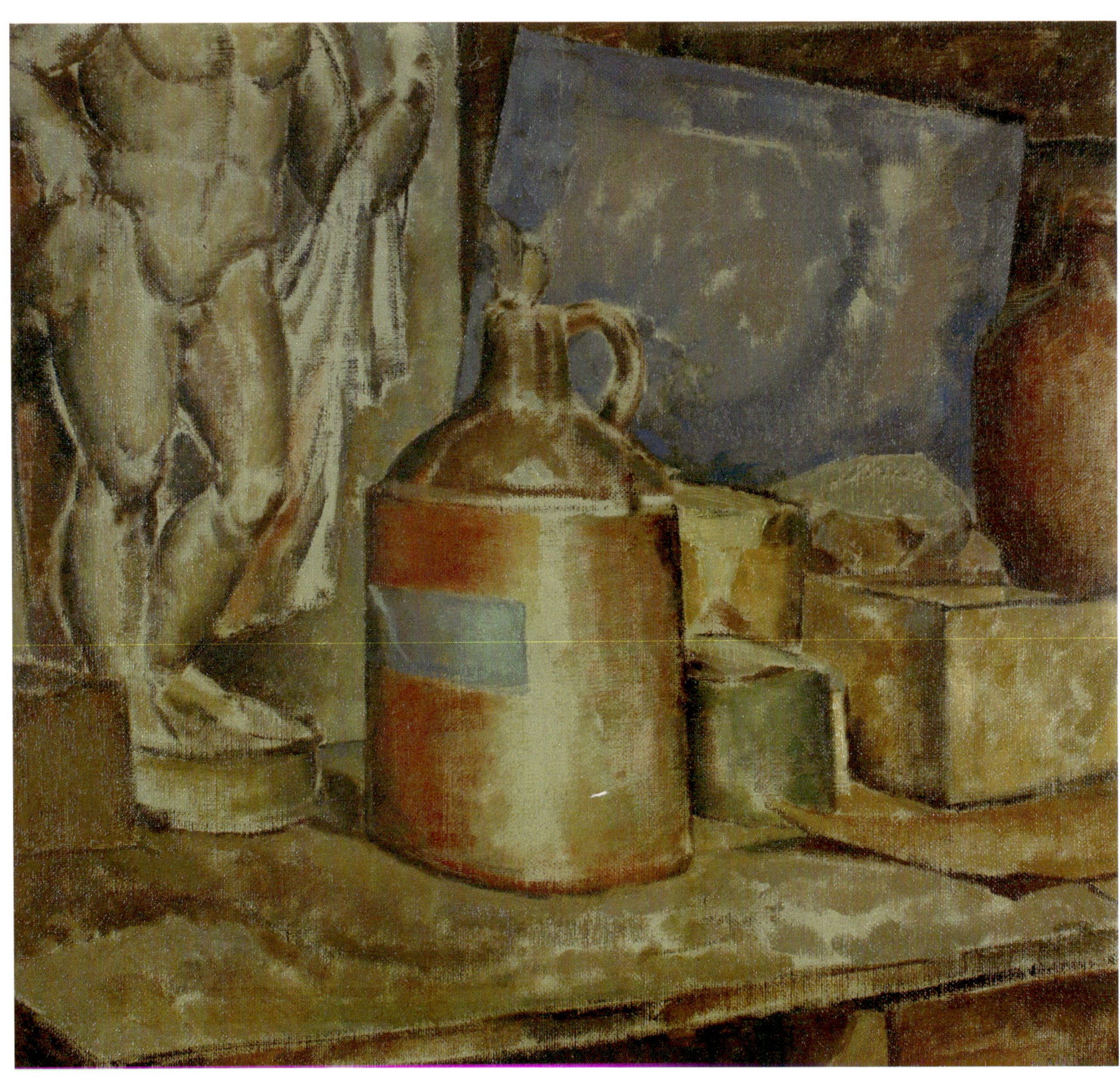

Still Life, c. 1924–25
oil on canvas
46.4 × 50.8 cm

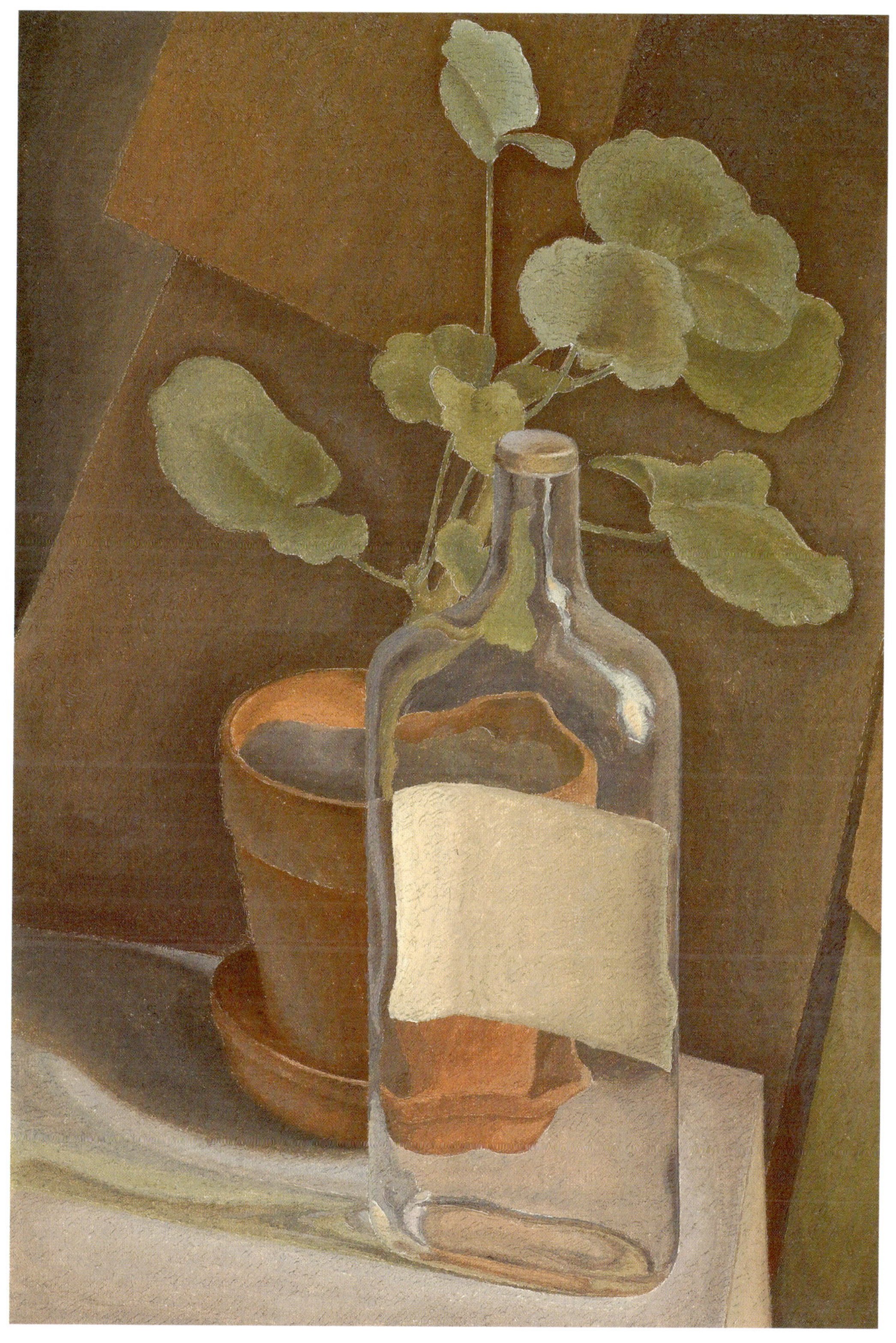

Geranium and Bottle, 1949
oil on canvas
45.6 × 30.1 cm

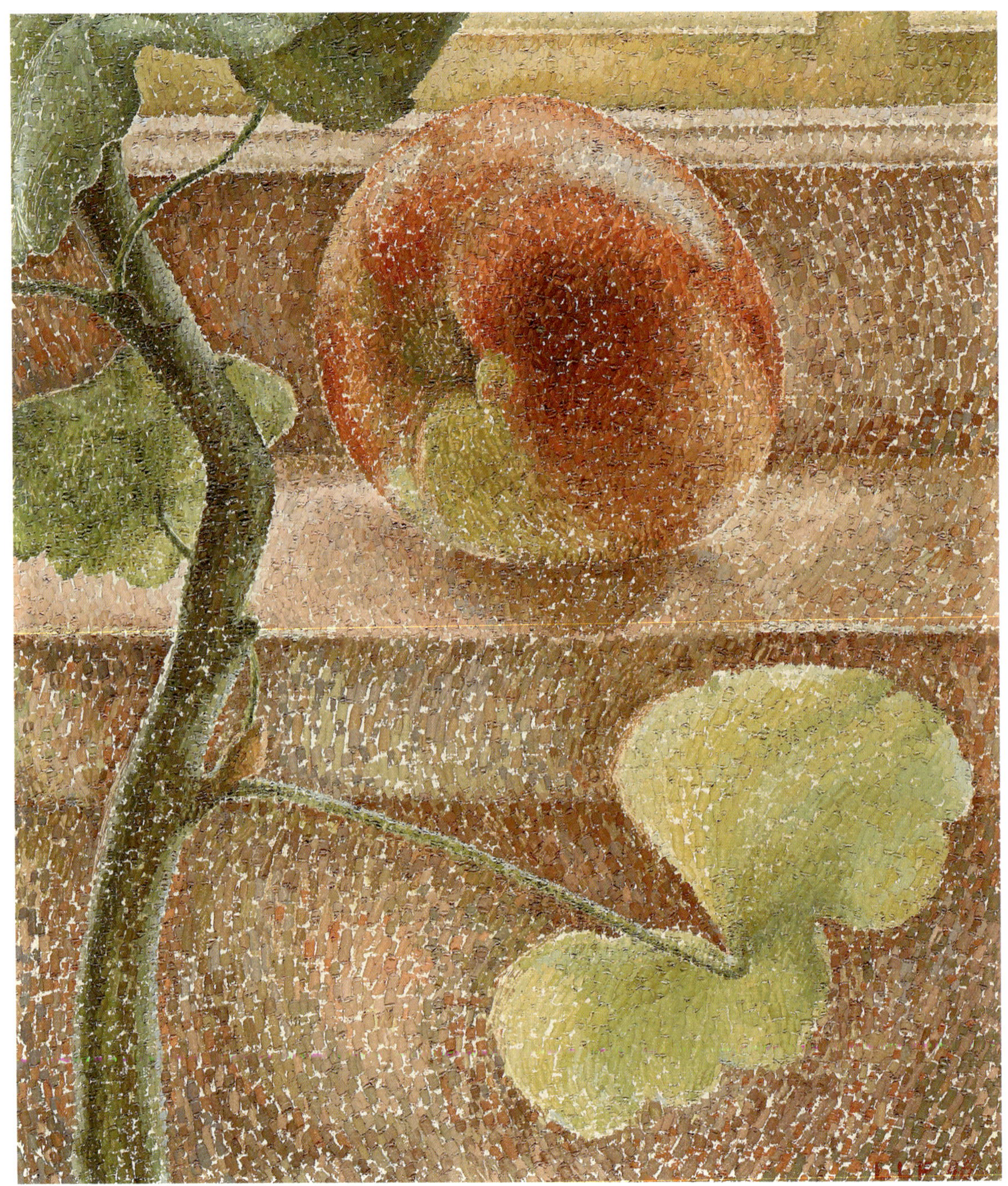

Still-life, 1941
oil on wood
40.9 × 35.5 cm

OPPOSITE
Still Life: Two Apples, c. 1940
oil on canvas
45.4 × 40.7 cm

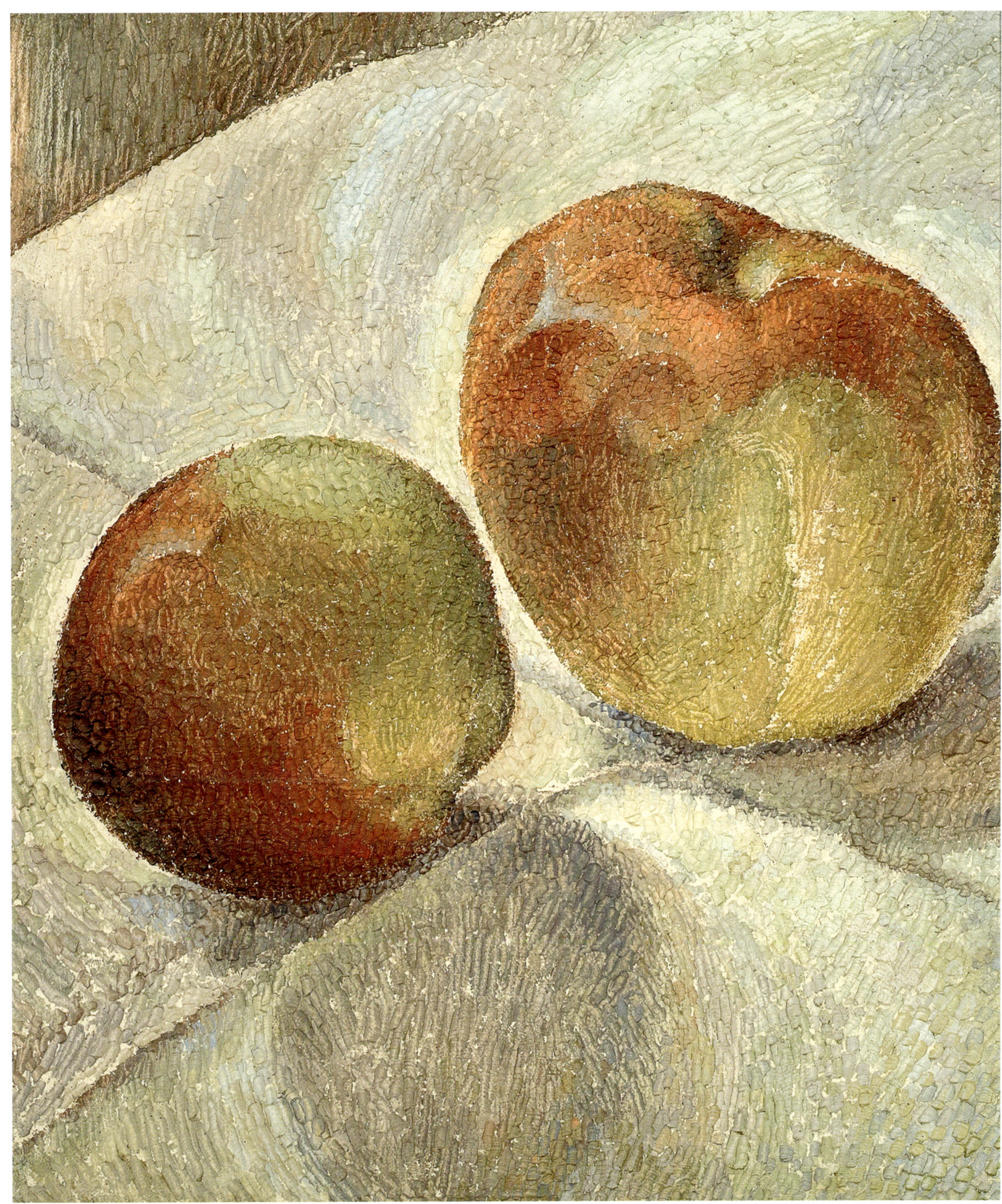

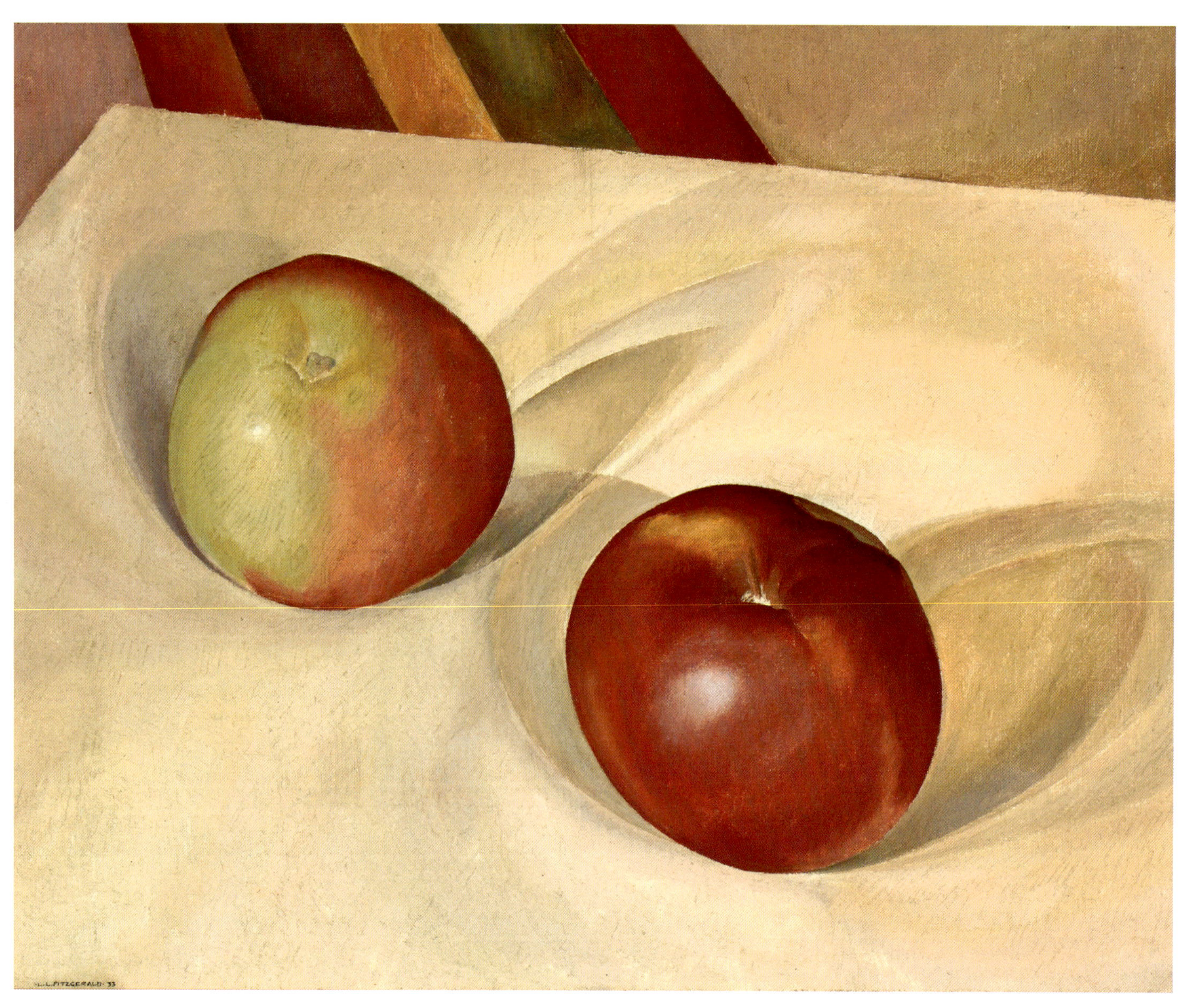

Apples, Still Life, 1933
oil on panel
30.5 × 38.1 cm

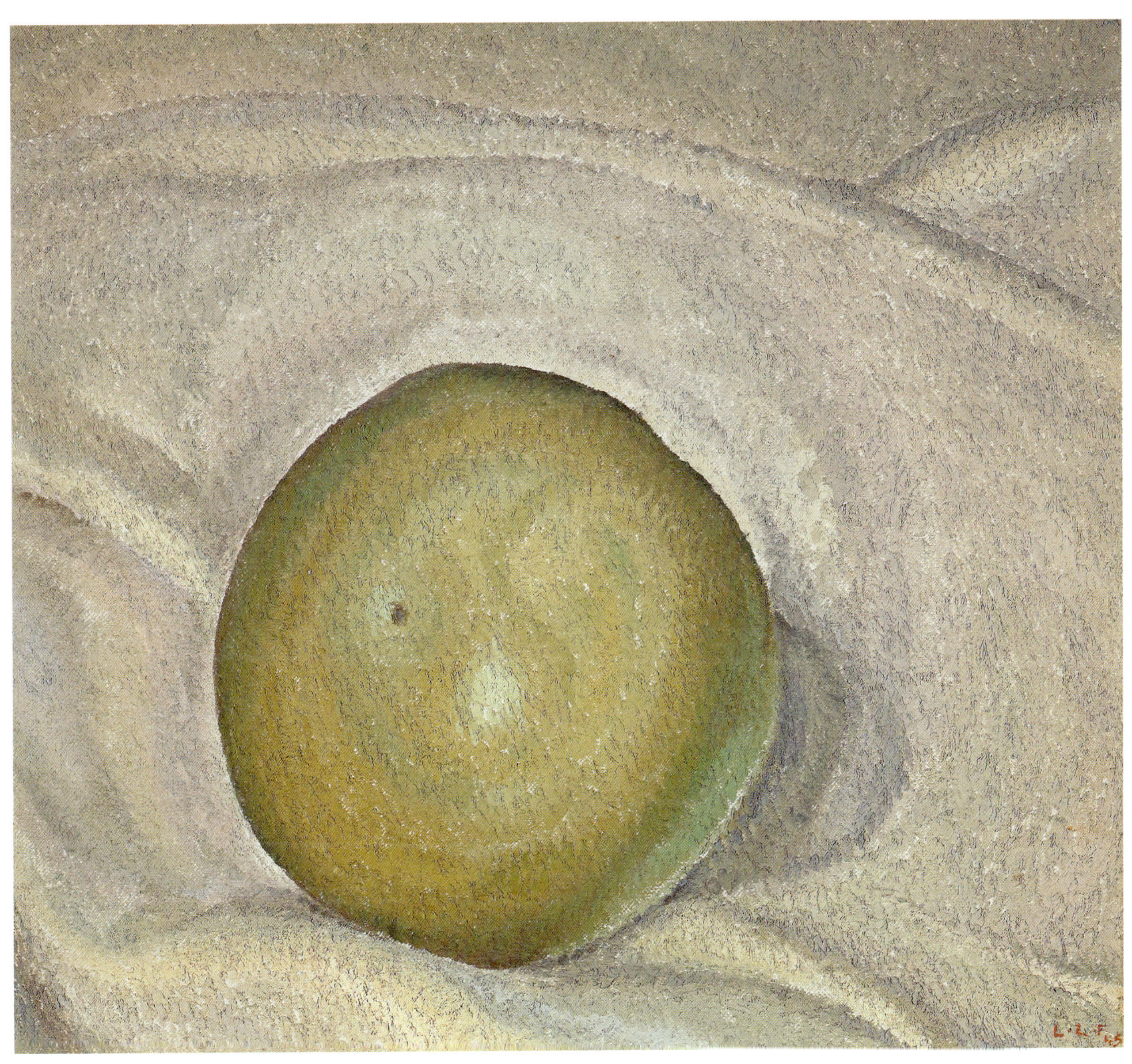

Green Apple, 1945
oil on canvas, mounted
on Masonite
29.6 × 33 cm

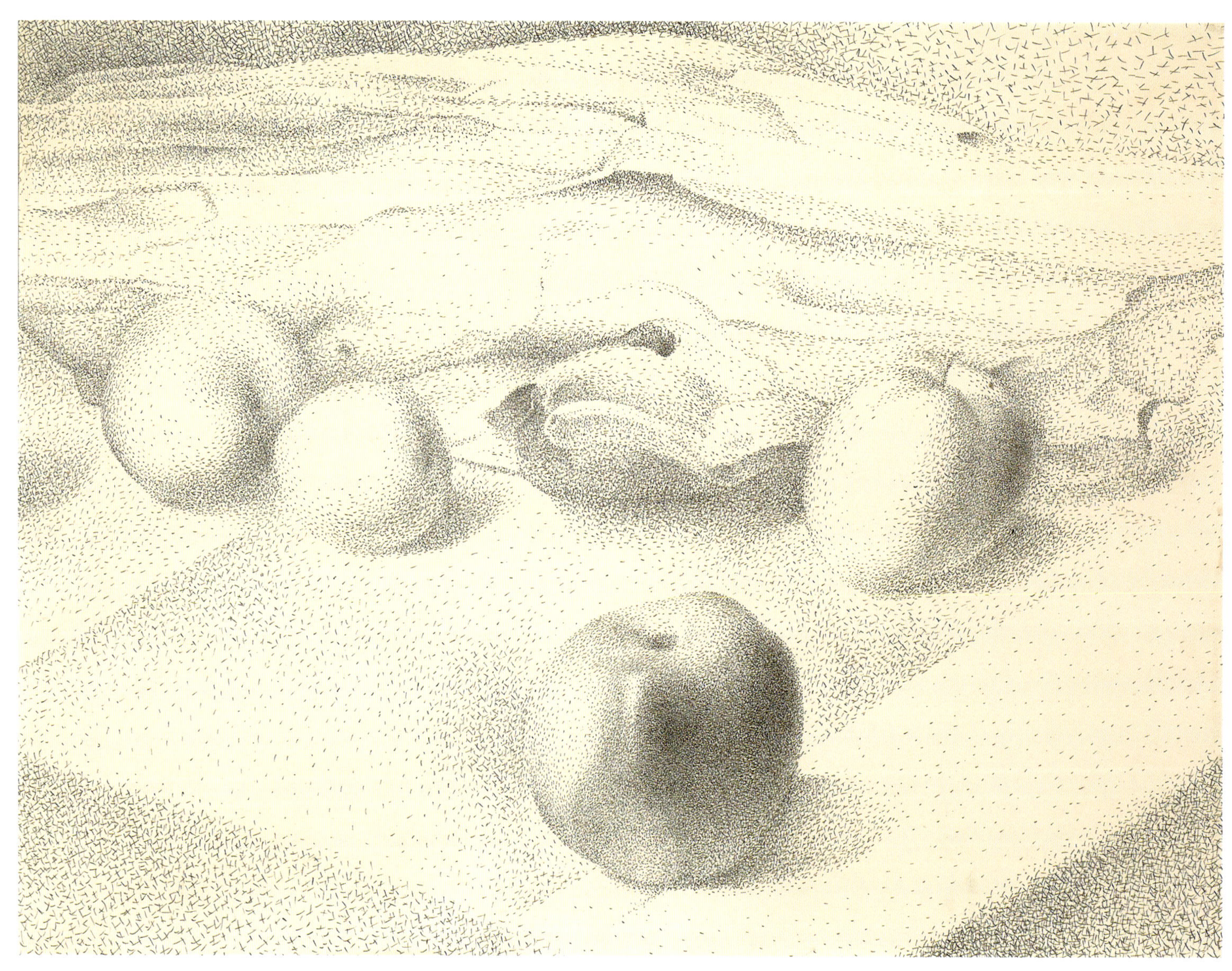

Four Apples on Tablecloth, 1947
ink on paper
46 × 60.9 cm

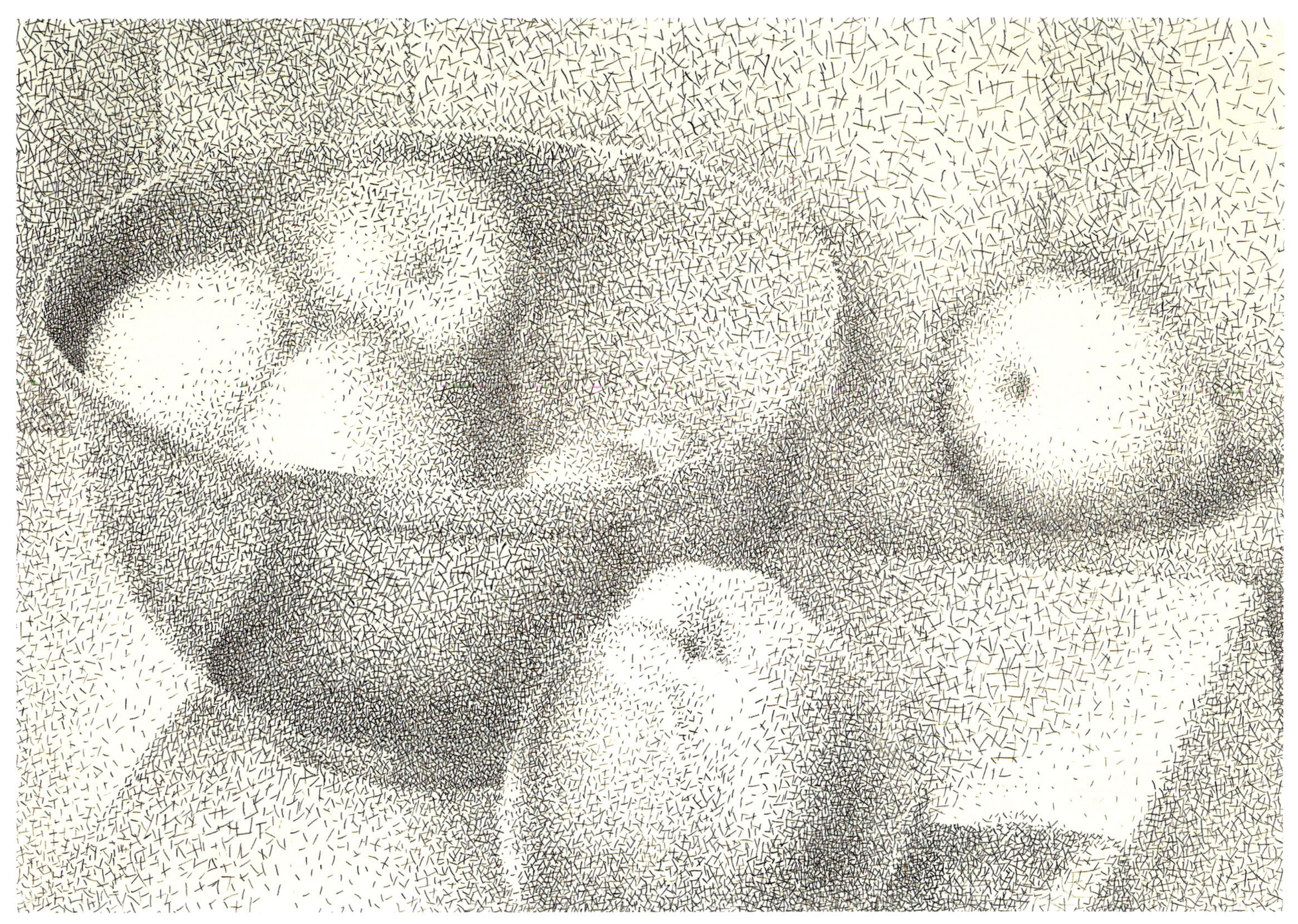

Apples in a Bowl, 1947
ink on paper
29.1 × 42 cm

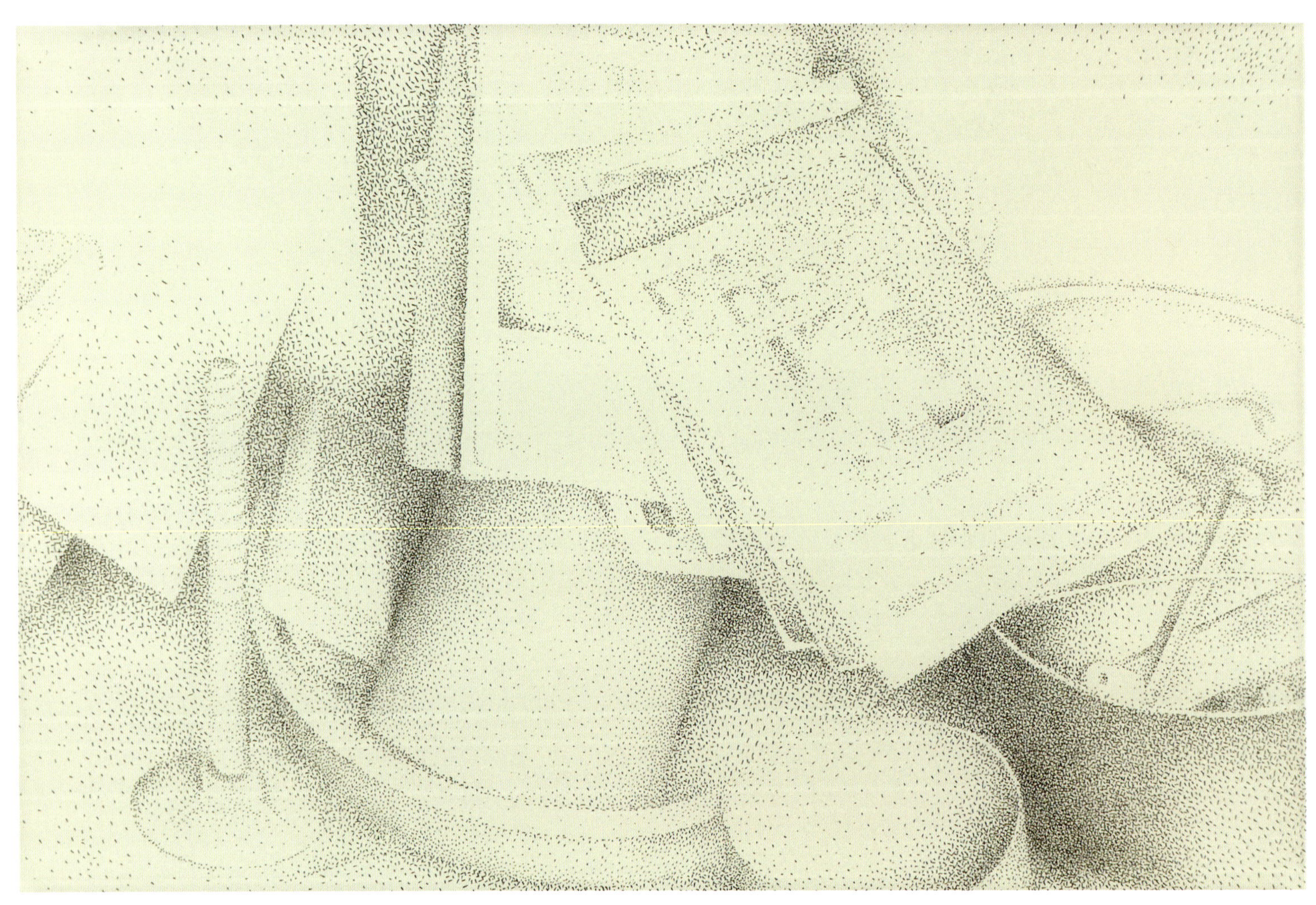

Book, 1948
ink on paper
30.5 × 46 cm

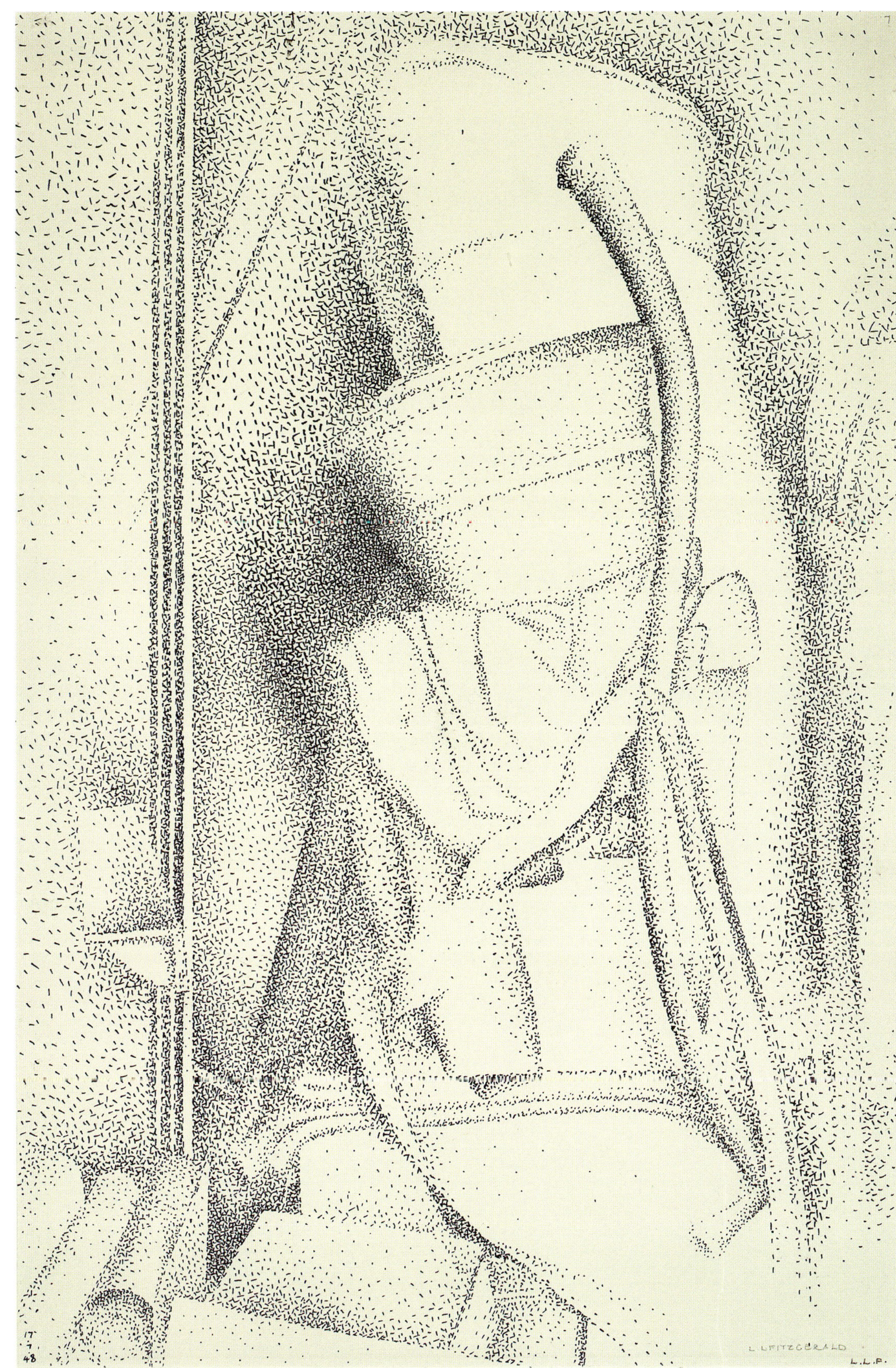

Still Life with Scythe, 1948
pen and ink on paper
sheet: 46.7 × 30.6 cm

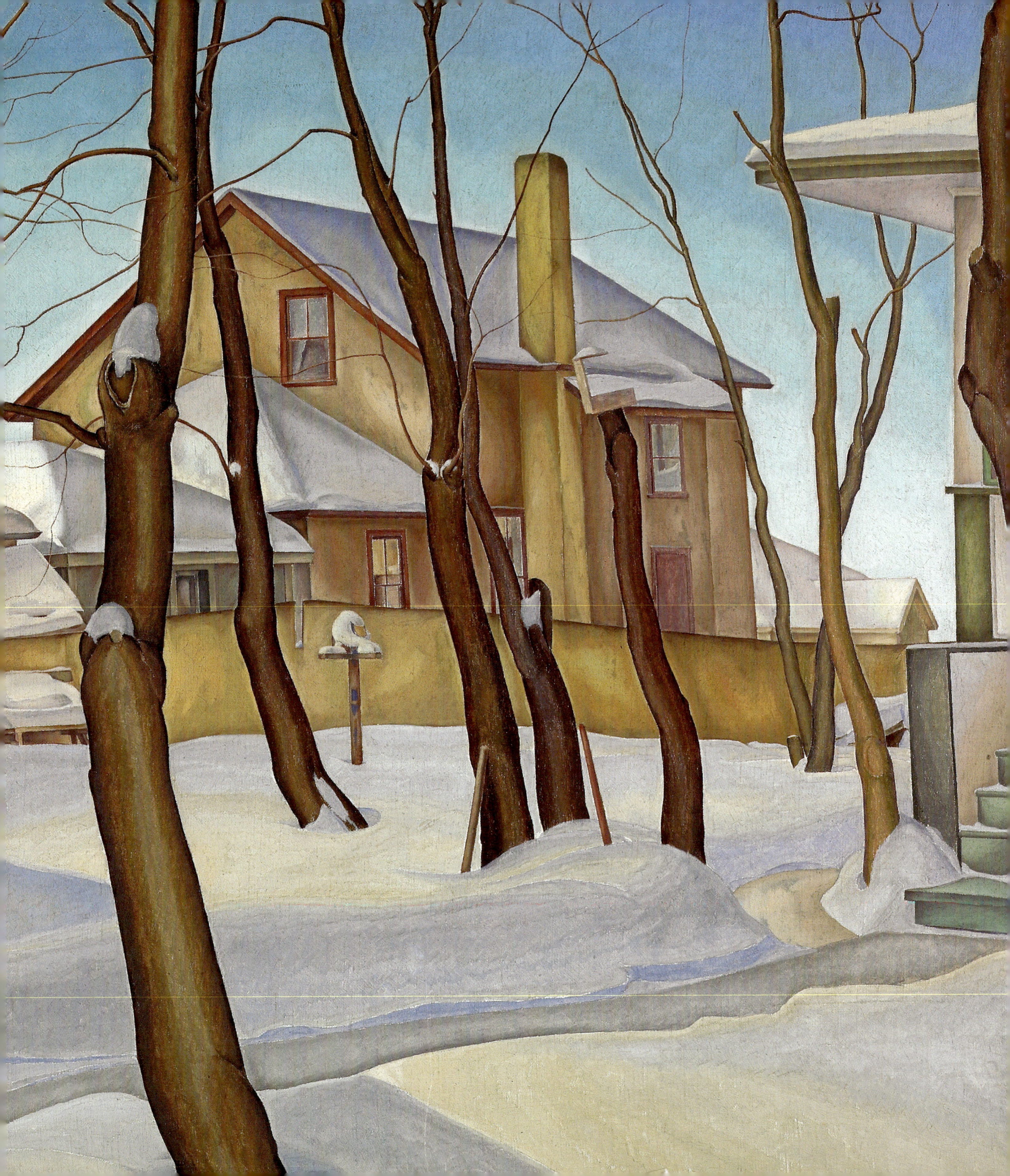

THE NEIGHBOUR-HOOD

While the members of the Group of Seven were out riding on boxcars or tramping in the woods, FitzGerald preferred encounters with his own Winnipeg neighbourhood and the urban forests of his native city. At times he would set up a kind of mobile studio-shack in his backyard, the better to work outdoors on cold winter days. The resulting works, such as *Doc Snyder's House*, are among the most beloved of Canadian paintings, recording FitzGerald's personal experience of his environment but also the play of light and colour on form. Each is a study in composition carefully wrought, evoking his quiet suburban world but also reflecting a sense of taut emotion and a fierce attentiveness to visual experience.

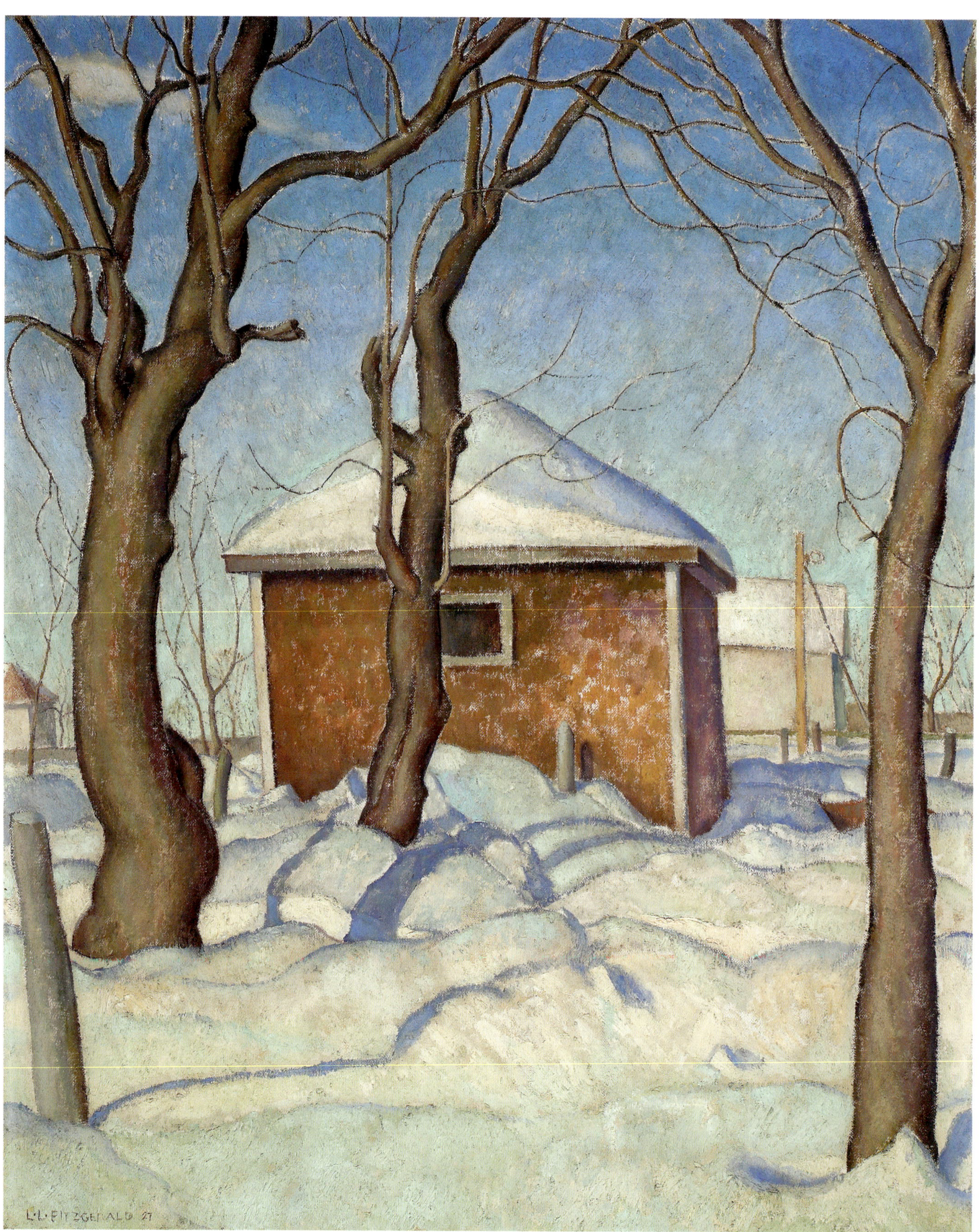
L·L·FITZGERALD 27

LE GARAGE DE M. WILLIAMSON

PIERRE DORION

Many years ago, when I was a young boy living in Quebec City, I participated in a drawing competition and won a prize, which consisted of art books. One of them, which I still own, was titled *Un siècle de peinture canadienne 1870–1970*, published by Les presses de l'université Laval in 1971 and written by Jean-René Ostiguy, then a curator at the National Gallery of Canada in Ottawa. This book was my introduction to Canadian art.

Among the illustrations were two paintings by Lionel LeMoine FitzGerald: *La maison du docteur Snyder*, 1931, and *Le garage de M. Williamson*, 1927—in English, *Doc Snyder's House* (p. 146) and *Williamson's Garage*. Like most of the images in the book, they were in black and white. My first impression of these paintings was thus of their formal qualities, as I was deprived of their colours and their texture. Still, I found something very powerful in looking at these images. Black-and-white reproductions leave a lot of room for the imagination, and that can trigger strong intuitive experiences, especially for a young person—I was eleven or twelve at the time.

I only saw the paintings in colour many years later, and I was surprised how different they look from what I had expected. The light is very different; what looked in black and white to be grey winter days was revealed to be the sunny, golden hour of late afternoon. Both paintings depict austere buildings, domestic structures surrounded by trees in a suburban setting.

I was particularly taken by the painting of the garage. This isolated little building, with no visible openings except for a small window out of reach, was very evocative for me. It embodied a kind of psychic space of isolation and privacy, attributes that I would ultimately come to identify with the artist's studio. The young boy that I was longed to be inside that little building, to make it his own. Unconsciously, I had developed an emotional bond to FitzGerald's painting.

A few years later in Montreal, when I was about sixteen, I came across a similar small structure, but this time it was in the real world. The encounter occurred during my years as a student in the Department of Visual Arts at the Cégep du

Williamson's Garage, 1927
oil on canvas
55.9 × 45.7 cm

Vieux Montréal. Close to that school, on the rue de Bullion just below Sherbrooke Street, was a small building with no door or point of access from the street side. It belonged to a vast property that had been abandoned. It must have been some kind of gardener's shed, and for many years I entertained a fascination with it. Although it was impossible to occupy or to rent, it became for me a fantasy studio, like the garage of M. Williamson.

I have been living in that same Montreal neighbourhood since then, and for decades I walked by that little building. In 2008, I made a small painting of it, *Remise (Rue de Bullion)*, working from a photograph I had taken some years before. My painting and FitzGerald's share surprisingly similar formal and emotional qualities. Both show a building in winter juxtaposed with a landscape of bare trees. I created *Remise* as a way of holding on to my feeling for that building, though I eventually surrendered the painting to the art market. It was bought by a Montreal collector. I like to think that he continues to have his own emotional response to my painting.

Looking at *Remise* now, some eleven years later, I find there is a singular atmosphere to that which I find in all of LeMoine FitzGerald's work, something that seems to me to be almost metaphysical, definitely northern, with a sentiment of melancholy that I can trace back to Caspar David Friedrich. More obscure, but sharing similar qualities, are the works of the Laethem-Saint-Martin group of painters in Belgium, especially Valerius de Saedeleer. These early twentieth-century artists combined late Symbolism with realism, projecting an almost mystical feeling in their depictions of landscape and small houses.

Le garage de M. Willamson also now reminds me of more contemporary works. The American artist Maureen Gallace comes to my mind, with her small paintings of isolated houses with no openings. I am reminded, too, of the American sculptor Robert Gober, with his distinctive interjection of the uncanny into the domestic. I, however, have been touched at first hand by FitzGerald's legacy, having gone on in the intervening years to make paintings inspired by architecture and the play of light, paintings imbued with a strange sense of absence and perhaps a similar metaphysical mood.

Today, the little building on rue de Bullion is gone, having made room for a condominium complex. I assume my painting is its only remaining witness. I am told that M. Williamson's garage also no longer stands. ■

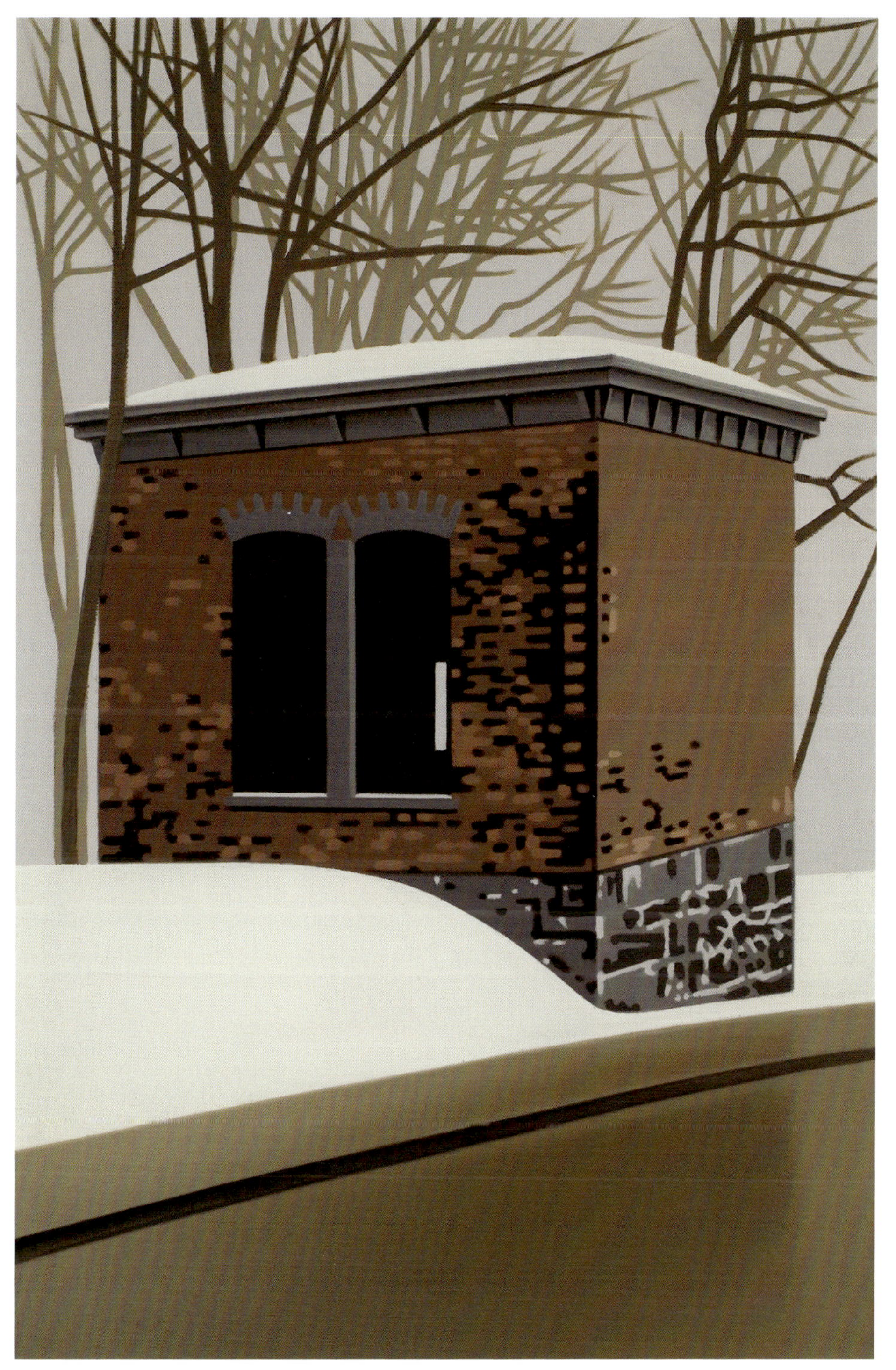

PIERRE DORION
(b. 1959)
Remise (Rue de Bullion), 2008
oil on linen
40.6 × 26.7 cm
Courtesy of the artist
Photo: Richard-Max Tremblay

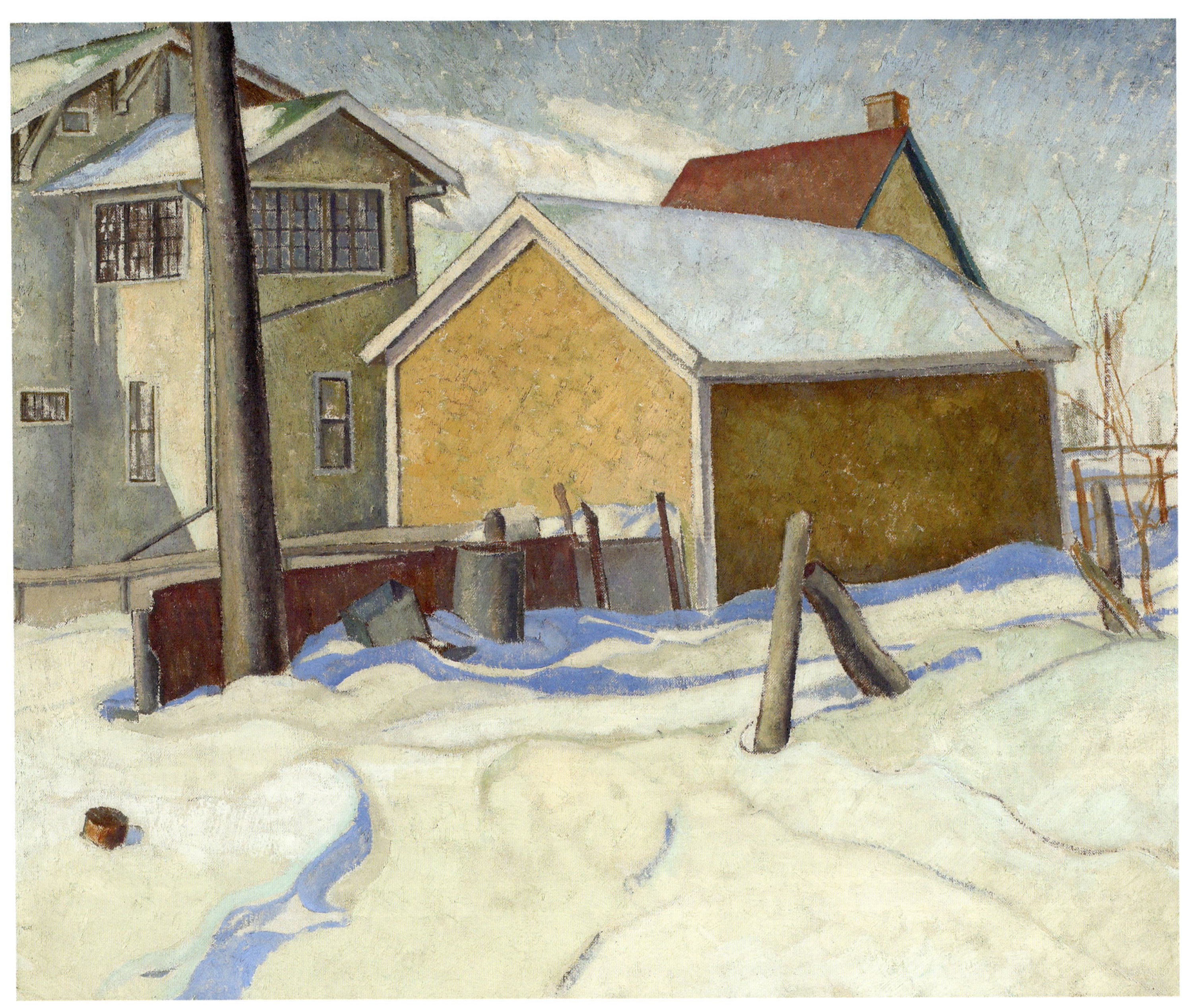

Garage and House,
1928
oil on canvas
46.1 × 56.7 cm

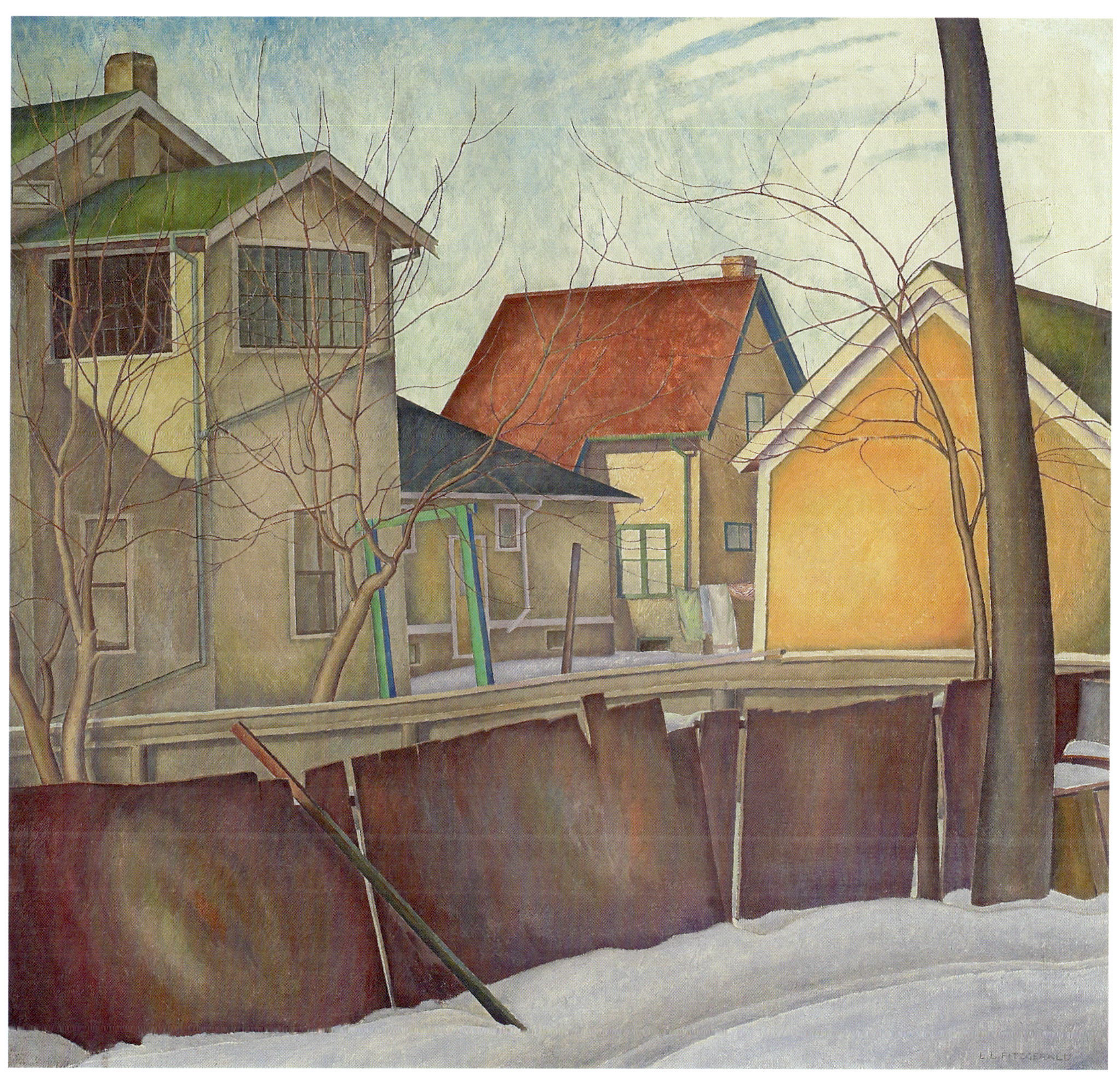

Pritchard's Fence,
c. 1928
oil on canvas
overall: 71.6 × 76.5 cm

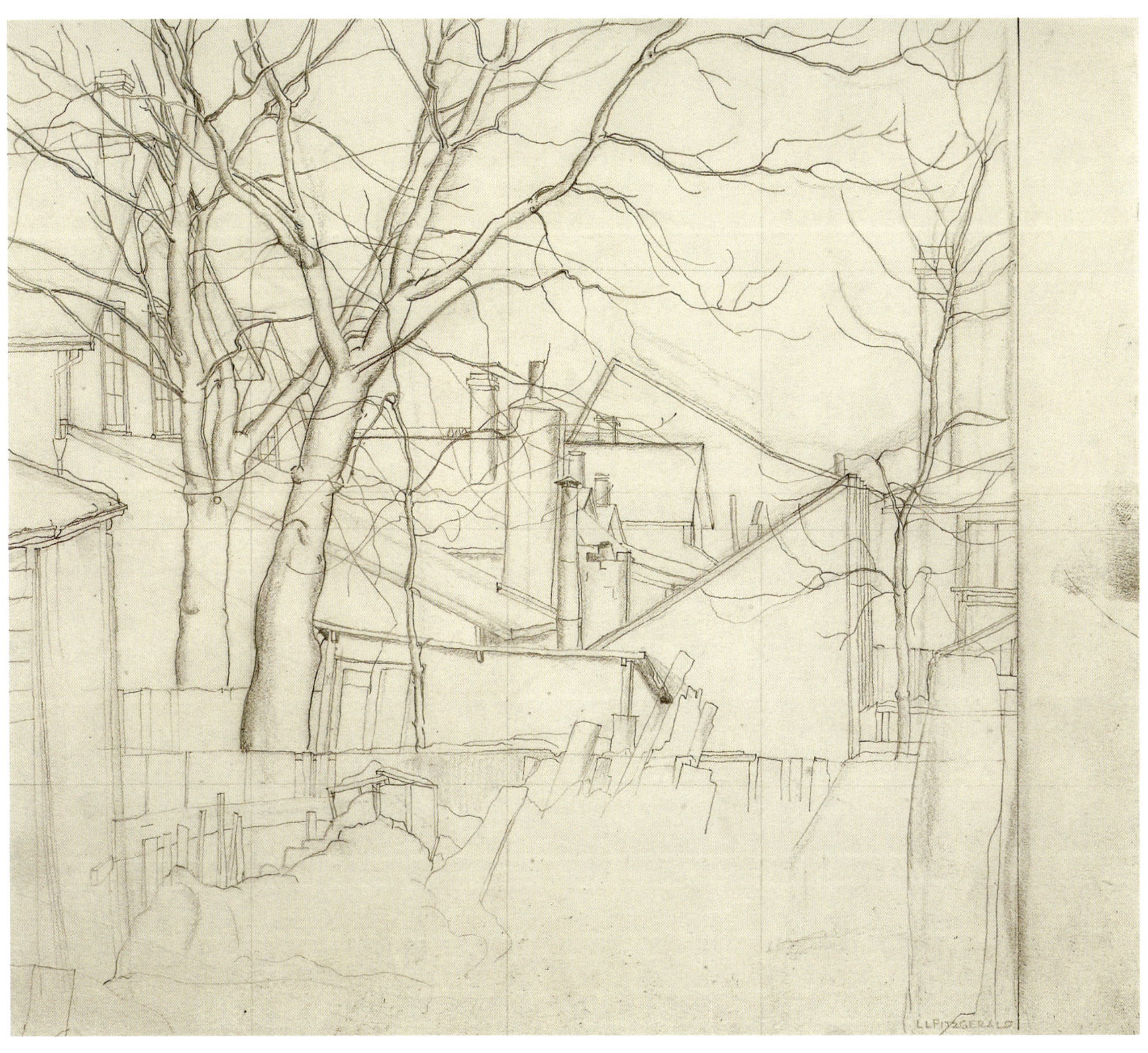

Transfer Drawing for "Backyards, Water Street," 1927
graphite on wove paper
22.4 × 25.8 cm

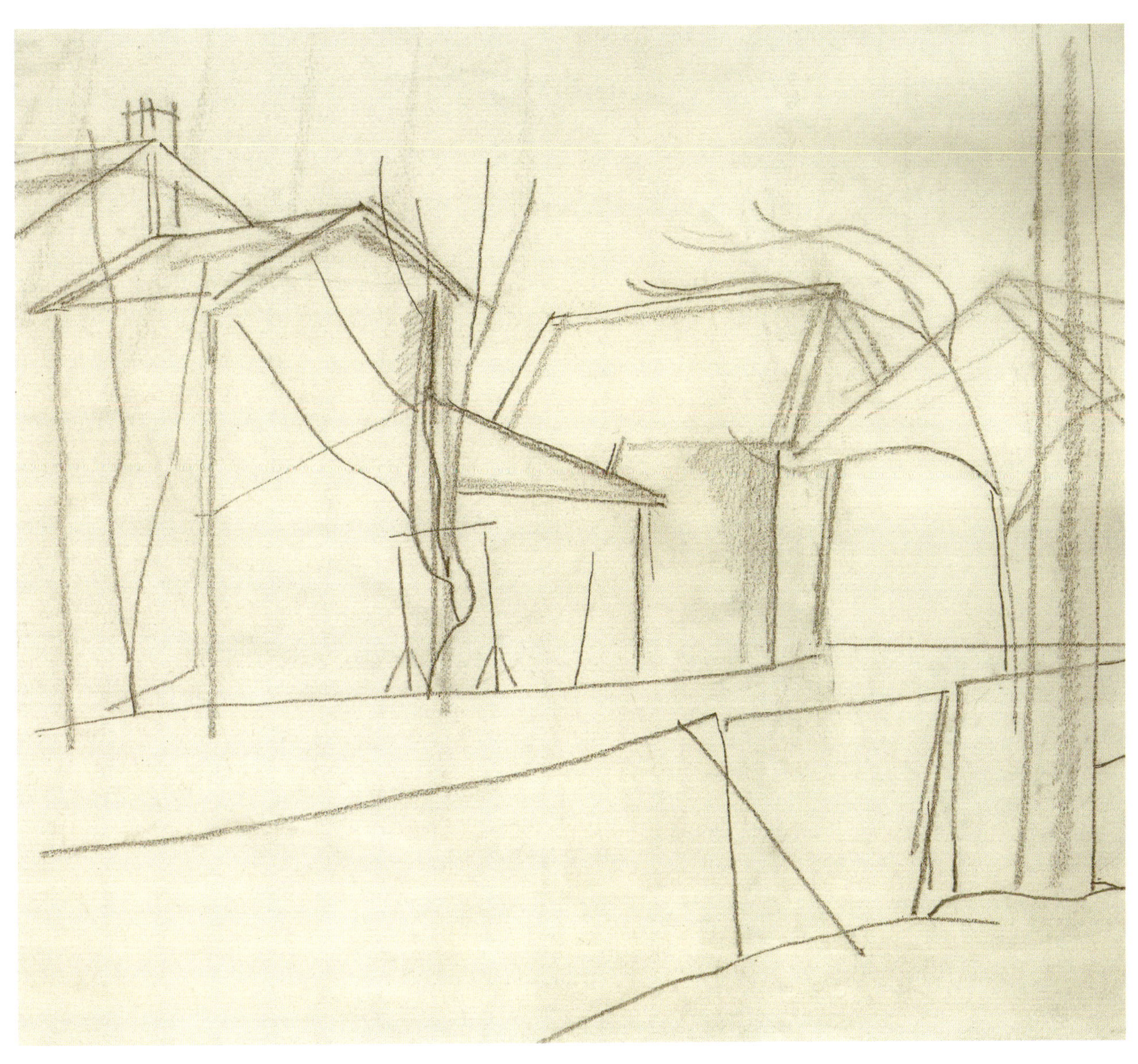

Study for "Pritchard's Fence," c. 1928
graphite on paper
24.2 × 26.9 cm

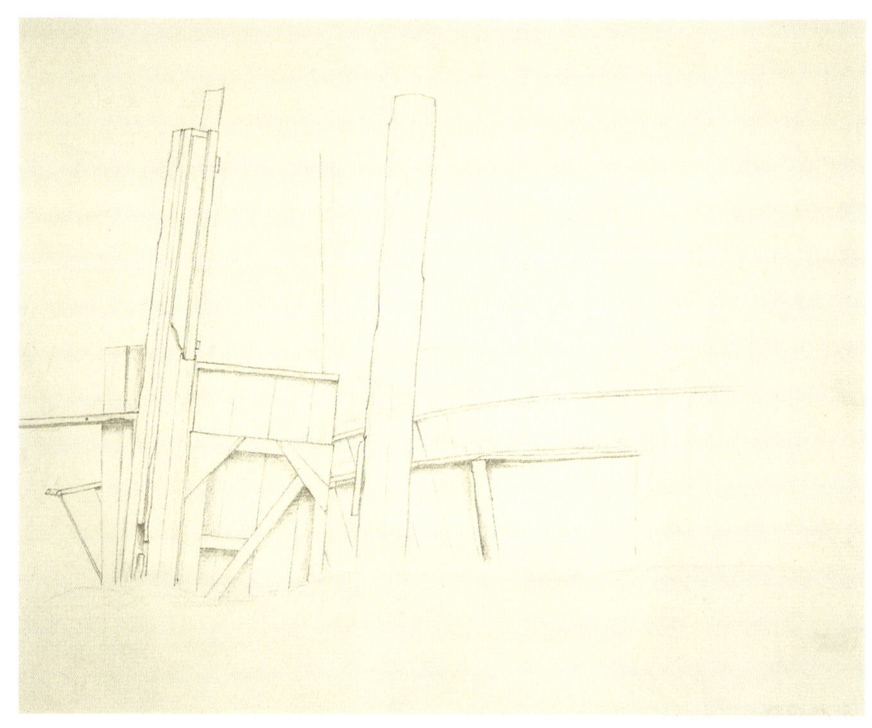

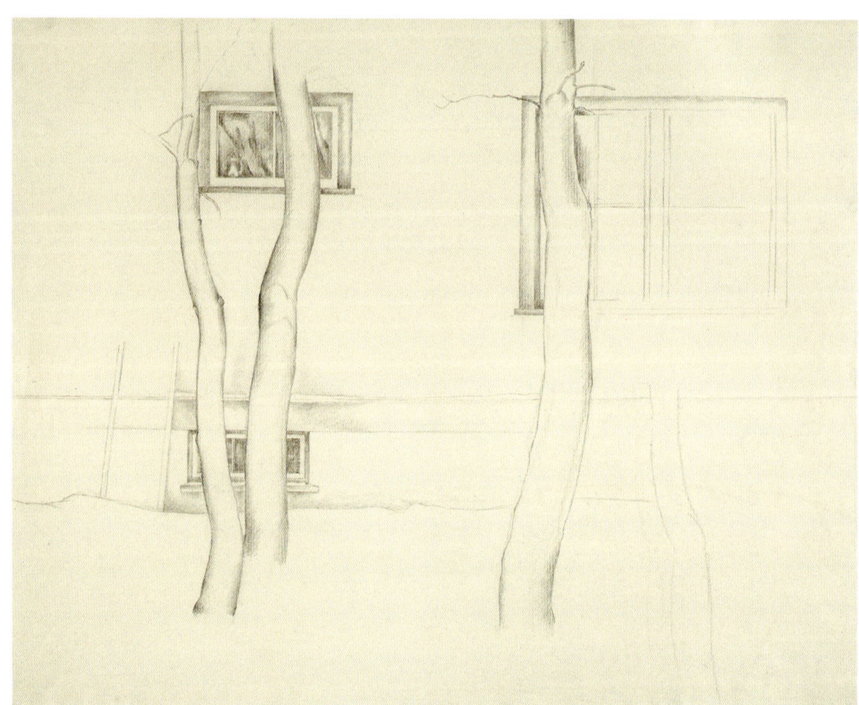

Construction, n.d.
graphite on paper
24 × 29 cm

Trees and House, c. 1937
graphite on laid paper
31.8 × 40.9 cm

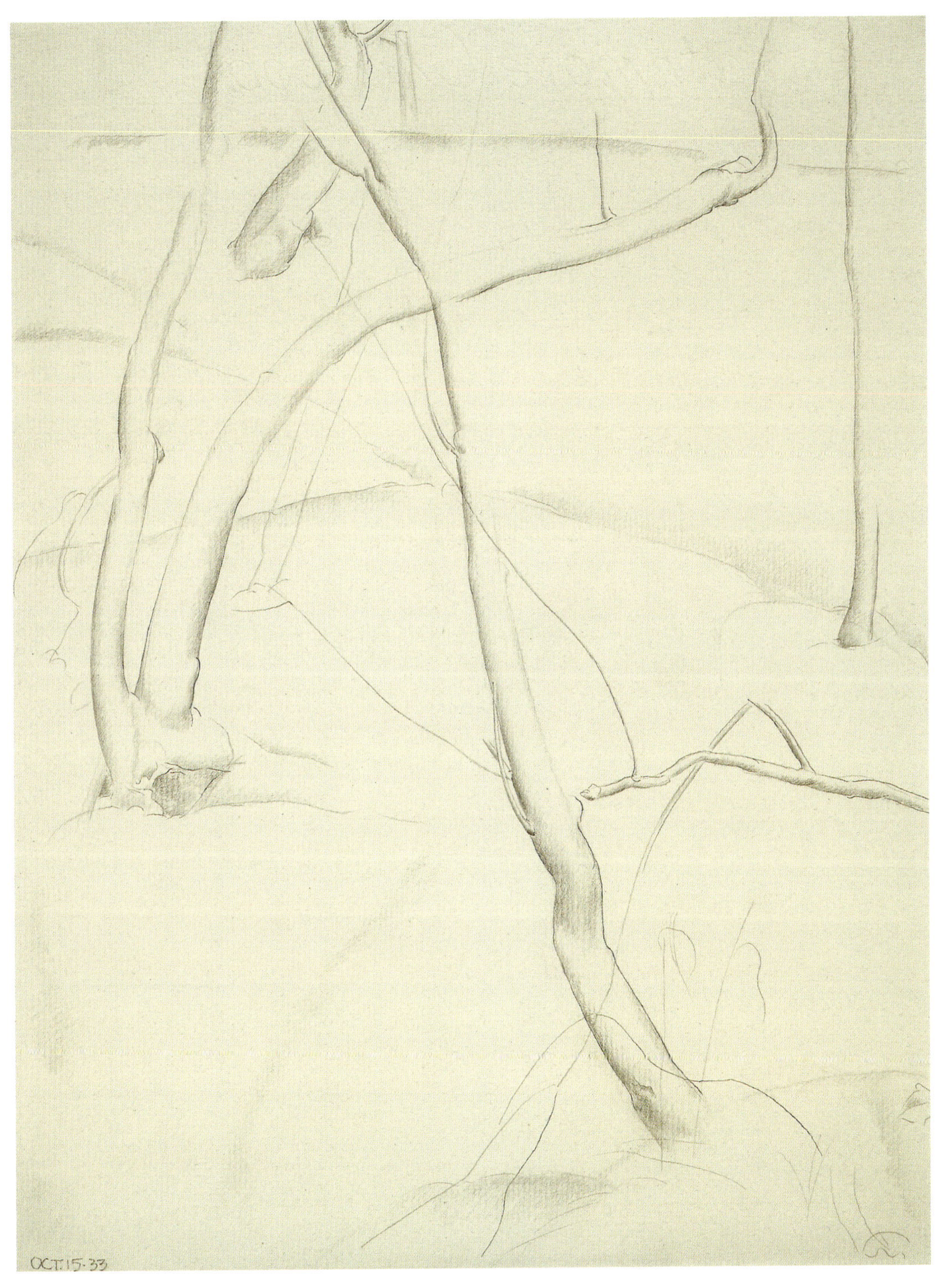

Trees in the Snow,
1933
graphite on laid paper
31.5 × 24.5 cm

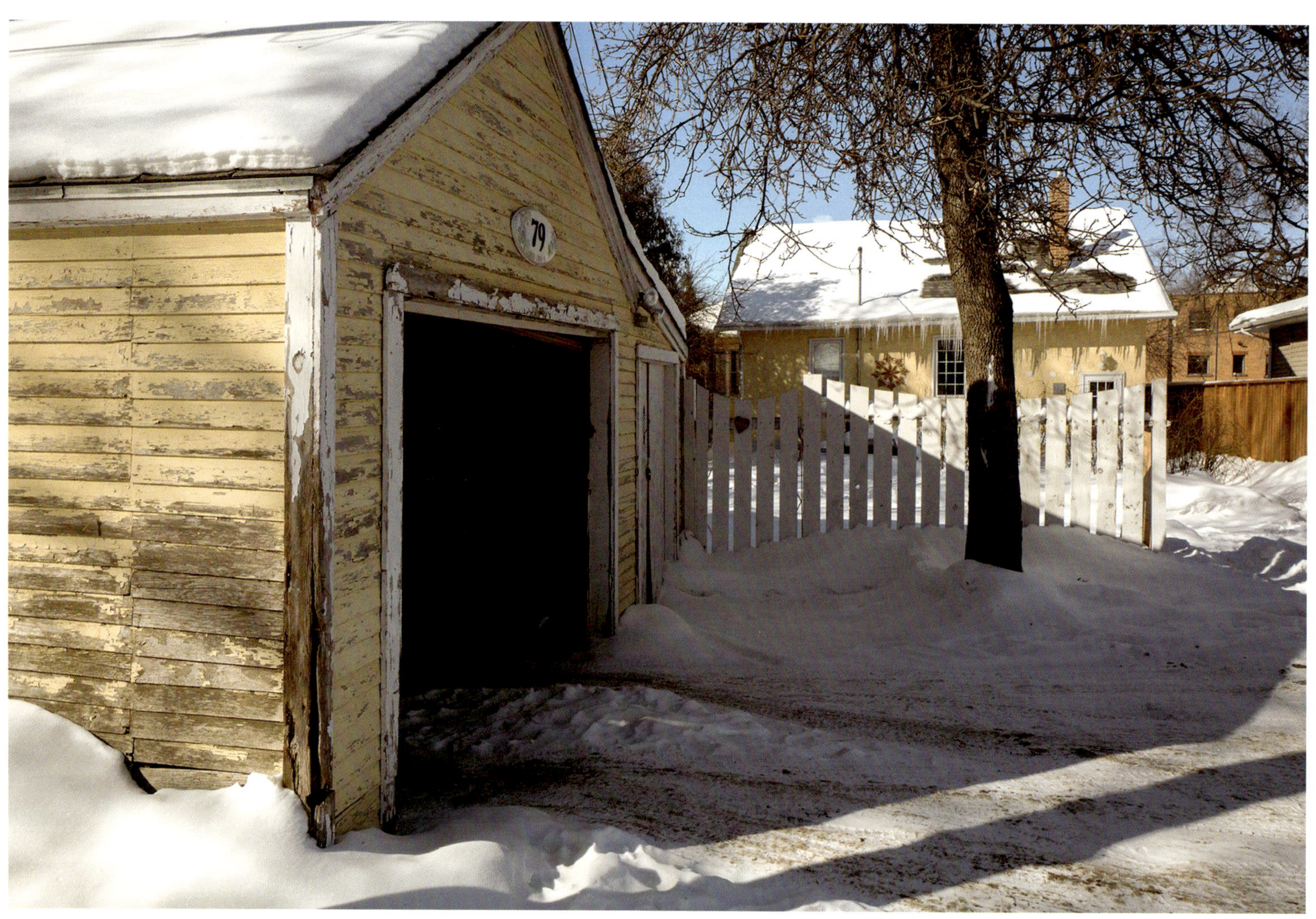

GEOFFREY JAMES
(b. 1942)
FitzGerald's Neighbourhood, 2019
Courtesy of the artist and Stephen Bulger Gallery, Toronto

IN FITZGERALD'S NEIGHBOURHOOD

GEOFFREY JAMES

I have always thought of Lionel LeMoine FitzGerald as belonging to that slightly nebulous category, the painter's painter. While there are clearly no rules about this, painters' painters can often be artists who abjure fashion, do not belong to schools, show a deep devotion to single subjects, and tend to be a little out of the mainstream, even provincial. (I have yet to meet a painter who does not admire the work of Giorgio Morandi.)

FitzGerald, of course, was out of the mainstream simply by virtue of living in Winnipeg, a city that, according to local lore, lost its commercial edge with the opening of the Panama Canal and never quite recovered. He was a somewhat solitary and intensely *local* artist—the source of many of his most important paintings was his own backyard, or those of his neighbours. His paintings are typically unpeopled—they are not uxorious in the manner of Pierre Bonnard or Edward Hopper, two other prime candidates for the painter's painter list. The idea of looking closely at his artistic territory was something that interested me greatly.

FitzGerald's neighbourhood is a twenty-minute bus ride from downtown Winnipeg along Portage, a classically nondescript street whose chief visual interest is in the tidal marks of the city's successive immigrant waves. In the neighbourhood abutting the small enclave where FitzGerald lived, Portage has a pierogi shop, a tapas bar, and Odin's Eye Tattoo parlour.

But Deer Lodge Place, the new name for what in FitzGerald's time was Lyle Street, is another world, largely unchanged. Perhaps the modest lot sizes, or proximity to the Assiniboine, or some more general lack of economic booms, has left the little neighbourhood intact—it covers no more than two blocks. It is easy to imagine FitzGerald working here. Except that, even with a map painstakingly marked up by the art historian Michael Parke-Taylor, I find it impossible to locate the actual subject of any of his paintings. The artist's house is there—the most handsome on the street—marked by a blue plaque placed not by a historical society or landmarks commission but by a real estate association. Doc Snyder's

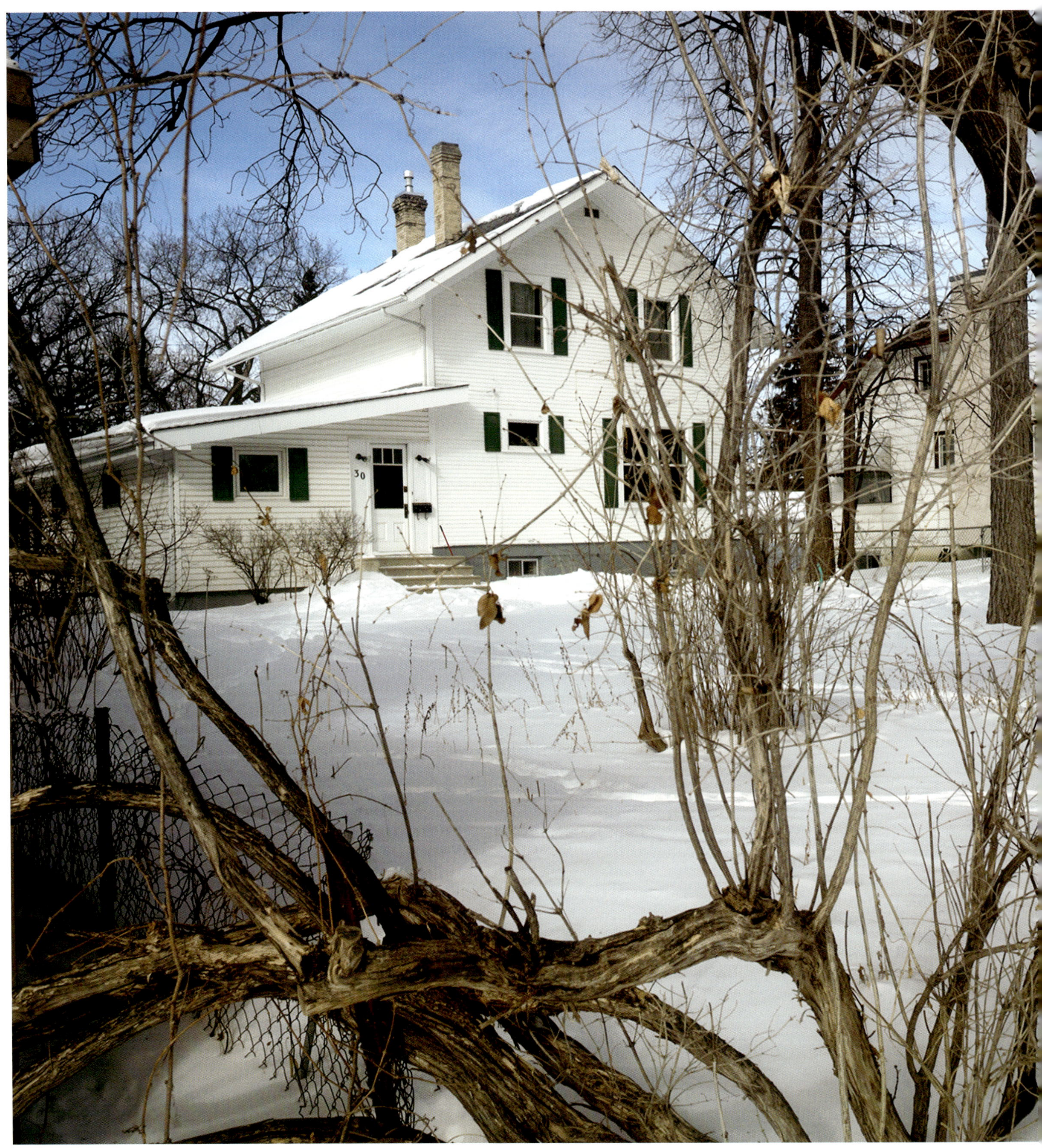
30

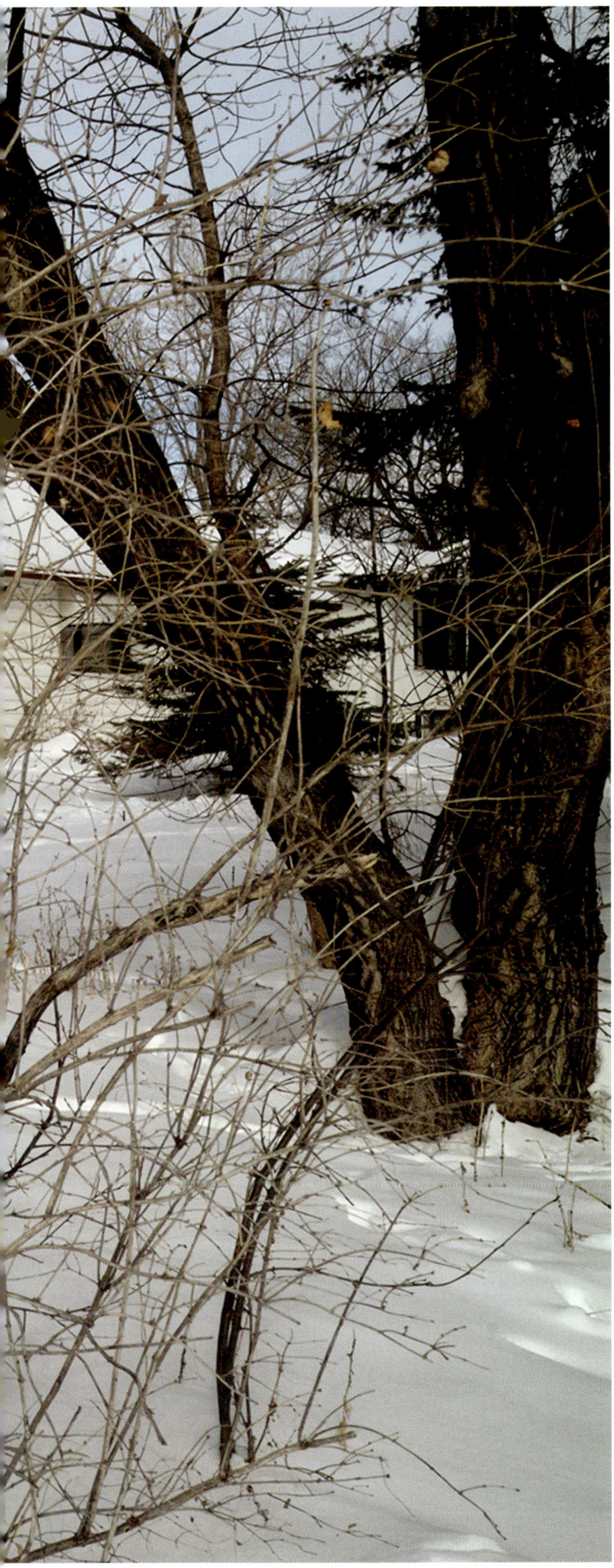

GEOFFREY JAMES
(b. 1942)
Lionel LeMoine FitzGerald's House, 2019
Courtesy of the artist and Stephen Bulger Gallery, Toronto

house is right next door. The alley behind bears the sign FitzGerald's Walk. But nowhere can I establish where the artist set up his easel to paint *Doc Snyder's House*, 1931 (p. 146), *Williamson's Garage*, 1927 (p. 132), or *Pritchard's Fence*, c. 1928 (p. 137).

I had, of course, never intended to try to remake a painting; you can't even remake a photograph. Everything has changed in subtle ways. Some houses have sprouted solariums or larger garages, and trees have grown and died. It was also apparent to me that FitzGerald's painting has less to do with any kind of topographical exactitude than with a moment of perception, a deep response to certain conditions of light. His light is winter light, usually early in the day; he clearly had no time for the impenetrable shadows of summer, when the trees become dense like broccoli. A preliminary drawing would show his feeling for the rhythm of the trees in front of him, and he would put their trunks close to the edge of the picture, giving the painting a special energy.

FitzGerald's aim, as he put it, was to render palpable his response to a luminous moment. The paradox, and what differentiates him from any photographer who responds to a particular moment or perception, is the slow, assiduous building up of paint, section by section, with great intensity of purpose. *Pritchard's Fence* took perhaps as long as a year to complete.

I spent two days in the neighbourhood, in clear February light, with fresh snow. There were photographs to be made, but it was hard to withstand the gentle tug of FitzGerald's vision. Wandering in this modest enclave, with its unspectacular architecture, its solid domesticity, I could only marvel at FitzGerald's clarity of purpose, his dogged ability to make something lasting and memorable out of what for almost everyone else would be the humdrum environment of the everyday. ■

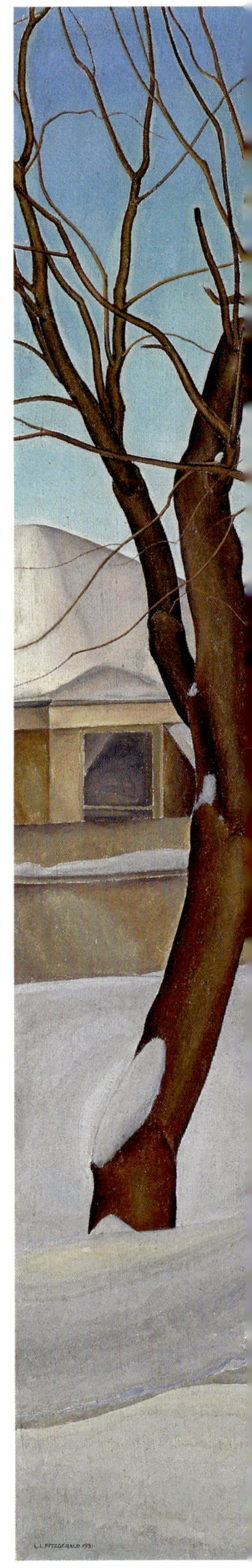

Doc Snyder's House, 1931
oil on canvas
74.9 × 85.1 cm

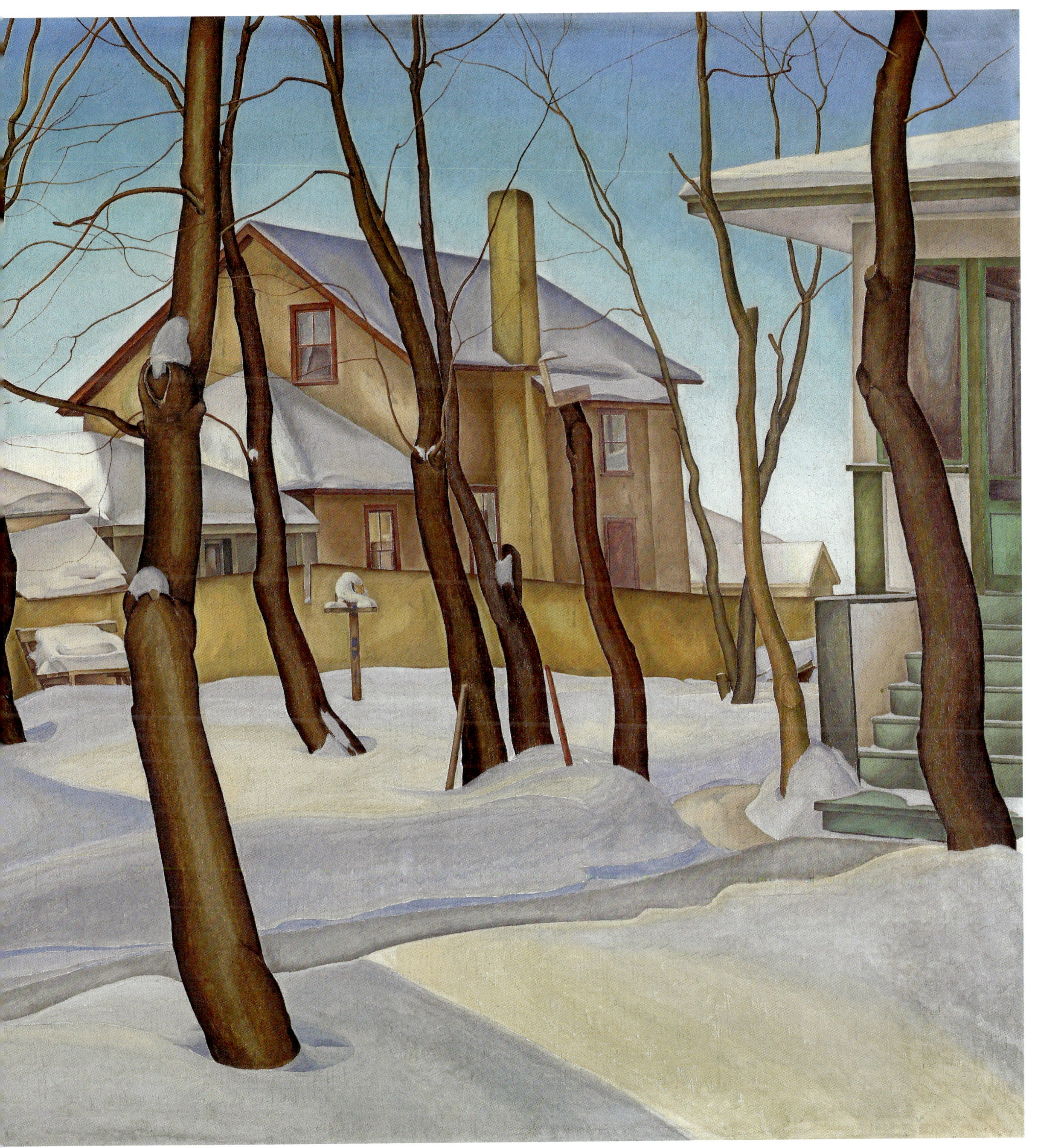

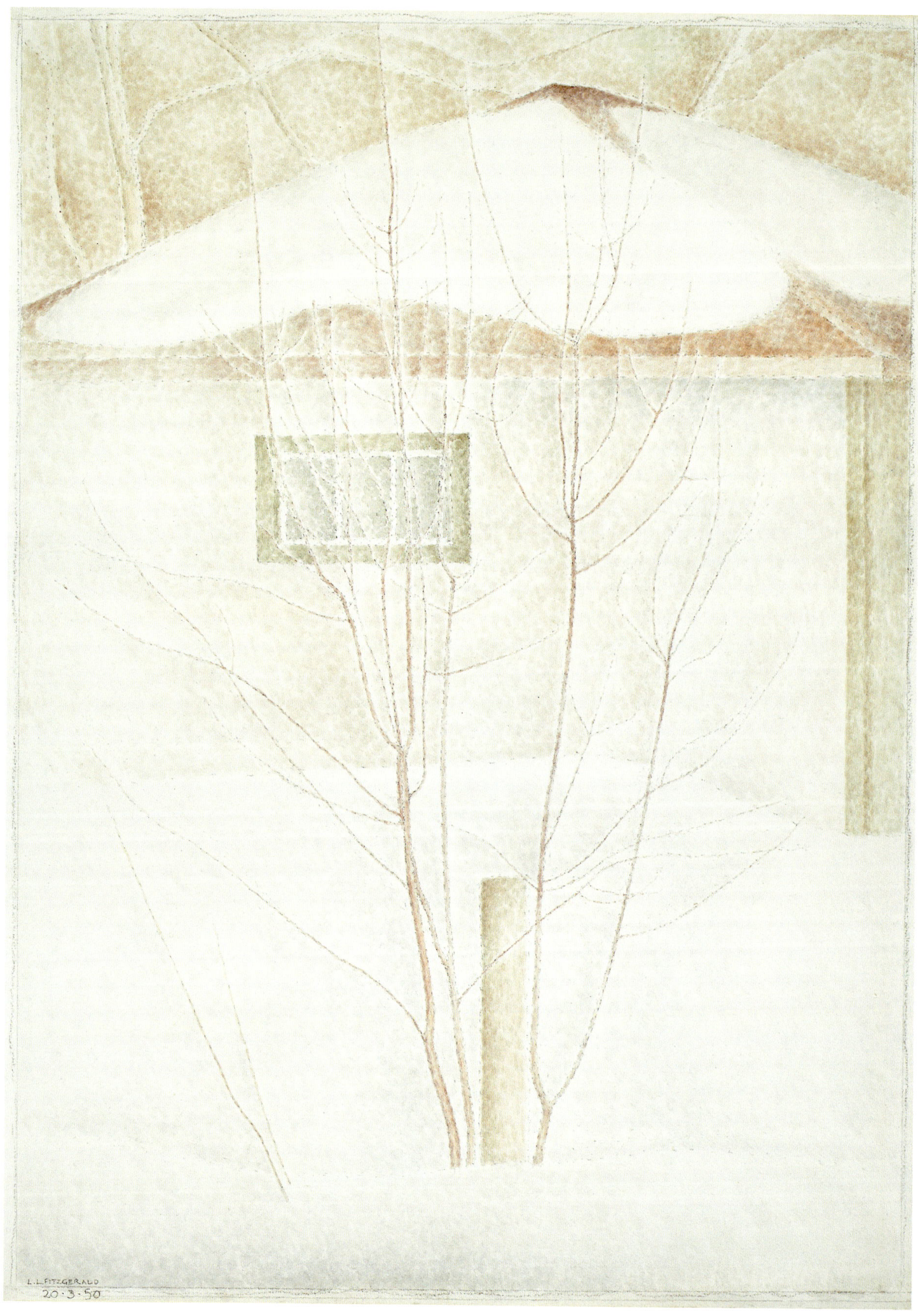
L.L.FITZGERALD
20·3·50

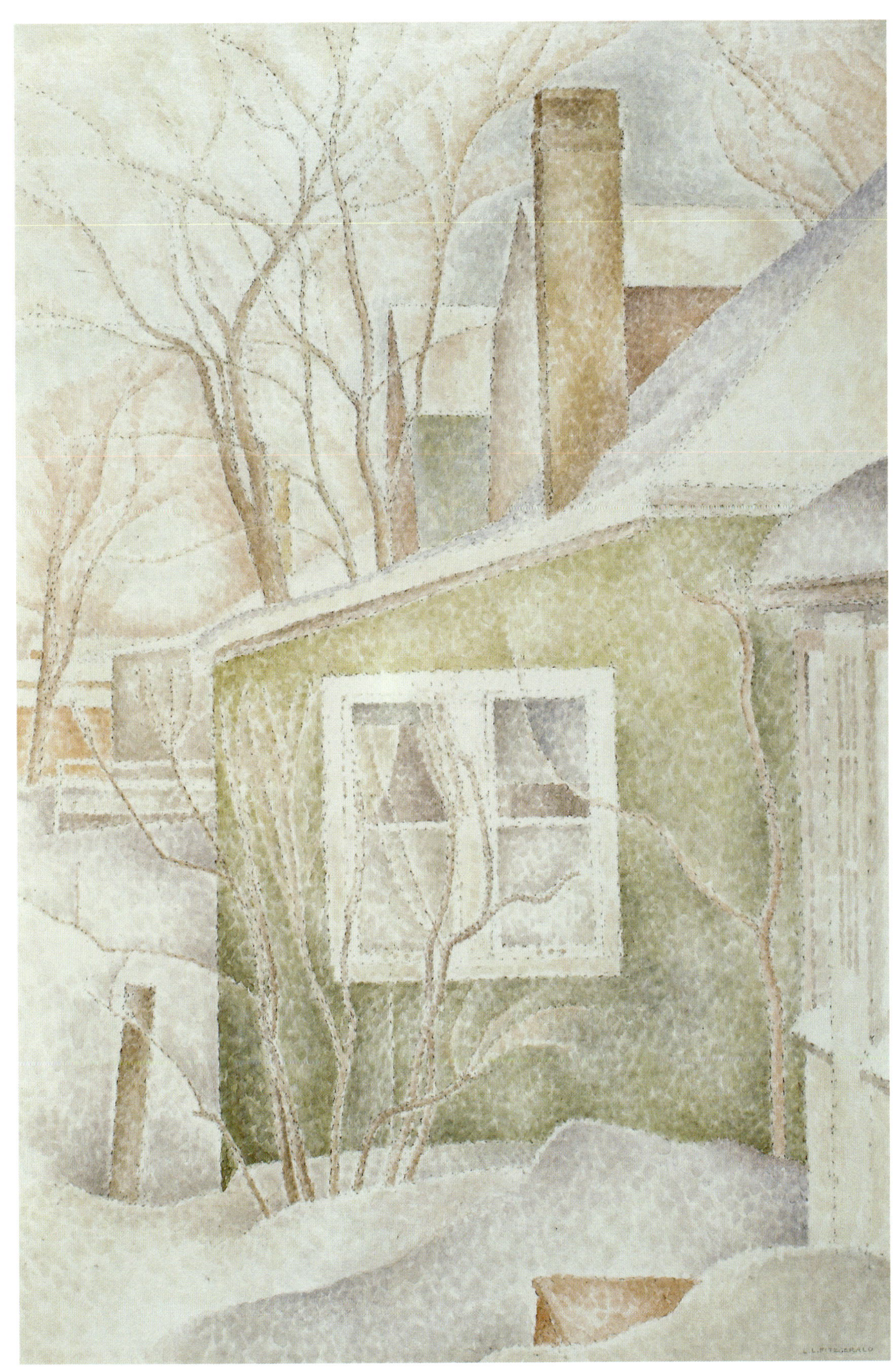

Campbell's House,
January 20, 1950
watercolour over
graphite on wove paper
56.3 × 38.8 cm

OPPOSITE
Barlow's Garage,
1950
watercolour with
charcoal and graphite
on paper
65.3 × 47.5 cm

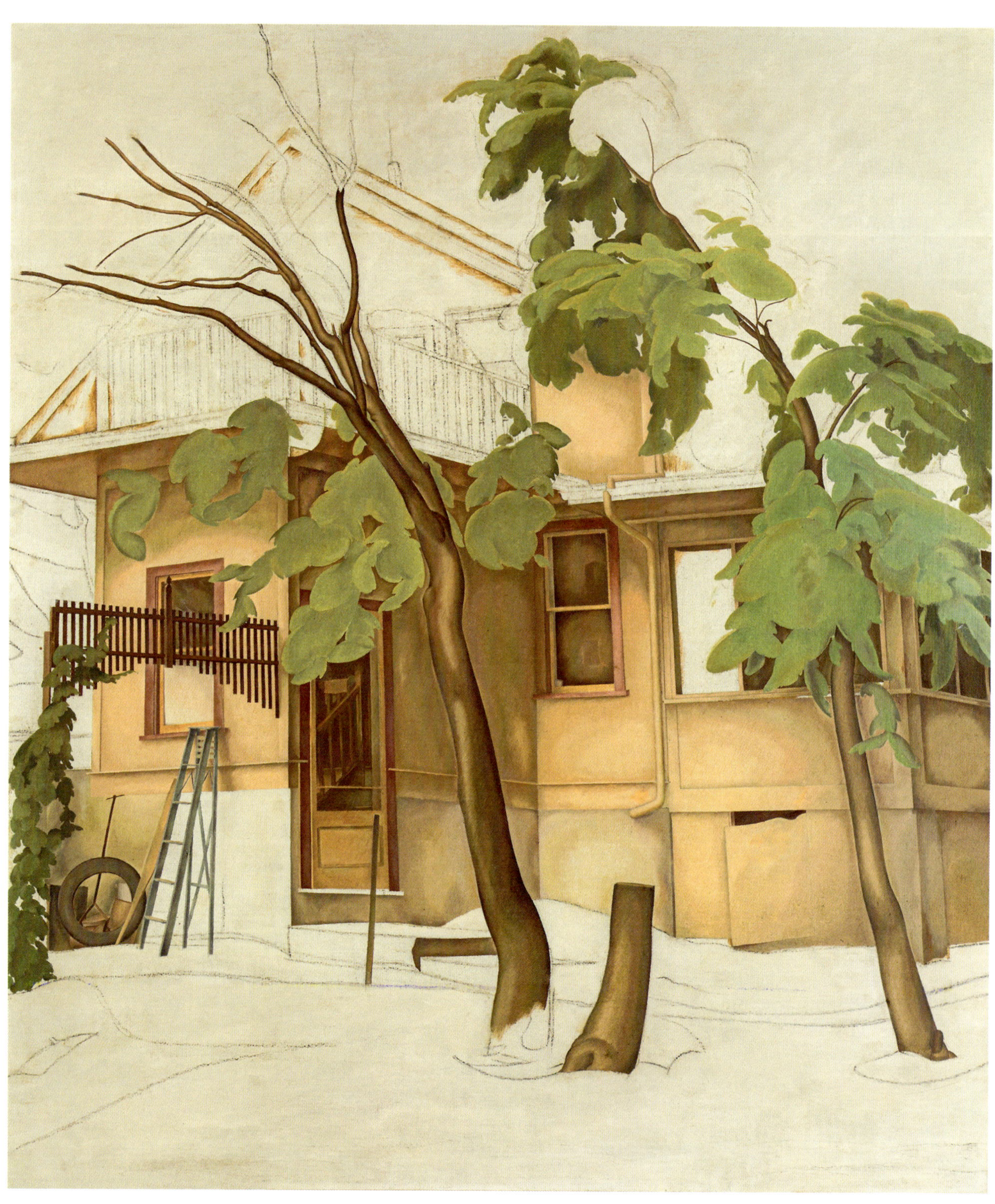

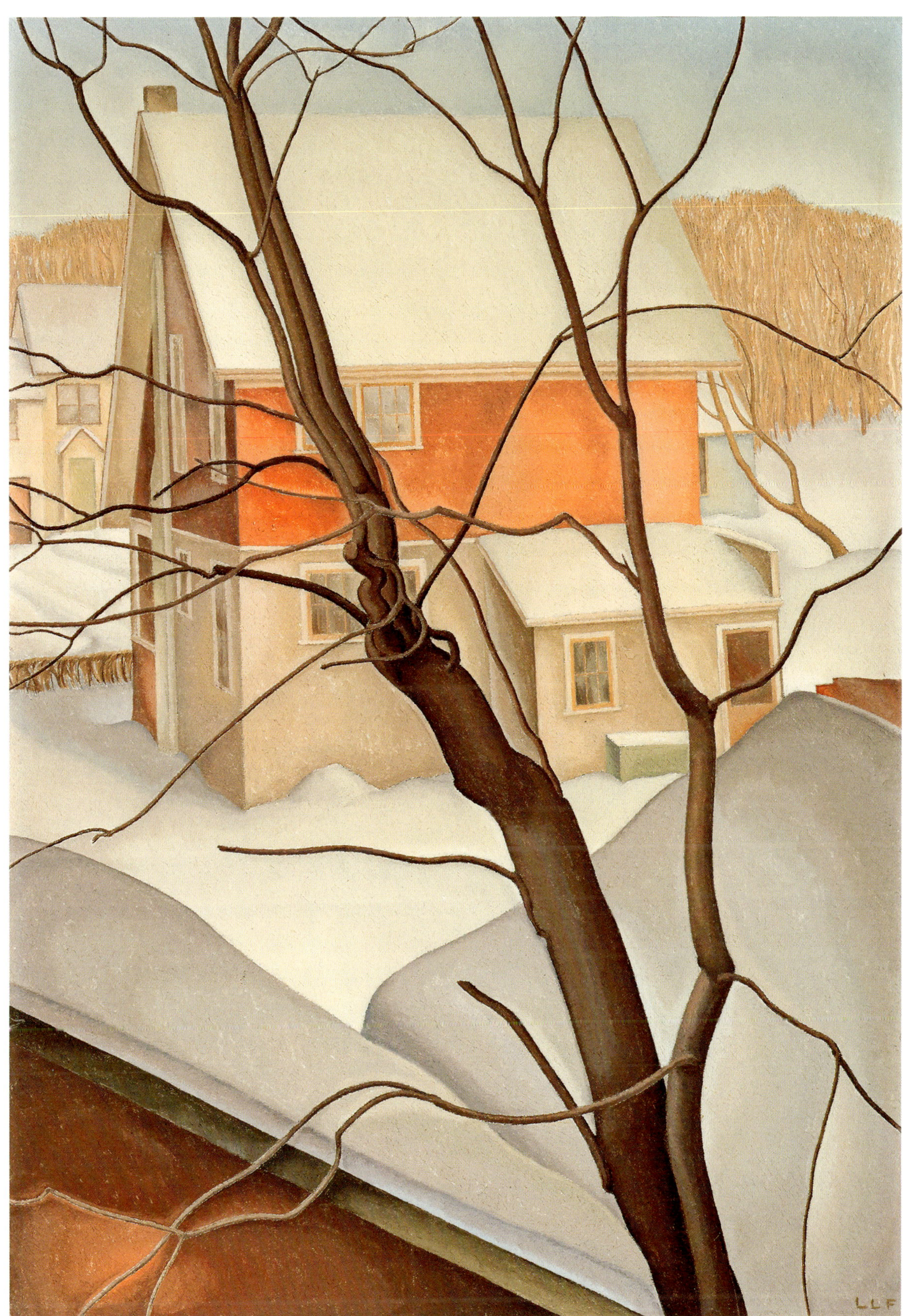

Oakdale Place,
c. 1950
oil on Masonite
59.7 × 42.4 cm

OPPOSITE
Backyard View of FitzGerald's House, 160 Lyle Street, c. 1930
oil on canvas
106.7 × 94 cm

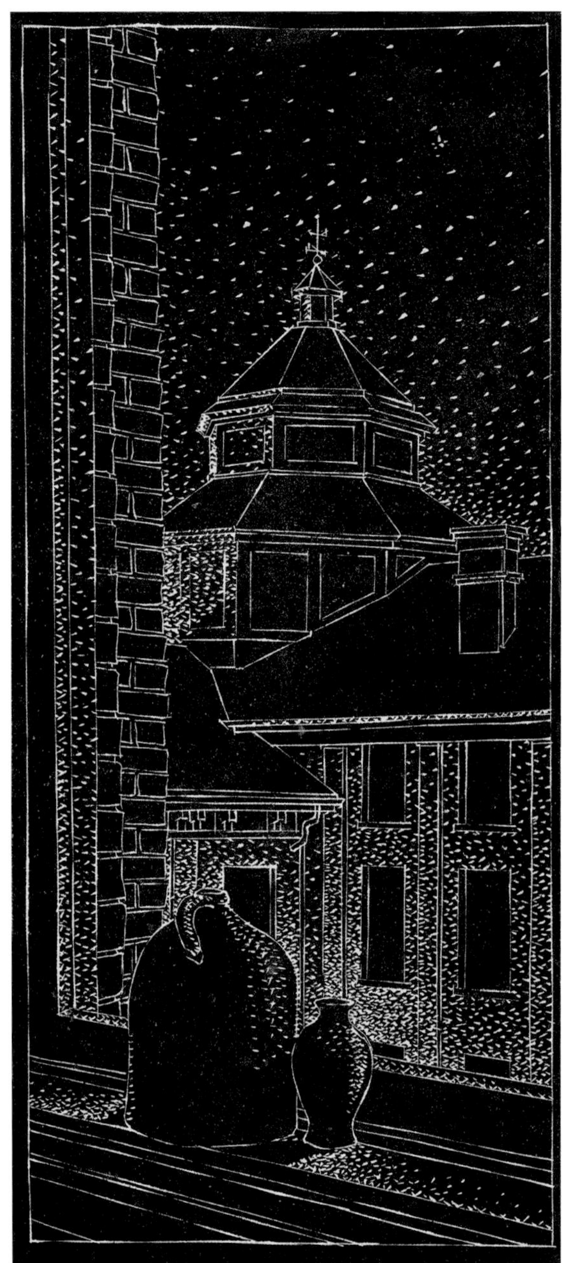

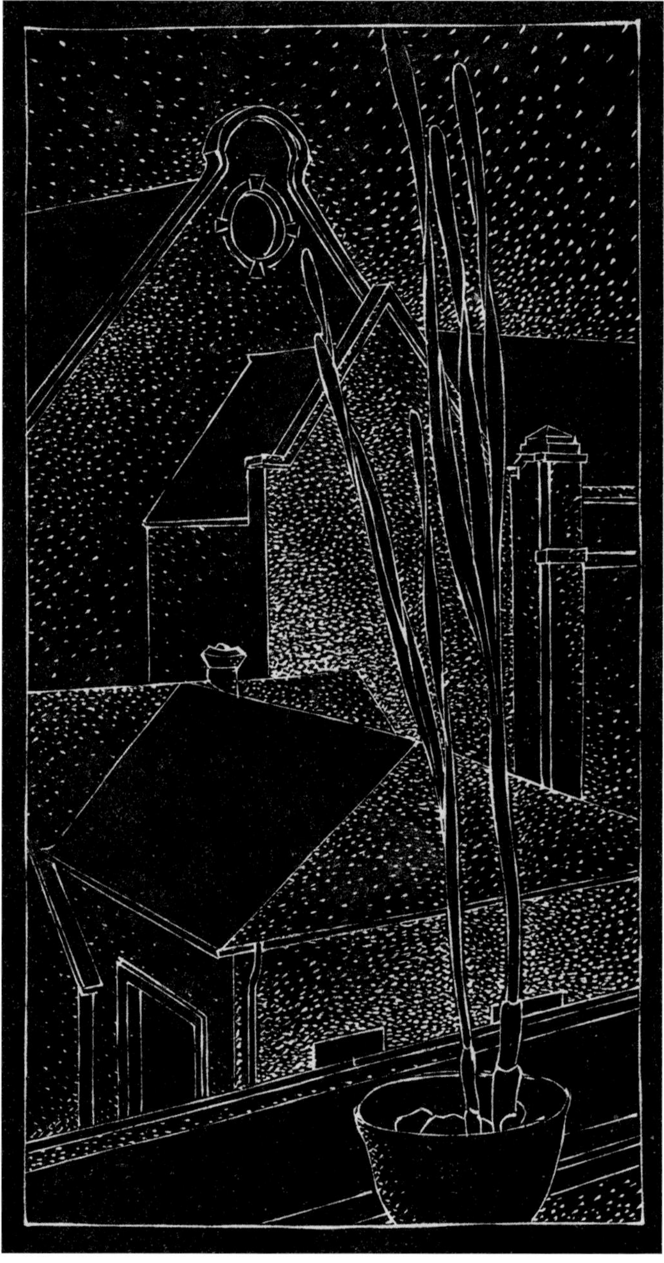

View from Window with Two Jugs, 1942
linocut on paper
26.2 × 10.8 cm;
image: 19.2 × 8.7 cm

View from Window with Potted Plant, c. 1938–39
linocut on paper
28.2 × 10.6 cm;
image: 16.7 × 9 cm

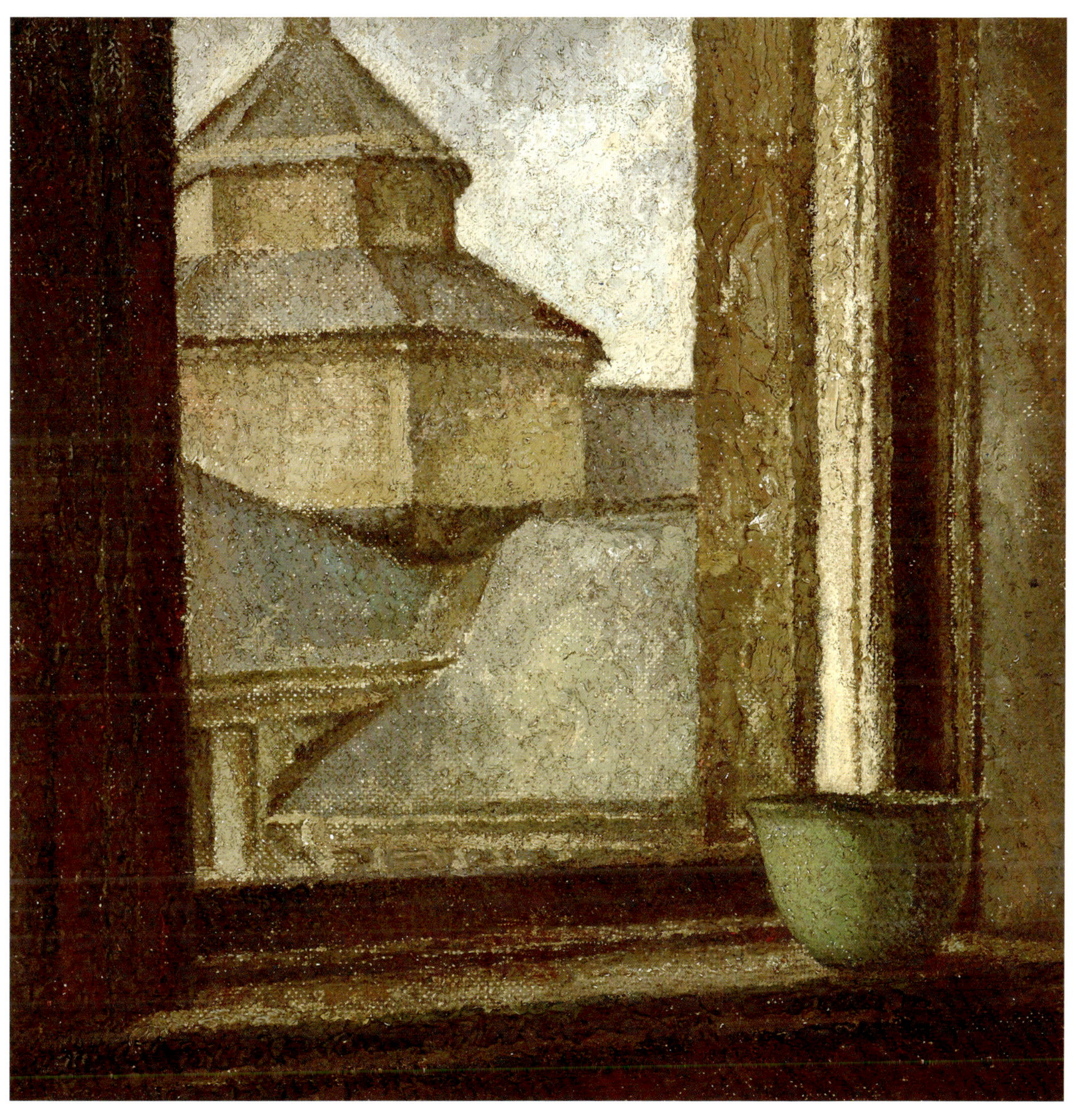

The Cupola, 1940
oil on canvas
26.7 × 26.7 cm

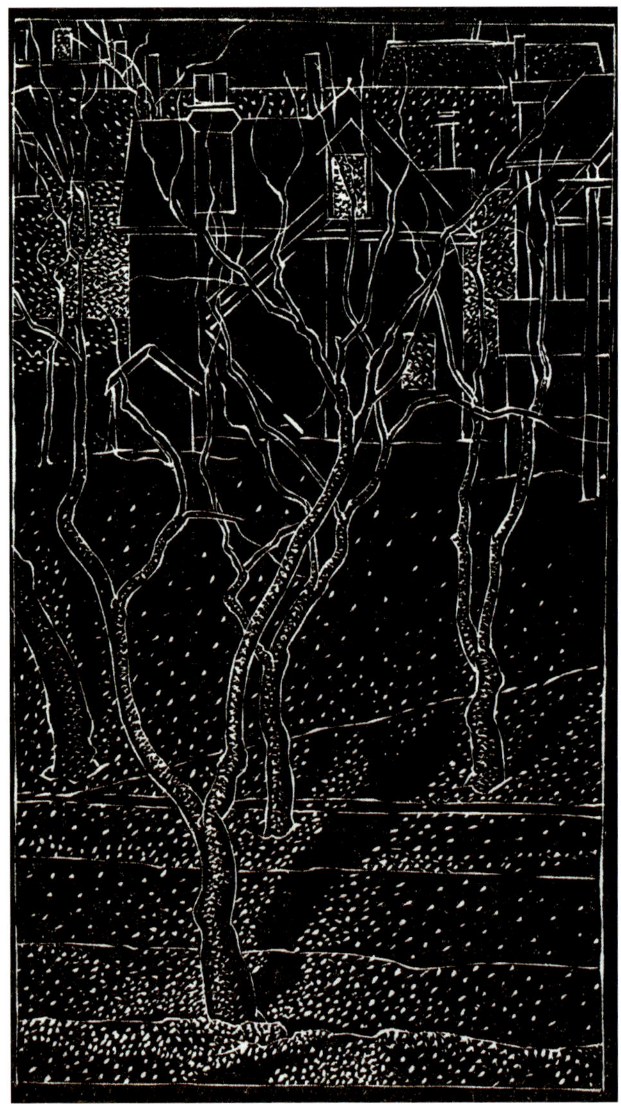

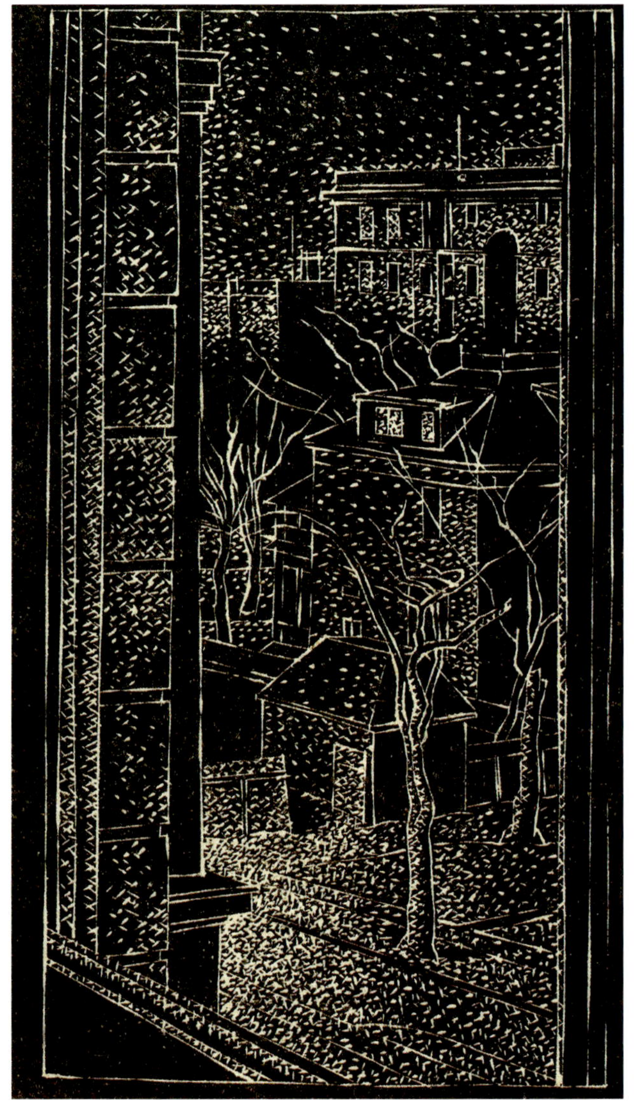

Trees and Houses, c. 1945
linocut on paper
14.5 × 18.2 cm;
image: 13.1 × 7.6 cm

View of City through a Window, 1946
linocut on paper
15.4 × 14.5 cm;
image: 13.2 × 7.5 cm

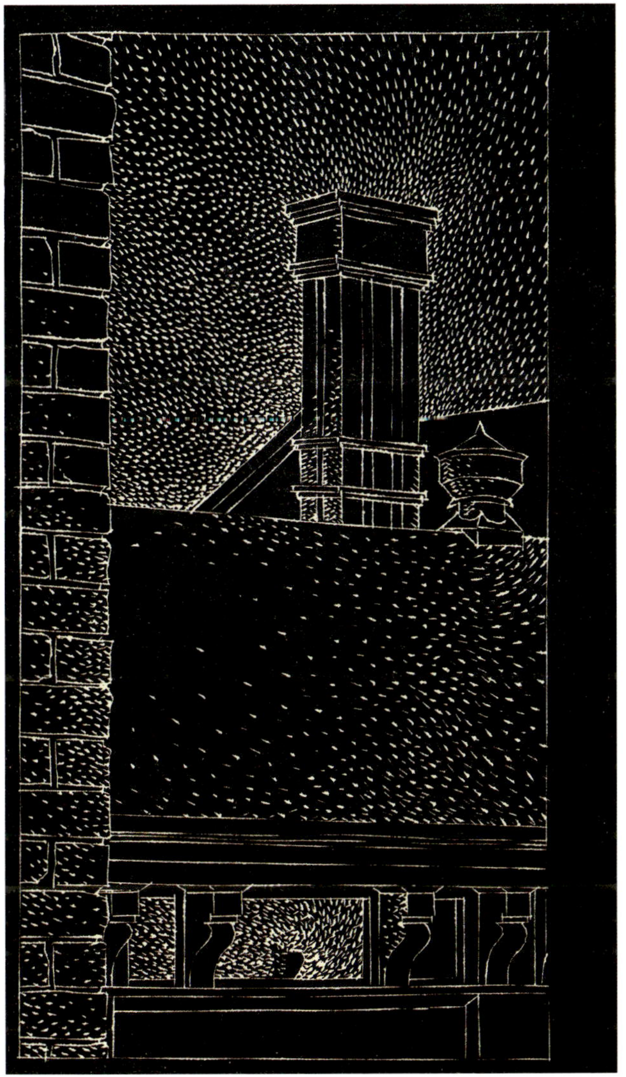

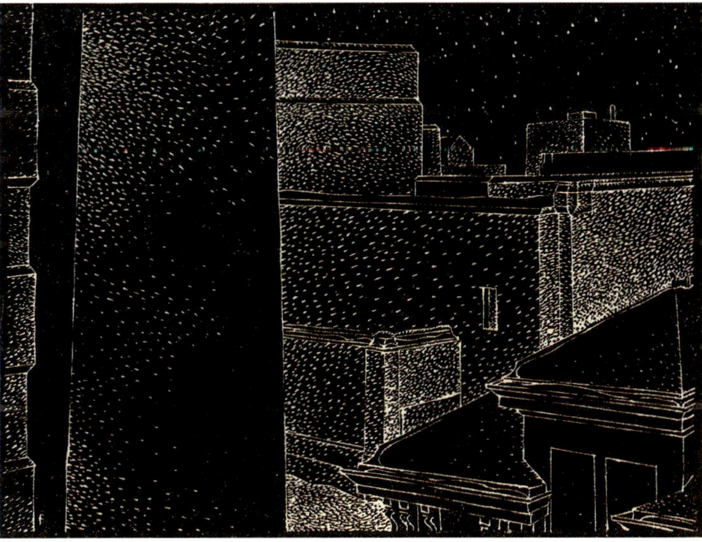

Arts Buildings, University of Manitoba, 1941
linocut on paper
28.9 × 14.4 cm;
image: 17.8 × 10.3 cm

Rooftops, Civic Auditorium, c. 1938–39
linocut on paper
13.3 × 26.1 cm;
image: 10.5 × 14.2 cm

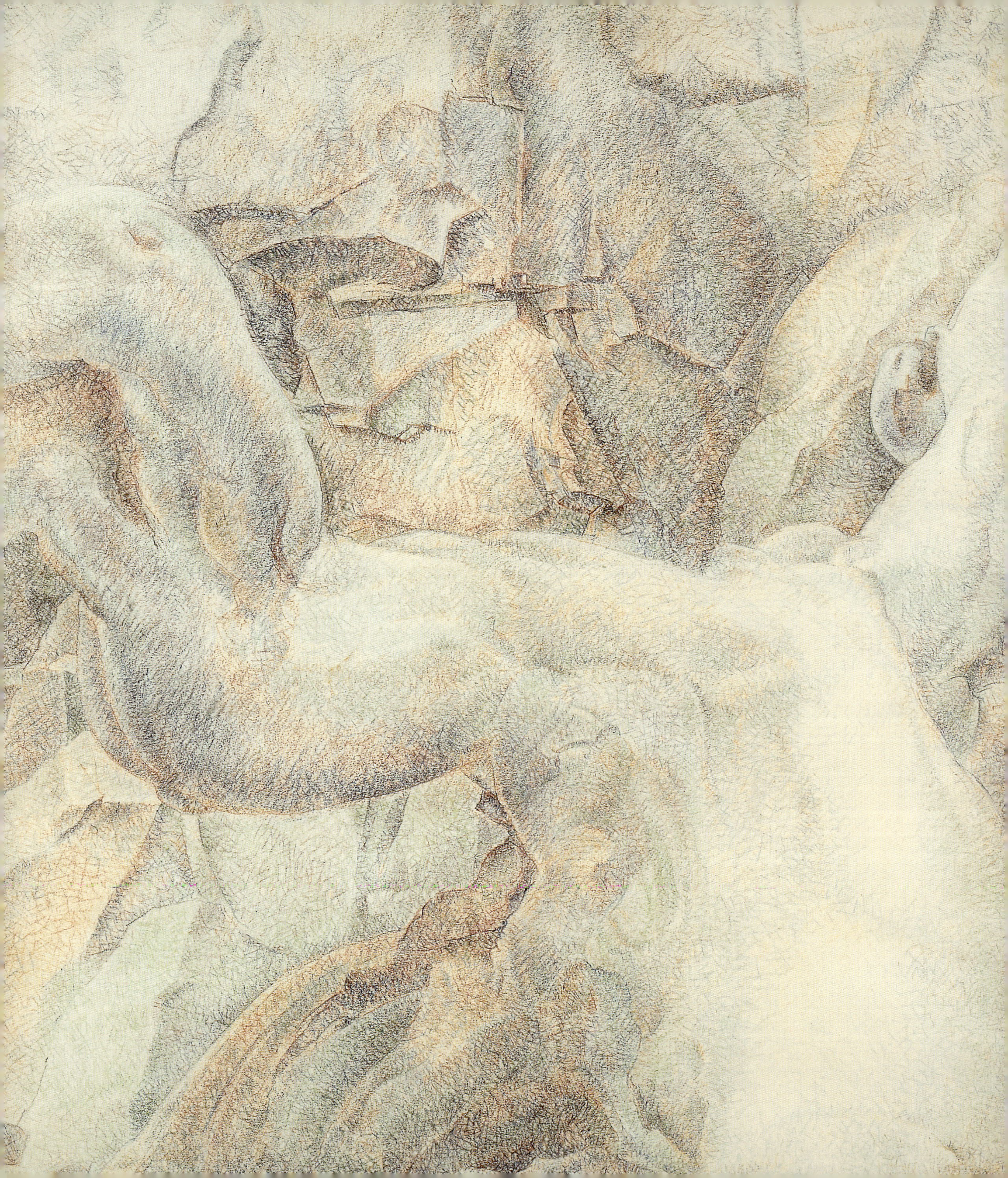

THE VOYAGE WEST

Like his fellow Group of Seven members Frederick Varley and Lawren Harris, FitzGerald was liberated both personally and artistically by his rapturous experience of the British Columbia landscape. FitzGerald spent the summers of 1942 through 1944 on Bowen Island; 1947 in Saseenos, on the southern tip of Vancouver Island; and the fall and winter of 1949 in Vancouver, revelling in his experience of the ocean and mountains. Here, FitzGerald investigated the microcosm and the macrocosm of the natural world in drawings and watercolours that conflate mountains with rocks, driftwood with bodies, and ocean tides with swelling clouds. Placing himself at the centre of this swirling mystical world, FitzGerald enjoyed a period of freedom from both domestic routine and the discipline of work at the Winnipeg School of Art. In 1949, following several leaves of absence, FitzGerald resigned from his teaching position to submerge himself at last in making art full time.

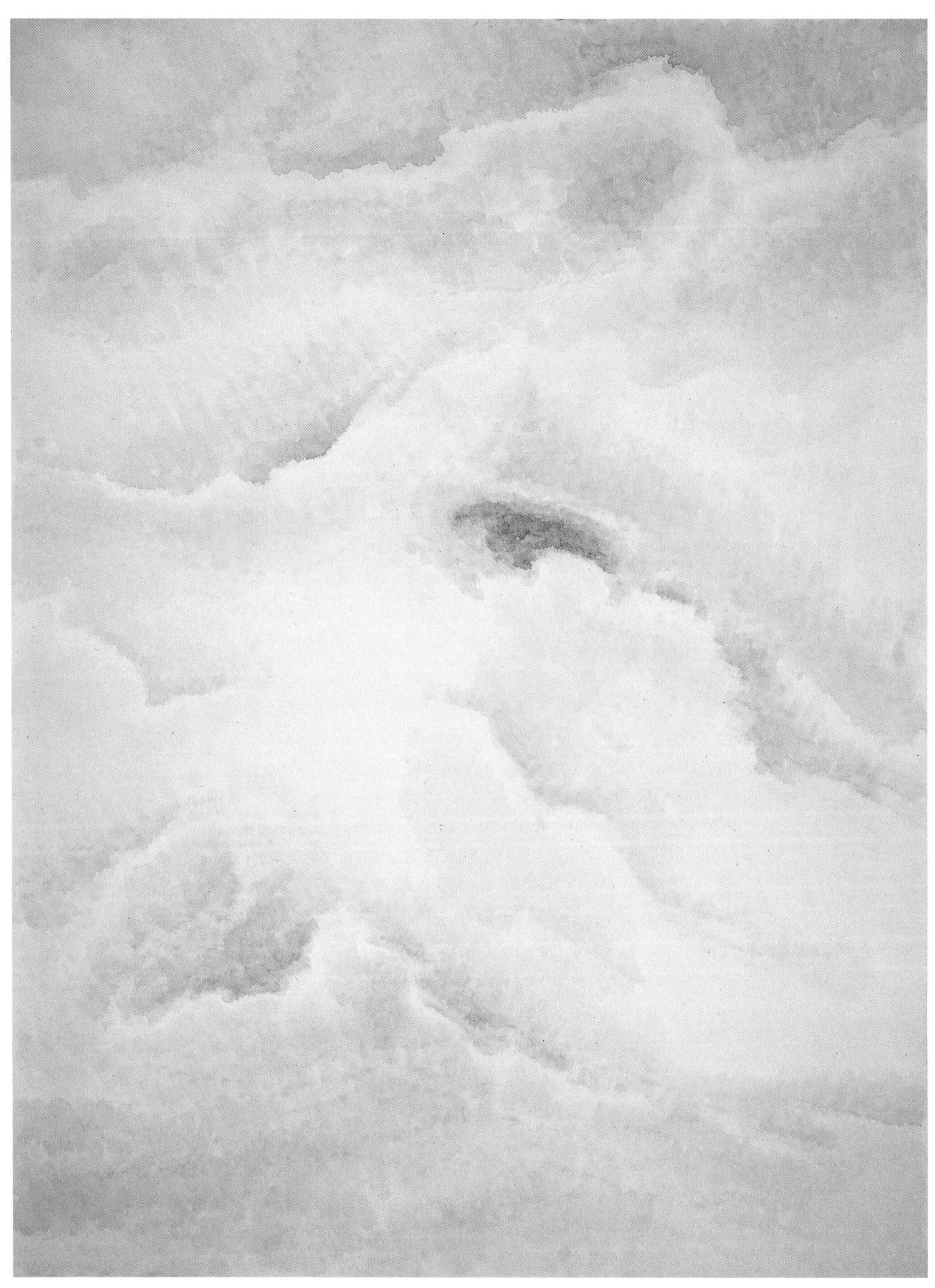

Clouds, 1943
watercolour on paper
61.1 × 45.8 cm

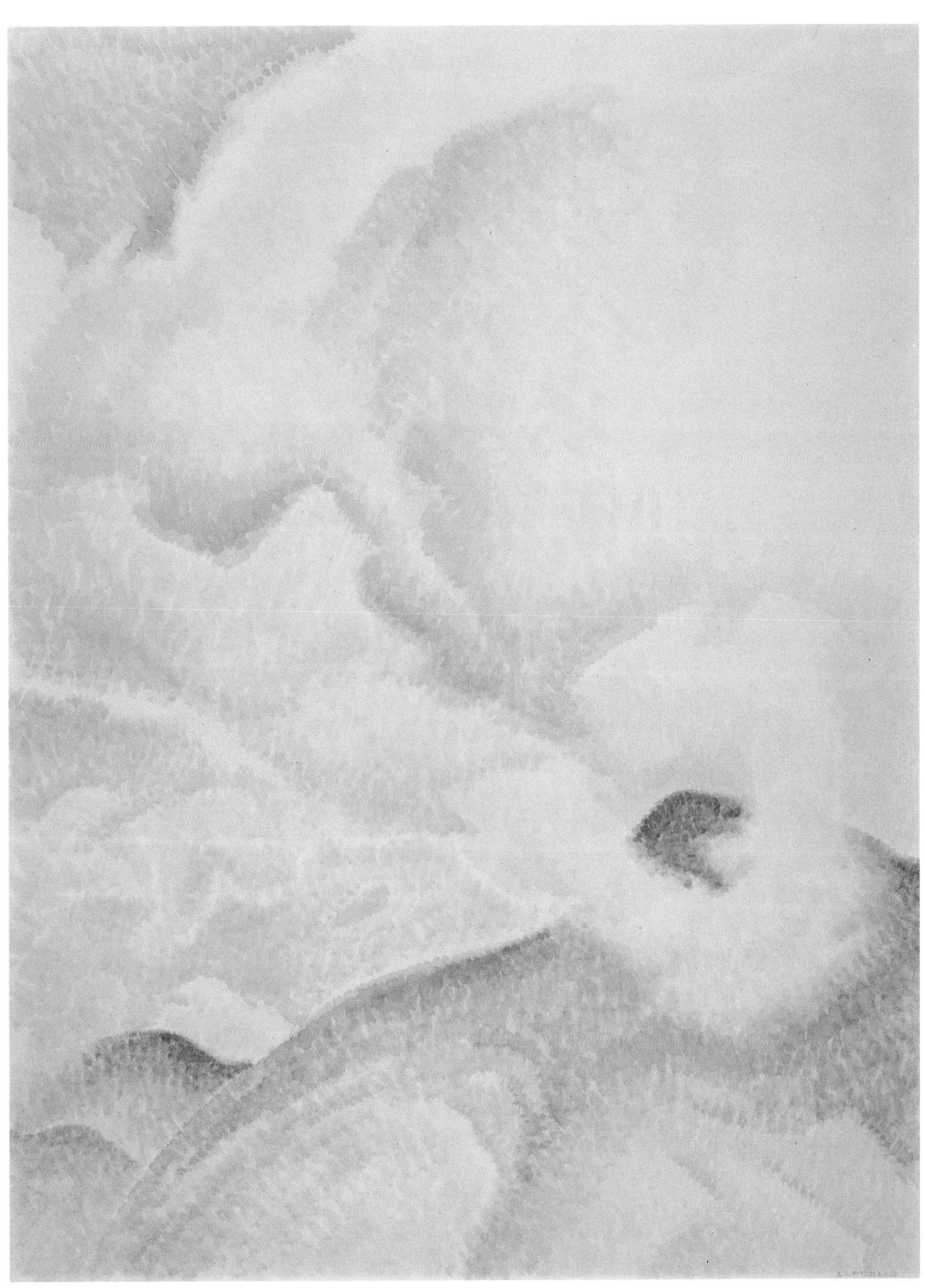

Cloud over Mountain, 1943/44
watercolour on paper
60 × 45.7 cm

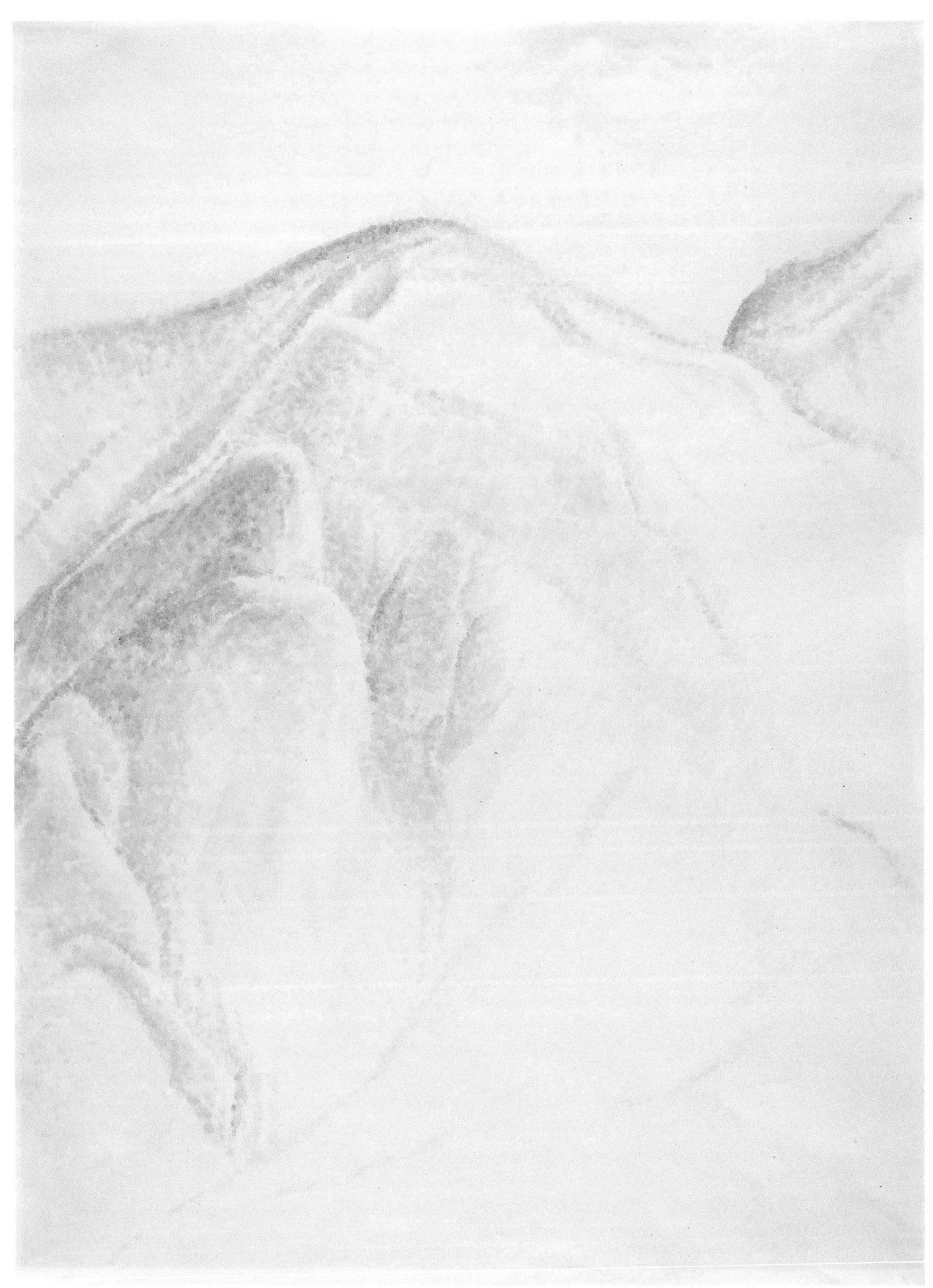

Mountains,
c. 1943–44
watercolour
on wove paper
60.9 × 45.7 cm

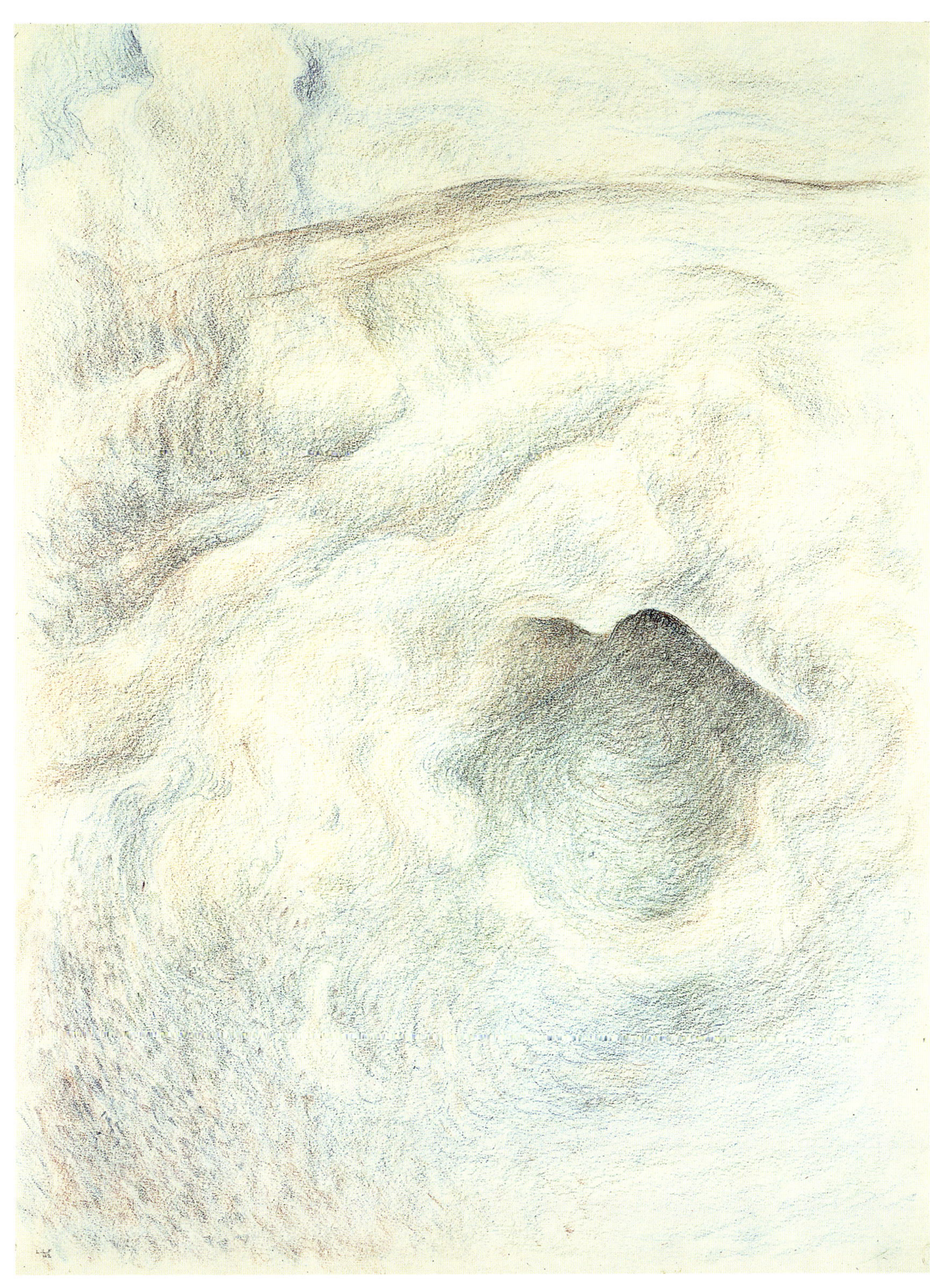

West Coast, Mountain in Mist, 1942
chalk on paper
61.1 × 46 cm

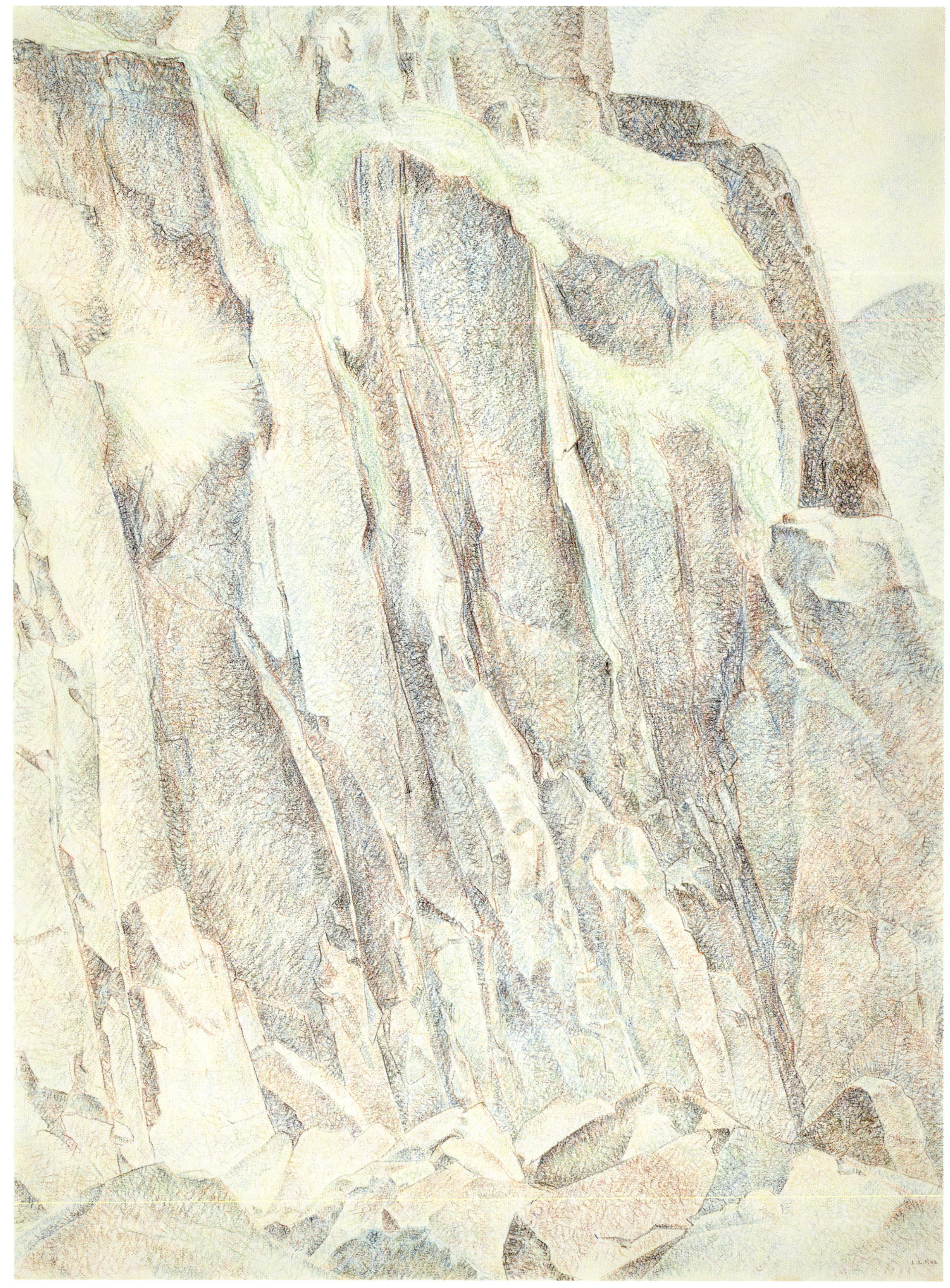

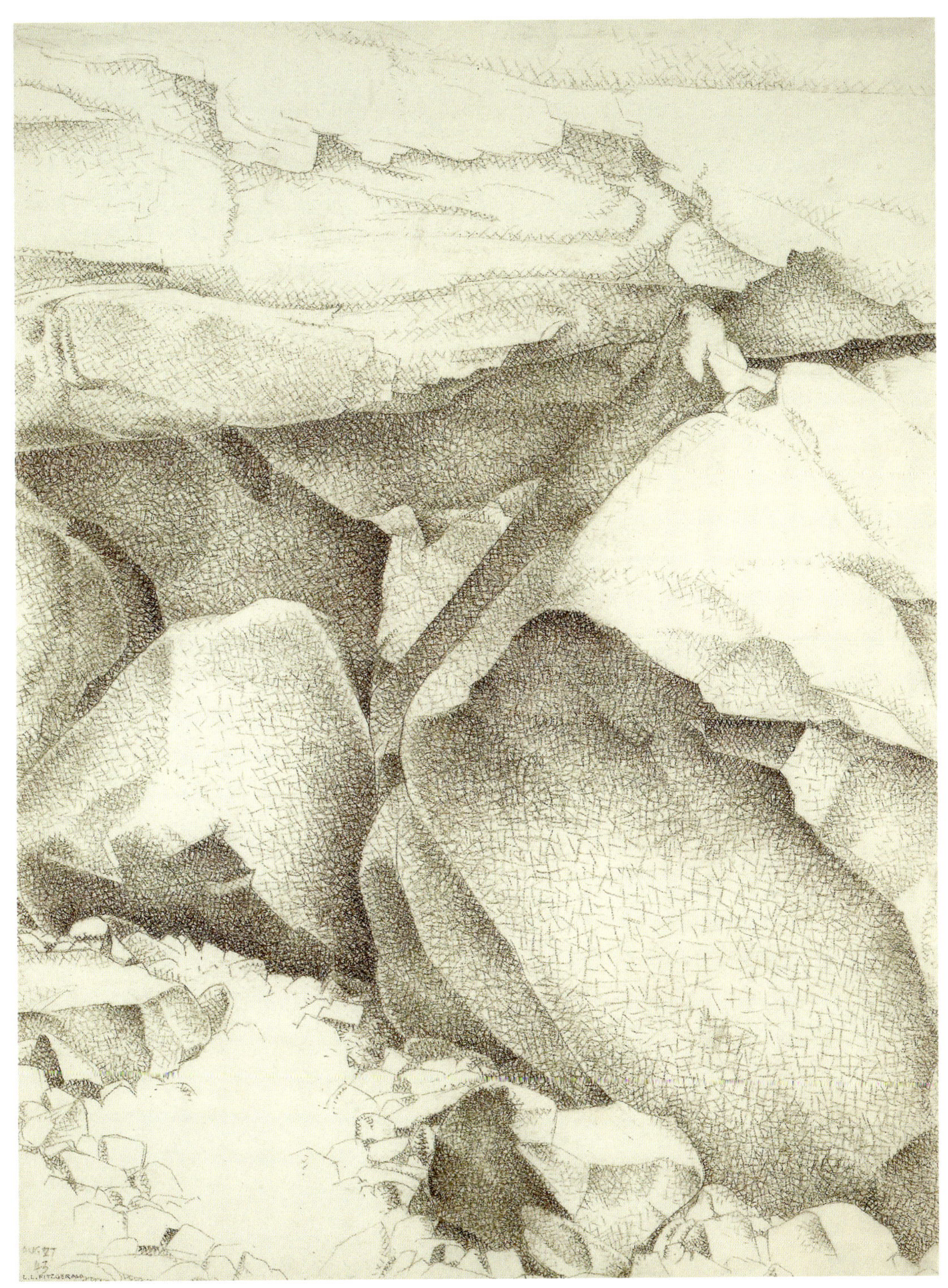

Rocks, 1943
coloured chalk on
wove paper
60.9 × 45.6 cm

OPPOSITE
Mountain Cliff,
1942
coloured pencil
with graphite on paper
sheet: 61 × 45.9 cm

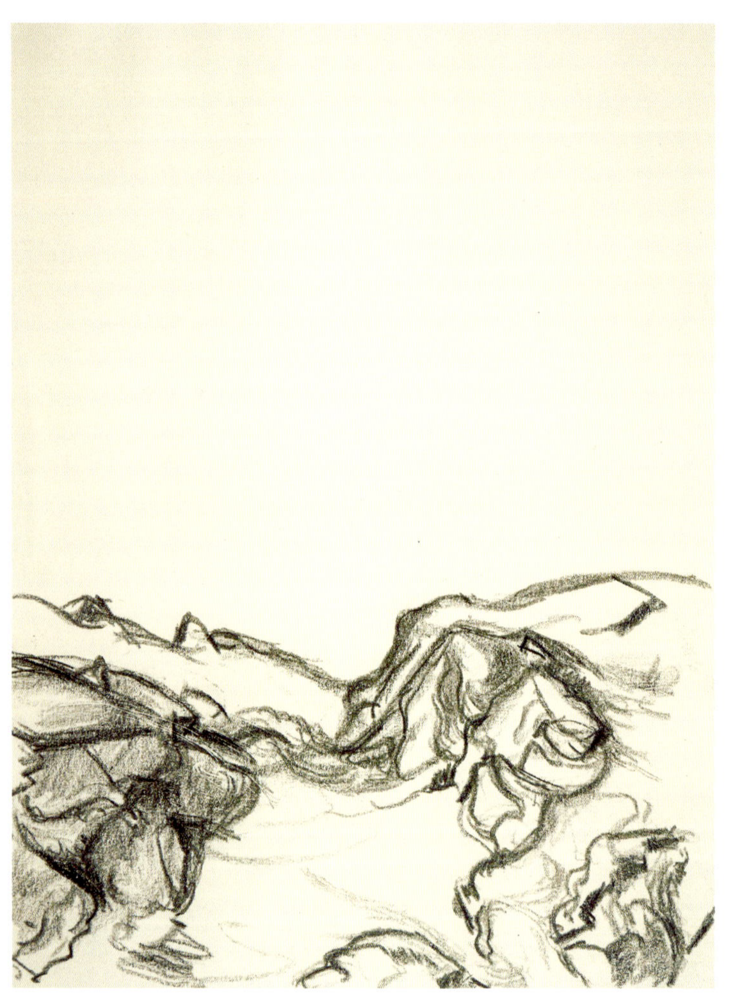

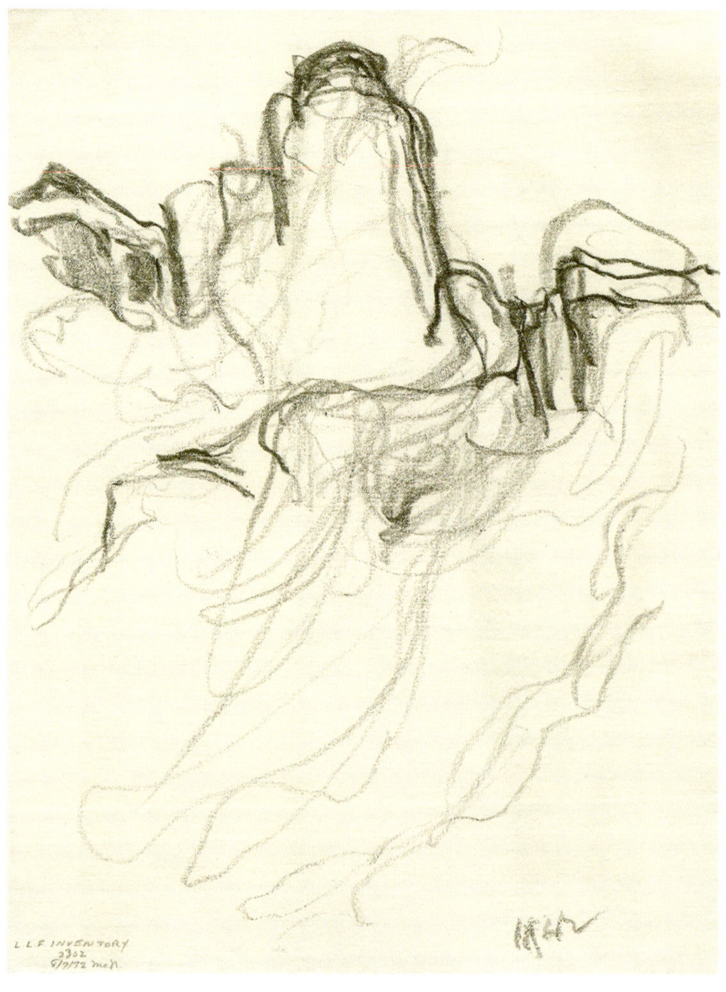

Untitled (West Coast Sketch), n.d.
graphite and chalk on paper
27.9 × 19.3 cm

Untitled (Rock Sketch), n.d.
graphite and chalk on paper
25.4 × 19 cm

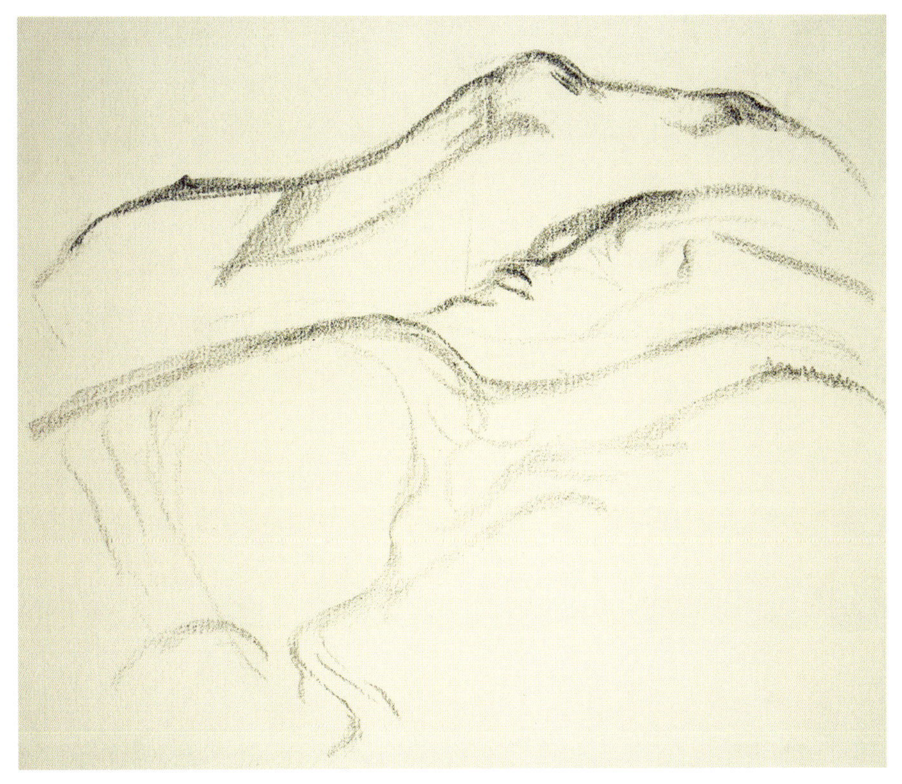

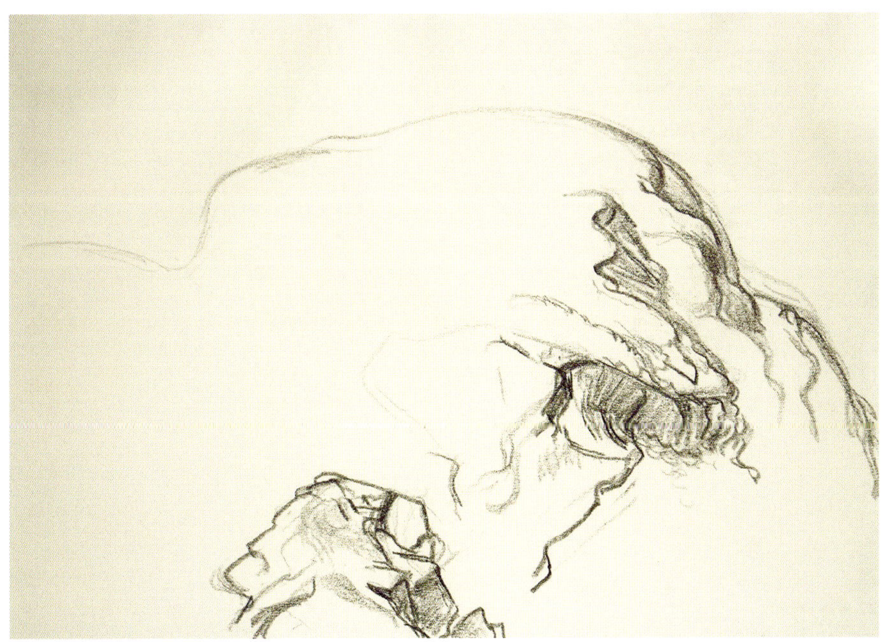

Untitled (Hills), n.d.
graphite and chalk on paper
22 x 25 cm

Untitled (West Coast Sketch), n.d.
graphite on paper
19.4 × 27.9 cm

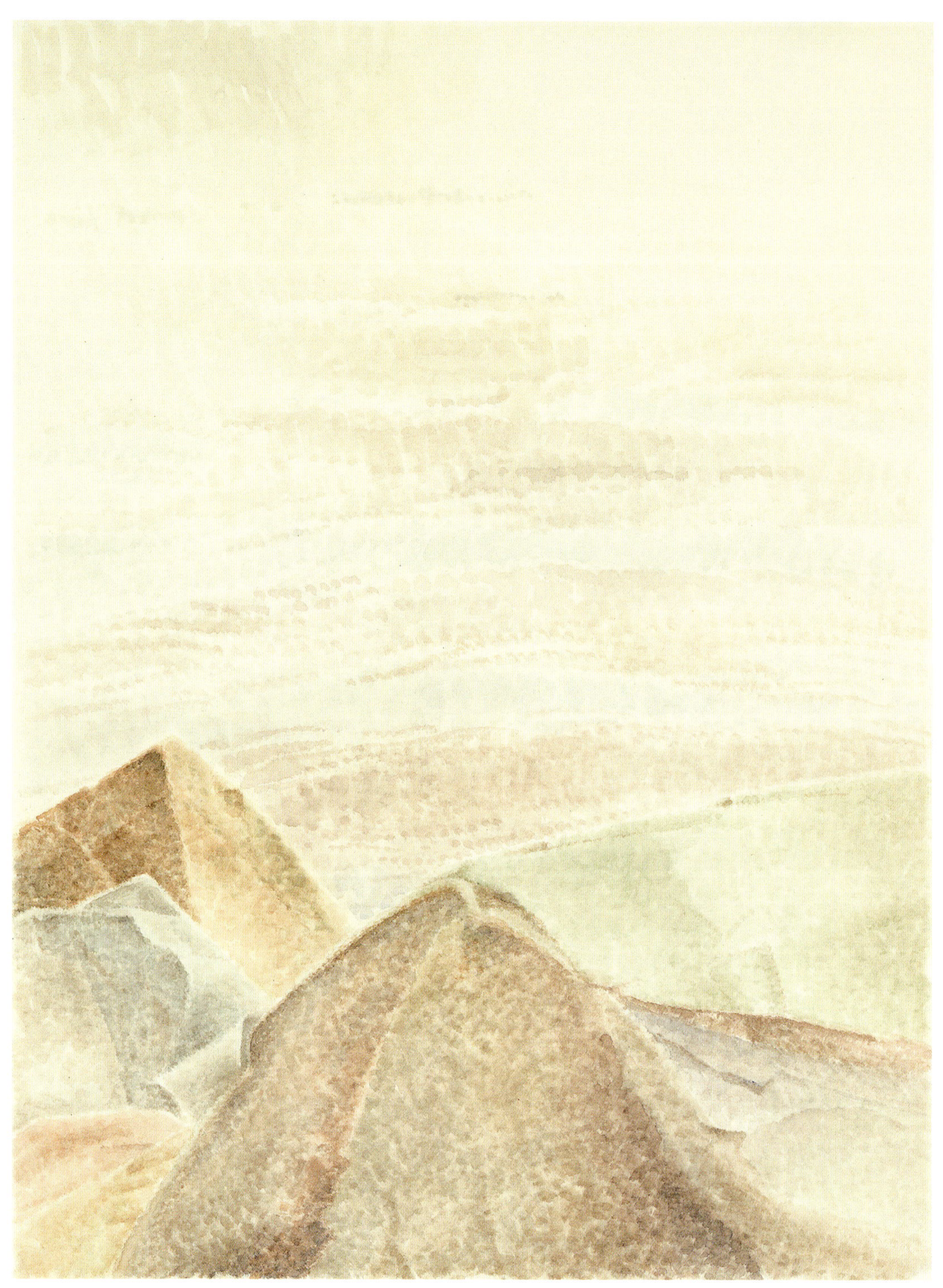

Rocky Shore, Howe Sound, 1943
watercolour on paper
61 × 45.8 cm

Rocks, 1944
watercolour on paper
61 × 45.7 cm

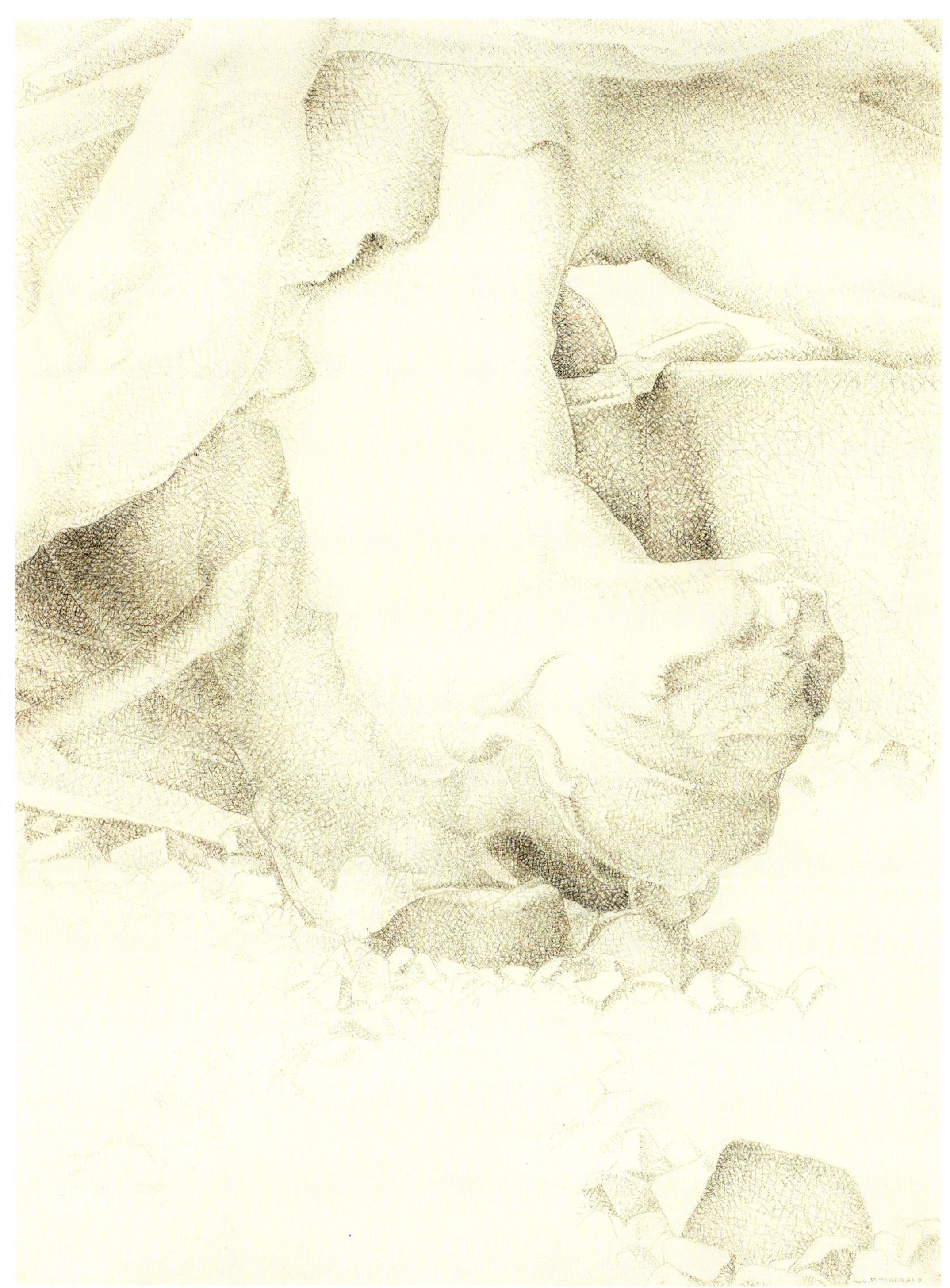

Driftwood, 1944
coloured pencil
on paper
sheet: 61.1 × 45.8 cm

OPPOSITE
Abstract Landscape, 1942
coloured chalk on
wove paper
61 × 46 cm

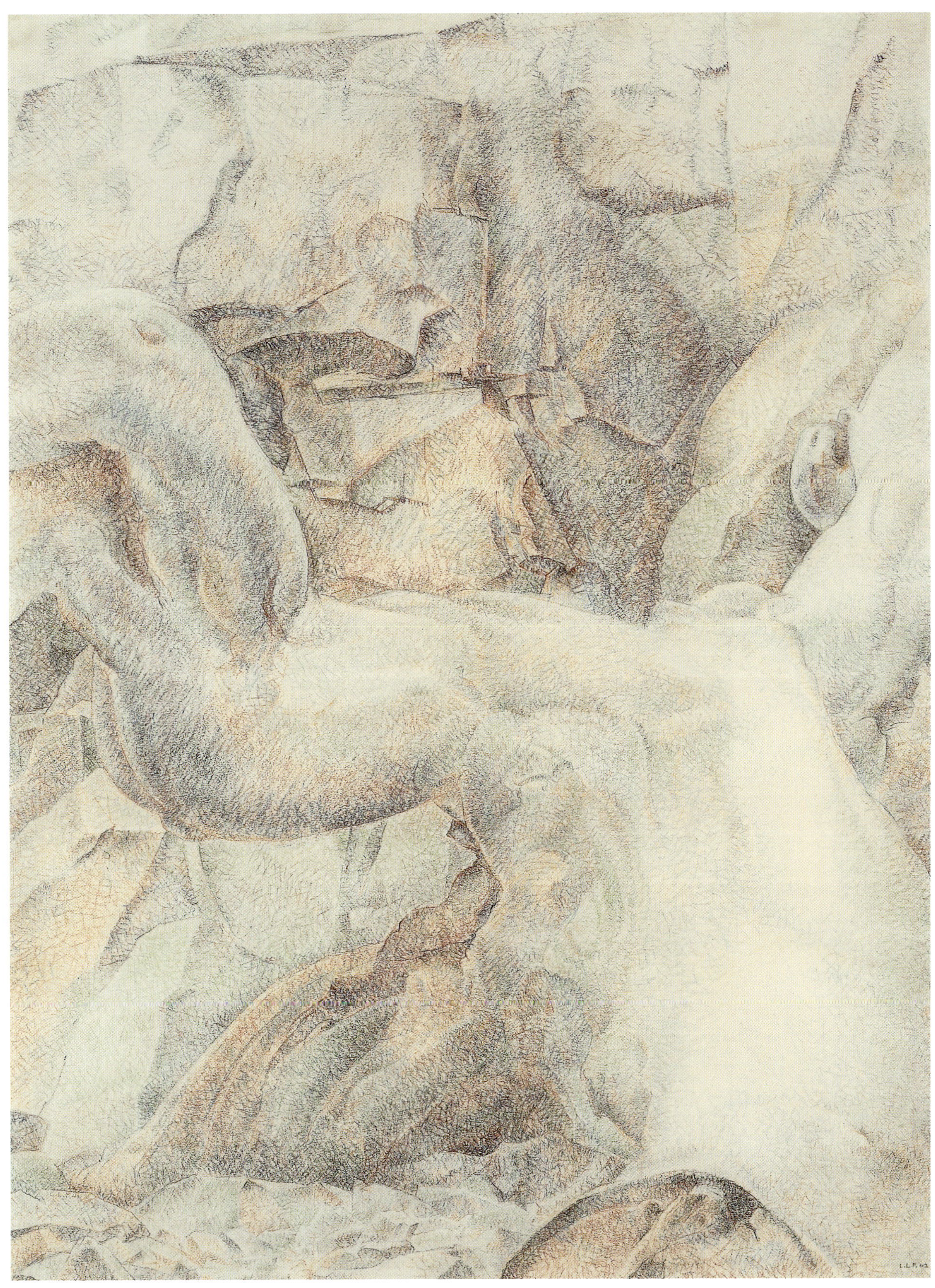

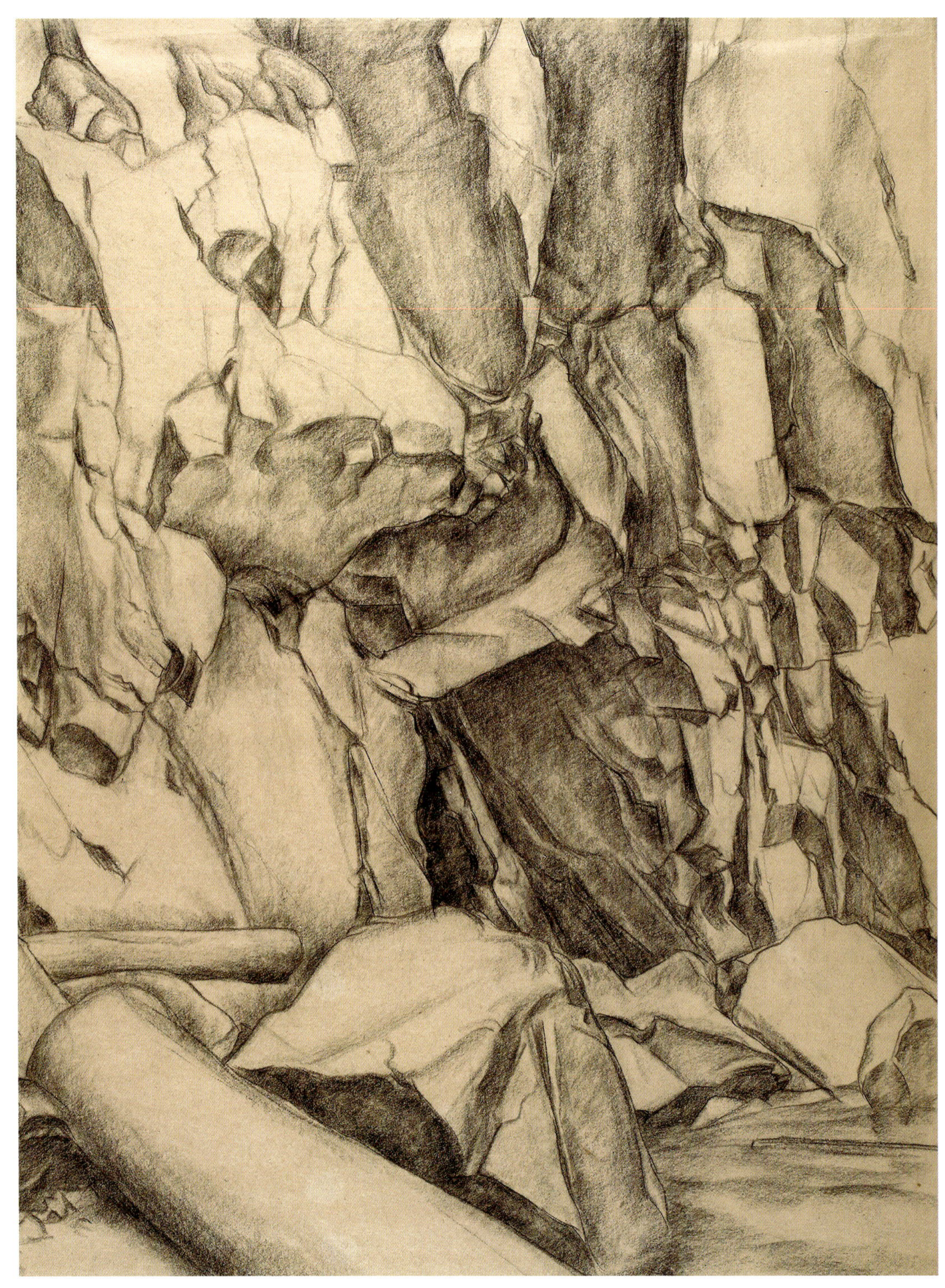

Rocks and Log, 1942
charcoal on paper
62.1 × 46.1 cm

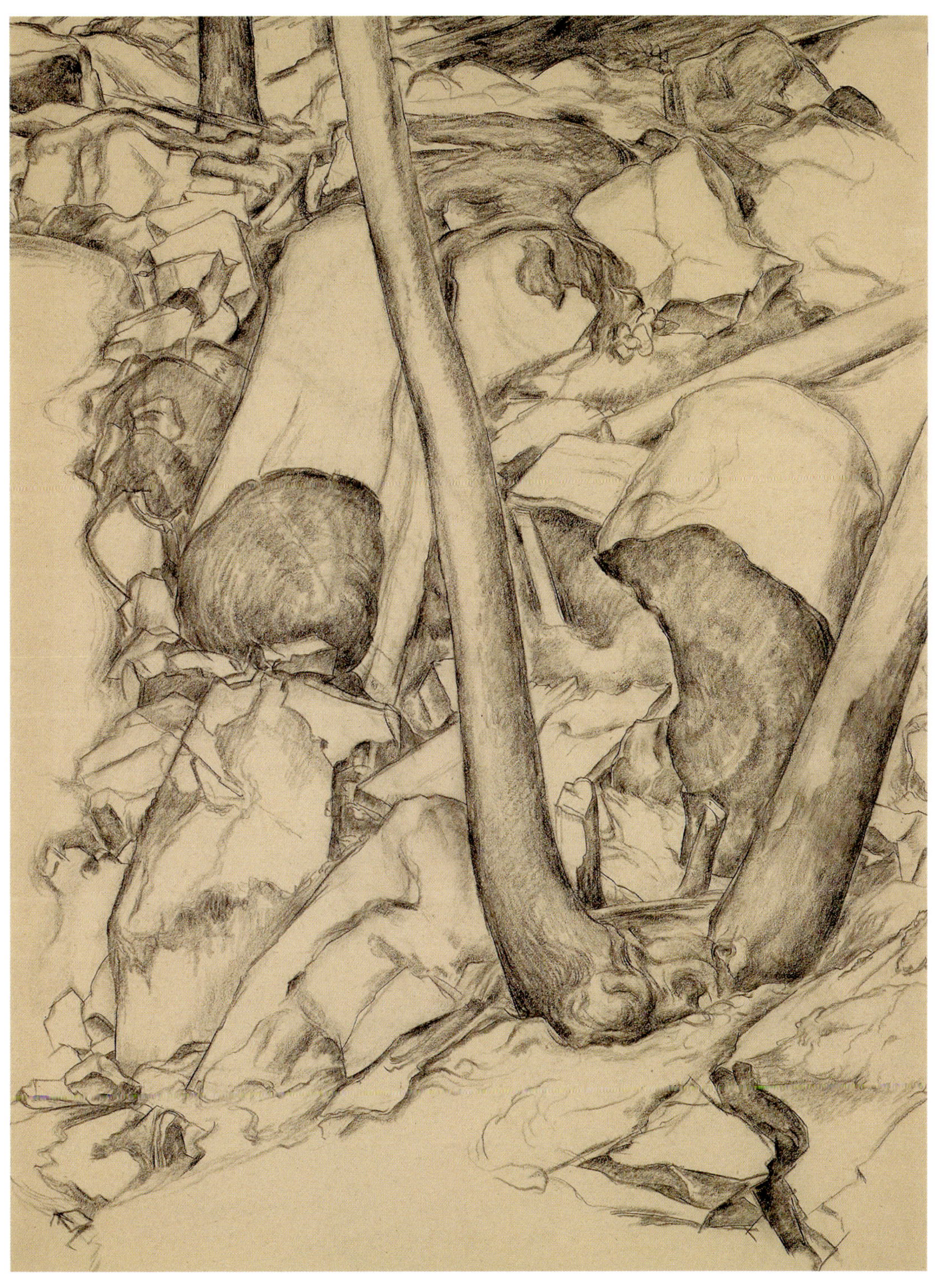

Driftwood and Rocks, 1942
charcoal on paper
62.2 × 46.5 cm

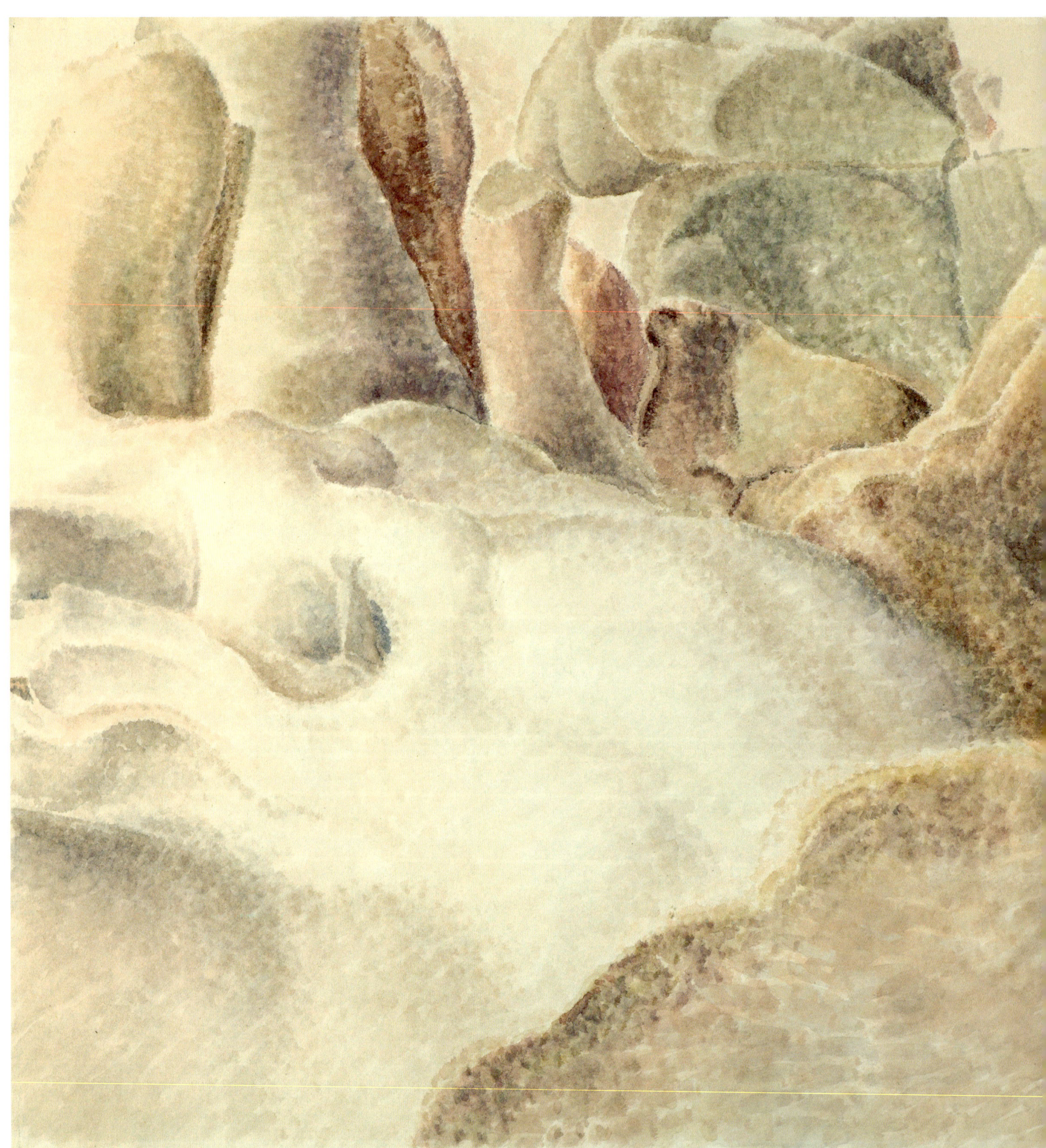

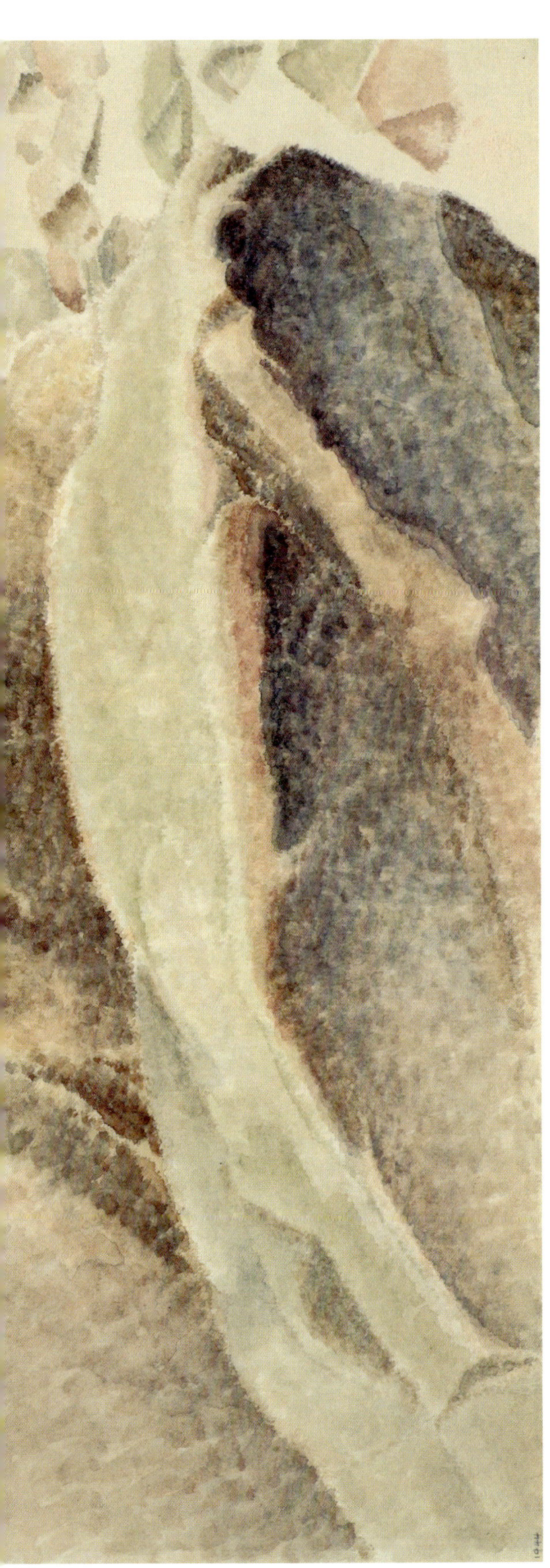

Rocks at the Water's Edge, 1944
watercolour on paper
46 × 61 cm

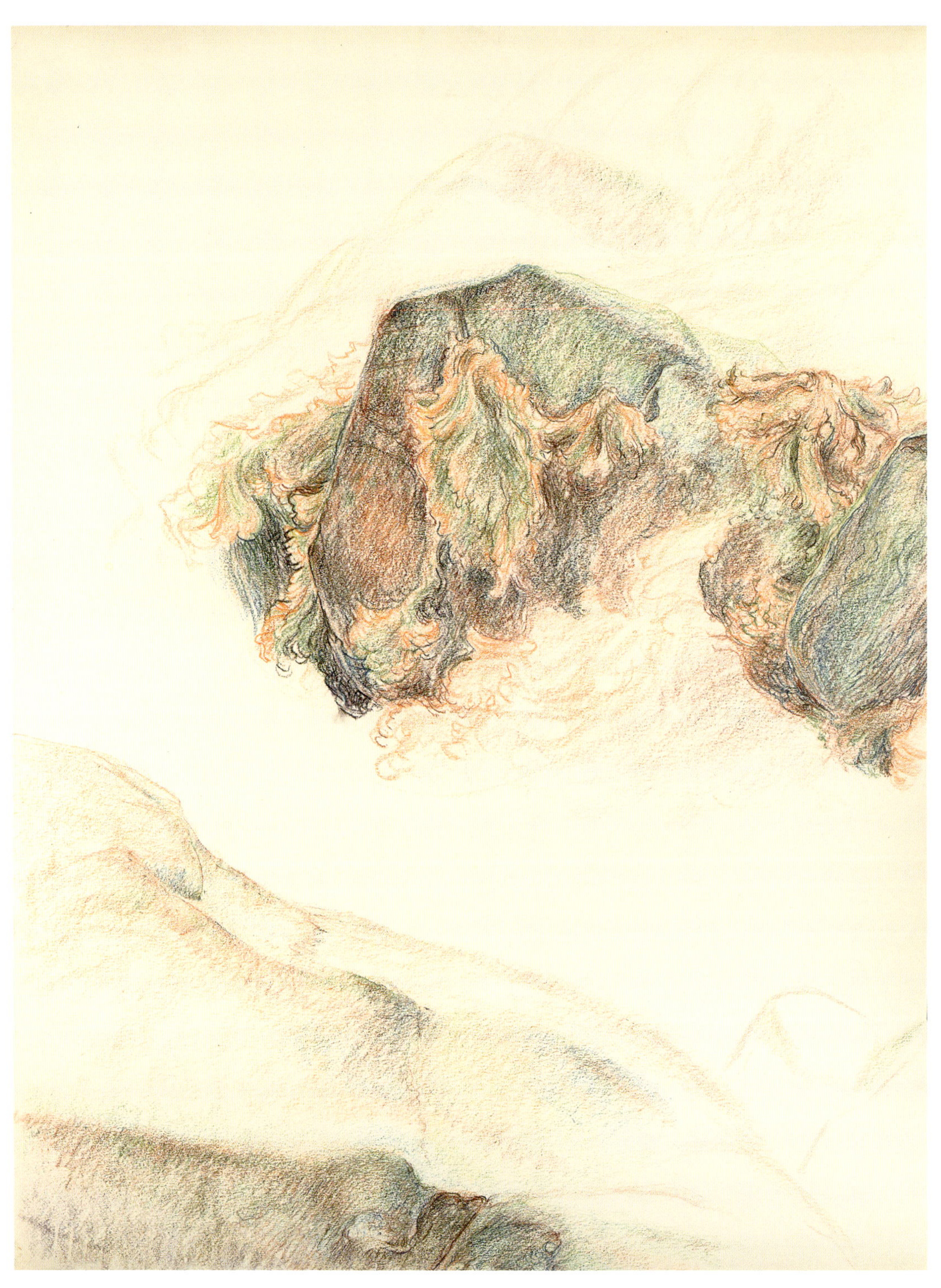

Organic Forms,
1942
crayon on paper
61.1 × 46 cm

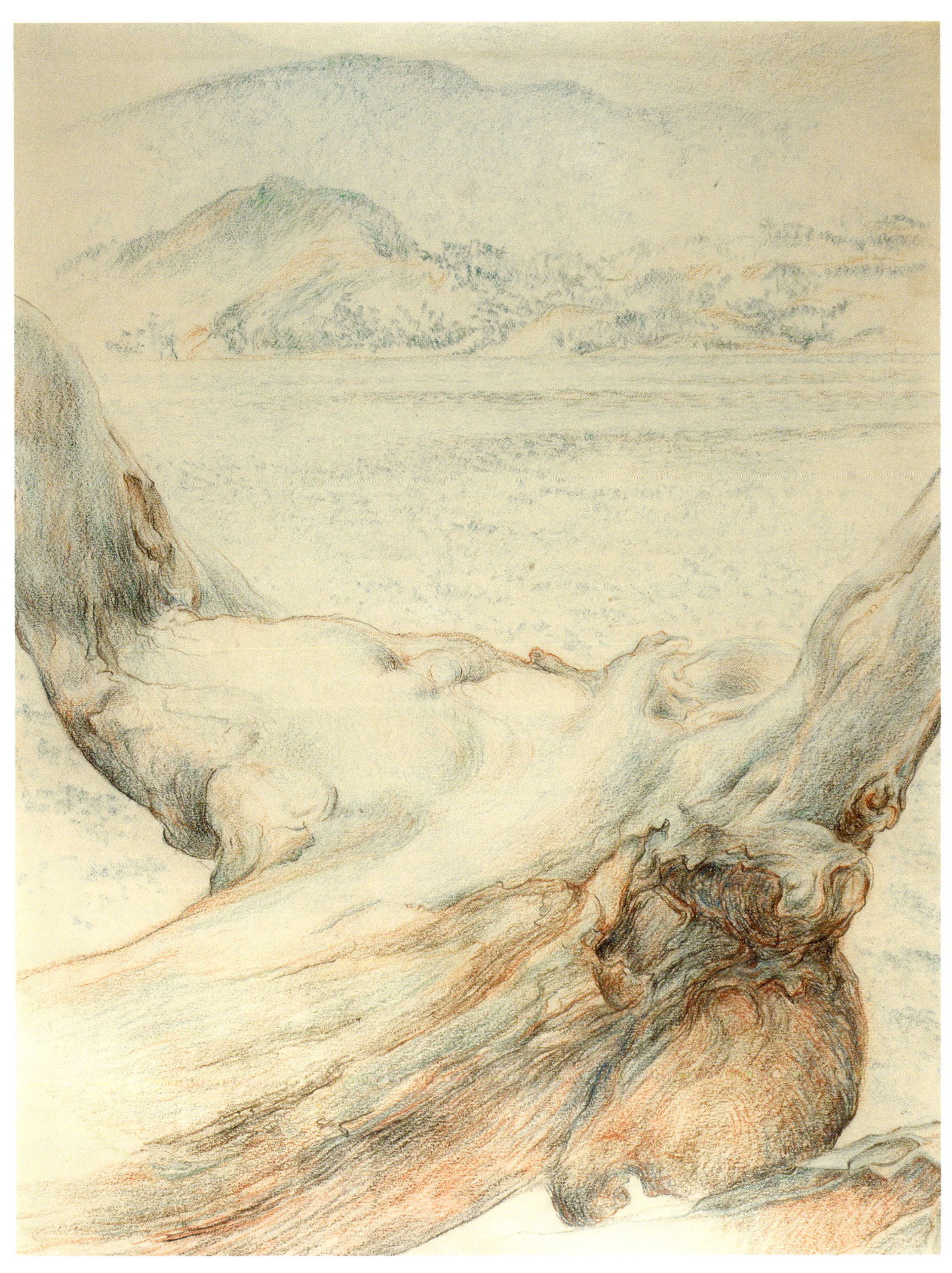

Driftwood, Bowen Island, BC, 1942
coloured pencil on paper
57.8 × 43.8 cm

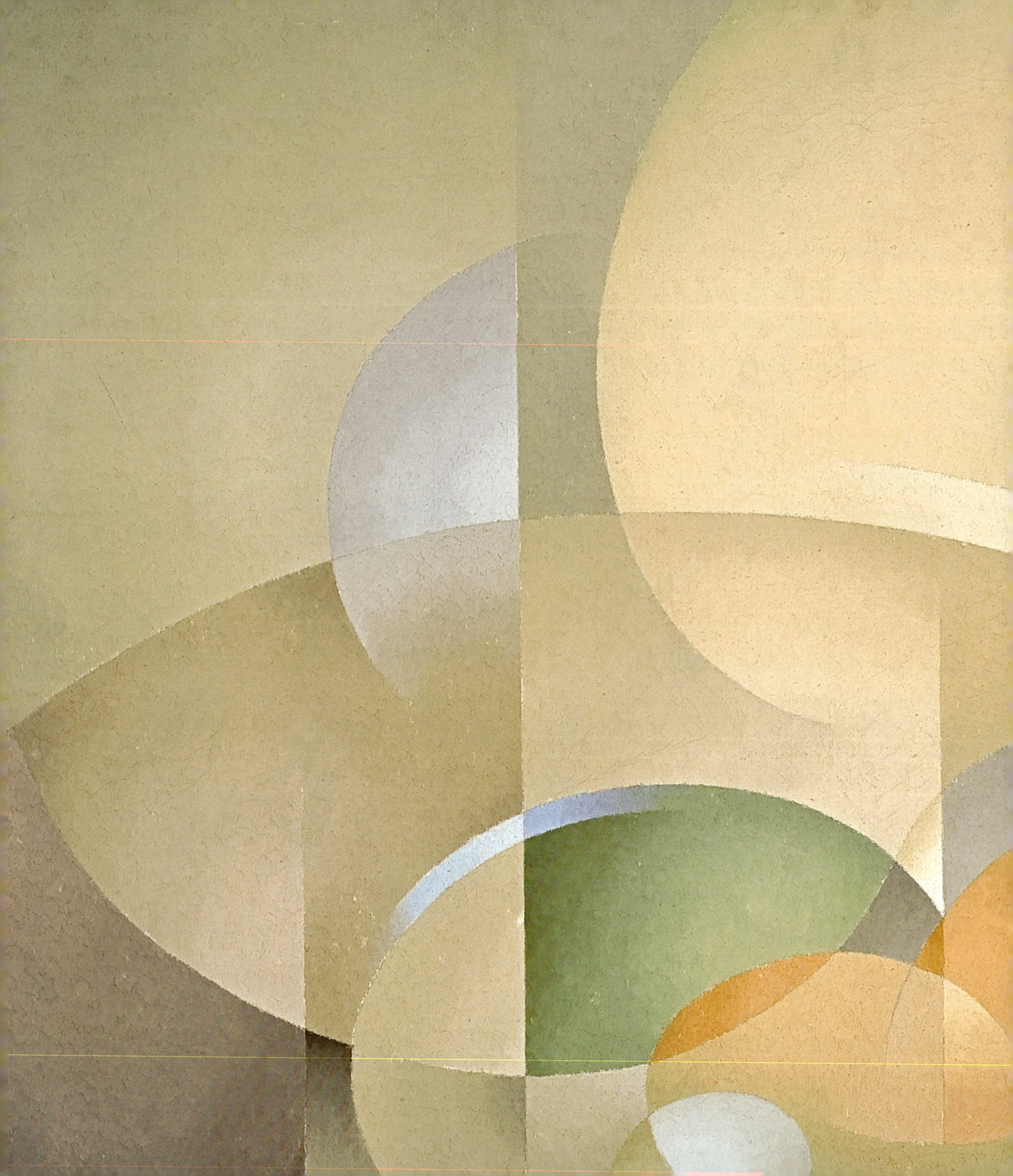

JOURNEY INTO ABSTRACTION

Throughout his career, FitzGerald sought to distill the essence of his subjects, stripping away inessential detail in the pursuit of pure form. In his earlier, representational paintings, the play of shadow had often been expressed through delicate abstract patterning, while his architectural paintings relied on carefully calibrated geometries. After 1950, however, FitzGerald began his experiments with abstraction in earnest, encouraged by his deep friendships begun in the late 1920s with Lawren Harris and Bertram Brooker—both pioneers of abstraction in Canadian art. Always, though, FitzGerald's abstracts retain a reference to the natural world, which was his muse, as is evident in his choice of colours and the play of forms evoking natural shapes or the movement of the wind.

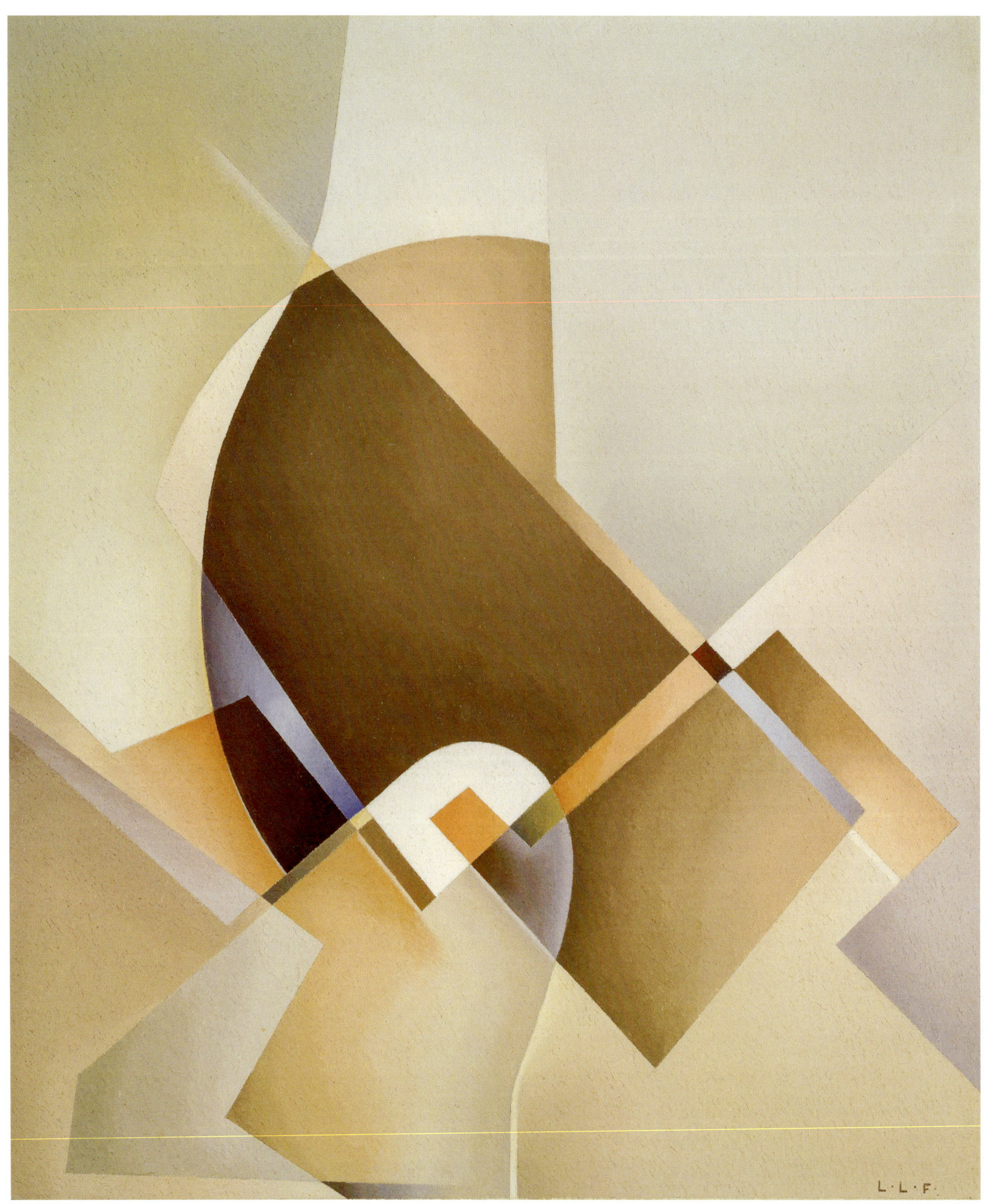
L·L·F.

CLOSE TO THE EARTH

FitzGerald's Path to Abstraction

MICHAEL PARKE-TAYLOR

Composition, c. 1952
oil on canvas
66 × 56 cm

Bertram Brooker, the Toronto writer and artist, and the legendary Canadian painter Lawren Harris did not always see eye to eye when it came to matters of art. But from their first encounter with the work of Lionel LeMoine FitzGerald, they agreed that the Winnipeg artist was extraordinary. In each case, a lifelong friendship with FitzGerald would be forged. This affiliation is germane to a discussion of FitzGerald's eventual arrival at abstraction because both Brooker and Harris were major exponents of abstract painting in Canada at different points in FitzGerald's career. How they intersected with FitzGerald is relevant: Brooker principally during the thirties, and Harris in the forties.[1] In each case, their interactions were a question not so much of influence but of mutual admiration, respect, and shared interests. Brooker and Harris do not "explain" FitzGerald's personal brand of abstraction. But they are significant as background support along the singular path FitzGerald travelled toward personal artistic discovery.

The Brooker/Harris/FitzGerald connection begins in January 1928 with FitzGerald's first one-person exhibition at the Arts and Letters Club, Toronto. The previous January, Brooker had mounted an exhibition of his own abstract paintings (inspired by music, not nature) at the Club. This is considered to be the first solo show of abstract art in Canada. Harris had been a member of the Group of Seven since its inception in 1920, their purpose to forge a strong Canadian identity through landscape depictions of the rugged Ontario northland. Harris's own adventure with abstraction would not take place until after 1934, when he left Toronto for the United States.

In response to FitzGerald's 1928 exhibition, Brooker purchased a pencil drawing for $12, which he wrote about in his Seven Arts newspaper column under the headline "The Joy of Ownership."[2] For his part, Harris felt compelled to write to FitzGerald: "I particularly like the way you extricate a suggestion of celestial structure and spirit from objective nature in

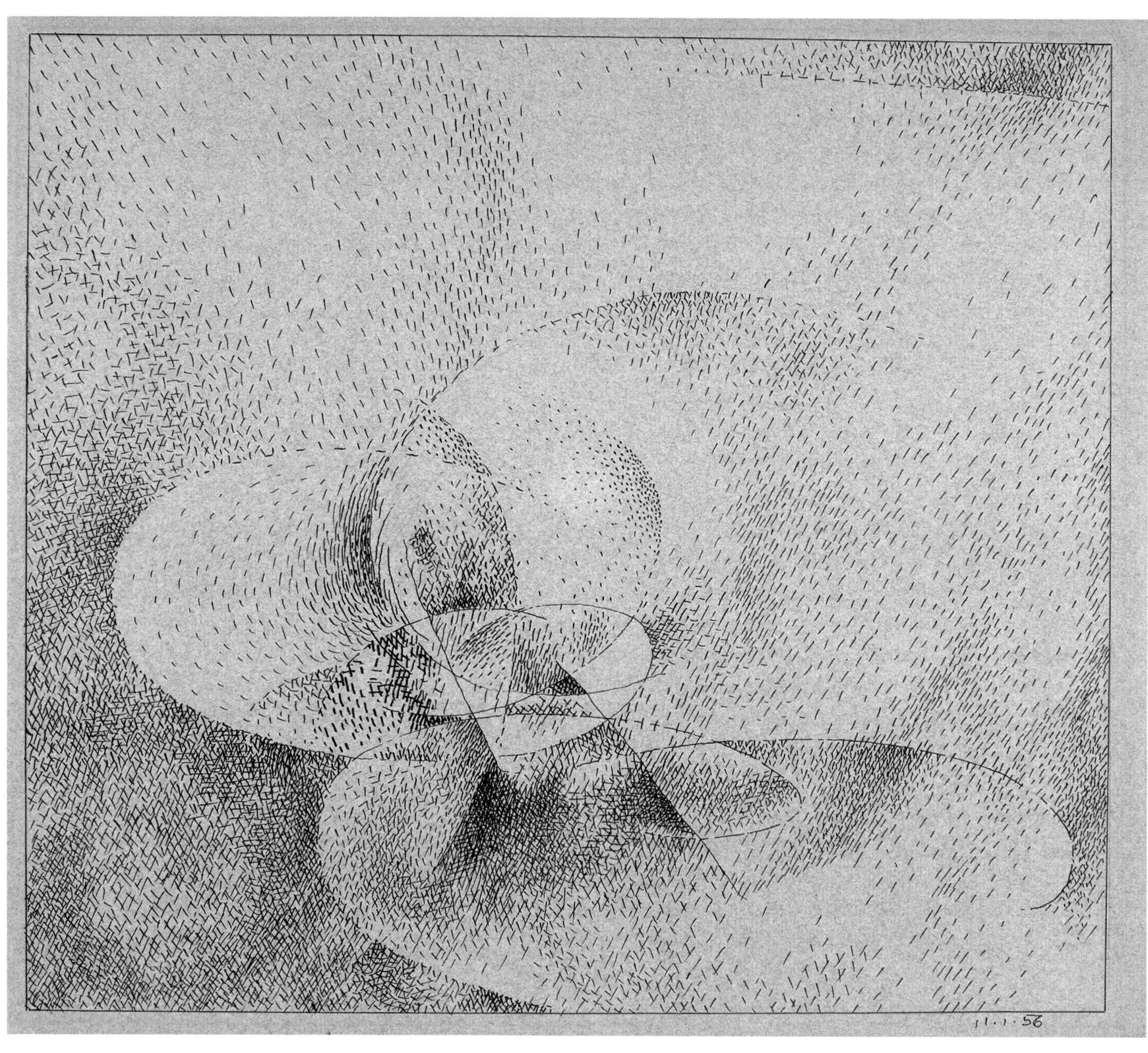

Abstract on Blue Paper, 1956
pen and black ink on
blue wove paper
32.5 × 37.8 cm

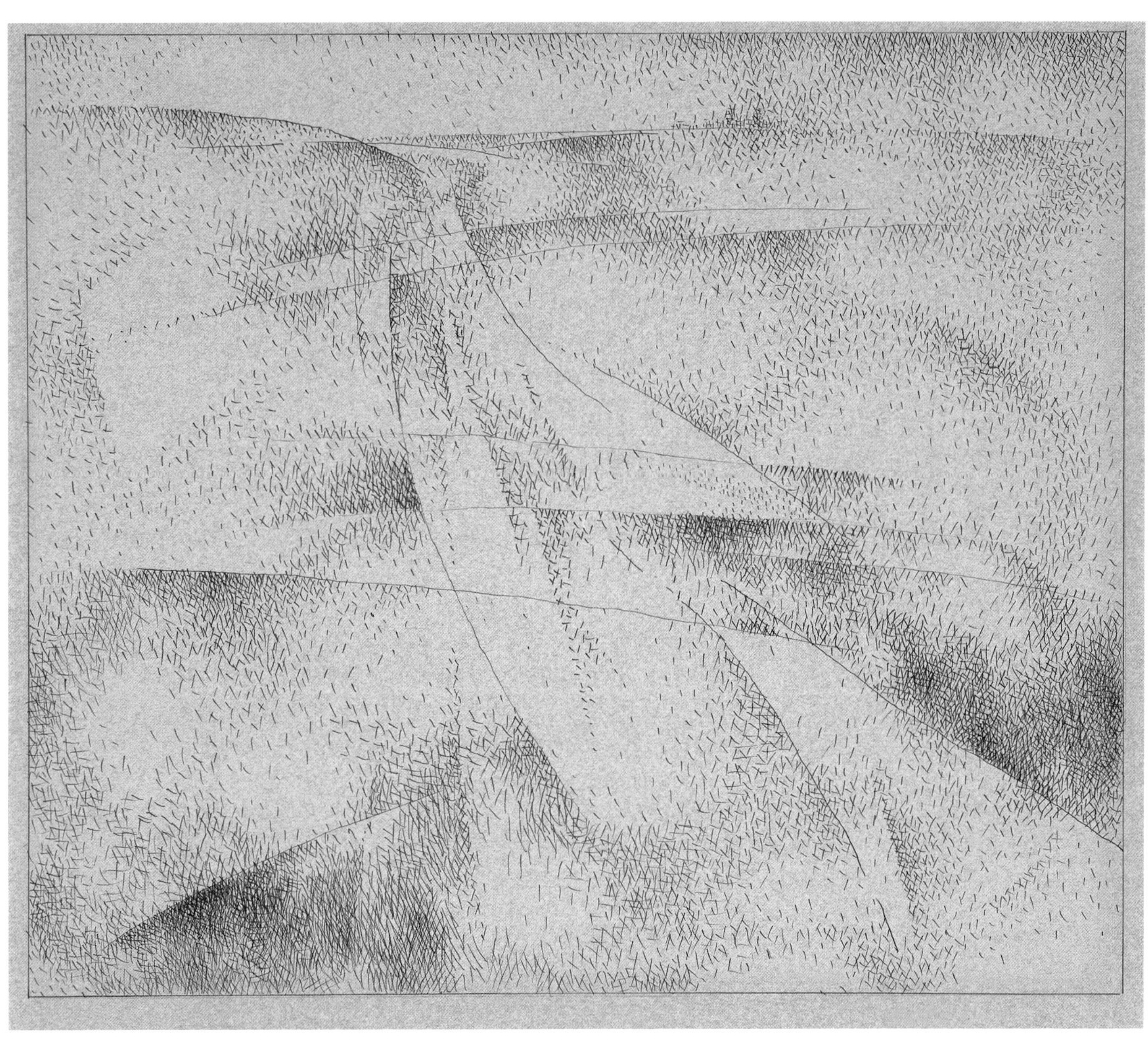

Path over the Hill, 1956
ink on paper
32.5 × 37.5 cm;
image: 30.1 × 35.3 cm

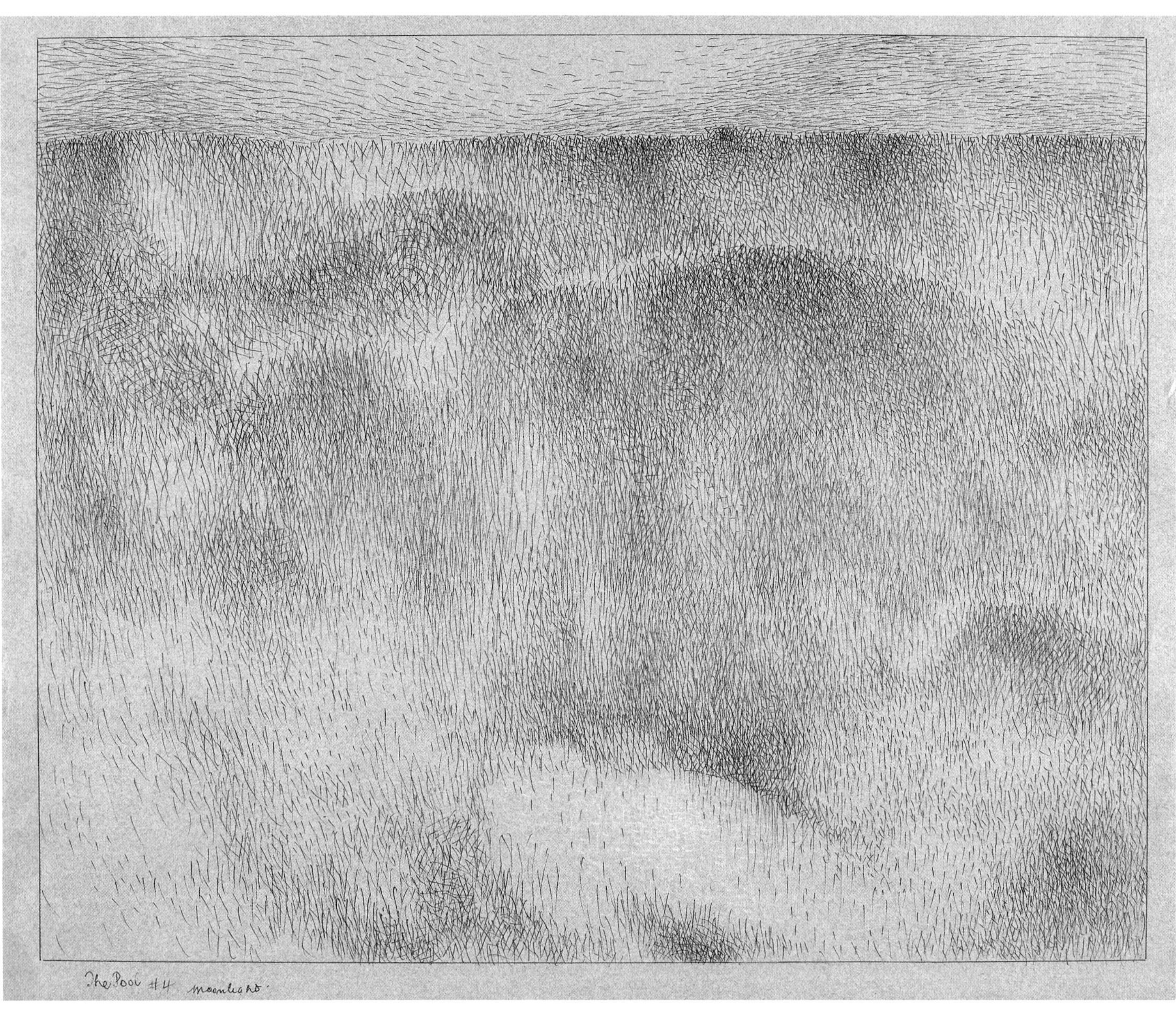

The Pool No. 4, Moonlight, 1956
pen and black ink
heightened with white
on blue wove paper
38.5 × 47.3 cm

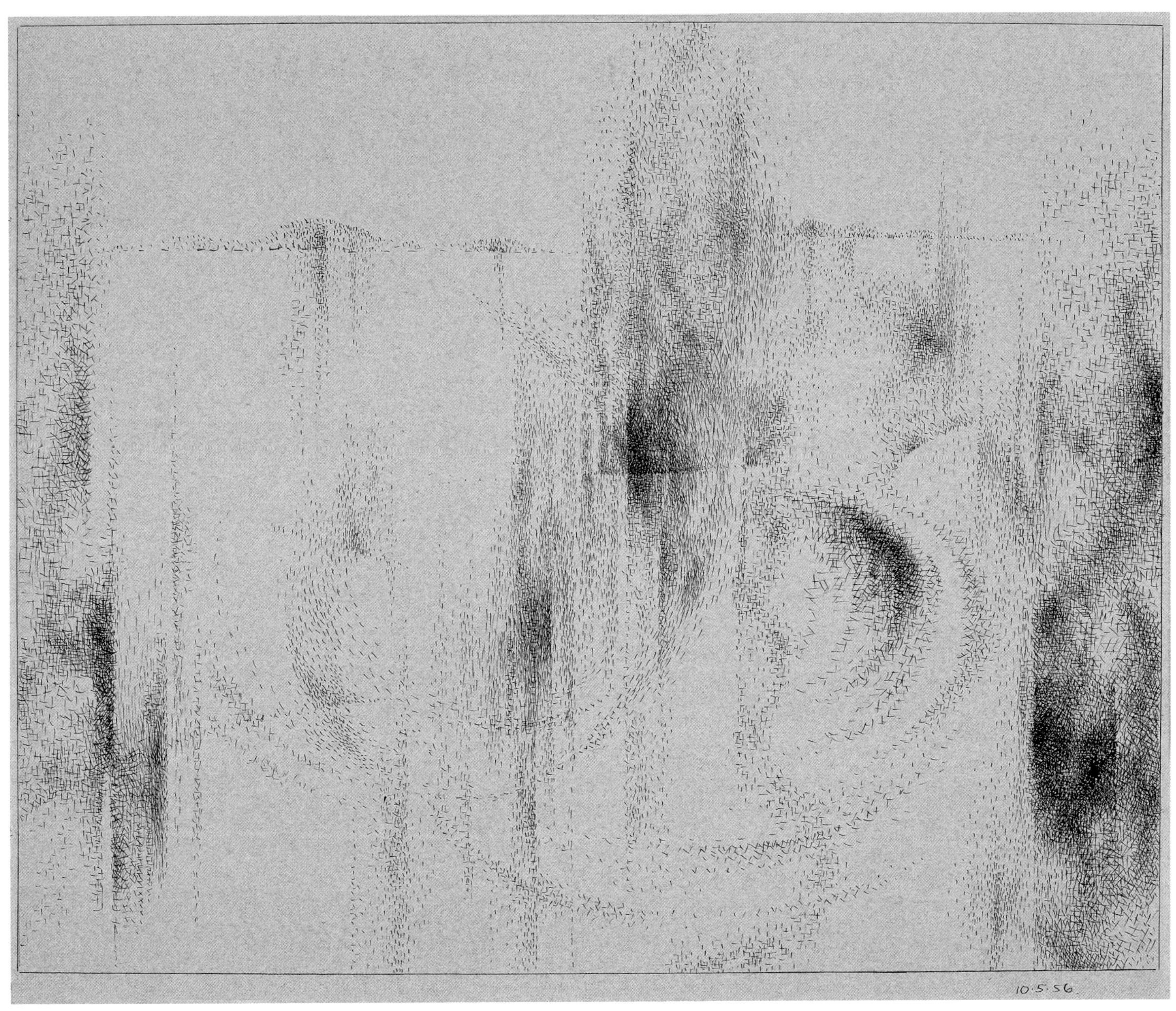

Abstract on Blue, 1956
ink on paper
47 × 48 cm

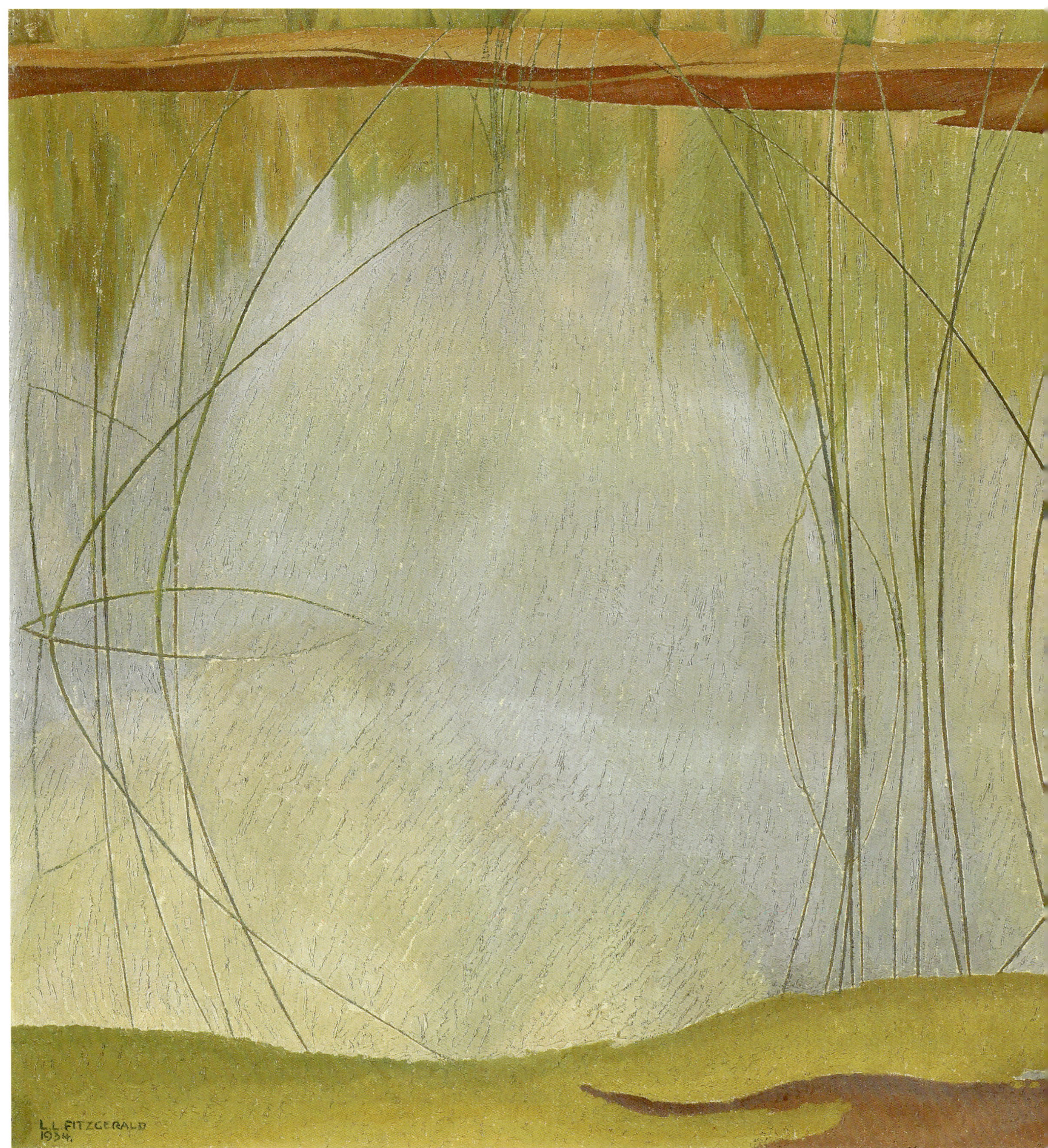
L.L. FITZGERALD
1934.

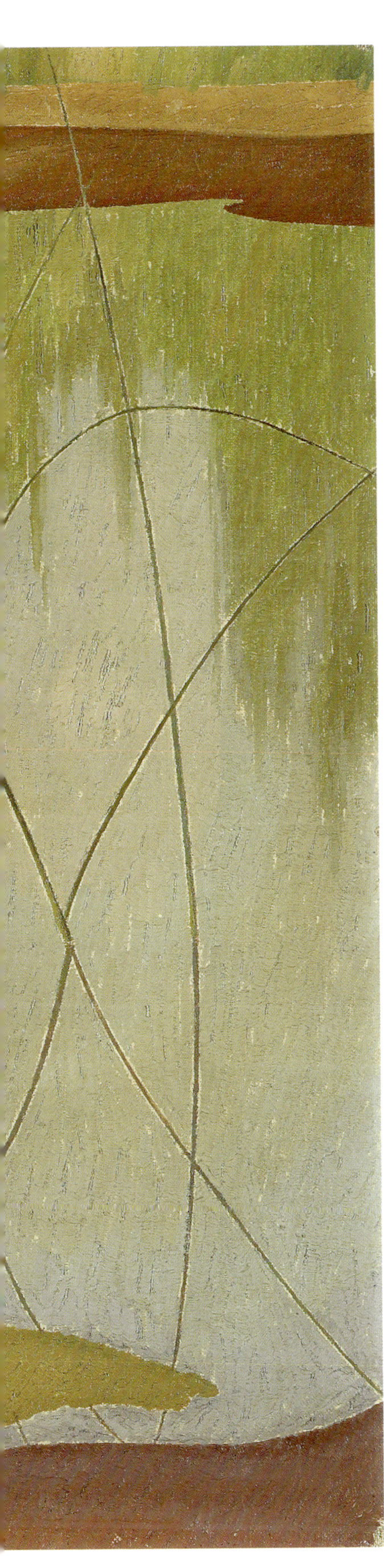

The Pool, 1934
oil on canvas
36.2 × 43.7 cm

Abstract: Green and Gold, 1954
oil on canvas
71.7 × 92 cm

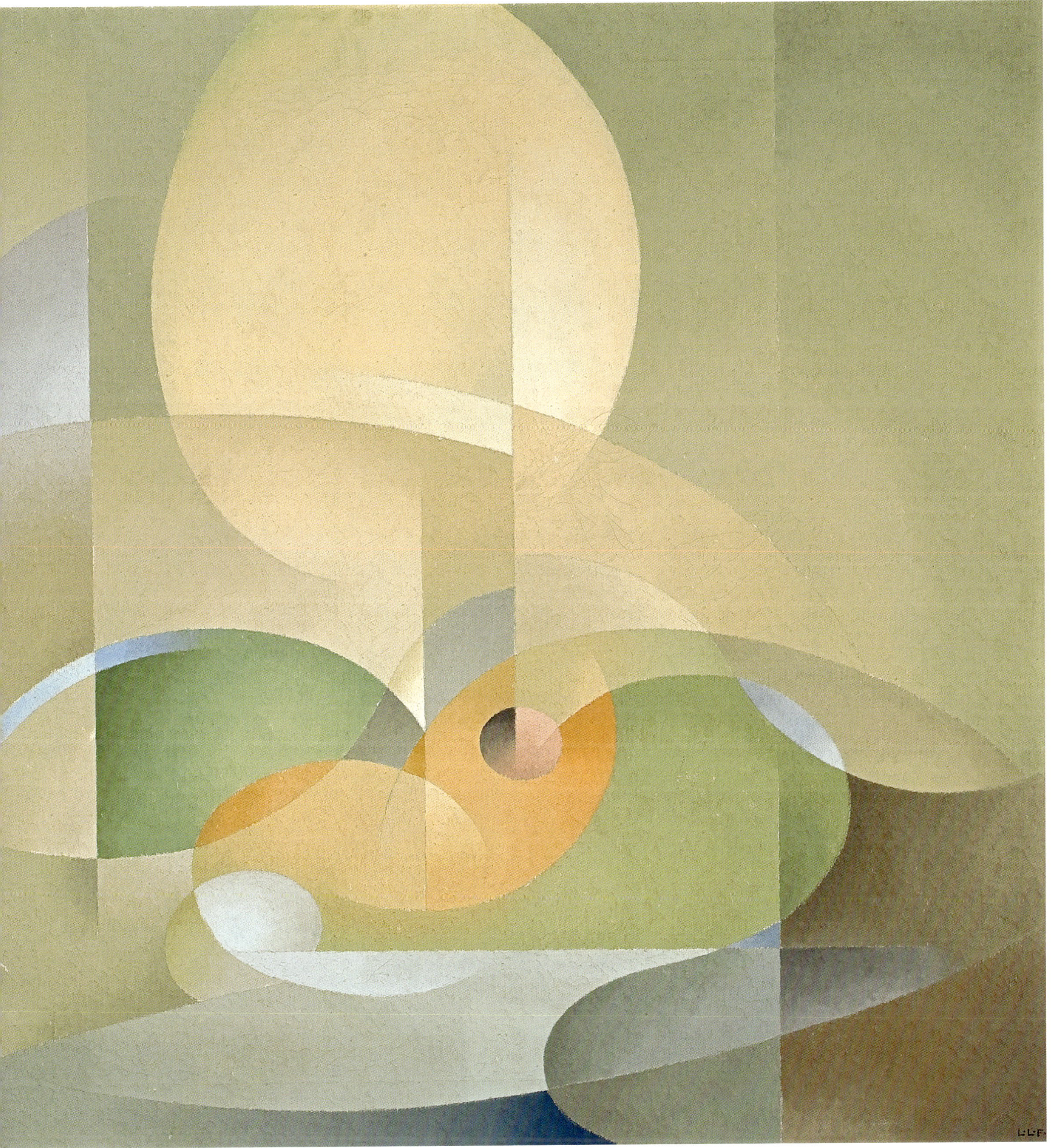
L·L·F·

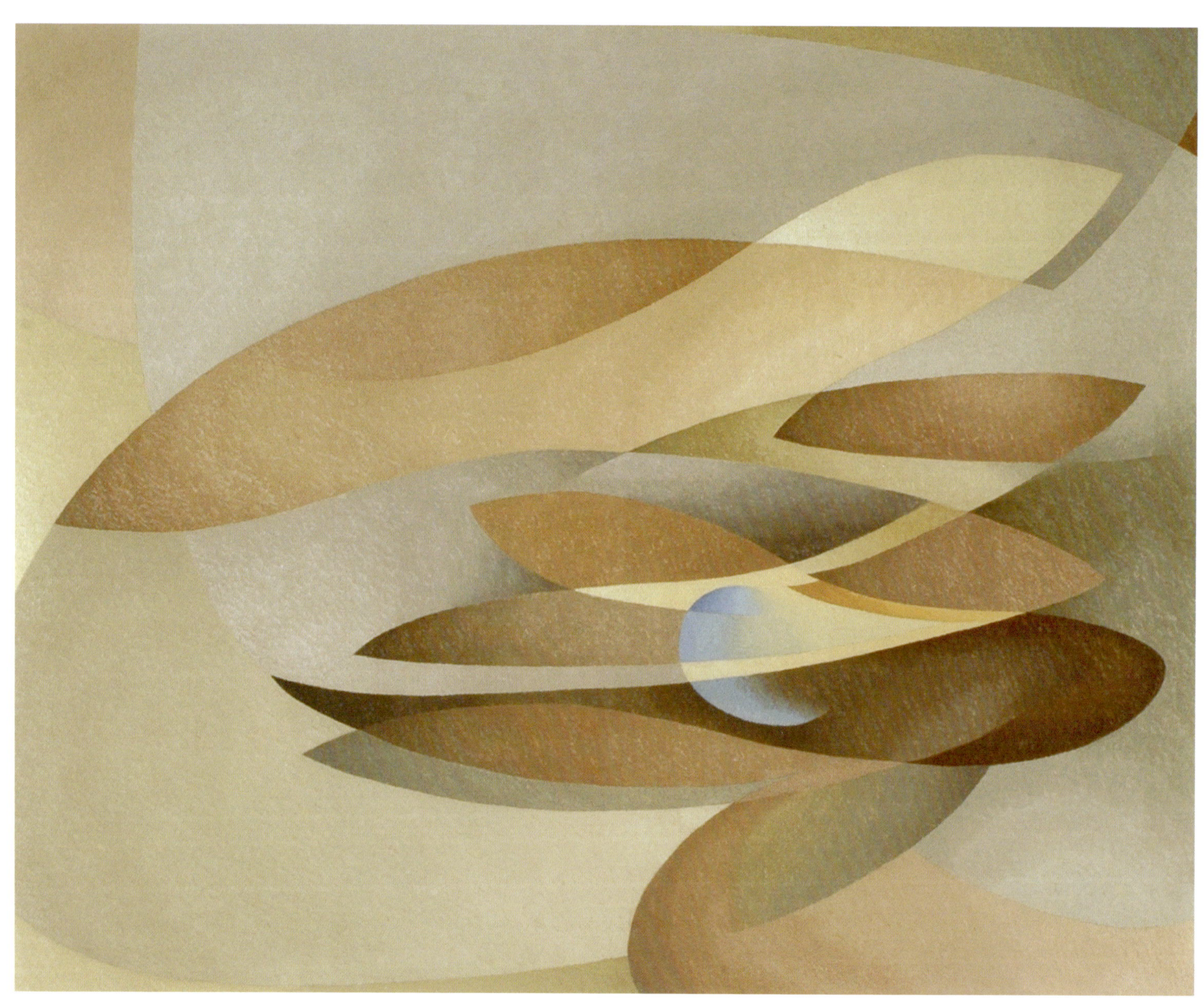

Autumn Sonata,
1953–54
oil on board
59.5 × 75 cm

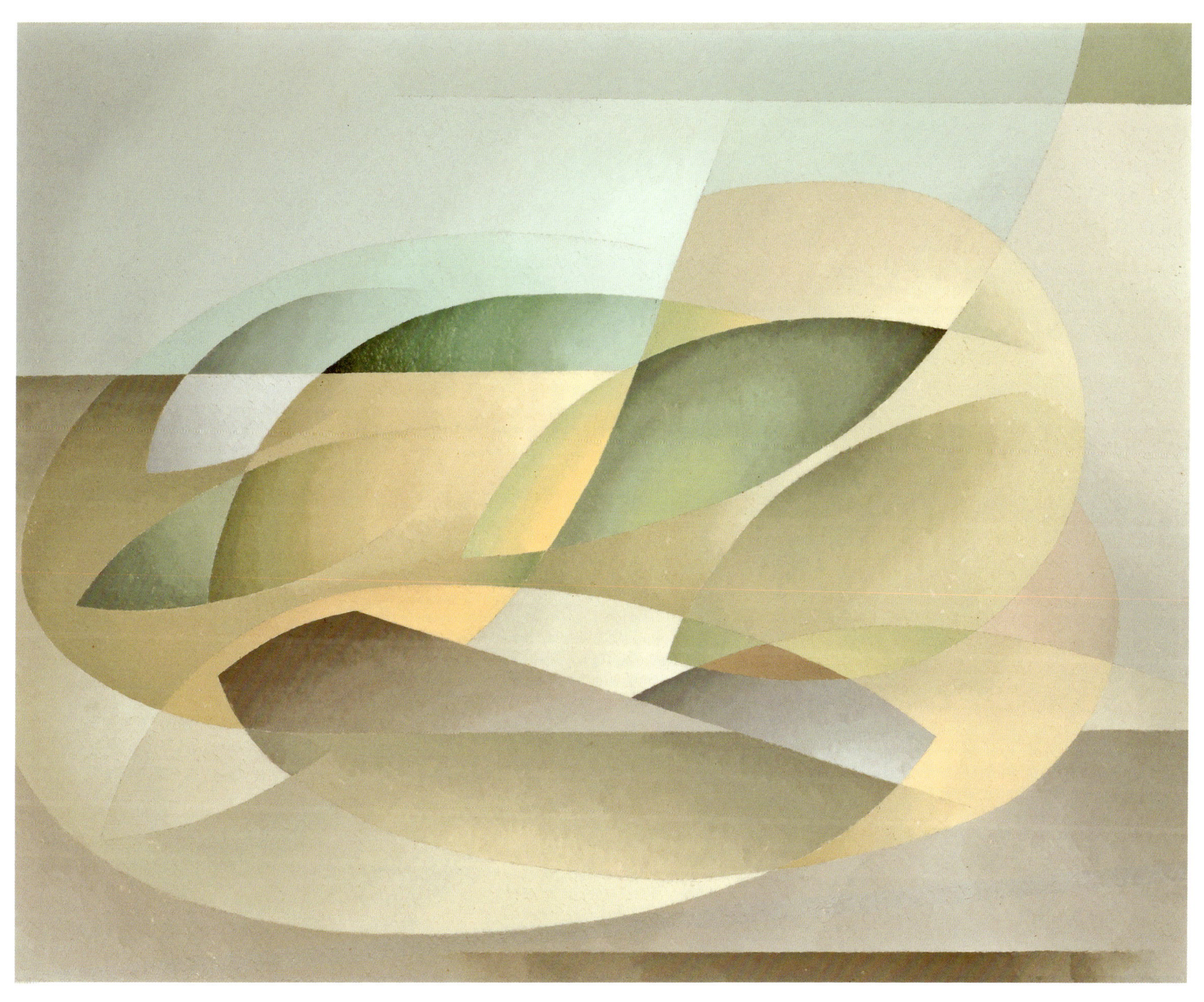

April Rhythm,
c. 1954
oil on Masonite
60.8 × 76 cm

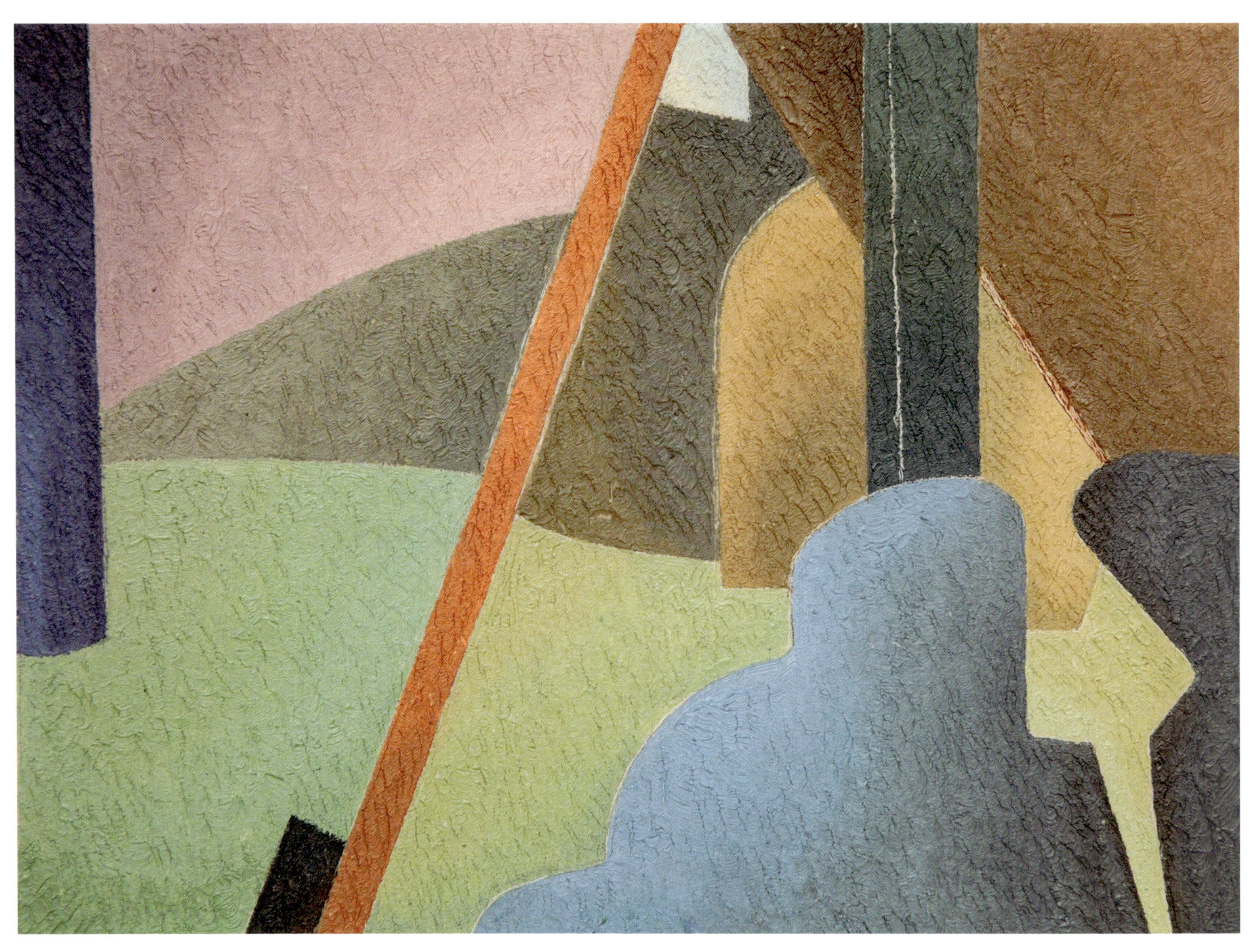

Composition, 1951
oil on panel
15.2 × 20.3 cm

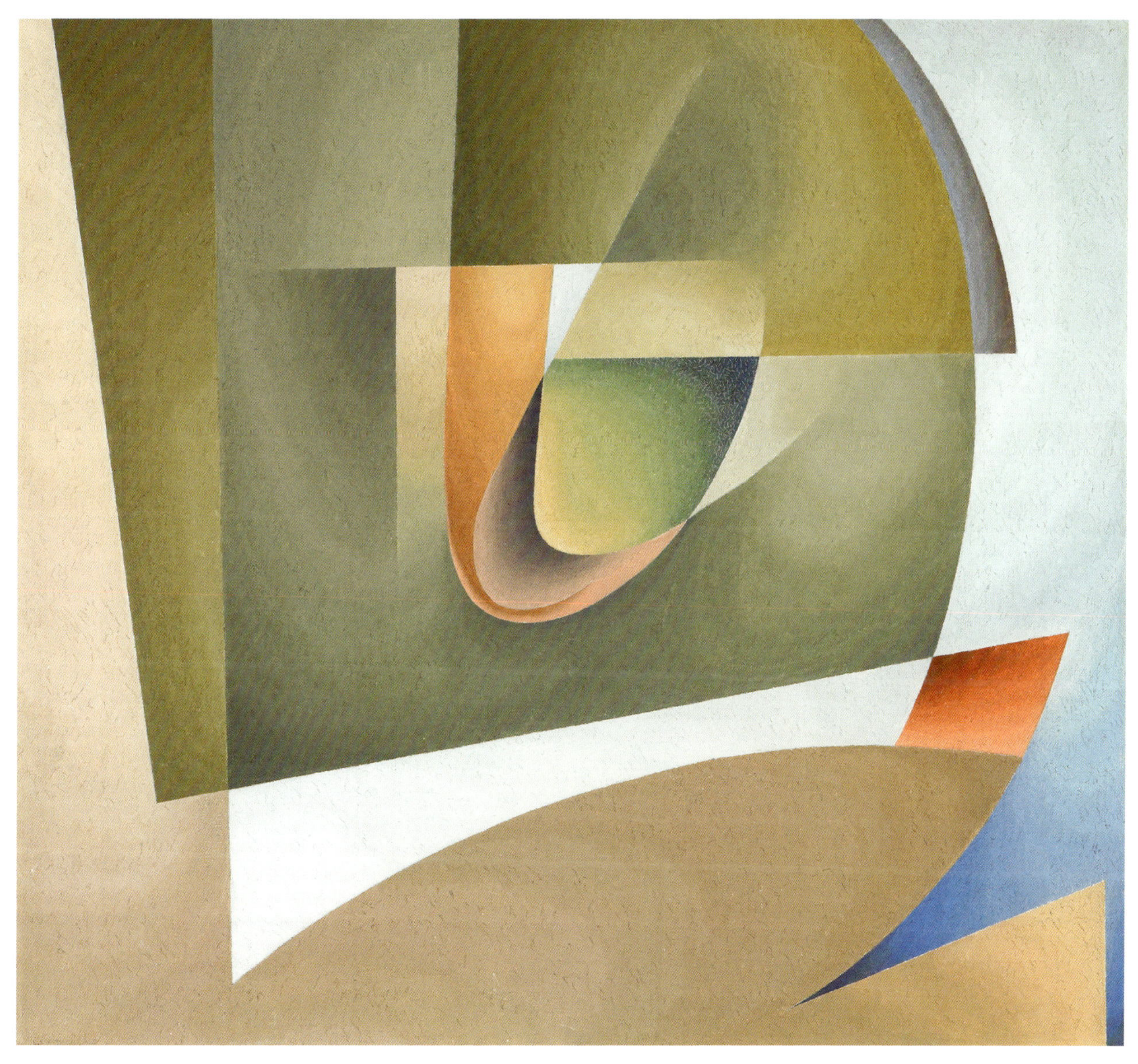

Brazil, c. 1950–51
oil on canvas
50.8 × 56 cm

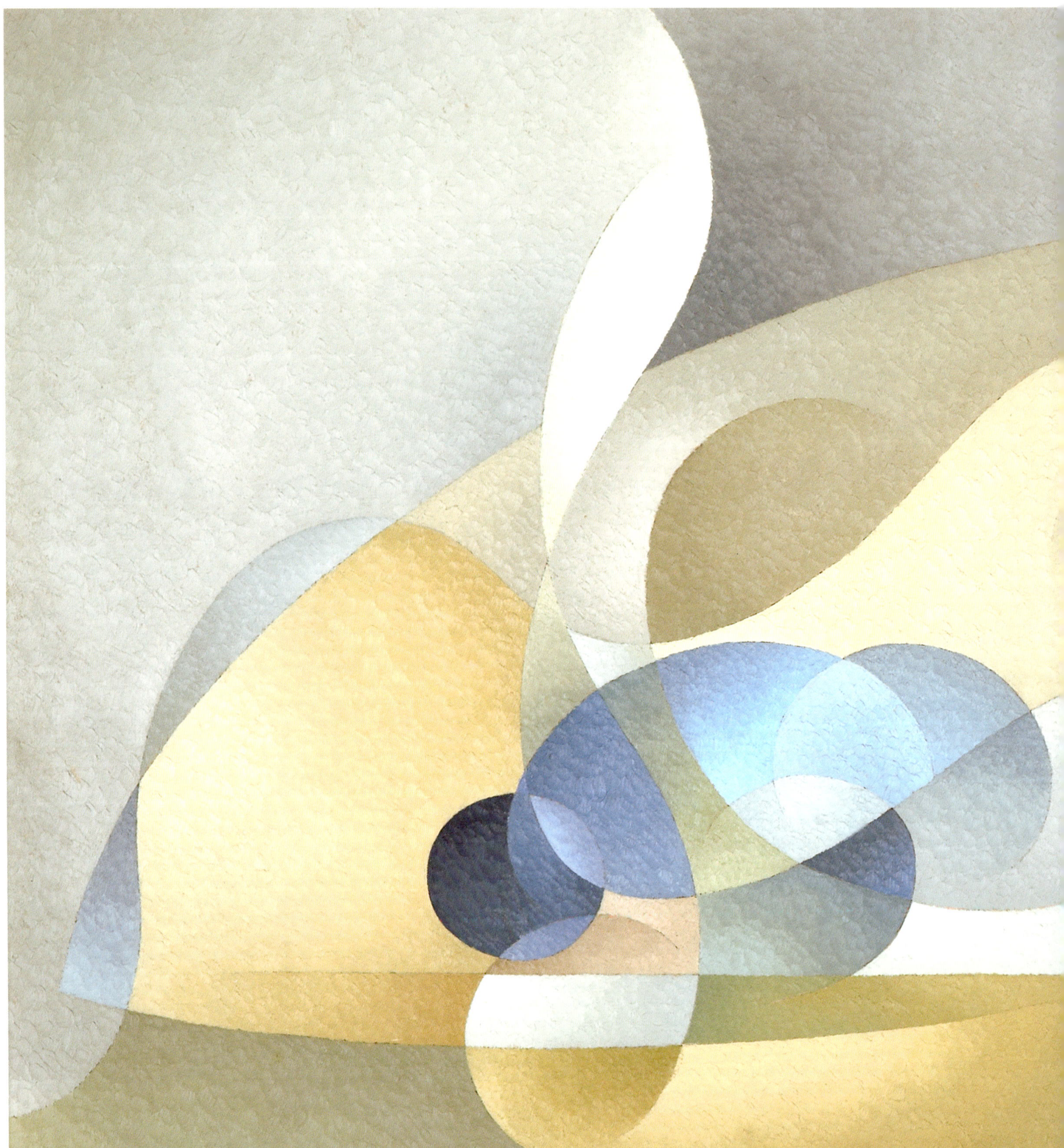

Abstract in Blue and Gold, 1954
oil on hardboard
44.5 × 69.5 cm

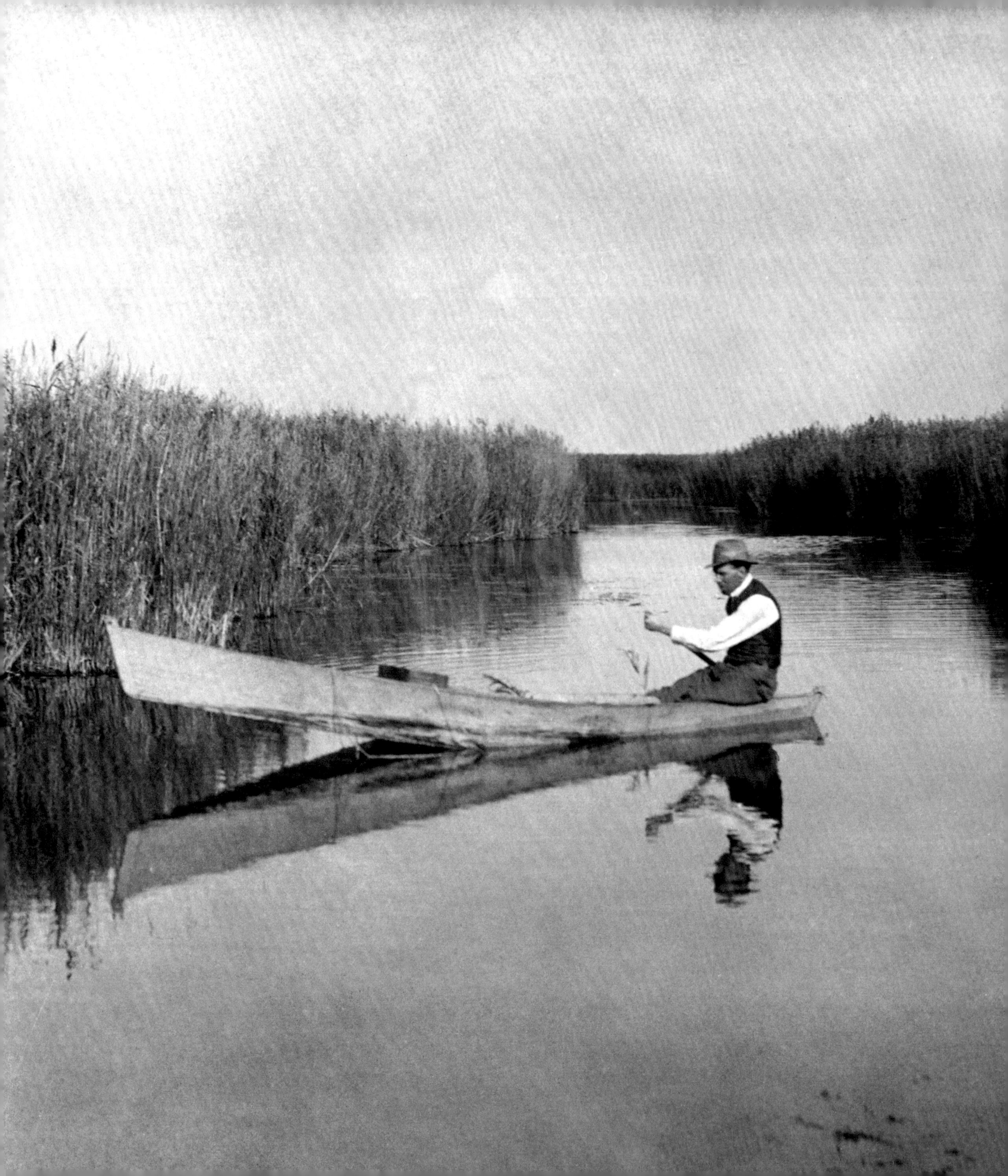

CHRONOLOGY

MICHAEL PARKE-TAYLOR

ABBREVIATIONS

AGT Art Gallery of Toronto (later Art Gallery of Ontario)
CGP Canadian Group of Painters
NGC National Gallery of Canada, Ottawa
OSA Ontario Society of Artists
RCA Royal Canadian Academy of Arts
WAG Winnipeg Art Gallery
WSA Winnipeg School of Art

1890

MARCH 17: Lionel LeMoine FitzGerald born in Winnipeg, MB, to Lionel Henry FitzGerald (1864–1943) and Isabella (Belle) Hicks (1864–1940).

1890–c. 1905

FitzGerald family, including LeMoine's siblings, Jack (1893–after 1969) and Geraldine (1896–1969), live in Winnipeg; childhood summer vacations spent at maternal grandparents' farm near Snowflake, MB.

1898

Attends Isbister Public School, 310 Vaughan Street. Grade 3 teacher introduces him to Perry Pictures, reproductions of art masterpieces.

1903

Attends Somerset School, 775 Sherbrook Street. In Grade 7 enjoys drawing lessons from exercise book *Prang's New Graded Course in Drawing for Canadian Schools.*

1904

AUGUST: Attends Victoria Public School, 110 Ellen Street, and graduates from Grade 8. Although passes entrance examinations for admission to a collegiate institute (August 10, 1904), FitzGerald works in August as an office boy in wholesale drug office of Martin, Bole and Wynne. Remains with this firm until 1906.

1905

OCTOBER: Winnipeg Public Library (then the Carnegie Library) opens at 380 William Avenue. FitzGerald discovers John Ruskin's *Elements of Drawing* and other books on art such as Holman Hunt's two-volume *Pre-Raphaelitism and the Pre-Raphaelite Brotherhood.* Studies reproductions of paintings by John Constable and J.M.W. Turner.

OPPOSITE
FitzGerald at Oak Point Lake, Manitoba, October 1915
University of Manitoba Archives & Special Collections 17.0190

1906

Makes watercolour copy of reproduction of a work thought to be by R.P. Bonington, *A Street in Rouen*, which he finds in an article by Henri Frantz, "The Art of Richard Parkes Bonington," in *The Studio: An Illustrated Magazine of Fine & Applied Art* 33, no. 140 (November 1904): 99–111. Later in life emphasizes to art critic Robert Ayre how important this text and illustrations were to his development.

MID-JULY 1906: At Winnipeg Industrial Exhibition wins second prize with *Drawing—Copy* (unidentified).

Works as a junior clerk with real estate and brokerage firm Osler, Hammond and Nanton, 440 Main Street, until 1908. Spends short period in a commercial art studio before returning to brokerage firm.

1908

LATE 1908: Shares studio expenses and rent in Chamber of Commerce Building with Nigel S. Wigston, an employee of Alexander Samuel Keszthelyi's School of Fine Arts, Winnipeg.

1909

MARCH 2–31; APRIL 1–30; JULY 1–31: Pays $6 monthly fee to register for evening life classes at Keszthelyi School of Fine Arts, Winnipeg. Keszthelyi gives instruction in "Drawing and Painting from the living model, Decorating, Designing and Portraiture." School is located on second floor, Stobart Block, on Portage Avenue.

DECEMBER: Meets Felicia (Vally) Wright (1883?–1962), a trained soprano from Ottawa.

1910

C. AUGUST 16–OCTOBER 26: FitzGerald stays with an aunt and uncle in Chicago while attempting to find work, most likely as a commercial artist. Probably visits Art Institute of Chicago. Has his photo portrait taken by Krauss Studio, Chicago (p. 199). No further details exist of this period other than letters from his parents. Is urged by his mother to return home and "give up the idea of going in for art" (October 26).

1911

In Winnipeg works again for Osler, Hammond and Nanton but lists his occupation in *Henderson's Winnipeg City Directory* as "artist" at Bijou Theatre Block, 494½ Main Street, rooms 27–28.

Exhibits professionally for first time at public library in group show organized by Women's Art Association. Contributes three pictures, including *Three Trees* (unidentified).

AUGUST 22–FEBRUARY 1912: Vally arrives home in Ottawa (August 22) and writes numerous letters to FitzGerald in Winnipeg (until February 1912).

NOVEMBER: Becomes friends with Scottish landscape painter Donald Macquarrie, who opened a studio in Winnipeg in 1910. In 1912 they share studio space at 416 Chamber of Commerce Building.

1912

Continues to work as junior clerk at Osler, Hammond and Nanton.

MARCH 15: Vally leaves Ottawa for Winnipeg.

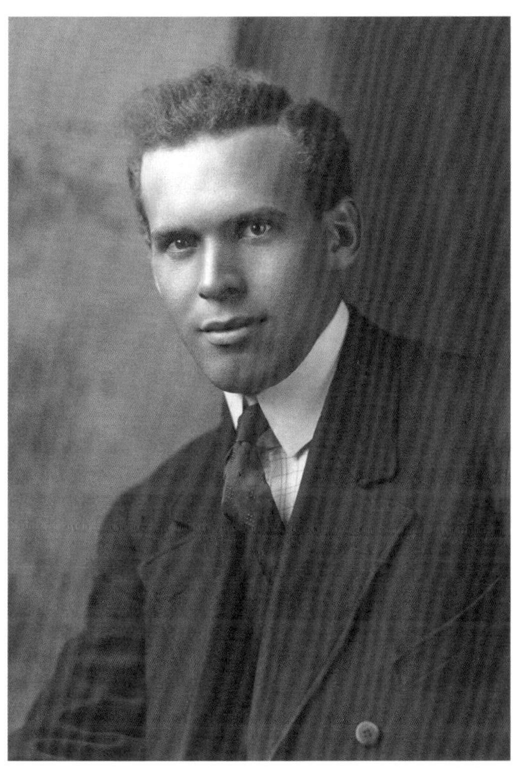

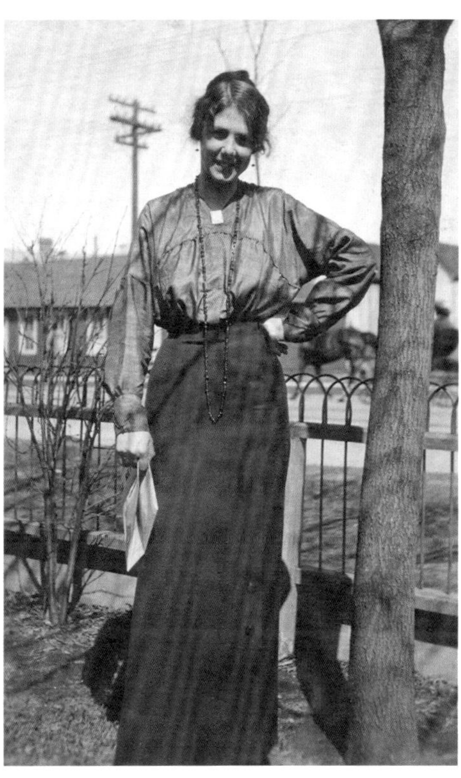

LEFT
LeMoine FitzGerald, 1910, Krauss Studio, Chicago
Lionel LeMoine FitzGerald fonds, PC 241 (A2009-016), Box 1, Folder 1 / University of Manitoba Archives & Special Collections, Winnipeg

RIGHT
Felicia (Vally) FitzGerald, c. 1912
Lionel LeMoine FitzGerald fonds, PC 241 (A2009-016), Box 1, Folder 3 / University of Manitoba Archives & Special Collections, Winnipeg

JULY–AUGUST: Sketching trip by canoe with Donald Macquarrie to Selkirk and Lockport, MB.

NOVEMBER 22: Marries Felicia (Vally) Wright at St. Andrew's Presbyterian Church, Winnipeg. The couple elopes to avoid interference from FitzGerald's parents. Live at 462 St. Mary Avenue.

Leaves office job around November 25 to work in commercial art, possibly for Stovel Company, an engraving, lithography, and printing firm. Describes this period as "the beginning of nine years spent in a wide variety of work, including advertising drawings, mural paintings and sketches for interior decorations, posters and window backgrounds, stage scenery, lettering and so on" (L.L. FitzGerald application for John Simon Guggenheim Memorial Foundation fellowship, 1940).

DECEMBER 16: Winnipeg Museum of Fine Arts (later called Winnipeg Art Gallery) opens at Main Street and Water Avenue. Contributes landscape painting (unidentified) to inaugural exhibition, *Royal Canadian Academy Exhibition of Paintings*.

Macquarrie appointed first curator of museum and holds position until March 1913, when he is replaced by artist Alexander Musgrove.

1913

SUMMER: FitzGerald and Vally live in tent on bank of Red River near Linden Avenue in suburb East Kildonan. Studio address is 108 Union Trust Building, Winnipeg.

WSA opens on Main Street next to museum, with Musgrove as first principal.

NOVEMBER 20: Exhibits for first time with RCA. Contributes *The Dying Embers of Autumn* (unidentified) to *Thirty-fifth Annual Exhibition of the Royal Canadian Academy of Arts* at the Art Association of Montreal.

Is included in eleven RCA exhibitions from 1913 to 1921 (excepting 1917).

1914

MAY 8–15: FitzGerald and Macquarrie close studio with private exhibition and sale of oils and watercolours.

JULY 16: Wins bronze medal at Winnipeg Industrial Fair.

AUGUST: Holidays in East and visits Ottawa.

Executes fourteen small monoprints that reflect a Barbizon/Corot influence possibly inspired by Macquarrie's painting and an *Exhibition of Scottish Watercolours and of a Loan Collection of Pictures* at WAG (September to November).

A.O. Brigden arrives from England to manage newly opened printing firm Brigdens of Winnipeg. Over the years Brigdens employs significant Winnipeg artists including Caven Atkins, Eric Bergman, Pauline Boutal, Fritz Brandtner, Charles Comfort, Alison Newton, Philip Surrey, and Gordon Smith. FitzGerald never works for Brigdens but is close friends with A.O. Brigden, soon his patron.

1915

FitzGerald and Vally move to 18 Evanson Street.

From 1915 to 1918, FitzGerald works as freelance commercial artist for clients such as Clark Brothers and Company, Richardson Brothers, Russell-Lang's Bookshop, Hudson's Bay Company, Canadian Pacific Railway, and Government of Manitoba. He is commissioned to design Rolls of Honour for La Verendrye School, Pilot Mound, Wesley College, and Red River Chapter of IODE to commemorate those who served in the First World War.

1916

MARCH 30: Son, Lionel Edward FitzGerald, born.

1918

FEBRUARY 18: Works in display department of T. Eaton Company for $30 a week. Describes wage as "slavery." Designs window and interior displays as well as annual Christmas parade.

APRIL 4–MAY 11: Exhibits painting *Late Fall, Manitoba*, 1917 (p. 10), at joint exhibition of RCA and OSA at Art Museum of Toronto. This leads to first major purchase of career when NGC buys picture for $275 (April 8). Exhibits with OSA in five exhibitions—1918, 1921, 1925, 1927, and 1931.

1919

MARCH 25: Daughter, Patricia LeMoine FitzGerald, born.

MAY 15: Winnipeg General Strike declared. Bloody Saturday, June 21.

1920

JANUARY 10–17: Visits Chicago; likely goes to Art Institute of Chicago.

MAY–JUNE: Assists American artist Augustus Vincent Tack with installing Tack's mural in dome of Manitoba Legislative Building, Winnipeg (unveiled July 15).

SEPTEMBER 17–26: Holidays in East Kildonan and makes at least eighteen sketches.

Works for interior decorating Studio of J.E. Dolen, 310 Assiniboine Avenue.

1921

MARCH 4–APRIL 10: Exhibits Impressionist-inspired painting *Summer, East Kildonan*, 1920 (no. 45, $375) (p. 34), at Forty-ninth Annual Exhibition of the Ontario Society of Artists at AGT.

SEPTEMBER 10–27: First solo exhibition at WAG. Designs catalogue listing forty-one works—thirty oils, nine pastels, and two decorative paintings. Sells first major painting, *The Prairie, Summer* (now *Summer Afternoon, The Prairie*), 1921 (p. ix), to WAG for $300. Exhibition reviewed by William Arthur Deacon, "Pastel Shades—A Few Impressions of the Work of a Young Winnipeg Artist" ([*Manitoba*] *Free Press Evening Bulletin*, September 12, 1921). Shorter version of text reprinted in William Arthur Deacon, *Pens and Pirates* (Toronto: Ryerson Press, 1923), 251–57.

SEPTEMBER: Group of Seven member Franz (Frank) H. Johnston appointed principal of WSA. Holds position until 1924.

OCTOBER 15–DECEMBER 10: Exhibits *Summer, East Kildonan*, in *Canadian Art Today* at WAG. Catalogue describes him as "Winnipeg's native son, whose studies have been greatly to his own credit. He specializes in the painting of light."

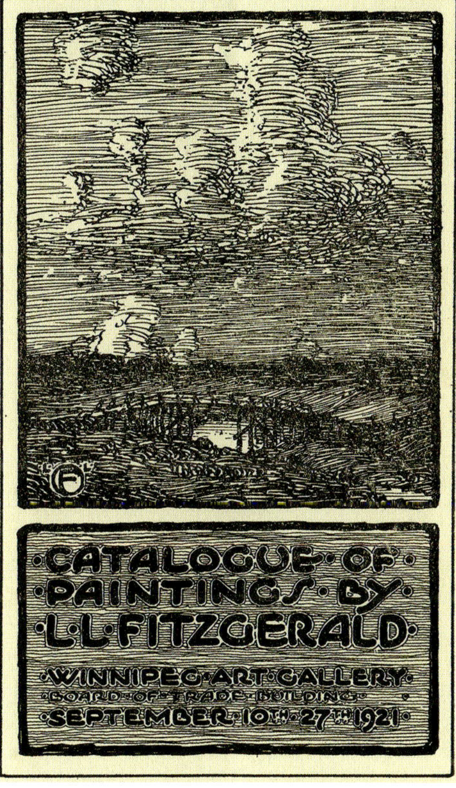

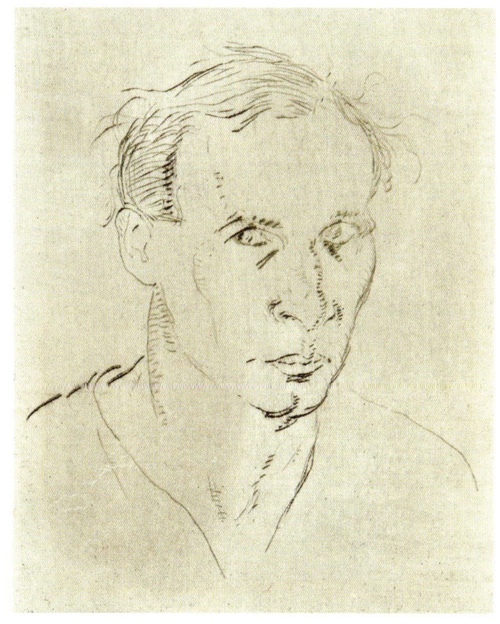

TOP
Winnipeg Art Gallery, *Catalogue of Paintings by L.L. FitzGerald*, September 10–27, 1921
Lionel LeMoine FitzGerald fonds, MSS 287 (A2009-016), Box 8, Folder 1 / University of Manitoba Archives & Special Collections, Winnipeg

BOTTOM
Self-Portrait No. 1, n.d.
drypoint on paper
sheet: 14.7 × 13 cm

OCTOBER 17–DECEMBER: Family leaves Winnipeg for Eastern Canada on October 17. Vally finds employment at Rip Van Winkle Tea Inn near Montreal. FitzGerald continues alone to New York, arriving around November 29. Rents room from Mrs. Rifflard, 178 West 81st Street. Starts classes at Art Students League December 5, taking four courses from Boardman Robinson, including "Drawing and Pictorial Design," December to March 1922.

Loan Exhibition of Impressionist and Post-Impressionist Paintings at Metropolitan Museum of Art had closed on September 15, a month prior to his arrival. Exhibition had created a furor around Cézanne's "degenerate" paintings.

1922

MARCH: Visits *Exhibition of Modern American and European Paintings* at Wanamaker Gallery of Modern Decorative Arts, New York (March 9–31). Sees works by American Precisionists (Charles Demuth, Charles Sheeler, and Preston Dickinson) as well as Pablo Picasso, André Derain, Albert Gleizes, Jean Metzinger, Louis Marcoussis, Diego Rivera, Mikhail Larionov, and Natalia Goncharova, among others.

Studies with Kenneth Hayes Miller at Art Students League, taking month-long course "Life Drawing and Painting for Men." Leaves New York March 31, although fees at Art Students League are paid until end of May 1922.

APRIL–JULY: Reunites with family in Montreal. In June paints Cézanne-inspired *Rivière-des-Prairies, P.Q.*, 1922, which features Rip Van Winkle Tea Inn. Family arrive home in Winnipeg July 19. Continues commercial work for Eaton's and interior decorations for J.E. Dolen.

1923

FEBRUARY 9: Mitchell and Copp (jewellery store) opens at 286 Portage Avenue with mural decoration by FitzGerald, under supervision of J.E. Dolen, representing origin of jewellery design (no longer extant).

APRIL: Begins to work seriously on drypoint prints. Submits to various print exhibitions in Canada and United States from 1924 to 1931. During career makes sixty-four drypoints and twenty-eight linocuts (see pp. 152, 154, 155).

SEPTEMBER: Advertises as L.L. FitzGerald Decorations, Studio 199 Oakdale Place.

SEPTEMBER 22: Baroni's café and tea room opens at Portage Avenue and Donald Street with mural decoration by FitzGerald featuring frieze with sixty figures (no longer extant).

1924

Moves to 160 Lyle Street (St. James neighbourhood) where resides until death in 1956. Lives directly opposite artist Hubert Valentine Fanshaw at 161 Lyle Street.

SEPTEMBER: Begins to teach "Antique, Still Life and Design" at WSA as assistant to principal C. Keith Gebhardt.

1925

FEBRUARY: From mid- to late 1920s designs sets and costumes for local theatre company known as the Community Players of Winnipeg. Designs stage setting for *Aria da Capo* by Edna St. Vincent Millay (February 19–21).

MAY 9–OCTOBER: Exhibits *Summer Afternoon, The Prairie*, 1921, in *British Empire Exhibition, Canadian Section of Fine Arts*, Fine Arts Galleries, Wembley Park, UK. Prestigious event noted in Winnipeg press: "This is not only a fine compliment to the artist, who made Winnipeg his choice as a fitting place to be born in, but also a reflex luster upon his native city" ("Around the Art Gallery," *Winnipeg Tribune*, March 21).

JUNE–JULY: Trip to Calgary. Sketches in Bowness Park (June 26) and visits Calgary Stampede (July 7). Sketches Lake Louise, Victoria Glacier (July 16), and spends summer in Banff, AB.

AUGUST 15: Writes Vally from Snowflake.

OCTOBER: Designs stage settings for *The Man Who Married a Dumb Wife* by Anatole France and *The Dark Lady of the Sonnets* by George Bernard Shaw (October 22–24), Community Players of Winnipeg.

1926

JANUARY 2: Manitoba Society of Artists established at studio of Walter J. Phillips and Alexander Musgrove, 310 Assiniboine Avenue. FitzGerald included in first exhibition at Richardson Brothers Gallery, 332 Main Street (February 20). Exhibits every year with this group from 1926 to 1956, excepting 1949.

AUGUST 11: Train trip to Snowflake; makes series of sketches in small-town Manitoba—Osborne, Morris, Rosenfeld, Altona, Gretna, Winkler, Morden, Horndean, Plum Coulee, Thornhill, Darlingford, Manitou, Domain, and other locations southwest of Winnipeg.

Writes Vally from Manitou and later, from Snowflake, sends sketches to her.[1]

AUGUST 12: Visits Hannah, ND.

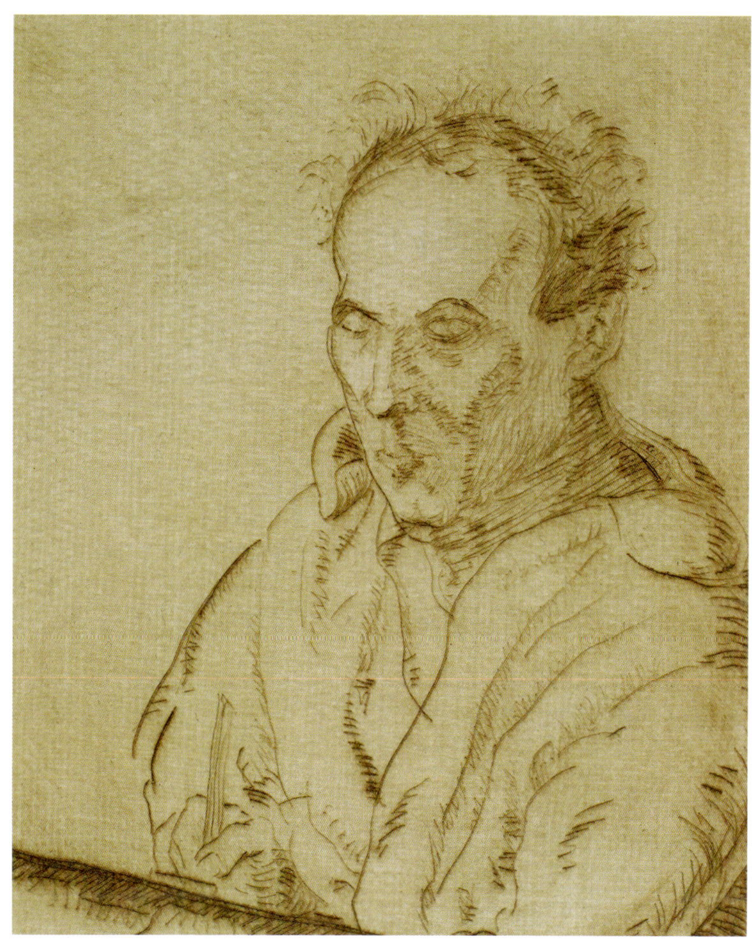

Self-Portrait No. 2, c. 1927
drypoint in brown on laid paper
23.1 × 16.5 cm;
plate: 10.5 × 8.9 cm

NOVEMBER 13: Meeting of Russian Rehearsal Club at FitzGerald's residence. Group discusses amateur movement in Russian theatre and studies *The Cherry Orchard* by Anton Chekhov.

1927

MARCH 3: Writes "Notes on Russian Art," which includes lengthy passage transcribed by FitzGerald from chapter 5 of Leo Tolstoy's *What Is Art?* (1897) for possible lecture series.

MARCH 4–27: Exhibits *Williamson's Garage*, 1927 (p. 132) ($200), in *Ontario Society of Artists: Fifty-fifth Annual Exhibition* at AGT.

APRIL 10–MAY 10: Exhibits *Après-midi d'été* (*Summer Afternoon, The Prairie*), no. 37, in *Exposition d'art canadien* at Musée du Jeu de Paume, Paris.

JULY 28–AUGUST 2: Snowflake.

1928

JANUARY: First solo exhibition in Eastern Canada presented at Arts and Letters Club, Toronto. Artist Bertram Brooker buys crayon drawing of tree trunks for $12, which he writes about months later in column The Seven Arts, *Ottawa Citizen*, August 17, 1929. Lawren Harris writes FitzGerald for first time: "I particularly like the way you extricate a suggestion of celestial structure and spirit from objective nature in your drawings" (undated letter, likely January 1928).

APRIL 11–14: Designs stage settings for *Sea Woman's Cloak* by Amélie Rives, Community Players of Winnipeg.

JULY 13–23: Writes Vally from Snowflake.

SUMMER: Visits Gebhardt's parents in Cheboygan, MI. On way home stops in Minneapolis, MN.

OCTOBER 17–20: Designs sets and costumes for *Henry IV* by Luigi Pirandello, Community Players of Winnipeg.

OCTOBER 27: Brooker mentions FitzGerald for first time in column: "Since writing my first letter I have been in Winnipeg for a few days . . . I had intended to look up the artist Fitzgerald [*sic*] while in Winnipeg, whose tree drawings I admire tremendously, but illness prevented me" (Brooker, The Seven Arts, *Winnipeg Tribune*, October 27, 1928).

Artist Fritz Brandtner emigrates from Danzig, Poland, to Winnipeg, working first as a house painter, then for Eaton's, and eventually for Brigdens. Enjoys friendship with FitzGerald, communicating a first-hand knowledge of German Expressionism, Constructivism, and the Bauhaus.

1929

JANUARY 28–FEBRUARY 28: Exhibits *Williamson's Garage* and *Winter, Oakdale Place* (unidentified) in [Fourth] Annual Exhibition of Canadian Art at NGC. Four months later NGC purchases *Williamson's Garage* (June 1929). Painting depicts garage owned by Milton J. Williamson, 172 Lyle Street. Exhibits in Annual Exhibition of Canadian Art at NGC every year from 1929 to 1933.

JANUARY 30–31; FEBRUARY 1–2: Consulting artist to set design by John Russell, *The Cradle Song*, Community Players of Winnipeg.

JULY–AUGUST: Brooker meets FitzGerald for first time when visiting Winnipeg in late July and August. Spend three days talking "voluminously" and sketch together on three occasions during Brooker's month-long trip to Manitoba.

AUGUST 19: Brooker reports to Harris about visit to FitzGerald: "He is greatly neglected in Winnipeg, but seems not to mind it—is very quiet, self-contained, controlled and quite resigned and even happy to be left alone. Nevertheless, I could see that he enjoyed talks with people of his own kind. It would do him good if you could see him. He seems to have little, if any, interest in metaphysics, but draws his sustenance from the ground and from his recognition of the relationship between all varieties

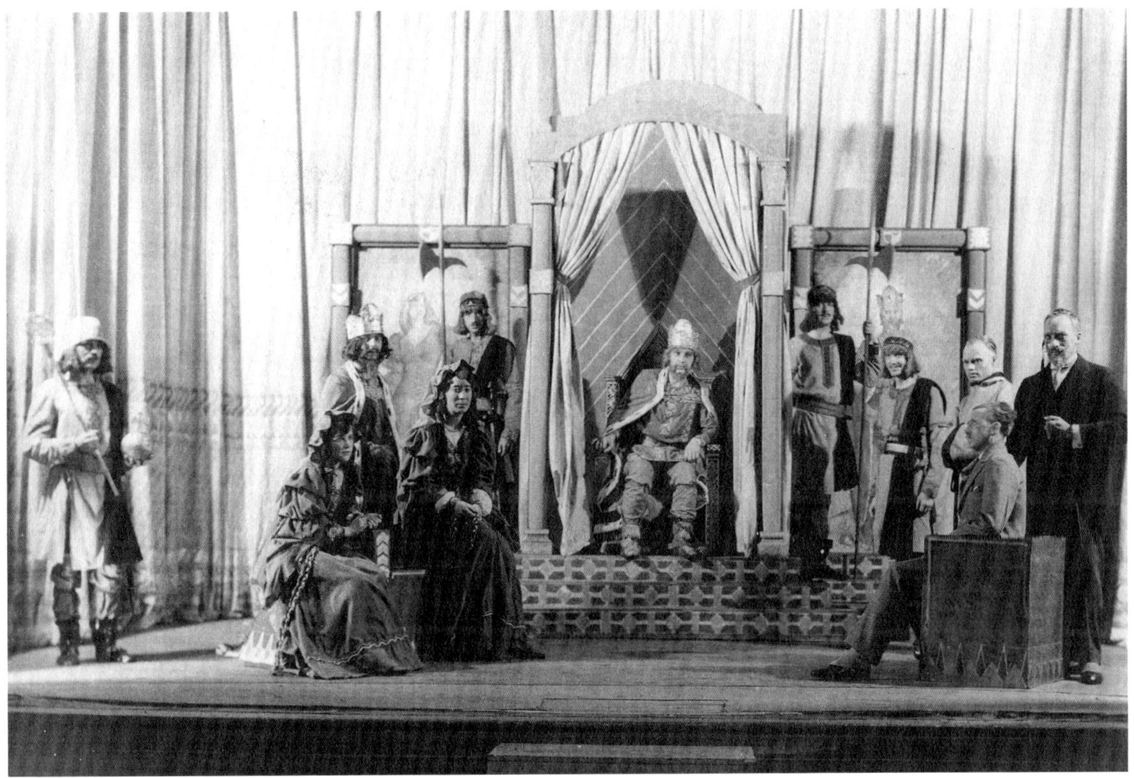

Cast of the Community Players of Winnipeg production of *Henry IV* by Luigi Pirandello, October 17–20, 1928
Lionel LeMoine FitzGerald fonds, PC 241 (A2009-016), Box 2, Folder 3 / University of Manitoba Archives & Special Collections, Winnipeg

of form—particularly the structure and rhythms in men and trees" (Brooker letter to Harris, August 19, 1929).

SEPTEMBER 2: Writes Vally from Snowflake.

SEPTEMBER 7: Appointed principal of WSA, replacing C. Keith Gebhardt, who returns to US.

SEPTEMBER 14: Brooker writes about meeting FitzGerald in Winnipeg during summer in column The Seven Arts, *Winnipeg Tribune*, September 14, 1929. Text is first published a week earlier in *Ottawa Citizen*, September 7, 1929.

FALL: FitzGerald completes decorative murals for room in St. Charles Hotel, Winnipeg.

C. DECEMBER 20–C. FEBRUARY 14, 1930: Second solo exhibition in Eastern Canada, at Aldine House, J.M. Dent and Sons, Toronto. Show includes three oil paintings, one watercolour, and twenty-three drawings. Brooker and Harris each buy a drawing, for $35 and $30, respectively. Brooker writes FitzGerald to report on purchases: "He took the one with the very large house in the centre with large trees at the left. I took the one of the trees just off Portage Ave.—the one you were painting up when I was there" (December 28, 1929). Exhibition is reviewed by Jehanne Bietry Salinger: "Here is beauty consciously created with subjects of practically no significance, yet the final achievement is arresting and important" ("Comment on Art," *Canadian Forum* 10, no. 114 [March 1930]: 209–11). Brooker writes about review in agreement with Salinger's observation that FitzGerald's drawings have a beauty akin to music of Bach and César Franck (Brooker, The Seven Arts, *Winnipeg Tribune*, March 15, 1930).

DECEMBER: Brooker publishes *Yearbook of the Arts in Canada 1928–1929* (Toronto: MacMillan, 1929) and includes reproduction of *Williamson's Garage* (plate XIII), 1927.

Begins painting *Doc Snyder's House*, 1931 (p. 146), outdoors in his yard in freezing temperatures during Christmas holidays. Dr. Victor L. Snyder lives at 152 Lyle Street.

DECEMBER 29: Harris writes FitzGerald to express interest in show at Dent's. "Sometime later I will try and write down what little I know about abstract painting. You seem to suggest a feeling in that direction. I would like to know what you feel."

1930

FEBRUARY: Organizes exhibition of fifteen oil sketches by Harris at WSA.

MARCH 9–30: Exhibits *Williamson's Garage*, 1927, and *Poplar Woods (Poplars)*, 1929 (p. 68), in *Exhibition of Paintings by Contemporary Canadian Artists under the Auspices of the American Federation of Arts*. Exhibition opens at Corcoran Art Gallery of Art, Washington, DC. FitzGerald visits show in June 1930 at Grand Central Art Galleries, New York.

APRIL 5–27: Invited to exhibit with Group of Seven for first time. Submits *Oakdale Place* and *Snow Laden Branches* (both paintings unidentified) to *Exhibition of the Group of Seven; Canadian Society of Painters in Water Colour; Society of Canadian Painter-Etchers; The Toronto Camera Club* at AGT.

JUNE 2: Departs Winnipeg to visit six major American cities and Eastern Canada. Itinerary includes Minneapolis, Chicago, Pittsburgh, Washington, Philadelphia, New York City, Montreal, Ottawa, and Toronto. Records events of American trip in daily diary ending on July 1 in New York. Travels to Montreal, Ottawa, and Toronto in July where spends week at Brooker's. Brooker describes Toronto stay in The Seven Arts, *Winnipeg Tribune*, September 6, 1930. FitzGerald meets J.E.H. MacDonald and Arthur Lismer and has photo portrait taken by M.O. Hammond (p. 207).

JULY 12: FitzGerald and Brooker sketch together at Dentonia Park, Toronto residence of art patrons Dr. Harold Tovell and his wife, Ruth Massey Tovell.

SUMMER: Playwright Herman Voaden and artist Lowrie Warrener visit FitzGerald in Winnipeg on way home to Toronto from California. Brooker writes FitzGerald to recount conversation with Voaden: "We talked much of you. He feels you are big and quiet and close to the earth—a real product of the prairies. We both feel you to be a very natural growth" (October 17, 1930).

NOVEMBER 10–DECEMBER: Organizes exhibition at WSA of forty-three sketches by Lismer. School purchases two drawings for permanent collection: *Pine Bough*, n.d., and *Cod Fishers Shacks—Paspébiac—P.Q.*, 1928. Lismer painting *Quebec Uplands*, 1926, gifted to WSA by its students 1928–29.

DECEMBER: Designs sets for *The Chester Mysteries*, produced by Community Players' director Edith Sinclair and presented at Church of St. Michael and All Angels.

1931

C. FEBRUARY–MID-MARCH: Exhibition of oil sketches (approximately twenty to twenty-five) by J.E.H. MacDonald at WSA.

MARCH 26: Brooker writes to ask FitzGerald about purchasing his *Still Life*, c. 1924–25 (p. 120). Painting is admired by Lismer, Harris, and Charles Comfort. Brooker eventually acquires picture by mailing $100 deposit in January 1932 with promise to send more. Lent by Brooker to 1936 retrospective exhibition of Group of Seven at NGC.

JUNE 13: Writes Brooker that has finished painting *Doc Snyder's House* started late December 1929.

AUGUST 4–25: Writes Vally from Snowflake.

SEPTEMBER: Irene Heywood (1912–1989) enrols in day classes at WSA, 1931–34, evening school, 1935–36. FitzGerald and Heywood become involved in secret love affair likely in 1939 when Heywood lives in Brandon, MB.

OCTOBER 29: Report to Board of Directors at WSA that Harris has donated oil sketch of *Lake McArthur, Rocky Mountains*, c. 1925, to permanent collection.

LATE NOVEMBER: Suffers from pneumonia until March 1932.

DECEMBER 4–24: Exhibits *Doc Snyder's House* for first time at invitation to show with Group of Seven for second time in *Seascapes and*

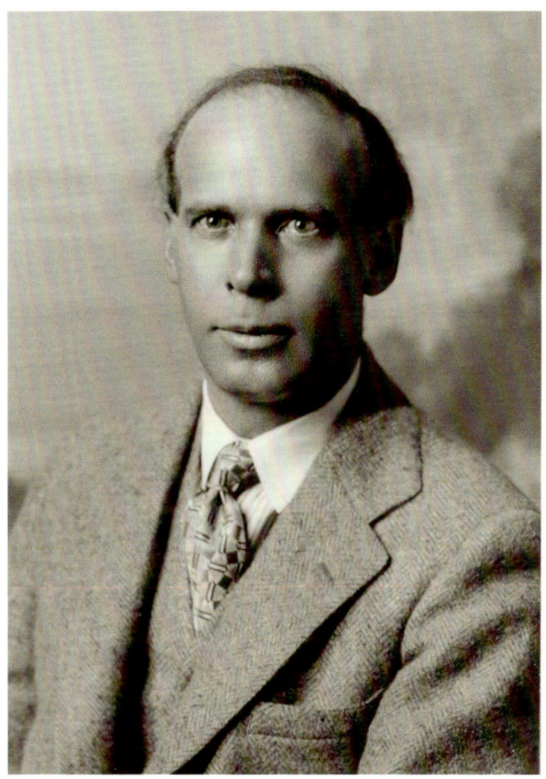

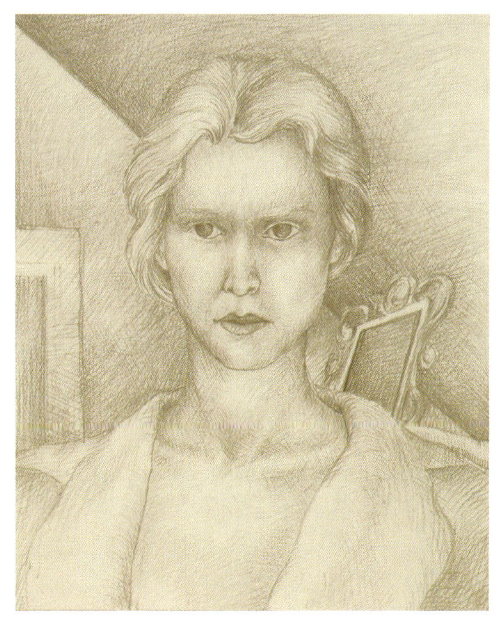

TOP
Photo of FitzGerald by M.O. Hammond, Toronto, 1930
Lionel LeMoine FitzGerald fonds, PC 241 (A2009-016), Box 1, Folder 1 / University of Manitoba Archives & Special Collections, Winnipeg

BOTTOM
IRENE HEYWOOD HEMSWORTH (1912–1989)
Self-Portrait, June 3, 1934
Gift of Irene Heywood Hemsworth and Wade Hemsworth / School of Art Gallery, University of Manitoba, Winnipeg / 37-0001

Dining room at Batterwood House, Vincent Massey residence near Port Hope, Ontario, 1932, showing two FitzGeralds, *Landscape with Trees* and *Farmyard*, both 1931, on the left

Canadian Art 21, no. 2 (March/April 1964): 100

Water-Fronts by Contemporary Artists; the Group of Seven at AGT.

1932

JANUARY 10: Brooker writes FitzGerald and notes that Toronto modernist painter Kathleen Munn admired *Doc Snyder's House* in Group of Seven exhibition. Brooker thinks canvas expresses "so perfectly the personality of the artist . . . it was almost like seeing your face and talking to you again to see it . . . long contemplation and patient workmanship in it."

JANUARY 16: W.J. Phillips reviews A.Y. Jackson exhibition organized by FitzGerald at WSA ("Art and Artists," *Winnipeg Tribune*, January 16, 1932). Jackson's painting *House at Cap aux Oies*, 1931, acquired by WSA.

MARCH 3: Art patron Vincent Massey of Toronto writes thank-you letter to FitzGerald regarding two paintings purchased from artist on recent trip to Winnipeg: *Farmyard*, 1931 (p. 49), and *Landscape with Trees*, 1931.

MARCH 5–APRIL 5: Exhibits *Doc Snyder's House* in *Exhibition of Paintings by Contemporary Canadian Artists* at International Art Center of Roerich Museum, New York. Receives letter from Eric Brown, director of NGC, regarding purchase of painting for $350 (March 21). FitzGerald notes price should have been $500. Writes to Brown: "I feel that it is the most complete thing that I have finished so far and it is nice that you are going to have it" (March 29).

MARCH 24: Lismer on lecture tour of eleven cities, including Winnipeg. Lismer visits WSA and FitzGerald has the "pleasure of a long chat with him" (by March 24). This meeting is followed by letter from Lismer to invite FitzGerald to

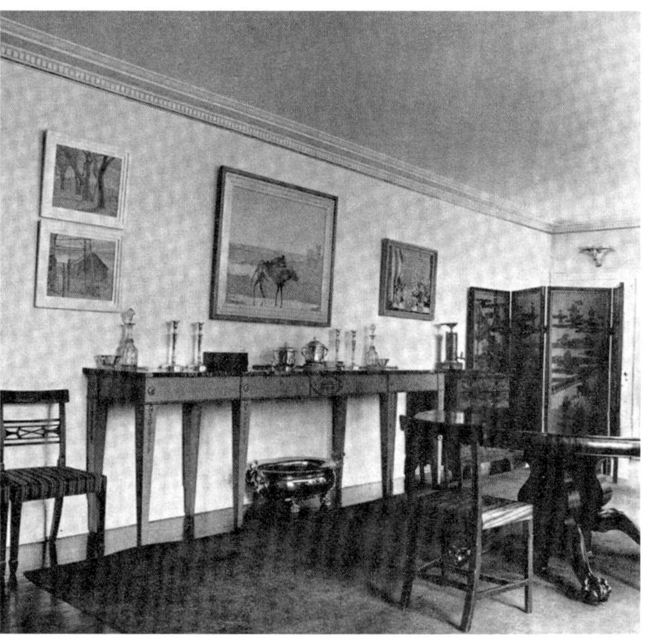

join Group of Seven (May 24, 1932). FitzGerald accepts membership June 21. Group now comprises nine artists (Frank Johnston left in 1924): Franklin Carmichael, Lawren Harris, A.Y. Jackson, Arthur Lismer, J.E.H. MacDonald, Frederick Varley, A.J. Casson, Edwin Holgate, and FitzGerald.

JULY 6: FitzGerald writes H.O. McCurry, assistant director, NGC, to note his membership in Group of Seven: "I have been exhibiting with them for the last three years, it is very much more interesting being one of them and to feel a definite connection."

NOVEMBER 26: Death of J.E.H. MacDonald.

DECEMBER–EARLY JANUARY 1933: Exhibits two small paintings (unidentified) with Group of Seven as an official member for first and only time before their dissolution. Exhibition takes place at Hart House, University of Toronto. No catalogue published.

1933

JANUARY 1: Harris writes FitzGerald that Group of Seven has disbanded "to form a society of all the so-called modern painters in the country" called the Canadian Group of Painters.

AUGUST: Reproduction of *Doc Snyder's House* in article in prestigious German publication: "Moderne Malerei in Kanada," *Die Kunst fur alle: Malerei, Plastik, Graphik, Architektur* 48, no. 11 (August 1933): 347.

JUNE: Joins CGP as founding member and contributes three paintings to first show, *Exhibition of Paintings by the Canadian Group of Painters*, Heinz Art Salon, Heinz Ocean Pier, Atlantic City, NJ. Critic Frank Bagnall writes that *Broken Tree in Landscape*, 1931 (p. 53), "has a purity of form akin to the work of Georgia O'Keeffe," and *Apples, Still Life*, 1933 (p. 124), "is one of the bright gems of the show" (Frank Bagnall, "Canadian Artists' Show," *Saturday Night* 48, no. 50 [October 21, 1933]: 16).

1934

MARCH 8: Writes Ayre in Montreal to introduce Brandtner, who is about to move there from Winnipeg. Brandtner later writes FitzGerald that he has been in Montreal for two weeks and has connected with Ayre (April 4).

NOVEMBER 1: Hart House String Quartet performs in Winnipeg. Fitzgerald visits with members Harry Adaskin and Milton Blackstone. Adaskin acquires *The Pool*, 1934 (p. 187).

DECEMBER: WSA moves to northwest corner of Portage Avenue and Main Street (until September 1938).

1935

MAY 18–JUNE 1: Brooker organizes *Exhibition of Drawings by Kathleen Munn, LeMoine FitzGerald, Bertram Brooker* at Galleries of J. Merritt Malloney, Toronto. FitzGerald is represented by eighteen drawings.

JUNE 17: Writes Brooker about drawings: "The only way I can account for the extreme delicacy of the pencil drawings is because of the terrific light we have here. The drawings always look strong enough when I am working on them outside, otherwise I wouldn't be able to do them but when I get them home they have the feeling of having faded on the short trip."

NOVEMBER 17: FitzGerald and Vally drive their son, Edward, to New York, where he is studying.

DECEMBER 5: Writes Lismer about drawings made summer 1935 for Group of Seven retrospective at NGC in February 1936: "I picked out what I thought were the best from the group of drawings I did during the summer. The whole outfit were experimental and being so close to them, I am rather hazy as to their quality. The spirit of the open prairie is rather illusive but maybe something of its real meaning has crept in unconsciously. I have never before had quite such a lengthy session with it at any one time before. That is day after day."

1936

FEBRUARY 20–APRIL 15: Exhibits five paintings and fifteen drawings in *Retrospective Exhibition of Painting by Members of the Group of Seven, 1919–1933* at NGC. Exhibition includes *Doc Snyder's House, Assiniboine River, Silver Heights*, 1931, lent by A.O. Brigden; *Summer*, 1931, lent by Hart House; and *Still Life*, c. 1924–25 (p. 120), lent by Brooker.

FitzGerald and Brooker, July 1936

Collection of the Winnipeg Art Gallery, Clara Lander Library, L.L. FitzGerald fonds, ACC700.005.1.2 C / Photo: Ronald Hooper, courtesy of the Winnipeg Art Gallery

APRIL 22: Writes Eric Brown, NGC, that he is working mainly on drawing and has no paintings for forthcoming exhibitions. "I find it very difficult to keep up with the shows. I seem to require so much time to do even a small drawing that I only get through a very few things during the year even though I am working all the spare time I have. Too bad it takes so much of one's time to make a living."

JULY 16: Brooker leaves Toronto by train for Winnipeg to meet FitzGerald July 18–19. During stay, Brooker and FitzGerald are photographed together by amateur photographer Ronald Hooper.

SEPTEMBER 15–APRIL 16: Exhibits *Doc Snyder's House* in *Exhibition of Contemporary Canadian Painting* arranged on behalf of Carnegie Corporation of New York for seven-month circulation in Southern Dominions of the British Empire. Exhibition travels to Johannesburg, South Africa.

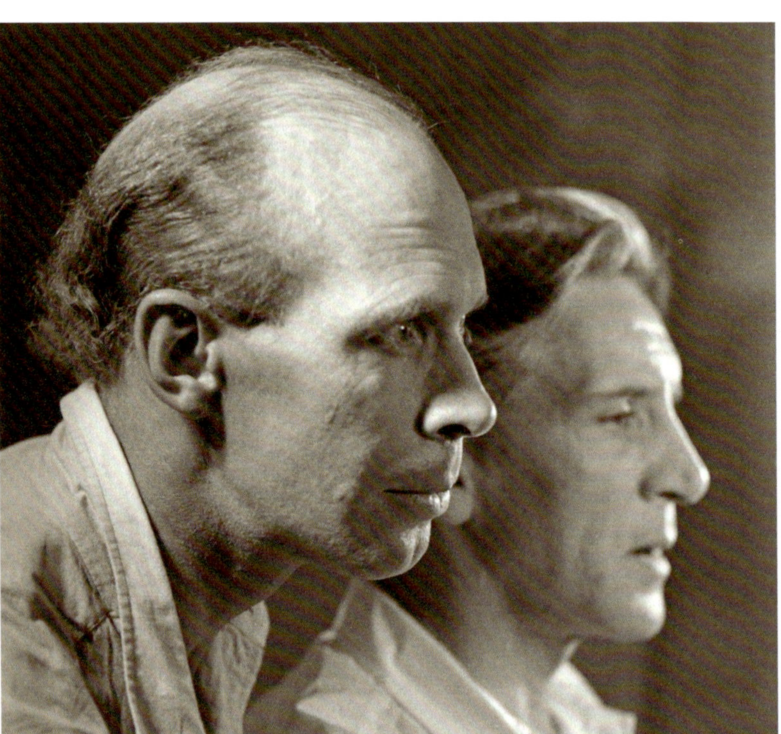

Brooker reproduces *Doc Snyder's House* in *Yearbook of the Arts in Canada, 1936* (Toronto: Macmillan, 1936), plate 1.

1937

MARCH 18: Writes H.O. McCurry, NGC, that has no paintings to contribute to forthcoming exhibitions because of focus on drawing. Notes that some recent drawings are "darn fine things with just as much in them as any painting I have done." Describes defined phases in development of an artist from growth to questioning and experiment.

DECEMBER 4: Writes Brooker to accept a painted plaster, *Linda*, 1932, by Elizabeth Wyn Wood, a gift from Brooker to WSA collection.

1938

AUGUST: Travels to Ottawa and Toronto. Stays with Brooker for six days. Hires Warren Luckcock as teaching assistant to replace George Overton, who taught at WSA from 1926 to 1938. Visits Lismer and A.Y. Jackson in Toronto. Reports on trip to H.O. McCurry: "Canada does not offer many rich plums to the artist but it does, for some unaccountable reason, seem to foster a great loyalty. Most of the artists are anxious to stay home in much less affluent circumstances, just to be here. There must be some magnetic force at work, that we are not aware of" (August 24).

AUGUST 14: Sketches in Minneapolis, MN.

SEPTEMBER: WSA reopens in new location in Old Law Courts building on Kennedy Street near Civic Auditorium (until 1965). Cupola of Juvenile Detention Hall on Memorial Boulevard visible from FitzGerald's studio and appears in painting *The Cupola*, 1940 (p. 153), and linocut *View from Window with Two Jugs*, 1942 (p. 152).

OCTOBER 15–DECEMBER 15: Exhibits paintings *Farmyard*, 1931 (p. 49); *Landscape with Trees*, 1931; *Summer*, 1931; and *The Jar*, 1938 (p. 118), in *A Century of Canadian Art* at Tate Gallery, London, organized by NGC.

OCTOBER 29–30: Jackson, en route to Toronto from southern Alberta, visits FitzGerald in Winnipeg.

MID-NOVEMBER–DECEMBER: Exhibits drawings in solo exhibition at Hart House, University of Toronto. Jackson and Lismer visit show. Exhibition travels to Art Association of Montreal (now Montreal Museum of Fine Arts), where reviewed by Ayre, *Montreal Standard*, December 31, 1938. Work consists of twenty-three drawings in different media that are sent February 1939 to NGC for purchase consideration.

1939

MARCH 8: Brandtner writes FitzGerald about formation of the Contemporary Arts Society in Montreal by John Lyman, Paul-Émile Borduas, Philip Surrey, and Brandtner. Offers membership but FitzGerald declines.

MARCH 15: Writes Eric Brown about selection of drawings NGC considering for purchase. "I have been hoping for a long time that you would purchase some of the drawings as I felt that they were very representative of the work I have been doing for the past few years. A great deal of that time was occupied in these studies and they come as close to what I was aiming for as anything that I did during that period. Also, I think I spent more time on them than the paintings for the purpose of making a much deeper study of nature."

APRIL 28: H.O. McCurry writes FitzGerald that NGC has selected four drawings for purchase: *Landscape with Trees*, charcoal ($40); *Barn with Trees and Tree Stumps*, watercolour ($60); *Pepper's Farm*, charcoal ($25); and *By the River*, pencil ($40).

AUGUST 1–SEPTEMBER 15: Exhibits *The Jar* ($450) in *Canadian Art/Canadian Group of Painters* at New York World's Fair, organized under supervision of NGC.

1940

JANUARY 12: Mother dies.

C. APRIL 22: Lismer visits FitzGerald in Winnipeg.

NOVEMBER: Submits application for fellowship to John Simon Guggenheim Memorial Foundation, New York.[2] Plans to spend following year painting and drawing in northern part of Midwestern states on works "that require longer continuous effort." Writes: "There is a particular character to the prairie country that has always had a strong appeal for me. The intimate attachment formed in childhood has remained and increased through the study of it, in painting." Is bitterly disappointed on learning that he is not successful applicant.

1941

DECEMBER 18: First surviving letter from FitzGerald to Irene Heywood (London, ON?). Writes thirteen letters or fragments of correspondence to Irene from 1941 to 1943. No known letters from Heywood to FitzGerald.

1942

FEBRUARY 1–MARCH 15: With A.O. Brigden organizes exhibition at the WAG of William Blake's drawings and engravings 1808–27. Loans from Brigden, Brooker, NGC, and others.

MAY 23: Writes to Irene Heywood (Toronto?): "We can only develop an understanding of the great forces behind the organization of nature by endless searching the outer manifestations. And we can only know ourselves better and still better by this search.... I want to go like the flower that contains the germ of a new life within the tangled, withered fragments left behind. I want to walk in the light that is never ending with open heart and open mind. When slipping into the great unknown I want to move always upward, ever seeking."[3]

JUNE 25: Brooker writes to thank FitzGerald for letter he has received "charged with beauty." Brooker explains: "if there is such a thing as emanation (as Blake certainly believed) there is an emanation in this letter that I have never before received from a human being. In some ways it almost tells me more about you than I have got from our long talks, and I suppose that is because this is entirely you, without any adulteration of myself in it, either as listener or contributor to a conversation. In any event, it was and is again today a more complete communication of a man's personality than anything I have known before." FitzGerald's letter to Brooker unlocated.

JULY–AUGUST: Makes first trip to West Coast to visit daughter, Patricia, at Bowen Island near Vancouver. Spends summer sketching rocks and mountains. Makes large drawings in black and white and series of coloured pencil crayons.

LATE AUGUST: Meets Harris in Vancouver for first time. Harris and his wife, Bess, had moved to Vancouver from Santa Fe, NM, in 1940.

1943

FEBRUARY 12–25: Harris arranges exhibition *FitzGerald Drawings* at Vancouver Art Gallery.

JULY–AUGUST: Summers at Bowen Island making drawings and watercolours.

LATE AUGUST: Spends four days in Vancouver. Visits Harris and artist J.W.G. (Jock) Macdonald before returning to Winnipeg.

DECEMBER 11: Father dies.

1944

MAY 5: Report to Board of Directors at WSA regarding acquisition of A.J. Casson, *Old Houses, Magnetawan*, n.d., and Florence Wyle, *Torso*, c. 1935.

JULY–AUGUST: Summers at Bowen Island. Paints watercolours (pp. 167, 173).

AUGUST: Visits Vancouver Art Gallery, Vancouver School of Art and principal Charles H. Scott. Meets with Jock Macdonald and Harris. Sees Jack Shadbolt's large mural *About Town with the United Services* at the United Services Centre (no longer extant).

Records visit in report to Board of Directors at WSA (October 31): "Report on a little journey around the art world of Vancouver in September [August] nineteen forty-four."

SEPTEMBER 2: Returns to Winnipeg from West Coast.

DECEMBER 2: Harris visits FitzGerald in Winnipeg in conjunction with lecture tour for Federation of Arts. FitzGerald becomes ill during winter and does not accomplish much painting.

1945

JANUARY 31: Writes to Ayre that he is "much troubled in mind . . ." Sequence of twelve self-portraits showing himself in torment may date from this period (pp. 90–93).

MAY 15: WSA acquires Emily Carr oil painting *Tree Movement*, 1937–38 (through Harris), and Franklin Carmichael's *Jack Pine*, 1942 (from exhibition of sixteen watercolours by Carmichael exhibited at WSA).

JUNE 11: Writes Harris that has been ill for three months and has not painted much.

JULY: Brooker visits FitzGerald in Winnipeg during summer. As memento of stay, Brooker sends facsimile of William Blake's *Songs of Innocence* and inscribes frontispiece: "To Lemoine [*sic*] in mutual reverence for Blake. Bert. 1945."

OCTOBER–NOVEMBER: Lawren Harris, "LeMoine FitzGerald, Western Artist: FitzGerald's Recent Work," *Canadian Art* 3, no. 1 (October–November 1945): 1–13. Article details FitzGerald's 1942–44 work at Bowen Island.

OCTOBER 10: Harris sends cheque to FitzGerald for three watercolours, which Harris had advised him to offer first to NGC, who decided not to purchase.

NOVEMBER 22: FitzGerald reports acquisition of Brooker's painting *Sounds Assembling*, 1928, by WSA.

NOVEMBER 24: Irene Heywood marries Canadian folksinger/songwriter Wade Hemsworth.

DECEMBER: Brooker purchases FitzGerald watercolour (unidentified).

1946

FEBRUARY 5: Adaskin writes Prime Minister Mackenzie King to request that FitzGerald receive a government pension to allow him to work on art full-time. This is not granted.

AUTUMN: Begins *The Little Plant* (p. 106), which is finished spring 1947.

1947

MAY 22: WSA Board of Directors grants FitzGerald one-year leave of absence.

SEPTEMBER 1: Begins one-year leave of absence from WSA, facilitated by efforts of Mary Ferguson, who arranges financial support from J.W. McConnell, president of Montreal Star Publishing Company.

NOVEMBER 5–APRIL 26, 1948: Spends winter on Vancouver Island at Saseenos (about thirty-one kilometres west of Victoria on the Sooke Basin) on an inlet of Strait of Juan de Fuca.

1948

MARCH: Requests extension of leave of absence for another year.

APRIL 10: Second year leave of absence granted by WSA Board of Directors.

APRIL 26: Leaves Saseenos for ten-day stay in West Vancouver, visiting Lawren and Bess Harris, B.C. Binning, and Harry Adaskin.

Vally and FitzGerald, Vancouver Island, sometime between November 1947 and April 1948

Photo by Frances Rhodes (FitzGerald's cousin)

Lionel LeMoine FitzGerald fonds, PC 241 (A2009-016), Box 1, Folder 1 / University of Manitoba Archives & Special Collections, Winnipeg

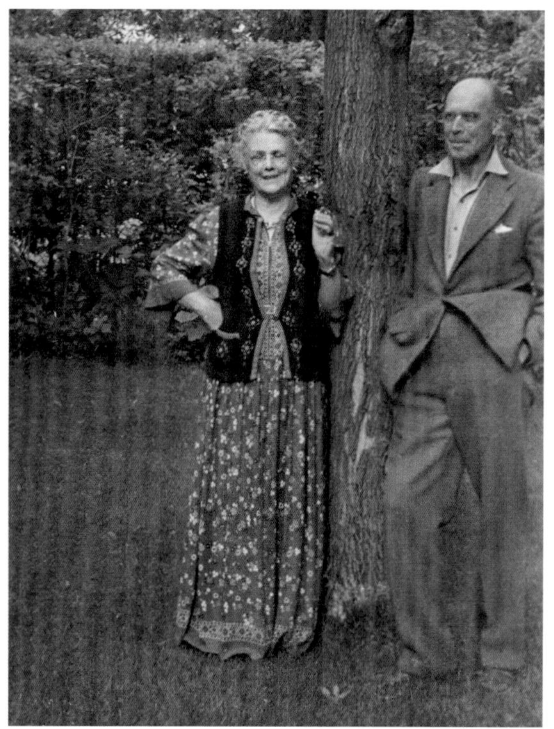

MAY: Returns to Winnipeg.

FALL: *Canadian Art* magazine publishes full-page colour photograph of *The Little Plant* (*Canadian Art* 6, no. 1 [Autumn 1948]: 28).

EARLY NOVEMBER: For two weeks prior to departure for Vancouver, lives with sister and husband at old family home at 672 Sherbrook Street (between Notre Dame and Sargent).

NOVEMBER 18: Leaves Winnipeg to spend winter in West Vancouver at 2749 Lawson Avenue. Lives near B.C. Binning in house owned by Barbara Munro (Vally's niece).

1949

JANUARY 15: While in Vancouver, resigns from position at WSA. Replaced by Joe Plaskett for one-year period.

APRIL–MAY: Visits Vancouver Art Gallery and Vancouver School of Art. Spends time with Harris, B.C. Binning, and Charles Scott.

MAY 6: Returns to Winnipeg.

SEPTEMBER 13–OCTOBER 2: Exhibition *FitzGerald Watercolours and Drawings* at Vancouver Art Gallery.

SEPTEMBER 20: Snowflake, MB.

NOVEMBER 17: Brooker lectures at Hart House, noting FitzGerald drawing he had acquired was "a verb—a picture of living."

DECEMBER 2–3: Exhibition *Drawings by B.C. Binning and LeMoine FitzGerald* at Vernon (Legion Centre) and Prince George, organized by Vancouver Art Gallery.

1950

Paints *From an Upstairs Window, Winter*, c. 1950–51, from attic window overlooking backyard of 160 Lyle Street.

Makes watercolour *Barlow's Garage*, 1950 (p. 148), named after Charles Barlow, who lived at 172 Lyle Street. This is the same building as *Williamson's Garage*, 1927. Milton J. Williamson lived at 172 Lyle Street from 1925 to 1926.

Makes three preparatory drawings for 1951 Canadian five-cent coin design competition to mark two-hundredth anniversary of identification of metal nickel. Charles Comfort and Fritz Brandtner receive honourable mention.

First abstract pictures. Meets Winnipeg physician E.J. Thomas, who becomes avid collector and patron. WSA becomes part of University of Manitoba.

1951

JANUARY 28–MAY 25: FitzGerald and Vally visit son, Edward, in Mexico City. Travel by bus to Laredo, TX, and fly to Mexico City. Sketches from plane over Tampico, Mexico (May 23). Sketches on flight home to Winnipeg over Fargo and Grand Forks, ND (inscribed 25.5.51).

FEBRUARY 4–17: Exhibition *L.L. FitzGerald Paintings and Drawings* at Winnipeg Art Gallery.

OCTOBER 11–27: Exhibits *Pritchard's Fence*, c. 1928 (p. 137), and *Still Life with Blue Book*, 1948, in *First Exhibition of Western Artists in Eastern Canada* at Dominion Gallery, Montreal, selected by Max Stern.

1952

OCTOBER 29: Receives Honorary LLD from University of Manitoba on occasion of its seventy-fifth anniversary.

1953

JULY 23–AUGUST 21: Flies to Toronto and sketches from plane (inscribed 23.7.53). Purpose of trip is to jury 1953 Canadian National Exhibition art show (July 25) with Paul Duval, Cleeve Horne, Lionel Thomas, Sydney Watson, and York Wilson.

JULY 26: Spends evening at Brooker's residence. Looks at Brooker's paintings July 28.

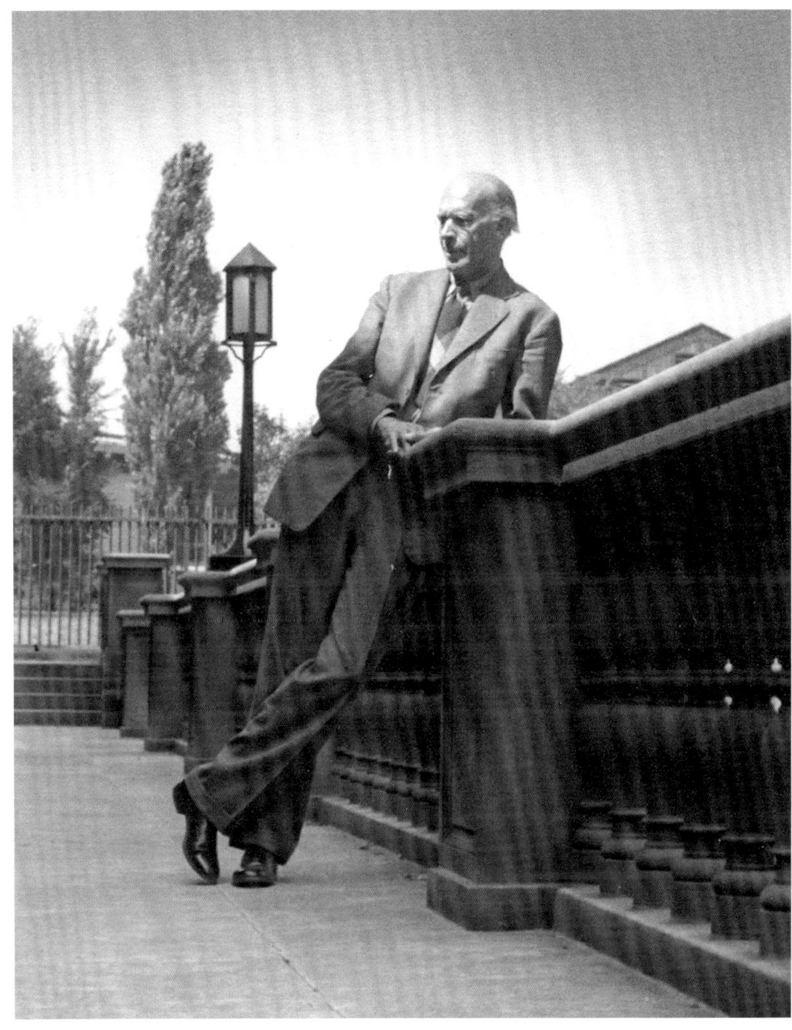

FitzGerald at Queen's Park, Toronto, July 1953

Collection of the Winnipeg Art Gallery, Clara Lander Library, L.L. FitzGerald fonds, ACC700.005 / Photo: Harold Sumberg, courtesy of the Winnipeg Art Gallery

JULY 30–31: Son-in-law, Hugh Morrison, takes photos (whereabouts unknown) of FitzGerald and Jackson at Jackson's studio.

AUGUST 2–5: Flies to Ottawa and sketches from plane (inscribed 2.8.53). Visits Parliament Hill, Sandy Hill, Beechwood Cemetery, and Hull, QC. Visits Montebello, QC, with Irene Heywood Hemsworth (August 4). Visits NGC to see H.O. McCurry, now director, and his secretary, Gertrude Ingall Matthewman, FitzGerald's cousin (August 5).

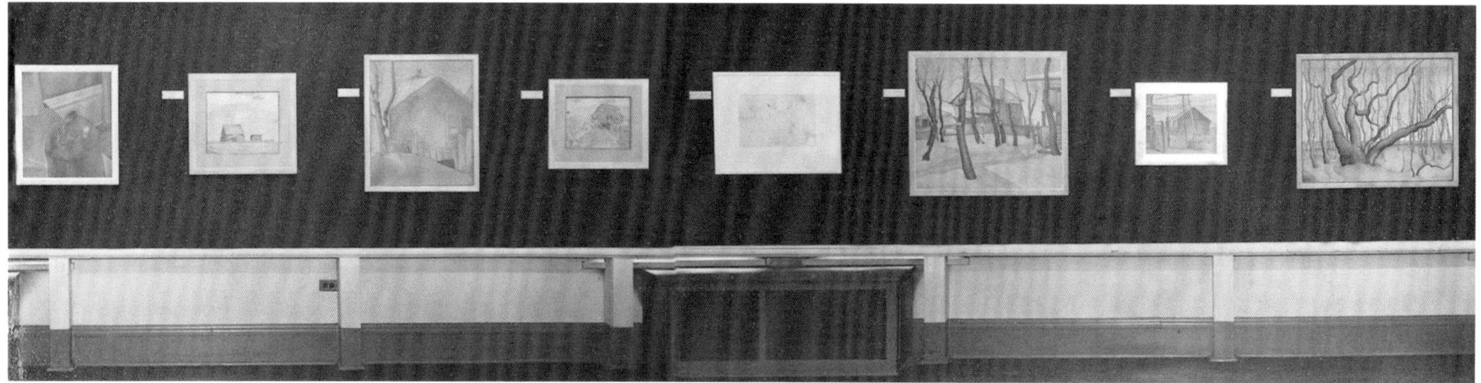

Installation view of *FitzGerald, 1890–1956: Memorial Exhibition* at the Winnipeg Art Gallery, February 23–March 23, 1958
Lionel LeMoine FitzGerald fonds, PC 241 (A2009-016), Box 2, Folder 17 / University of Manitoba Archives & Special Collections, Winnipeg

AUGUST 8: Publication of FitzGerald interview with Toronto art critic Pearl McCarthy: "Mr. FitzGerald: Rare Visitor but His Horizon Is National," *Globe and Mail*, August 8, 1953.

AUGUST 9: Flies to Toronto and sketches from plane (inscribed 9.8.53).

AUGUST 13–21: An evening at Brooker's to look at FitzGerald's drawings. Spend time together again looking at drawings August 15 and visit for final time on August 19.

AUGUST 16: Visits artists Florence Wyle and Frances Loring at their country residence. Visits studio of Rody Kenny Courtice.

AUGUST 21: Returns to Winnipeg. Sketches from plane (inscribed 21.8.53).

1954

JULY 28: Ayre visits FitzGerald for afternoon in Winnipeg and takes photographs of him in yard (frontispiece).

OCTOBER 29: Travels by train to Regina to judge works for NGC exhibition. Visits artist Kenneth Lougheed in Balgonie, SK.

OCTOBER 31: Visits Fort Qu'Appelle, SK.

DECEMBER 1: Gives radio interview to CBC Midwest Network for broadcast "Painters of the Prairie." This is only in-depth interview of his career.

1955

MARCH 22: Learns of Brooker's death that day on radio broadcast.

NOVEMBER 5: Lawren and Bess Harris visit FitzGerald in Winnipeg. Examine *Still Life with Hat*, 1955, and the "long narrow" pen-and-ink abstract drawings.

1956

FEBRUARY 17–MARCH 18: Memorial exhibition for Brooker held at eighty-fourth Annual Exhibition of OSA at AGT. FitzGerald tribute to Brooker in introduction to catalogue.

MARCH 28: Visits Henry Moore exhibition organized by British Council at WAG. Notes in diary that Moore's sculpture and drawings are "very fine things."

APRIL 2: Visit from Norah McCullough, executive secretary, Saskatchewan Arts Board, in Winnipeg to see Moore exhibition.

APRIL 19: Attends reception for British art historian Anthony Blunt at home of Joseph Harris, owner of *Abstract: Green and Gold*, 1954 (p. 188). Blunt in Winnipeg to lecture on Picasso in anticipation of exhibition *A Half Century of Picasso Prints* organized by Museum of Modern Art, New York, which opens at WAG July 5.

JULY 20: Visits Picasso exhibition of etchings, drypoints, and lithographs at WAG. Notes in diary, "the living quality of the line and what it contains—amazing variety of composition and the same searching for the aliveness of the human figure as in the Matisse drawings I saw so recently—even the smallest detail is given the same care—the selection marvelous."

AUGUST 5: Suffers heart attack and dies in hospital at age sixty-six. Cremation in Minneapolis followed by memorial service in Winnipeg. Ashes scattered at grandparents' former farm in Snowflake.

November 9–December 16: Lawren Harris, "Lemoine [*sic*] Fitzgerald [*sic*]" in *Canadian Group of Painters 56/57*, catalogue for exhibition held at AGT and Vancouver Art Gallery. In memorial tribute, Harris describes FitzGerald "by nature and by necessity somewhat of a recluse . . . . He had a pervading gentleness which cloaked a constant inner firmness. He influenced others by his presence which was that of a saintly artist."

1957

MARCH 30: FitzGerald Memorial Room opens at WAG.

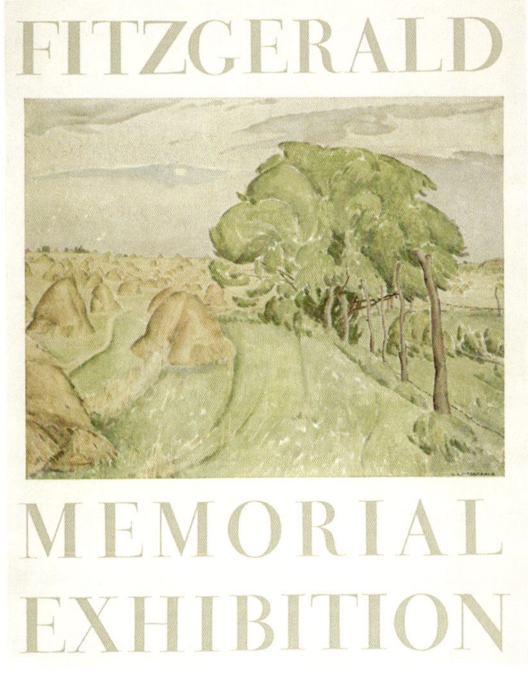

FitzGerald, 1890–1956: Memorial Exhibition catalogue cover (Ottawa: National Gallery of Canada, 1958)

1958

FEBRUARY 23–MARCH 23: Fifty-eight works in *FitzGerald, 1890–1956: Memorial Exhibition* organized by Ferdinand Eckhardt, Alan Jarvis, Douglas Duncan, Lawren Harris, A.O. Brigden, and Dr. E.J. Thomas opens at WAG. Exhibition tours to Montreal, Toronto, and Ottawa.

Notes

INTO THE LIGHT | *Sarah Milroy*

1 FitzGerald to Robert Ayre, August 27, 1954. Robert Ayre fonds, Queen's University Archives, Kingston.

2 Robert Ayre, "Lionel LeMoine FitzGerald," unpublished article, n.d., typescript, 6, Ayre fonds.

3 L.L. FitzGerald, "Notes on Russian Art," March 3, 1927. Excerpt from Leo Tolstoy, *What Is Art*, chapter 5, transcribed by FitzGerald. L.L. FitzGerald fonds, University of Manitoba Archives and Special Collections, 11-0184, 8.

AN ART OF ADAPTATION: RETHINKING FITZGERALD'S EARLY CAREER | *Andrew Kear*

1 Robert Ayre, "Painter of the Prairies," *Weekend Magazine* 8 no. 12 (1958): 29.

2 L.L. FitzGerald radio interview, "Painters of the Prairie," Canadian Broadcasting Corporation Midwest Network, December 1, 1954. Transcript reproduced in Michael Parke-Taylor, *In Seclusion with Nature: The Later Works of L. LeMoine FitzGerald, 1942–1956* (Winnipeg: Winnipeg Art Gallery, 1988), 49. Alternatively, given FitzGerald's brief, midcareer, membership in the Group of Seven, one might be tempted to interpolate a broader nationalist bent to the landscape works. But a statement like "what they were doing in the east, I was trying to work out on the western prairie" should be understood less as FitzGerald's endorsement of the Group's ardent nationalism and more as an appeal to the prosaic observation "that we have, in our own country, ample material for any form of pictorial expression." See Helen Coy, *FitzGerald as Printmaker: A Catalogue Raisonné of the First Complete Exhibition of the Printed Works* (Winnipeg: University of Manitoba Press, 1982), 3; FitzGerald to Robert Ayre, July 25, 1949, Robert Ayre fonds, Queen's University Archive, Kingston.

3 FitzGerald, quoted in Ferdinand Eckhardt, *FitzGerald, 1890–1956: Memorial Exhibition* catalogue (Winnipeg: Winnipeg Art Gallery, 1958), n.p.

4 FitzGerald writes that New York gave him "a sudden jolt into everything." See Robert Ayre, "Lionel LeMoine FitzGerald," unpublished article, n.d., typescript, p. 6, Ayre fonds; Ayre, "Painter of the Prairies," 29.

5 Ayre, "Painter of the Prairies," 26.

6 Patricia Bovey, "Lionel LeMoine FitzGerald: Some European Influences on His Work," in Bovey, *Lionel LeMoine FitzGerald: The Development of an Artist* (Winnipeg: Winnipeg Art Gallery, 1978), 78.

7 FitzGerald to Ayre, July 25, 1949. Ayre fonds.

8 FitzGerald to Ayre, July 25, 1949, Ayre fonds.

9 John Ruskin, *The Elements of Drawing* (Toronto: J.M. Dent and Sons, 1932 [1857]), xvi.

10 Ruskin, *Elements*, 3–4.

11 Jonathan Crary, *Techniques of the Observer: On Vision and Modernity in the Nineteenth Century* (Cambridge, MA: MIT, 1990), 95, 96.

12 Ogden Rood, *Modern Chromatics: Students' Text-Book of Color with Applications to Art and Industry* (New York: Van Nostrand Reinhold, 1973 [1879]), 163.

13 For further discussion of Ruskin's influence on Neo-Impressionism, see Robyn S. Roslak, *Neo-Impressionism and Anarchism in Fin-de-Siècle France: Painting, Politics, and Landscape* (London: Ashgate, 2007), 186ff.

14 John House, *Impressionism: Paint and Politics* (New Haven, CT: Yale University Press, 2004), 148.

15 Adam Parkes, A *Sense of Shock: The Impact of Impressionism on Modern British and Irish Writing* (Oxford: Oxford University Press, 2011), 25.

16 Christian Brinton, "Fashions in Art," *International Studio* 49, no. 193 (March 1913): iii–x.; Brinton, "Evolution Not Revolution in Art," *International Studio* 49, no. 194 (April 1913): xxxii.

17 Willard Huntington Wright, "Modern Art: The New Spirit in America," *International Studio* 60, no. 238 (December 1916): lxiv–lxv; Wright, "Modern Art: A Full Harvest of the New Painting," *International Studio* 61, no. 242 (April 1917): 62–64.

18 Christine Lalonde, *Beauty in a Common Thing: Drawings and Prints by L.L. FitzGerald* (Ottawa: National Gallery of Canada, 2004), 11–12.

19 FitzGerald, "Painters of the Prairie," radio interview, quoted in Michael Parke-Taylor, *In Seclusion with Nature*, 50.

20 Jeff Richmond-Moll, email to Andrew Kear, May 21, 2013.

21 Marilyn Baker claims that Ewart studied with Whistler and Sargent at the Pennsylvania Academy of the Fine Arts, yet according to her class records she took classes with neither at the PAFA. Whether Ewart studied with either artist elsewhere is unknown. See *The Winnipeg School of Art: The Early Years* (Winnipeg: University of Manitoba, 1984), 24; Jeff Richmond-Moll email to Andrew Kear, May 21, 2013.

22 See Jessie Lemont, "Old Subjects in New Vestments," *International Studio* 54, no. 213 (November 1914): iii–x; Duncan Phillips, "The Romance of a Painter's Mind," *International Studio* 58, no. 229 (March 1916): xix–xiv.

23 However, Tack did not create his first completely abstract work until 1924, several years after his Winnipeg commission. See Eleanor Green, "Augustus Vincent Tack," *Artforum* 11, no. 2 (October 1972): 56, 58.

24 L.L. FitzGerald, Diary, June 12, 1930. L.L. FitzGerald fonds, University of Manitoba Archives and Special Collections, Winnipeg, Box 1, Folder 12, 1-0183.

25 *Canadian Art of Today* (Winnipeg: Winnipeg Art Gallery, 1921), 5.

26 FitzGerald was in correspondence with his family while in Chicago. See File Correspondence—Family, 1863–1956, MSS 287, PC 241, TC 139 (A. 09.16), L.L. FitzGerald fonds. See also Kendall Banning, *Citadels of Commerce*, c. 1909 or 1910, in Collected Art Publications 1920–1956, Box 4, File 17, Articles Collected by FitzGerald 1906–1956, MSS 287, PC 241, TC 139 (A.09.16), FitzGerald fonds.

27 We know FitzGerald was in Chicago at this time based on an entry in his account book. See Photocopies and Typed Transcripts 1977–1982, Box 14, Folder 1, Account Book 1913–1925, January 10–17, 1920, FitzGerald fonds.

28 James N. Wood and Katharine C. Lee, *Master Paintings in the Art Institute of Chicago* (Boston: Little, Brown, 1988), 8–9.

29 Sarah Kelly Oehler, a curator at the Art Institute of Chicago, confirms that *Centre Bridge* was on permanent display at the AIC in both 1910 and 1920. "In 1910, our Bulletin listed the works by American artists in the collection, including the Redfield, and the museum just didn't have a lot yet. Redfield was a regular exhibitor at our annuals, which suggests it was very likely that *Centre Bridge* would have been equally valued, and therefore installed. Moreover, from what I can interpret from our cryptic early records, it looks like it was on view continuously from March 1921 through 1930, when it went out on loan to Europe; it then went back on view until the late 1930s, when it went on a long-term loan to the Evanston Public Library. We don't have records before 1921 of gallery locations, but I cannot imagine that they would put it back on view in 1921 if it hadn't been on view before that. It just wasn't what they did .... Finally, and this might be the best confirmation, it's also listed in the 1920 handbook [p. 54]. A note at the beginning of the catalogue states that paintings with an asterisk were not on view when compiled, and the Redfield does not have an asterisk, so it must have been on view .... So, all in all, I'm comfortable saying it was likely on view ... [in] both 1910 and 1920." Sarah Kelly Oehler email to Andrew Kear, October 5, 2015.

30 See "Exhibition History," Art Institute of Chicago, http://www.artic.edu/research/1920-exhibition-history. According to AIC archivist Bart Ryckbosch, "It was not uncommon for Chicago collectors to deposit their private collection at the Art Institute. That's probably why there's no shipping or receiving documents specifically for the 1920 show [*Paul Schulze Collection of Paintings*], since three pieces were already in storage." Ryckbosch provided the author with a document showing "the inventory of the Schulze collection at the Art Institute on October of 1919, 17 paintings in all," in which *The Northwest Wind* is listed. A second document, "a request by Paul Schulze to the museum to send 14 paintings of his to the Hamilton Club for exhibition during the spring of 1919," clearly states, "pictures which are now in your possession." According to Ryckbosch, "by 'possession' [Schulze] meant that [the AIC] was holding on to them for him, as the actual transfer of ownership did not happen until 1924." Bart Ryckbosch email to Andrew Kear, December 23, 2014.

31 FitzGerald arrived in New York in late November 1921. He narrowly missed the Metropolitan Museum of Art's *Loan Exhibition of Impressionist and Post-Impressionist Paintings* (May 3–September 15, 1921), which included twenty-four paintings by the French artist whose work deeply influenced FitzGerald throughout his subsequent career—Paul Cézanne. The show generated controversy around the artist, who became the subject of an invective-laced pamphlet, *Degenerate "Modernistic" Works in the Metropolitan Museum of Art*, that circulated shortly before the show ended. This likely prompted lively discussion of Cézanne's work among those at the Art Students League when FitzGerald arrived on the scene. Thanks to Michael Parke-Taylor for bringing this information to the author's attention.

32 Karen Linda Sens, "A Discussion of the Stylistic Development in the Dated Oil Paintings of Lionel LeMoine FitzGerald (1890–1956)" (master's thesis, University of British Columbia, 1978), 31–32.

33 The *Exhibition of Paintings by French Cubists and Post Impressionists* ran from November 22 to December 17, 1921. Thanks to Alison Reid for bringing this to the author's attention.

34 Exhibition Catalogues 1921–1992, Box 8, File 10, Art Catalogues of Other Artists 1922–1980, SS 287, PC 241, TC 139 (A. 09.16), FitzGerald fonds.

35 Although he returned from New York in 1922, FitzGerald did not resume his artistic practice fully until 1924, when he was finally able to leave commercial work for a teaching job at the Winnipeg School of Art, which afforded him more time for his own work. See Ayre, "Lionel LeMoine FitzGerald," 9.

A CANADIAN ARTIST IN AMERICA, 1930: FITZGERALD'S TRAVEL DIARY | *Michael Parke-Taylor*

1 L.L. FitzGerald, Diary, June 15, 1930, 63. L.L. FitzGerald fonds, University of Manitoba Archives and Special Collections, Winnipeg, Box 1, Folder 12, 1-0183.

2 L.L. FitzGerald report to the board of directors, Winnipeg School of Art, January 15, 1931, photocopy. Winnipeg Art Gallery Library.

3 FitzGerald visited the Grand Central Art Galleries, Grand Central Terminal, 15 Vanderbilt Avenue, New York, on June 18, 1930. Two of his paintings were installed in their *Exhibition of Paintings by Contemporary Artists under the Auspices of the American Federation of Arts*, organized by the American Federation of Arts, Corcoran Art Gallery of Art,

Washington, DC. In addition to *Williamson's Garage*, 1927 (p. 133), the show included *Poplar Woods (Poplars)*, 1929 (p. 68).

4 Unfortunately, the diary for the 1930 trip ends in New York and thus does not detail what FitzGerald did in Montreal, Ottawa, and Toronto. The only known account of his Toronto visit is given by Bertram Brooker: "Lemoine [*sic*] Fitzgerald [*sic*] was here for a week or more from Winnipeg in the course of a lengthy trip to investigate what colleges and galleries are doing in Minneapolis, Chicago, New York, Montreal, Ottawa and Toronto. When Arthur Lismer took him around the college here the students all thought he was Lismer's brother they look so much alike. He made the acquaintance of a good many artists here, admired much that is being done, and did some sketching—to say nothing of talking till three or four a.m. nearly every night of his visit. Like so many people who come to Toronto—including those from the States and abroad—he was astonished at the number of things to see and talk about, the number of people to meet, and perhaps particularly the atmosphere of friendliness and interest in one another's work which pervades the art atmosphere here." Brooker, The Seven Arts, *Winnipeg Tribune*, September 6, 1930.

After the 1930 trip, FitzGerald used the diary to record a chronology of his life from 1921 to 1951 (pp. 97–98), followed by brief entries from 1953 until August 3, 1956 (pp. 99–116), two days before his death. The back pages of the diary list various addresses of people relevant to the 1930 trip (pp. 154–55). For a complete digital photographic record of the diary, see http://digitalcollections.lib.umanitoba.ca/islandora/object/uofm%3Afitzgerald_ll?page=1.

5 Although FitzGerald's diary offers a unique view of art in America from a Canadian perspective, by the thirties many Canadian artists had either travelled or studied in the United States, where they were exposed to the most recent developments in American and European modern art. See Christine Boyanoski, "The Canadian View of American Art," in Boyanoski, *Permeable Border: Art of Canada and the United States 1920–1940* (Toronto: Art Gallery of Ontario, 1989), 15–20.

6 FitzGerald, Diary, June 15, 1930, 55.

7 On June 8, FitzGerald spent five hours at the Field Museum in Chicago. In his diary he mentioned looking at Chinese masks, costumes, carvings, and models of pagodas. He visited the Mexican and Peruvian sections of the museum but found the religious decorative wooden carvings from the South Sea Islands "intensely interesting." (FitzGerald, Diary, June 8, 23.) On June 20, he spent the morning at the American Museum of Natural History, New York, where he noted that "one of the many remarkable things" was the enormous Aztec Sun Stone commonly known as the Calendar Stone (FitzGerald, Diary, June 20, 67).

8 FitzGerald, Diary, June 7, 1930, 18.

9 FitzGerald, Diary, June 7, 1930, 20 (emphasis in original).

10 FitzGerald, Diary, June 7, 1930, 20.

11 FitzGerald, Diary, June 7, 1930, 19.

12 FitzGerald, Diary, June 12, 1930, 42.

13 FitzGerald, Diary, June 21, 1930, 70.

14 Robert Ayre, "Lionel LeMoine FitzGerald," unpublished article, n.d., typescript, 6. Robert Ayre fonds, Queen's University Archives, Kingston.

15 FitzGerald, Diary, June 7, 1930, 20.

16 See Sandra Shaul, "Lionel LeMoine FitzGerald: The Search for Structural Unity in Abstract Art," in Shaul, *The Modern Image: Cubism and the Realist Tradition* (Edmonton: Edmonton Art Gallery, 1982), 21.

17 FitzGerald, Diary, June 20, 1930, 68. The drawing is inscribed in graphite, lower right, "June 20/30/ New York Life." FitzGerald fonds, MSS 287 (A2009-016), Box 3, Folder 11, Item 43.

18 FitzGerald notes in his diary for his 1930 trip seeing the work of numerous American artists, including Abbott Handerson Thayer, Boardman Robinson, John White Alexander, Howard Giles, George Luks, Eugene E. Speicher, Leon Kroll, Henry Lee McFee, John Wesley Carroll, George Bellows, Charles Rosen, Bernard Karfiol, Charles Burchfield, Edward Hopper, George de Forest Brush, John Singer Sargent, Maurice Sterne, Gifford Beal, and Kenneth Hayes Miller.

19 FitzGerald, Diary, June 23, 1930, 79.

20 In a later text, FitzGerald instructed that it was through the study of historical art that the student could "reach back into the artists' minds and reach an understanding of what they really were searching for resulting in a better understanding of self." He continued: "It is noticeable that your problems have been their problems in another age; theirs assisting you to march forward and face the difficulties that always attend any form of self expression." L.L. FitzGerald, November 9, 1933, photocopy, Ferdinand Eckhardt Papers, Winnipeg Art Gallery Library.

21 FitzGerald, Diary, June 21, 1930, 71. The reception of Cézanne by American artists in the early decades of the twentieth century has been analyzed by the art historian Gail Stavitsky. She notes that the attitude of American artists toward Cézanne prior to the First World War "tended to focus on the innovative, radical aspects of Cézanne's work which validated their own experimentation with abstraction and new perceptions of art and the world around them." She continues: "During the 1920s, a greater concern for more stable arrangements of smoothly rendered, volumetric, essential forms coincided with the international postwar classicism/'return to order,' in which Cézanne served as the primary bridge between the old masters and modernism. He continued to play this vital role at a time when many artists turned away from European-derived abstraction toward representation as a way of redefining their relationship to America, their native soil." This latter approach parallels the case of FitzGerald, who also used Cézanne to reconcile Old Master and modern—representation and abstraction, except

that FitzGerald's native soil was prairie Canadian. See Gail Stavitsky, "Cézanne and American Modernism," in Stavitsky, *Cézanne and American Modernism* (New Haven, CT: Yale University Press, 2009), 52. Although he does not mention the notion of "significant form" in Cézanne as formulated by Roger Fry and Clive Bell, FitzGerald was probably in agreement with Bertram Brooker that it was this aspect of making something solid and enduring out of the art of the museums that marked Cézanne's legacy. For broader implications of this in Canadian art, see Lora Senechal Carney, *Canadian Painters in a Modern World 1925–1955* (Montreal/Kingston: McGill-Queen's University Press, 2017), xxix.

22 FitzGerald, Diary, June 12, 1930, 42–43.

23 Pieter Brueghel the Younger added the h to the family name.

24 The Philadelphia Museum of Art also owns a similar painting: Follower of Pieter Bruegel the Elder, *Wedding Dance*, c. 1575–1600, oil on panel, 80.3 × 106.4 cm, John G. Johnson Collection, 1917 (cat. 420). It is possible that FitzGerald might have been referring to this picture rather than the smaller painting by Pieter Brueghel the Younger.

25 FitzGerald, Diary, June 15, 1930, 53. FitzGerald expanded on the notion of keeping the eye within the picture in a text he wrote three years later: "Another part of the picture that should be carefully studied are the four sides next to the frame. Everything should be worked out here so that the eye is arrested and not allowed to go outside but rather to be tempted to revolve within the area. This does not necessarily mean that it will be a circular motion but so subtle that the attention will inevitably be drawn back to the main theme again thus to wander through, over again." L.L. FitzGerald, November 9, 1933, photocopy, Ferdinand Eckhardt fonds, Winnipeg Art Gallery Library.

26 FitzGerald, Diary, June 15, 1930, 53.

27 FitzGerald, Diary, June 15, 1930, 54.

28 The American painter Lucile E. Blanch (1895–1981) studied at the Art Students League after 1918 under Boardman Robinson and Kenneth Hayes Miller. She likely met FitzGerald when he studied at the Art Students League with her husband, Arnold Blanch—also a pupil of Robinson's.

29 FitzGerald, Diary, June 29, 1930, 94.

30 Although FitzGerald was about to enter the abstract phase of his career in 1950, he noted in correspondence to Robert Ayre in 1949 the relevance of historical British artists Constable, Turner, Blake, and Palmer as leaving "some indelible marks for American art of the future." He continued: "Perhaps the starkness of living today is forcing the artist, the poet to find a counter balance and these men seem to offer a starting point. It is a possibility. Art is not design, structure, volume, tensions and all the modern vocabulary only. Surely there are some human values as well that don't have to be sweet sentimentality . . ." See L.L. FitzGerald to Ayre, July 25, 1949, Robert Ayre fonds, Queen's University Archives, Kingston.

31 FitzGerald, Diary, June 30, 1930, 93.

32 FitzGerald later expanded on how the artist arrives at self-expression: "the greater the artist the more intense his study of his predecessors combined with his study of nature. He absorbs everything that he can from them, that is useful to the fuller expression of his own ideas and finally after years of work and study prolonged effort and many failures, they become congealed into one powerful unit that is the individual and the world has a new addition to its ever enlarging treasure house." L.L. FitzGerald, May 23, 1935, photocopy, Ferdinand Eckhardt fonds, Winnipeg Art Gallery Library.

FEELINGS OF VOLUPTUOUSNESS: FITZGERALD'S EROTIC BIOCENTRISM | *Oliver A.I. Botar*

EPIGRAPH: L.L. FitzGerald, "Notes on Russian Art," March 3, 1927. Excerpt from Leo Tolstoy, *What Is Art*, chapter 5, transcribed by FitzGerald. L.L. FitzGerald fonds, University of Manitoba Archives and Special Collections, 11-0184, p. 8. This passage also appears in his sketch for a lecture on "Russian art" that consists of comments on Tolstoy's book.

1 Oliver Botar, "Prolegomena to the Study of Biomorphic Modernism: Biocentrism, László Moholy-Nagy's 'New Vision' and Ernő Kállai's *Bioromantik*" (PhD dissertation, University of Toronto, 1998).

2 The circumstances under which these erotic drawings were kept, transferred to his son, Edward, and then marketed (mainly, it seems, through Laing Galleries in Toronto) remain unclear. There are stories but no proof (conversation with Michael Parke-Taylor, February 25, 2019). According to labels on its verso, the drawing in my possession was originally sold through Laing Galleries by Edward FitzGerald.

3 Ferdinand Eckhardt, "A New FitzGerald," exhibition brochure (Winnipeg: Winnipeg Art Gallery, 1963). There may well be more such works.

4 The date of 1945 was first suggested by Christine Lalonde, *Beauty in a Common Thing: Drawings and Prints by L.L. FitzGerald* (Ottawa: National Gallery of Canada, 2004), 53. On them, see also Michael Parke-Taylor, *Lionel LeMoine FitzGerald: Life and Work* (Toronto: Art Canada Institute, 2018), 52–53. Heywood had an extraordinary life, has left a memoir, was a good artist, and deserves scholarly attention. Late in life she was preparing a monograph and film on FitzGerald, both left unrealized.

5 Eckhardt-Gramatté Foundation, Winnipeg, catalogue number 2417.

6 FitzGerald's relationship to Surrealism awaits analysis.

7 FitzGerald to Heywood, February 1, 1943. Irene Heywood Hemsworth fonds, Library and Archives Canada, Ottawa (IHHF LAC), R814 Box 310, file on FitzGerald Correspondence.

8 There are a number of FitzGerald works in the collections of the Winnipeg Art Gallery and the School of Art Gallery at the University of Manitoba that depict hovering nude couples

embracing, as well as frankly erotic images of nude women, that date from the early to mid-1940s.

9 Like Lawren Harris, Irene Heywood, and Elizabeth Wylie before him, Michael Parke-Taylor has established that FitzGerald was profoundly nature-centric. See Parke-Taylor, *In Seclusion with Nature: The Later Work of L. LeMoine FitzGerald, 1942 to 1956* (Winnipeg: Winnipeg Art Gallery, 1988), 17, 20. Heywood wrote of his nature-centrism in her sketches for a monograph on FitzGerald. See IHHF LAC, R814 Box 310, file on Manuscripts: The School. Harris wrote of this affiliation in his article "FitzGerald's Recent Work," in *Canadian Art* 3 (November 1945): 13. For the unabridged text of this article, see Parke-Taylor, *In Seclusion with Nature*, 47–48. Wylie was the first art historian to emphasize FitzGerald's nature-centrism, and she attributed it to Theosophical beliefs, but her struggle with this notion is reflected in her statement that "FitzGerald never chose Theosophy as a belief system and likely did not want to produce didactic art promoting it." See Elizabeth Wylie, "The Development of Spirituality in the Work of Lionel LeMoine FitzGerald" (master of fine arts thesis, Concordia University, November 1981), 42.

10 Botar, "Prolegomena to the Study of Biomorphic Modernism," chap. 2. See also Botar, "Defining Biocentrism," in Oliver Botar and Isabel Wünsche, eds., *Biocentrism and Modernism* (Farnham, UK: Ashgate, 2011), 15–45. As Sherrye Cohn notes, "Transcendentalism is Romanticism in its American guise." See Cohn, *Arthur Dove: Nature as Symbol* (Ann Arbor: UMI Research Press, 1985), 2.

11 Botar, "Defining Biocentrism." According to my definition, there were further components such as anarchism, biologism, neo-Lamarckism, life philosophy (*Lebensphilosophie*), organicism, and "organismic biology" that cannot be entered into here. The original German term for Life Reform Movement is *Lebensreformbewegung*.

12 *Vitalmystik* and *kosmovitale Einsfühlung* in the German original.

13 Botar, "Prolegomena to the Study of Biomorphic Modernism," chap. 2. See also Christopher Partridge, *The Re-Enchantment of the West*, vol. 1 of *Alternative Spiritualities, Sacralization, Popular Culture and Occulture* (London: T&T Clark International, 2004).

14 Botar, introduction to "Prolegomena to the Study of Biomorphic Modernism."

15 Brooker employs the rhetoric of holism throughout his writings: his copy of the South African politician and philosopher Jan Smuts's *Holism and Evolution* (London: Macmillan, 1926), one of the central texts of Bergsonian holism, is heavily annotated, as is his copy of the Swedish-American philosopher John Elof Boodin's *Cosmic Evolution: Outlines of Cosmic Idealism* (c. 1943), a deist version of holist evolutionary theory. Both copies are in the University of Manitoba Archives and Special Collections. Joyce Zemans refuted Theosophical origins for Brooker's art in "First Fruits: The World and Spirit Paintings," in *Provincial Essays*, no. 7 (1989): 17–37. Carole Luff demonstrates that Brooker had read Bergson in "Progress Passing through the Spirit: The Modernist Vision of Bertram Brooker and Lionel LeMoine FitzGerald as Redemptive Art" (master's thesis, Carleton University, 1991), 94. Adam Lauder first brought Bergson's vitalist thinking into concrete connection with Brooker's oeuvre in his "It's Alive! Bertram Brooker and Vitalism," in Cassandra Getty, ed., *The Logic of Nature, the Romance of Space* (Oshawa, ON: Robert McLaughlin Gallery and Art Gallery of Windsor, 2010), 81–105.

16 Brooker Smith to Birk Sproxton, February 28, 1981, quoted in Luff, "Progress Passing through the Spirit," 116.

17 FitzGerald to Heywood, September 24, 1942. IHHF LAC, R814 Box 310, file on FitzGerald Correspondence.

18 Indeed, the biocentric frame has been convincingly applied to Brooker's thinking by my former student Brennan Smith: "Past, Future, World and Spirit: Bertram Brooker's Enchanted Modernism" (Advanced Research Paper for master's degree, Queen's University, August 2011), 40ff. Brooker's list of "Books That Have Influenced Me" includes foundational biocentric texts such as Goethe, Emerson, Darwin, Schopenhauer, Ernst Haeckel, Nietzsche, Maurice Maeterlinck, and Oswald Spengler. See Brooker fonds, University of Manitoba Archives and Special Collections, Box 10, Folder 9. I cannot delve into possible sources of FitzGerald's biocentrism here, but it would have been Brooker who introduced FitzGerald to biocentric ideas once their intimate friendship had commenced in 1929. On this friendship, see Brooker's letters to FitzGerald among the Brooker fonds, in which Brooker repeatedly expressed his desire to meet, make art with, and converse with FitzGerald. Lauder has connected FitzGerald to a "Canadian vitalist Modernism." See Lauder, "It's Alive!," 95.

19 FitzGerald to Heywood, January 6 and 12, 1943. IHHF LAC, R814 Box 310, file on FitzGerald Correspondence.

20 FitzGerald to Heywood, December 19, 1942. IHHF LAC, R814 Box 310, file on FitzGerald Correspondence. He may be referring here to his 1927 essay "Excerpt from Tolstoy's What is Art Chapter 5. Mar. 3/1927," where he expressed disagreement with the view that "[a]rt is an activity arising even in the animal kingdom, and springing from sexual desire and the propensity to play (Schiller, Darwin, Spencer)." Instead, he inverts it, examining what art can express, which he pinpoints as "feeling." This is how he comes to the conclusion (borrowed from Tolstoy) that among other things, art can "infect" the viewer with "feelings of voluptuousness." The original is in the FitzGerald fonds. The copy I saw was in IHHF LAC, R814 Box 310, file on Research Material on L.L. FitzGerald.

21 Kenneth James Hughes, *Lionel LeMoine FitzGerald: A Reappraisal* (Winnipeg: Manitoba Cultural Studies Group, St. John's College, University of Manitoba, 1983), 33–36, referring to the Canadian social and medical historian

Michael Bliss. In the publications of the German novelist Wilhelm Bölsche, whose bestseller *Das Liebesleben in der Natur*, 1898 (*The Love Life in Nature* [New York: Albert and Charles Boni, 1926]), sold in the millions, the sex drive is identified with the life force.

22 Heywood relates in her memoir that a man she accepted a ride from in Brandon, Manitoba, attempted to rape her, though elsewhere she reports that she contracted gonorrhea, suggesting that he had succeeded. In either case, she was traumatized and expressed concern that she might be unable to have a healthy relationship with a man if she didn't try to overcome her trauma. FitzGerald "was the only one I could tell and until now the only one I have told fully," she wrote. IHHF LAC, R814 Box 310, file on Manuscripts: Memoir.

23 FitzGerald to Heywood, September 24, 1942. IHHP LAC, R814 Box 310, file on FitzGerald Correspondence.

24 *Freikörperkultur* or FKK (nudism) in German. It is possible that FitzGerald's good friend the German Danziger Fritz Brandtner, who moved to Winnipeg in 1928, told him about the Life Reform Movement or its tenets such as nudism, vegetarianism, body culture, and so on. FitzGerald was Brandtner's friend and mentor in Winnipeg, and the friendship continued beyond Brandtner's move to Montreal in 1934, at FitzGerald's suggestion. Brandtner brought at least one drawing of a nude woman on a beach with him from Danzig that FitzGerald would have seen: *Bather, Baltic Sea*, 1925, ink and gouache on paper, National Gallery of Canada, Accession No. 42976.

25 Parke-Taylor, *In Seclusion with Nature*, 16.

FITZGERALD AND THE MORPHOLOGY OF DESIRE
Robert Enright

1 FitzGerald to Brooker, February 19, 1937. Brooker fonds, University of Manitoba Archives and Special Collections, Winnipeg (emphasis in original).

CLOSE TO THE EARTH: FITZGERALD'S PATH TO ABSTRACTION
Michael Parke-Taylor

1 The relevant literature on FitzGerald/Brooker/Harris is Patricia E. Bovey, *L.L. FitzGerald and Bertram Brooker: Their Drawings* (Winnipeg: Winnipeg Art Gallery, 1975), exhibition catalogue; Carole Luff, "Progress Passing through the Spirit: The Modernist Vision of Bertram Brooker and Lionel LeMoine FitzGerald as Redemptive Art" (master's thesis, Carleton University, 1991); Ann Davis, "Celestial Spirit and Objective Nature: FitzGerald's and Harris's Adventures in Abstraction," in Catherine M. Mastin, ed., *The Group of Seven in Western Canada* (Toronto: Key Porter Books; Calgary: Glenbow Museum, 2002).

2 Bertram Brooker, "The Joy of Ownership," The Seven Arts, *Ottawa Citizen*, August 17, 1929.

3 Harris to FitzGerald, n.d. [c. February 1928], University of Manitoba Archives and Special Collections, Winnipeg, 12-0749.

4 Richard Maurice Bucke, *Cosmic Consciousness: A Study in the Evolution of the Human Mind* (Philadelphia: Innes and Sons, 1901).

5 Brooker to FitzGerald, December 28, 1929, University of Manitoba Archives and Special Collections, 11-0271.

6 Harris to FitzGerald, December 29, 1929, University of Manitoba Archives and Special Collections, 12-0752.

7 FitzGerald, Diary, June 29, 1930, 94. L.L. FitzGerald fonds, University of Manitoba Archives and Special Collections, Winnipeg, Box 1, Folder 12, 1-0183.

8 Bertram Brooker, The Seven Arts, *Ottawa Citizen*, August 24, 1929.

9 Brooker to FitzGerald, October 17, 1930, University of Manitoba Archives and Special Collections, 11-0270.

10 L.L. FitzGerald, "Plans for Work," John Simon Guggenheim Memorial Foundation, New York (file for L.L. FitzGerald), 1940. Published in Helen Coy, *FitzGerald as Printmaker: A Catalogue Raisonné of the First Complete Exhibition of the Printed Works* (Winnipeg: University of Manitoba Press, 1982), 4.

11 FitzGerald to Ayre, July 25–September 6, 1949, Robert Ayre fonds, Queen's University Archives, Kingston.

12 FitzGerald to Ayre, August 27, 1954, Ayre fonds.

13 L.L. FitzGerald, "Painters on the Prairie," radio interview, Canadian Broadcasting Corporation Midwest Network, December 1, 1954, in Michael Parke-Taylor, *In Seclusion with Nature: The Later Work of L. LeMoine FitzGerald, 1942 to 1956* (Winnipeg: Winnipeg Art Gallery, 1988), appendix B, 51.

CHRONOLOGY | *Michael Parke-Taylor*

1 The document that references FitzGerald's railway trip from Winnipeg to Snowflake is in the Lionel LeMoine FitzGerald fonds, University of Manitoba Archives and Special Collections, Box 6, Folder 5, 21-0074. It is a nine-page illustrated letter (very humorous) from FitzGerald to Vally postmarked "MANITOU Aug. 11 [19]26," written on the train as he stopped in various small towns in Manitoba.

2 Fitzgerald's Guggenheim application is quoted in Helen Coy, *FitzGerald as Printmaker: A Catalogue Raisonné of the First Complete Exhibition of the Printed Works* (Winnipeg: University of Manitoba Press, 1982), 3–4.

3 FitzGerald to Heywood, May 23, 1942. Irene Heywood Hemsworth fonds, Library and Archives Canada, Ottawa, R814 Box 310, file on FitzGerald correspondence.

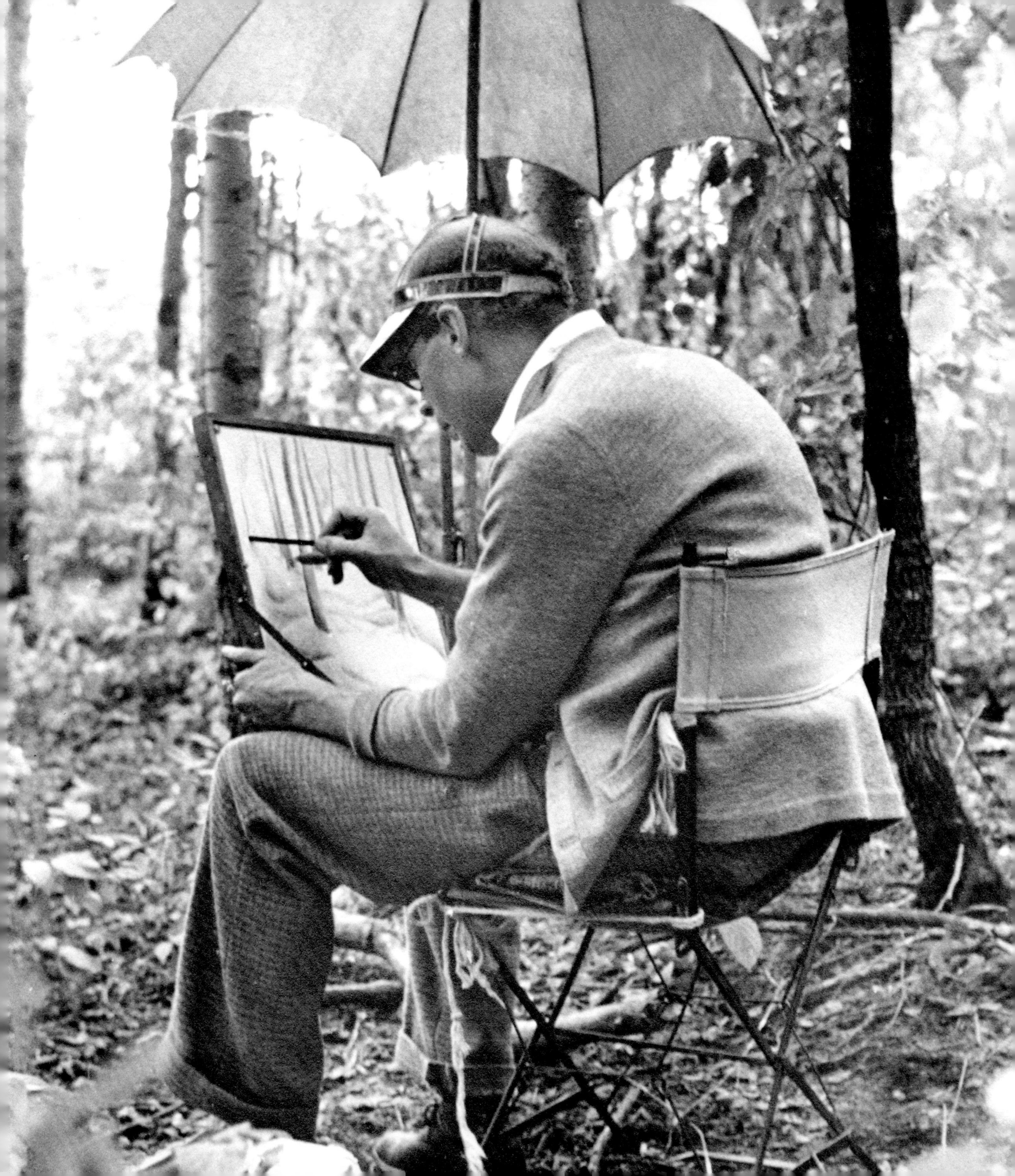

List of Works

Those with an asterisk * are not in the exhibition

Abstract, n.d.
graphite, crayon on paper
22.7 × 30.6 cm;
image: 17.4 × 23.2 cm
Gift from the Douglas M. Duncan Collection / Collection of the Winnipeg Art Gallery / G-70-422
Photo: Alexandra Cousins, courtesy of the Winnipeg Art Gallery

Abstract, n.d.
graphite, charcoal on paper
23 × 30.6 cm;
image: 17.5 × 23.2 cm
Gift from the Douglas M. Duncan Collection / Collection of the Winnipeg Art Gallery / G-70-415
Photo: Leif Norman, courtesy of the Winnipeg Art Gallery

Abstract, n.d.
graphite on paper
15.3 × 22.8 cm;
image: 11.5 × 15.4 cm
Gift from the Douglas M. Duncan Collection / Collection of the Winnipeg Art Gallery / G-70-440
Photo: Alexandra Cousins, courtesy of the Winnipeg Art Gallery

Abstract, n.d.
graphite on paper
10.7 × 13.2 cm;
image: 10.2 × 12.7 cm
Gift from the Douglas M. Duncan Collection / Collection of the Winnipeg Art Gallery / G-70-459
Photo: Alexandra Cousins, courtesy of the Winnipeg Art Gallery

Abstract, n.d.
graphite on paper
10 × 17.3 cm; image:
6.5 × 7 cm
Gift from the Douglas M. Duncan Collection / Collection of the Winnipeg Art Gallery / G-70-467
Photo: Alexandra Cousins, courtesy of the Winnipeg Art Gallery

Abstract, n.d.
graphite on paper
10.6 × 13 cm
Gift from the Douglas M. Duncan Collection / Collection of the Winnipeg Art Gallery / G-70-468
Photo: Alexandra Cousins, courtesy of the Winnipeg Art Gallery

Abstract, n.d.
graphite on paper
19.7 × 14.6 cm;
image: 19 × 14 cm
Gift from the Douglas M. Duncan Collection / Collection of the Winnipeg Art Gallery / G-70-469
Photo: Alexandra Cousins, courtesy of the Winnipeg Art Gallery

Abstract, n.d.
graphite on paper
framed: 49 × 39 cm
Collection of Oliver A.I. Botar
p. 82

Abstract, n.d.
pen and ink on paper
sheet: 31.5 × 37 cm
Canada Council Joint Drawings Purchase Fund, 1961 / Art Gallery of Ontario, Toronto / 61/15
Courtesy of the Art Gallery of Ontario

Abstract, 1950
graphite on paper
14.2 × 19.5 cm;
image: 13.7 × 19.1 cm
Gift from the Douglas M. Duncan Collection / Collection of the Winnipeg Art Gallery / G-70-474
Photo: Alexandra Cousins, courtesy of the Winnipeg Art Gallery

Abstract, 1950
graphite on paper
8.9 × 16.9 cm;
image: 8.4 × 16.4 cm
Gift from the Douglas M. Duncan Collection / Collection of the Winnipeg Art Gallery / G-70-478
Photo: Alexandra Cousins, courtesy of the Winnipeg Art Gallery

Abstract, 1950
watercolour over graphite on paper
20.5 × 15.3 cm
Purchase 1986 / McMichael Canadian Art Collection, Kleinburg 1986.26 / **p. vii**

Abstract, 1950
graphite on paper
19.1 × 14 cm
Gift from the Douglas M. Duncan Collection / Collection of the Winnipeg Art Gallery / G-70-465
Photo: Alexandra Cousins, courtesy of the Winnipeg Art Gallery

Abstract, 1950/55
graphite on paper
13 × 10.6 cm;
image: 12.7 × 10.1 cm
Gift from the Douglas M. Duncan Collection / Collection of the Winnipeg Art Gallery / G-70-460
Photo: Alexandra Cousins, courtesy of the Winnipeg Art Gallery

Abstract: Green and Gold, 1954
oil on canvas
71.7 × 92 cm
Gift of Mr. and Mrs. Joseph Harris Collection of the Winnipeg Art Gallery G-63-287 / Photo: Ernest Mayer, courtesy of the Winnipeg Art Gallery
p. 188

Abstract in Blue and Gold, 1954
oil on hardboard
44.5 × 69.5 cm
Gift of the Volunteer Committee, 1990 / Art Gallery of Hamilton 1990.2 / **p. 195**

Abstract Landscape, 1942
coloured chalk on wove paper
61 × 46 cm
Gift from the Douglas M. Duncan Collection, 1970 / National Gallery of Canada, Ottawa / 16473 / Photo: NGC
p. 169

Abstract on Blue, 1956
ink on paper
47 × 48 cm
The Jack and Frances Barwick Collection, 1985 / Carleton University Art Gallery, Ottawa / 1985.9
Photo: Justin Wonnacott / **p. 185**

Abstract on Blue Paper, 1956
pen and black ink on blue wove paper
32.5 × 37.8 cm
Gift from the Douglas M. Duncan Collection, 1970 / National Gallery of Canada, Ottawa / 16482
Photo: NGC / **p. 182**

Aerial View, from the series Small Pencil Sketches 1953 Made on a Trip by Plane to Toronto and Ottawa, 1953
graphite on paper
18.2 × 14 cm
Gift of Mr. Edward FitzGerald Collection of the Winnipeg Art Gallery G-63-188 p
Photo: Alexandra Cousins, courtesy of the Winnipeg Art Gallery

Aerial View, from the series Small Pencil Sketches 1953 Made on a Trip by Plane to Toronto and Ottawa, 1953
graphite on paper
18.1 × 14.2 cm
Gift of Mr. Edward FitzGerald Collection of the Winnipeg Art Gallery G-63-188 q / Photo: Alexandra Cousins, courtesy of the Winnipeg Art Gallery

OPPOSITE
FitzGerald sketching at Silver Heights, Winnipeg, August 23, 1934
Gift of Earl and Patsy Green from the Estate of Patricia Morrison / School of Art Gallery, University of Manitoba, Winnipeg / 1-0228 / Photo: Arnold O. Brigden

Aerial View, from the series Small Pencil Sketches 1953 Made on a Trip by Plane to Toronto and Ottawa, 1953
graphite on paper
18.1 × 14.1 cm
Gift of Mr. Edward FitzGerald
Collection of the Winnipeg Art Gallery G-63-188 e / Photo: Alexandra Cousins, courtesy of the Winnipeg Art Gallery

Aerial View, from the series Small Pencil Sketches 1953 Made on a Trip by Plane to Toronto and Ottawa, 1953
graphite on paper
18.1 × 14 cm
Gift of Mr. Edward FitzGerald
Collection of the Winnipeg Art Gallery G-63-188 a / Photo: Alexandra Cousins, courtesy of the Winnipeg Art Gallery

Aerial View, from the series Small Pencil Sketches 1953 Made on a Trip by Plane to Toronto and Ottawa, 1953
graphite on paper
18.1 × 14 cm
Gift of Mr. Edward FitzGerald
Collection of the Winnipeg Art Gallery G-63-188 d / Photo: Alexandra Cousins, courtesy of the Winnipeg Art Gallery

Aerial View, from the series Small Pencil Sketches 1953 Made on a Trip by Plane to Toronto and Ottawa, 1953
graphite on paper
18.1 × 14.1 cm
Gift of Mr. Edward FitzGerald
Collection of the Winnipeg Art GalleryG-63-188 r / Photo: Alexandra Cousins, courtesy of the Winnipeg Art Gallery

Apples in a Bowl, 1947
ink on paper
29.1 × 42 cm
Gift of the Women's Committee
Collection of the Winnipeg Art Gallery G-57-152 / Photo: Leif Norman, courtesy of the Winnipeg Art Gallery
p. 127

Apples, Still Life, 1933
oil on panel
30.5 × 38.1 cm
Private collection, Mississauga
p. 124

April Rhythm, c. 1954
oil on Masonite
60.8 × 76 cm
Private collection / Photo: Toni Hafkenscheid, courtesy of Art Canada Institute / **p. 191**

Arts Buildings, University of Manitoba, 1941
linocut on paper
28.9 × 14.4 cm;
image: 17.8 × 10.3 cm
Gift of Mr. C.C. Sinclair / Collection of the Winnipeg Art Gallery G-65-173 / Photo: Alexandra Cousins, courtesy of the Winnipeg Art Gallery
p. 155

Autumn Sonata, 1953–54
oil on board
59.5 × 75 cm
Gift of the Estate of Patricia Morrison and Victor Brooker, 1976
School of Art Gallery, University of Manitoba, Winnipeg / 76.158
p. 190

Backyard View of FitzGerald's House, 160 Lyle Street, c. 1930
oil on canvas
106.7 × 94 cm
Collection of I. Gaspard
Photo: Leif Norman / **p. 150**

Barlow's Garage, 1950
watercolour with charcoal and graphite on paper
65.3 × 47.5 cm
Gift from the Fund of the T. Eaton Co. Ltd. for Canadian Works of Art, 1953
Art Gallery of Ontario, Toronto 52/52 / Courtesy of the Art Gallery of Ontario / **p. 148**

The Barn, c. 1930
oil on board
29.7 × 36.4 cm
Gift from the Estate of Arnold O. Brigden / Collection of the Winnipeg Art Gallery / G-73-327 / Photo: Leif Norman, courtesy of the Winnipeg Art Gallery / **p. 43**

Book, 1948
ink on paper
30.5 × 46 cm
Gift of Mr. and Mrs. John H. Moore, London, Ontario, through the Ontario Heritage Foundation, 1978
Collection of Museum London 78.A.64 / **p. 128**

* *Brazil*, c. 1950–51
oil on canvas
50.8 × 56 cm
Gift from the Douglas M. Duncan Collection, 1970 / National Gallery of Canada, Ottawa / 16467
Photo: NGC / **p. 193**

Broken Tree in Landscape, 1931
oil on canvas
35.5 × 42.8 cm
Gift of the Women's Committee
Collection of the Winnipeg Art Gallery G-56-29 / Photo: Ernest Mayer, courtesy of the Winnipeg Art Gallery
p. 53

Broken Tree, Kildonan Park, 1920
oil on canvas
83.8 × 88.9 cm
Private collection, Ontario
p. 35

Campbell's House, January 20, 1950
watercolour over graphite on wove paper
56.3 × 38.8 cm
Purchased 1957 / National Gallery of Canada, Ottawa / 6721 / Photo: NGC
p. 149

Cloud over Mountain, 1943/44
watercolour on paper
60 × 45.7 cm
Collection of Leo and Margaret Yau
p. 159

Clouds, 1931
graphite on paper
30.5 × 22.9 cm
Gift of the Douglas M. Duncan Collection, 1970 / Carleton University Art Gallery, Ottawa / 1970.12
Photo: Justin Wonnacott / **p. 61**

Clouds, 1943
watercolour on paper
61.1 × 45.8 cm
Gift of John and Helen O'Brian
Collection of the Vancouver Art Gallery VAG 97.35.7 / Photo: Trevor Mills, Vancouver Art Gallery / **p. 158**

Clouds, from the series Sketches Made in Mexico 1951, 1951
graphite on paper
17.6 × 12 cm
Gift of Mr. Edward FitzGerald
Collection of the Winnipeg Art Gallery G-63-230 x / Photo: Alexandra Cousins, courtesy of the Winnipeg Art Gallery

Clouds and Fence, from the series Sketches Made in Mexico 1951, 1951
graphite on paper
10.6 × 14.6 cm
Gift of Mr. Edward FitzGerald
Collection of the Winnipeg Art Gallery G-63-230 q / Photo: Alexandra Cousins, courtesy of the Winnipeg Art Gallery

Composition, 1951
oil on panel
15.2 × 20.3 cm
Collection of Robert Hucal, Winnipeg
Photo: Leif Norman
p. 192

Composition, c. 1952
oil on canvas
66 × 56 cm
Purchase, Horsley and Annie Townsend Bequest / The Montreal Museum of Fine Arts / 1964.1496
Photo: The Montreal Museum of Fine Arts / **p. 178**

Conception, May 31, 1956
ink on paper
23 × 16.1 cm
The Eckhardt-Gramatté Foundation, Winnipeg / Photo: Leif Norman
p. 85

Construction, n.d.
graphite on paper
24 × 29 cm
Gift from the Douglas M. Duncan Collection / Collection of the Winnipeg Art Gallery / G-70-374 / Photo: Leif Norman, courtesy of the Winnipeg Art Gallery / **p. 140**

The Cupola, 1940
oil on canvas
26.7 × 26.7 cm
Gift of the Founders, Robert and Signe McMichael / McMichael Canadian Art Collection, Kleinburg / 1973.14.2
p. 153

Daffodil, c. 1940
coloured chalk on paper
63 × 48 cm
The Jack and Frances Barwick Collection, 1985 / Carleton University Art Gallery, Ottawa / Photo: Justin Wonnacott / 1985.1 / **p. 111**

Dance Emporium Purves, from the series Trip to Snowflake 1926, August 11, 1926
graphite on paper
12 × 16 cm
Gift of Mr. Edward FitzGerald
Collection of the Winnipeg Art Gallery
G-63-191

Dead Trees, c. 1930
oil on canvas
50.5 × 55.5 cm;
framed: 53.7 × 58.6 cm
Gift from the Douglas M. Duncan Collection, 1970 / National Gallery of Canada, Ottawa / 16446 / Photo: NGC
p. 54

Doc Snyder's House, 1931
oil on canvas
74.9 × 85.1 cm
Gift of P.D. Ross, Ottawa, 1932
National Gallery of Canada, Ottawa
3993 / Photo: NGC / **p. 146**

Domain, from the series Trip to Snowflake 1926, August 11, 1926
graphite on paper
12 × 16 cm
Gift of Mr. Edward FitzGerald
Collection of the Winnipeg Art Gallery
G-63-207

Driftwood, 1944
coloured pencil on paper
sheet: 61.1 × 45.8 cm
Gift from the Douglas M. Duncan Collection, 1970 / Art Gallery of Ontario, Toronto / 70/57 / Courtesy of the Art Gallery of Ontario
p. 168

Driftwood and Rocks, 1942
charcoal on paper
62.2 × 46.5 cm
Gift from the Douglas M. Duncan Collection / Collection of the Winnipeg Art Gallery / G-70-100 / Photo: Leif Norman, courtesy of the Winnipeg Art Gallery / **p. 171**

Driftwood, Bowen Island, BC, 1942
coloured pencil on paper
57.8 × 43.8 cm
Private collection / **p. 175**

Evening, The Red River, Winnipeg, c. 1920
oil on canvas
133.7 × 93.1 cm
The Power Corporation of Canada Art Collection / **p. 6**

Fallen Tree (Uprooted Tree), c. 1926
drypoint on paper
sheet (irregular):
24.4 × 31.6 cm
Gift from the Douglas M. Duncan Collection, 1970 / Art Gallery of Ontario, Toronto / 70/78 / Courtesy of the Art Gallery of Ontario / **p. 79**

Farmyard, 1931
oil on canvas
34.9 × 42.6 cm
Vincent Massey Bequest, 1968
National Gallery of Canada, Ottawa
15474 / Photo: NGC / **p. 49**

Figure in the Woods, 1920
oil on canvas
91.4 × 61 cm
Collection of the Sinclair Family
p. 32

Flooded Landscape, 1956
pen and ink on paper
sheet (irregular):
32.7 × 38.1 cm
Gift from J.S. McLean, Canadian Fund, 1957 / Art Gallery of Ontario, Toronto 56/31 / Courtesy of the Art Gallery of Ontario

Four Apples on a Window Sill, c. 1943
coloured chalk on paper
46 × 61 cm
Collection of the Winnipeg Art Gallery
G-89-1541 / Photo: Leif Norman, courtesy of the Winnipeg Art Gallery
p. 113

Four Apples on Tablecloth, 1947
ink on paper
46 × 60.9 cm
Collection of the Winnipeg Art Gallery
L-47 / Photo: Leif Norman, courtesy of the Winnipeg Art Gallery
p. 126

Fragments, from the series Trip to Snowflake 1926, August 11, 1926
graphite on paper
12 × 16 cm
Gift of Mr. Edward FitzGerald
Collection of the Winnipeg Art Gallery
G-63-208

* *From an Upstairs Window, Winter*, c. 1950–51
oil on canvas
61 × 45.7 cm
Purchased 1951 / National Gallery of Canada, Ottawa / 5800
Photo: NGC / **p. 115**

Garage and House, 1928
oil on canvas
46.1 × 56.7 cm
Gift from the Douglas M. Duncan Collection, 1970 / National Gallery of Canada, Ottawa / 16367 / Photo: NGC
p. 136

Geranium and Bottle, 1949
oil on canvas
45.6 × 30.1 cm
Collection of the Winnipeg Art Gallery
L-9 / Photo: Leif Norman, courtesy of the Winnipeg Art Gallery
p. 121

Grain Silos, Saskatchewan, n.d.
oil on canvas, laid down on board
30.5 × 27.9 cm
Private collection, Toronto / Courtesy of Oeno Gallery / **p. 38**

Green Apple, 1945
oil on canvas, mounted on Masonite
29.6 × 33 cm
Gift from the Douglas M. Duncan Collection, 1970 / National Gallery of Canada, Ottawa / 16361 / Photo: NGC
p. 125

Green Self-Portrait with Two Nudes, c. 1942
watercolour on paper
60.9 × 45.7 cm
Acquired with funds from the Women's Committee and The Winnipeg Foundation / Collection of the Winnipeg Art Gallery / G-63-19
Photo: Lianed Marcoleta, courtesy of the Winnipeg Art Gallery

Haystacks and Clouds, from the series Trip to Snowflake 1926, August 11, 1926
graphite on paper
12 × 16 cm
Gift of Mr. Edward FitzGerald
Collection of the Winnipeg Art Gallery
G-63-200

Hilly Landscape, from the series Sketches Made in Mexico 1951, 1951
graphite on paper
10.5 × 14.6 cm
Gift of Mr. Edward FitzGerald
Collection of the Winnipeg Art Gallery
G-63-230 f

Horndean, from the series Trip to Snowflake 1926, August 11, 1926
graphite on paper
12 × 16 cm
Gift of Mr. Edward FitzGerald
Collection of the Winnipeg Art Gallery
G-63-201

Interior with Chair, c. 1930
oil on canvas
75 × 70 cm
The Power Corporation of Canada Art Collection / **p. 16**

Into the Poplar Woods, n.d.
hand-lettered folder with title page and six drawings in graphite on paper
Library and Archives Canada, Ottawa, Irene Heywood Hemsworth fonds, e011192288-e011192294
p. 94

The Jar, 1938
oil on canvas
61.3 × 53.9 cm
Gift of the Women's Committee Collection of the Winnipeg Art Gallery G-56-25 / Photo: Leif Norman, courtesy of the Winnipeg Art Gallery
p. 118

Jug on the Window Sill, 1943
chalk on paper
60.8 × 45.7 cm
Gift of the Women's Committee Collection of the Winnipeg Art Gallery G-56-27 / Photo: Alexandra Cousins, courtesy of the Winnipeg Art Gallery
p. 114

Lake Louise, 1925
graphite on paper
13.3 × 17.8 cm
Gift from the Douglas M. Duncan Collection / Collection of the Winnipeg Art Gallery / G-70-434

Lake Winnipeg, 1929
oil on canvas
29.8 × 36.2 cm
Private collection
Photo: Leif Norman / **p. 44**

Landscape, 1925
graphite on paper
13.5 × 17.8 cm
Gift from the Douglas M. Duncan Collection / Collection of the Winnipeg Art Gallery / G-70-476

* *Landscape*, from the series Sketches Made in Mexico 1951, 1951
graphite on paper
14.5 × 10.5 cm
Gift of Mr. Edward FitzGerald Collection of the Winnipeg Art Gallery G-63-230 e / Photo: Alexandra Cousins, courtesy of the Winnipeg Art Gallery

Landscape, from the series Small Pencil Sketches 1953 Made on a Trip by Plane to Toronto and Ottawa, 1953
graphite on paper
18.1 × 14 cm
Gift of Mr. Edward FitzGerald Collection of the Winnipeg Art Gallery G-63-188 c

Landscape, from the series Small Pencil Sketches 1953 Made on a Trip by Plane to Toronto and Ottawa, 1953
graphite on paper
18.1 × 14.1 cm
Gift of Mr. Edward FitzGerald Collection of the Winnipeg Art Gallery G-63-188 j

Landscape, from the series Small Pencil Sketches 1953 Made on a Trip by Plane to Toronto and Ottawa, 1953
graphite on paper
17.8 × 14 cm
Gift of Mr. Edward FitzGerald Collection of the Winnipeg Art Gallery G-63-188 k

Landscape with Barn, n.d.
oil on canvas
25.4 × 36.2 cm
Courtesy of Loch Gallery, Winnipeg
p. 42

Landscape with Clouds, 1937
graphite on laid paper
24 × 32 cm
Gift from the Douglas M. Duncan Collection, 1970 / National Gallery of Canada, Ottawa / 16297 / Photo: NGC
p. 59

Landscape with House and Haystacks, from the series Trip to Snowflake 1926, August 11, 1926
graphite on paper
12 × 16 cm
Gift of Mr. Edward FitzGerald / Collection of the Winnipeg Art Gallery G-63-205

Landscape with River, 1955
ink on paper
sheet: 27.9 × 42.9 cm; image: 25.5 × 41.8 cm
Gift of Michael and Sonja Koerner McMichael Canadian Art Collection, Kleinburg / 2018.9.1 / **p. 64**

Large Trees and Bridge, June 17, 1937
graphite on laid paper
31.5 × 24 cm
Gift from the Douglas M. Duncan Collection, 1970 / National Gallery of Canada, Ottawa / 16315 / Photo: NGC
p. 77

* *Late Fall, Manitoba*, 1917
oil on canvas
76.7 × 91.7 cm
Purchased 1918 / National Gallery of Canada, Ottawa / 1483
Photo: NGC / **p. 10**

Leaves, n.d.
chalk on paper
63 × 48.2 cm
Gift from the Douglas M. Duncan Collection, 1970 / Collection of Museum London / 70.A.88
p. 112

Leaves, 1937
graphite on paper
31.7 × 24 cm
Gift from the Douglas M. Duncan Collection / Collection of the Winnipeg Art Gallery / G-74-96 / Photo: Alexandra Cousins, courtesy of the Winnipeg Art Gallery
p. 81

The Little Plant, 1947
oil on canvas
60.5 × 45.7 cm
Gift of Mr. R.A. Laidlaw / McMichael Canadian Art Collection, Kleinburg 1969.2.4 / **p. 106**

Morris, from the series Trip to Snowflake 1926, August 11, 1926
graphite on paper
12 × 16 cm
Gift of Mr. Edward FitzGerald Collection of the Winnipeg Art Gallery G-63-204 / Photo: Alexandra Cousins, courtesy of the Winnipeg Art Gallery

Mountain Cliff, 1942
coloured pencil with graphite on paper
sheet: 61 × 45.9 cm
Gift from the Douglas M. Duncan Collection, 1970 / Art Gallery of Ontario, Toronto / 70/59 / Courtesy of the Art Gallery of Ontario
p. 162

Mountains, c. 1943–44
watercolour on wove paper
60.9 × 45.7 cm
Purchased 1957 / National Gallery of Canada, Ottawa / 6724 / Photo: NGC
p. 160

* *Mountains*, from the series Sketches Made in Mexico 1951, 1951
graphite on paper
15.3 × 11.5 cm
Gift of Mr. Edward FitzGerald Collection of the Winnipeg Art Gallery G-63-230u / Photo: Alexandra Cousins, courtesy of the Winnipeg Art Gallery

* *New York Life Building*, June 20, 1930
pencil on paper
20 × 20.5 cm
Lionel LeMoine FitzGerald fonds, MSS 287 (A2009-016), Box 3, Folder 11, Item 43 / University of Manitoba Archives & Special Collections, Winnipeg / **p. 21**

Night Movement over Fargo, from the series Sketches Made in Mexico 1951, 1951
graphite on paper
12 × 17.8 cm
Gift of Mr. Edward FitzGerald Collection of the Winnipeg Art Gallery G-63-230 w / Photo: Alexandra Cousins, courtesy of the Winnipeg Art Gallery

Nude, n.d.
graphite on paper
28 × 19.2 cm
Gift of Mr. Edward FitzGerald Collection of the Winnipeg Art Gallery G-63-107 / Photo: Alexandra Cousins, courtesy of the Winnipeg Art Gallery

Nude Reclining on Bed, 1928
chalk on paper
22.9 × 30.5 cm
Gift of Mr. Edward FitzGerald Collection of the Winnipeg Art Gallery G-63-137 / Photo: Ernest Mayer, courtesy of the Winnipeg Art Gallery
p. 96

Oakdale Place, c. 1950
oil on Masonite
59.7 × 42.4 cm
Private collection / Photo: Toni Hafkenscheid, courtesy of Art Canada Institute / **p. 151**

Organic Forms, 1942
crayon on paper
61.1 × 46 cm
Gift from the Douglas M. Duncan Collection / Collection of the Winnipeg Art Gallery / G-70-114 / Photo: Lianed Marcoleta, courtesy of the Winnipeg Art Gallery / **p. 174**

Over Grand Forks, from the series Sketches Made in Mexico 1951, 1951
graphite on paper
12 × 17.5 cm
Gift of Mr. Edward FitzGerald Collection of the Winnipeg Art Gallery G-63-230 bb / Photo: Alexandra Cousins, courtesy of the Winnipeg Art Gallery

Over St. Jo, Mi., from the series Sketches Made in Mexico 1951, 1951
graphite on paper
17.7 × 11.9 cm
Gift of Mr. Edward FitzGerald Collection of the Winnipeg Art Gallery G-63-230 z / Photo: Alexandra Cousins, courtesy of the Winnipeg Art Gallery

Over Tampico, Noon, from the series Sketches Made in Mexico 1951, 1951
graphite on paper
17.6 × 11.7 cm
Gift of Mr. Edward FitzGerald Collection of the Winnipeg Art Gallery G-63-230 y / Photo: Alexandra Cousins, courtesy of the Winnipeg Art Gallery

Park (Abstract), n.d.
graphite on paper
15.1 × 22.8 cm;
image: 11.5 × 15.2 cm
Gift from the Douglas M. Duncan Collection / Collection of the Winnipeg Art Gallery / G-70-439 / Photo: Alexandra Cousins, courtesy of the Winnipeg Art Gallery

Path over the Hill, 1956
ink on paper
32.5 × 37.5 cm;
image: 30.1 × 35.3 cm
Gift of the Women's Committee Collection of the Winnipeg Art Gallery G-57-153 / Photo: Leif Norman, courtesy of the Winnipeg Art Gallery
p. 183

Pembina Valley, 1923
oil on canvas
46 × 56 cm
Given in memory of Richard A. Graybiel by his family, 1979 / Art Gallery of Windsor / 1979.073
p. 57

The Pool, 1934
oil on canvas
36.2 × 43.7 cm
Purchased 1973 / National Gallery of Canada, Ottawa / 17612 / Photo: NGC
p. 187

The Pool No. 4, Moonlight, 1956
pen and black ink heightened with white on blue wove paper
38.5 × 47.3 cm
Gift from the Douglas M. Duncan Collection, 1970 / National Gallery of Canada, Ottawa / 16335 / Photo: NGC
p. 184

Poplar Woods (Poplars), 1929
oil on canvas
71.8 × 91.5 cm
Acquired in memory of Mr. and Mrs. Arnold O. Brigden / Collection of the Winnipeg Art Gallery / G-75-88 Photo: Lianed Marcoleta, courtesy of the Winnipeg Art Gallery
p. 68

* *Potato Patch, Snowflake*, 1925
oil on canvas on board
43.4 × 52.2 cm
Gift of Dr. Bernhard Fast / Collection of the Winnipeg Art Gallery / G-98-279 / Photo: Lianed Marcoleta, courtesy of the Winnipeg Art Gallery
p. 15

Prairie, c. 1921
oil on canvas, laid down on paperboard
18.2 × 22.2 cm
Gift of The Robert and Signe McMichael Trust / McMichael Canadian Art Collection, Kleinburg 2011.2.15 / **p. 36**

The Prairie, 1929
oil on canvas
28.7 × 33.6 cm
Gift from the Estate of Arnold O. Brigden / Collection of the Winnipeg Art Gallery / G-73-332 / Photo: Leif Norman, courtesy of the Winnipeg Art Gallery / **p. 41**

Prairie Farm, 1931
oil
35.9 × 43.2 cm
Private collection
Photo: Leif Norman / **p. 46**

Prairie Landscape, 1935
graphite on paper
sheet: 30.7 × 23 cm
Gift of the Kudelka Family, 1990 / Art Gallery of Ontario, Toronto / 90/94 Courtesy of the Art Gallery of Ontario
p. 28

Prairie Sky, June 29, 1935
graphite on wove paper
30.5 × 22.9 cm
Gift from the Douglas M. Duncan Collection, 1970 / National Gallery of Canada, Ottawa / 16305 / Photo: NGC
p. 62

Prairie Town, 1931
oil
35.9 × 43.5 cm
Private collection
Photo: Leif Norman / **p. 47**

Prairie Trail No. 2, 1956
ink on paper
45.7 × 57.1 cm;
image: 43 × 50.5 cm
Acquired with funds from the Naylor Bequest / Collection of the Winnipeg Art Gallery / G-86-145 / Photo: Alexandra Cousins, courtesy of the Winnipeg Art Gallery / **p. 5**

Prairie Trail No. 3, July 17, 1956
pen and black ink on laid paper
45.2 × 56.7 cm
Gift from the Douglas M. Duncan Collection, 1970 / National Gallery of Canada, Ottawa / 16355 / Photo: NGC
p. 65

Pritchard's Fence, c. 1928
oil on canvas
overall: 71.6 × 76.5 cm
Bequest of Isabel E.G. Lyle, 1951 Art Gallery of Ontario, Toronto / 51/19 / Courtesy of the Art Gallery of Ontario / **p. 137**

Railway Station, c. 1930–31
graphite on paper
Sheet: 31.4 × 35.8 cm
Canada Council Joint Drawings Purchase Fund, 1961 / Art Gallery of Ontario, Toronto / 61/13 / Courtesy of the Art Gallery of Ontario
p. 48

Reclining Nude, n.d.
pen and ink on paper
Sheet: 26.8 × 39.5 cm
Canada Council Joint Drawings Purchase Fund, 1961 / Art Gallery of Ontario, Toronto / 61/14 / Courtesy of the Art Gallery of Ontario
p. 89

Recumbent Daphne, c. 1926
drypoint on buff laid paper
11.5 × 13 cm;
plate: 7.4 × 8.3 cm
Gift from the Douglas M. Duncan Collection, 1970 / National Gallery of Canada, Ottawa / 16227 / Photo: NGC
p. 98

Recumbent Daphne, c. 1926
drypoint on buff laid paper
15.5 × 23.3 cm;
plate: 7.4 × 8.3 cm
Gift from the Douglas M. Duncan Collection, 1970 / National Gallery of Canada, Ottawa / 16222 / Photo: NGC
p. 98

Recumbent Daphne, c. 1926
drypoint on wove paper
12 × 15.5 cm;
plate: 7.4 × 8.3 cm
Gift from the Douglas M. Duncan Collection, 1970 / National Gallery of Canada, Ottawa / 16225 / Photo: NGC
p. 99

Recumbent Daphne, c. 1926
drypoint on wove paper
12.1 × 15.5 cm;
plate: 7.4 × 8.3 cm
Gift from the Douglas M. Duncan Collection, 1970 / National Gallery of Canada, Ottawa / 16226 / Photo: NGC
p. 99

Red Barn, c. 1934
oil on canvas
43.2 × 35.8 cm
Gift from the Douglas M. Duncan Collection, 1970 / National Gallery of Canada, Ottawa / 16425 / Photo: NGC
p. 25

The Red House, c. 1925
oil on canvas
50.8 × 41.9 cm
The Power Corporation of Canada Art Collection / **p. 39**

Remarks by FitzGerald, from the series *Trip to Snowflake 1926*, August 11, 1926
graphite on paper
12 × 16 cm
Gift of Mr. Edward FitzGerald Collection of the Winnipeg Art Gallery G-63-209 / Photo: Alexandra Cousins, courtesy of the Winnipeg Art Gallery

Road in the Country, 1927
oil on canvas
30 × 38 cm
Gift from the Douglas M. Duncan Collection, 1970 / National Gallery of Canada, Ottawa / 16529 / Photo: NGC
p. 52

Road to Snowflake, 1923
oil on panel
19.1 × 15.9 cm
Collection of Cara and Murray Sinclair Photo: Rachel Topham Photography
p. 37

Rocks, 1943
coloured chalk on wove paper
60.9 × 45.6 cm
Gift from the Douglas M. Duncan Collection, 1970 / National Gallery of Canada, Ottawa / 16347 / Photo: NGC
p. 167

Rocks, 1944
watercolour on paper
61 × 45.7 cm
Private collection / Photo: Toni Hafkenscheid, courtesy of Art Canada Institute / **p. 167**

Rocks and Log, 1942
charcoal on paper
62.1 × 46.1 cm
Gift from the Douglas M. Duncan Collection / Collection of the Winnipeg Art Gallery / G-70-99 / Photo: Alexandra Cousins, courtesy of the Winnipeg Art Gallery / **p. 170**

Rocks at the Water's Edge, 1944
watercolour on paper
46 × 61 cm
Gift from the Douglas M. Duncan Collection, 1970 / Art Gallery of Windsor / 1970.031
p. 173

Rocky Shore, Howe Sound, 1943
watercolour on paper
61 × 45.8 cm
Gift from the Douglas M. Duncan Collection / Collection of the Vancouver Art Gallery / VAG 70.68 Photo: Maegan Hill-Carroll, Vancouver Art Gallery / **p. 166**

Rooftops, Civic Auditorium, c. 1938–39
linocut on paper
13.3 × 26.1 cm;
image: 10.5 × 14.2 cm
Gift of C.C. Sinclair / Collection of the Winnipeg Art Gallery / G-65-174 Photo: Alexandra Cousins, courtesy of the Winnipeg Art Gallery
p. 155

Rosenfeld, from the series Trip to Snowflake 1926, August 11, 1926
graphite on paper
12.1 × 15.9 cm
Gift of Mr. Edward FitzGerald Collection of the Winnipeg Art Gallery G-63-202 / Photo: Alexandra Cousins, courtesy of the Winnipeg Art Gallery

Scene with Clouds, from the series Sketches Made in Mexico 1951, 1951
graphite on paper
11.5 × 15.2 cm
Gift of Mr. Edward FitzGerald Collection of the Winnipeg Art Gallery G-63-230 n / Photo: Alexandra Cousins, courtesy of the Winnipeg Art Gallery

Seated Nude Torso, 1937
graphite on paper
30.5 × 22.8 cm
Gift of Mr. Edward FitzGerald Collection of the Winnipeg Art Gallery G-63-128 / Photo: Alexandra Cousins, courtesy of the Winnipeg Art Gallery
p. 103

Self-Portrait No. 1, n.d.
drypoint on paper
sheet: 14.7 × 13 cm
Gift from the Douglas M. Duncan Collection, 1970 / Art Gallery of Ontario / 70/67 / Courtesy of the Art Gallery of Ontario / **p. 201**

Self-Portrait No. 2, c. 1927
drypoint in brown on laid paper
23.1 × 16.5 cm;
plate: 10.5 × 8.9 cm
Gift from the Douglas M. Duncan Collection, 1970 / National Gallery of Canada, Ottawa / 16250 / Photo: NGC
p. 203

Self-Portrait, c. 1945
watercolour on paper
60.9 × 45.7 cm
Acquired with funds from the Women's Committee and The Winnipeg Foundation / Collection of the Winnipeg Art Gallery / G-63-23 Photo: Alexandra Cousins, courtesy of the Winnipeg Art Gallery
p. 92

Self-Portrait, c. 1945
watercolour on paper
45.7 × 60.9 cm
Acquired with funds from the Women's Committee and The Winnipeg Foundation / Collection of the Winnipeg Art Gallery / G-63-24 Photo: Alexandra Cousins, courtesy of the Winnipeg Art Gallery

Self-Portrait, c. 1945
watercolour on paper
45.7 × 60.9 cm
Acquired with funds from the Women's Committee and The Winnipeg Foundation / Collection of the Winnipeg Art Gallery / G-63-20 Photo: Alexandra Cousins, courtesy of the Winnipeg Art Gallery

Self-Portrait (3 Nudes), c. 1945
watercolour on paper
45.7 × 60.9 cm
Acquired with funds from the Women's Committee and The Winnipeg Foundation / Collection of the Winnipeg Art Gallery / G-63-26 Photo: Alexandra Cousins, courtesy of the Winnipeg Art Gallery
p. 90

Self-Portrait (Unfinished), c. 1945
oil on canvas
54.5 × 44.5 cm
Gift of the Alumni Association of the University of Manitoba / School of Art Gallery, University of Manitoba, Winnipeg / 77.433 / **p. 93**

Self-Portrait (with Nude in Upper Left Corner), c. 1945
watercolour on paper
60.9 × 45.7 cm
Acquired with funds from the Women's Committee and The Winnipeg Foundation / Collection of the Winnipeg Art Gallery / G-63-21 Photo: Alexandra Cousins, courtesy of the Winnipeg Art Gallery / **p. 91**

Silo, 1928
watercolour and graphite on paper
13.7 × 17 cm
Gift from the Estate of Arnold O. Brigden / Collection of the Winnipeg Art Gallery / G-73-323 / Photo: Alexandra Cousins, courtesy of the Winnipeg Art Gallery

Sketch for "Poplar Woods," 1927
graphite, ink on paper
23.7 × 31.8 cm
Acquired in memory of Mr. and Mrs. Arnold O. Brigden / Collection of the Winnipeg Art Gallery / G-75-65 Photo: Leif Norman, courtesy of the Winnipeg Art Gallery / **p. 71**

Slavic Nude, 1933
graphite on paper
48.3 × 27.9 cm
University of Toronto Art Collection, Gift of Dr. Norman Bell, 2008 Art Museum University of Toronto 2008-003 / **p. 103**

Smokestack and Clouds, 1935
graphite on paper
30.5 × 22.9 cm
The Hart House Collection, Bequest of the B. Bickersteth Estate, 1978 Art Museum University of Toronto HH1978.001 / **p. 63**

Snowflake, 1949
charcoal on laid paper
31.4 × 47.6 cm
Gift from the Douglas M. Duncan Collection, 1970 / National Gallery of Canada, Ottawa / 16480 / Photo: NGC **p. 60**

Spring Bulbs, 1944
coloured chalk on wove paper
60.9 × 45.8 cm
Gift from the Douglas M. Duncan Collection, 1970 / National Gallery of Canada, Ottawa / 16353 / Photo: NGC **p. 110**

Still Life, c. 1924–25
oil on canvas
46.4 × 50.8 cm
Collection of Salah Bachir and Jacob Yerex / **p. 120**

Still-life, 1941
oil on wood
40.9 × 35.5 cm
Purchased 1973 / National Gallery of Canada, Ottawa / 17611 Photo: NGC /**p. 122**

Still Life from Window, 1952
oil on canvas
36.3 × 44.2 cm
Vancouver Art Gallery Acquisition Fund / Collection of the Vancouver Art Gallery / VAG 87.32 / Photo: Vancouver Art Gallery / **p. 117**

Still Life: Two Apples, c. 1940
oil on canvas
45.4 × 40.7 cm
Gift of the Women's Committee Collection of the Winnipeg Art Gallery G-56-28 / Photo: Lianed Marcoleta, courtesy of the Winnipeg Art Gallery **p. 123**

Still Life with Bulbs, 1938
pastel on paper
sheet: 46 × 30.6 cm
Gift from the Douglas M. Duncan Collection, 1970 / Art Gallery of Ontario, Toronto / 70/39 / Courtesy of the Art Gallery of Ontario **p. 109**

Still Life with Jars, 1924
oil on canvas
76.5 × 61 cm
Gift from the Douglas M. Duncan Collection, 1970 / Art Gallery of Ontario, Toronto / 70/35 / Courtesy of the Art Gallery of Ontario **p. 119**

Still Life with Plant, 1948
oil on canvas, laid down on board
47.9 × 35.6 cm
Private collection Photo: Frank Tancredi /**p. 116**

Still Life with Scythe, 1948
pen and ink on paper
sheet: 46.7 × 30.6 cm
Gift from the Douglas M. Duncan Collection, 1970 / Art Gallery of Ontario, Toronto / 70/51 / Courtesy Art Gallery of Ontario / **p. 129**

Stooks and Trees, 1930
oil on canvas
29 × 37.7 cm
Gift from the Estate of Florence Brigden / Collection of the Winnipeg Art Gallery / G-75-13 / Photo: Leif Norman, courtesy of the Winnipeg Art Gallery /**p. 51**

Stooks near Snowflake, Manitoba, 1923
oil on canvas
38.1 × 48.3 cm
Taylor B. Somers Collection / Photo: Rachel Topham Photography / **p. 50**

Storm on Prairies, 1935
graphite on paper
22.1 × 29.4 cm
Gift of the Founders, Robert and Signe McMichael / McMichael Canadian Art Collection, Kleinburg / 1976.25.4 **p. 40**

Study for "Pritchard's Fence," c. 1928
graphite on paper
24.2 × 26.9 cm
Gift of Earl and Patsy Green from the Estate of Patricia Morrison / School of Art Gallery, University of Manitoba, Winnipeg 12-0493 / **p. 139**

* *Summer Afternoon, The Prairie*, 1921
oil on canvas
107.2 × 89.5 cm
Collection of the Winnipeg Art Gallery L-90 / Photo: Lianed Marcoleta, courtesy of the Winnipeg Art Gallery **p. ix**

Summer, East Kildonan, 1920
oil on canvas
127.6 × 107.3 cm; framed: 148.6 × 128.3 × 10.2 cm
Private collection, Montreal **p. 34**

Transfer Drawing for "Backyards, Water Street," 1927
graphite on wove paper
22.4 × 25.8 cm
Gift from the Douglas M. Duncan Collection, 1970 / National Gallery of Canada, Ottawa / 16769 / Photo: NGC **p. 138**

Tree, n.d.
graphite on paper
31.6 × 24 cm
Gift of Mr. Edward FitzGerald Collection of the Winnipeg Art Gallery G-63-80 / Photo: Alexandra Cousins, courtesy of the Winnipeg Art Gallery **p. 54**

Tree Roots, 1939
graphite on paper
27.6 × 38.1 cm
Gift of Dr. F. Eckhardt / Collection of the Winnipeg Art Gallery / G-87-305 Photo: Leif Norman, courtesy of the Winnipeg Art Gallery / **p. 74**

Tree Study, 1928
graphite on paper
24.4 × 31.7 cm
Gift of Mr. Edward FitzGerald Collection of the Winnipeg Art Gallery G-63-82 / Photo: Alexandra Cousins, courtesy of the Winnipeg Art Gallery

Tree Study, 1928
graphite on paper
24 × 31.6 cm
Gift of Mr. Edward FitzGerald Collection of the Winnipeg Art Gallery G-63-83 / Photo: Alexandra Cousins, courtesy of the Winnipeg Art Gallery

Tree Trunk, 1936
graphite on wove paper
30.4 × 22.8 cm
Gift from the Douglas M. Duncan Collection, 1970 / National Gallery of Canada, Ottawa / 16312 / Photo: NGC **p. 76**

Tree Trunk, 1939
graphite on paper
28.3 x 37.1 cm
Gift from the Douglas M. Duncan Collection / McMichael Canadian Art Collection, Kleinburg / 1981.41.5 **p. 72**

Tree Trunk Study, 1937
graphite on paper
29.4 × 22 cm
Gift of Marita LaFlech Kehoe / School of Art Gallery, University of Manitoba, Winnipeg / 18-0010 / **p. 77**

Tree Trunk with Flower, July 10, 1936
graphite on wove paper
30.3 × 22.8 cm
Gift from the Douglas M. Duncan Collection, 1970 / National Gallery of Canada, Ottawa / 16308 / Photo: NGC
p. 76

Trees, n.d.
graphite on paper
31 × 24 cm
Gift from the Douglas M. Duncan Collection, 1970 / Art Gallery of Windsor / 1970.036 / **p. 78**

Trees and Clouds, from the series Sketches Made in Mexico 1951, 1951
graphite on paper
10.6 × 14.6 cm
Gift of Mr. Edward FitzGerald
Collection of the Winnipeg Art Gallery G-63-230 k / Photo: Alexandra Cousins, courtesy of the Winnipeg Art Gallery

Trees and House, c. 1937
graphite on laid paper
31.8 × 40.9 cm
Gift from the Douglas M. Duncan Collection, 1970 / National Gallery of Canada, Ottawa / 16325 / Photo: NGC
p. 140

Trees and Houses, c. 1945
linocut on paper
14.5 × 18.2 cm;
image: 13.1 × 7.6 cm
Collection of the Winnipeg Art Gallery G-66-49 / Photo: Alexandra Cousins, courtesy of the Winnipeg Art Gallery
p. 154

Trees and Stumps, June 12, 1935
graphite on wove paper
22.9 × 30.2 cm
Gift from the Douglas M. Duncan Collection, 1970 / National Gallery of Canada, Ottawa / 16296 / Photo: NGC
p. 73

Trees in the Snow, 1933
graphite on laid paper
31.5 × 24.5 cm
Gift from the Douglas M. Duncan Collection, 1970 / National Gallery of Canada, Ottawa / 16293 / Photo: NGC
p. 141

Tulip Leaves, c. 1947
watercolour on wove paper
61 × 45.8 cm
Gift from the Douglas M. Duncan Collection, 1970 / National Gallery of Canada, Ottawa / 16352 / Photo: NGC
p. 80

Two Blades of Grass, 1936
graphite on laid paper
31.1 × 24 cm
Gift from the Douglas M. Duncan Collection, 1970 / National Gallery of Canada, Ottawa / 16307 / Photo: NGC
p. x

Two Branches with Leaves, n.d.
graphite on paper
22.2 × 29.8 cm
Gift of Mr. Edward FitzGerald
Collection of the Winnipeg Art Gallery G-63-61 / Photo: Alexandra Cousins, courtesy of the Winnipeg Art Gallery
p. 54

Two Leaves, June 3, 1937
graphite on laid paper
30.8 × 23.5 cm
Gift from the Douglas M. Duncan Collection, 1970 / National Gallery of Canada, Ottawa / 16311 / Photo: NGC
p. 81

Unidentified Landscape, from the series Small Pencil Sketches 1953 Made on a Trip by Plane to Toronto and Ottawa, 1953
graphite on paper
18.1 × 14 cm
Gift of Mr. Edward FitzGerald
Collection of the Winnipeg Art Gallery
G-63-188 b / Photo: Alexandra Cousins, courtesy of the Winnipeg Art Gallery

Unidentified Landscape, from the series Small Pencil Sketches 1953 Made on a Trip by Plane to Toronto and Ottawa, 1953
graphite on paper
18 × 14 cm
Gift of Mr. Edward FitzGerald
Collection of the Winnipeg Art Gallery G-63-188 i / Photo: Alexandra Cousins, courtesy of the Winnipeg Art Gallery

Unidentified Scene, from the series Sketches Made in Mexico 1951, 1951
graphite on paper
11.3 × 15.3 cm
Gift of Mr. Edward FitzGerald
Collection of the Winnipeg Art Gallery G-63-230 a / Photo: Alexandra Cousins, courtesy of the Winnipeg Art Gallery

* *Unidentified Scene*, from the series Sketches Made in Mexico 1951, 1951
graphite on paper
15.4 × 11.5 cm
Gift of Mr. Edward FitzGerald
Collection of the Winnipeg Art Gallery G-63-230 t / Photo: Alexandra Cousins, courtesy of the Winnipeg Art Gallery

Untitled, n.d.
oil on canvas
90.5 × 130.5 cm; framed: 102.2 × 142.2 × 5.7 cm
Private collection / **p. 33**

Untitled, n.d.
graphite on paper
29.1 × 38.1 cm
Gift from the Douglas M. Duncan Collection / Collection of the Winnipeg Art Gallery / G-74-94 / Photo: Leif Norman, courtesy of the Winnipeg Art Gallery / **p. 75**

Untitled, 1955
pen and ink on paper
sheet: 23 × 30 cm
Gift of Mrs. Nora E. Vaughan, Toronto, 1988 / Art Gallery of Ontario, Toronto 88/123 / Courtesy of the Art Gallery of Ontario / **p. 88**

Untitled (Figure Crouching before Mirror), 1924
ink on paper
23.1 × 18.6 cm
Gift of Michael and Sonja Koerner
McMichael Canadian Art Collection, Kleinburg / 2018.9.2 / **p. 87**

Untitled (Hills), n.d.
graphite and chalk on paper
22 × 25 cm
Gift of Earl and Patsy Green from the Estate of Patricia Morrison / School of Art Gallery, University of Manitoba, Winnipeg / 12-0304, 2303
p. 165

Untitled (Landscape), 1923
ink on paper
30.4 × 37 cm
Gift of Earl and Patsy Green from the Estate of Patricia Morrison School of Art Gallery, University of Manitoba, Winnipeg / 12-0473/2472
p. 56

Untitled (Reclining Male Nude), n.d.
graphite on paper
19.2 × 27.9 cm
Gift of Earl and Patsy Green from the Estate of Patricia Morrison / School of Art Gallery, University of Manitoba, Winnipeg / 26-0120

Untitled (Rock Sketch), n.d.
graphite and chalk on paper
25.4 × 19 cm
Gift of Earl and Patsy Green from the Estate of Patricia Morrison School of Art Gallery, University of Manitoba, Winnipeg / 12-0303, 2302
p. 164

Untitled (Seated Female Nude), n.d.
graphite on paper
19.2 × 27.9 cm
Gift of Earl and Patsy Green from the Estate of Patricia Morrison / School of Art Gallery, University of Manitoba, Winnipeg / 26-0032

Untitled (Seated Female Nude), n.d.
graphite on paper
27.9 × 19.2 cm
Gift of Earl and Patsy Green from the Estate of Patricia Morrison / School of Art Gallery, University of Manitoba, Winnipeg / 26-0163

Untitled (Seated Female Nude), n.d.
graphite on paper
27.9 × 19.2 cm
Gift of Earl and Patsy Green from the Estate of Patricia Morrison / School of Art Gallery, University of Manitoba, Winnipeg / 26-0159

Untitled (Seated Male Nude from Rear), n.d.
graphite on paper
19.2 × 27.9 cm
School of Art Gallery, University of Manitoba, Winnipeg / Gift of Earl and Patsy Green from the Estate of Patricia Morrison / 26-0010

Untitled (Standing Female Nude), n.d.
graphite on paper
27.9 × 19.2 cm
Gift of Earl and Patsy Green from the Estate of Patricia Morrison / School of Art Gallery, University of Manitoba, Winnipeg / 26-0014

Untitled (Standing Female Nude), n.d.
graphite on paper
27.9 × 19.2 cm
Gift of Earl and Patsy Green from the Estate of Patricia Morrison / School of Art Gallery, University of Manitoba, Winnipeg / 26-0074

Untitled (Standing Female Nude), n.d.
graphite on paper
27.9 × 19.2 cm
Gift of Earl and Patsy Green from the Estate of Patricia Morrison / School of Art Gallery, University of Manitoba, Winnipeg / 26-0008

Untitled (Standing Female Nude), n.d.
graphite on paper
27.9 × 19.2 cm
Gift of Earl and Patsy Green from the Estate of Patricia Morrison / School of Art Gallery, University of Manitoba, Winnipeg / 26-0015

Untitled (Standing Male Nude), n.d.
graphite on paper
27.9 × 19.1 cm
Gift of Earl and Patsy Green from the Estate of Patricia Morrison / School of Art Gallery, University of Manitoba, Winnipeg / 26-0166

Untitled (Standing Male Nude from Back, Rear), n.d.
graphite on paper
27.9 × 19.1 cm
School of Art Gallery, University of Manitoba, Winnipeg / 26-0196

Untitled (Standing Male Nude, Hand on Hip), n.d.
graphite on paper
27.9 × 19.1 cm
School of Art Gallery, University of Manitoba, Winnipeg / 26-026

Untitled (Trees), n.d.
graphite on paper
25.4 × 18.9 cm
Gift of Earl and Patsy Green from the Estate of Patricia Morrison School of Art Gallery, University of Manitoba, Winnipeg / 12-0192, 2191

Untitled (Trees), n.d.
graphite on paper
22.3 × 29.8 cm
Gift of Earl and Patsy Green from the Estate of Patricia Morrison School of Art Gallery, University of Manitoba, Winnipeg / 12-0291, 2290
p. 54

Untitled (Trees), n.d.
graphite on paper
22.2 × 29.8 cm
Gift of Earl and Patsy Green from the Estate of Patricia Morrison / School of Art Gallery, University of Manitoba, Winnipeg / 12-0294, 2293

Untitled (West Coast Sketch), n.d.
graphite and chalk on paper
27.9 × 19.3 cm
Gift of Earl and Patsy Green from the Estate of Patricia Morrison / School of Art Gallery, University of Manitoba, Winnipeg / 12-0272, 2271
p. 164

Untitled (West Coast Sketch), n.d.
graphite on paper
27.9 × 19.4 cm
Gift of Earl and Patsy Green from the Estate of Patricia Morrison School of Art Gallery, University of Manitoba, Winnipeg / 12-0273, 2272
p. 165

View from Window with Potted Plant, c. 1938–39
linocut on paper
28.2 × 10.6 cm;
image: 16.7 × 9 cm
Collection of the Winnipeg Art Gallery G-66-57 / Photo: Alexandra Cousins, courtesy of the Winnipeg Art Gallery
p. 152

View from Window with Two Jugs, 1942
linocut on paper
26.2 × 10.8 cm;
image: 19.2 × 8.7 cm
Gift of C.C. Sinclair / Collection of the Winnipeg Art Gallery / G-65-172 Photo: Alexandra Cousins, courtesy of the Winnipeg Art Gallery
p. 152

View of City through a Window, 1946
linocut on paper
15.4 × 14.5 cm;
image: 13.2 × 7.5 cm
Collection of the Winnipeg Art Gallery G-66-47 / Photo: Alexandra Cousins, courtesy of the Winnipeg Art Gallery
p. 154

West Coast, Mountain in Mist, 1942
chalk on paper
61.1 × 46 cm
Gift from the Douglas M. Duncan Collection / Collection of the Vancouver Art Gallery / VAG 70.74 Photo: Vancouver Art Gallery
p. 161

Williamson's Garage, 1927
oil on canvas
55.9 × 45.7 cm
Purchased 1929 / National Gallery of Canada, Ottawa / 3682 / Photo: NGC
p. 132

Winkler, from the series Trip to Snowflake 1926, August 11, 1926
graphite on paper
12 × 16 cm
Gift of Mr. Edward FitzGerald Collection of the Winnipeg Art Gallery G-63-198 / Photo: Alexandra Cousins, courtesy of the Winnipeg Art Gallery

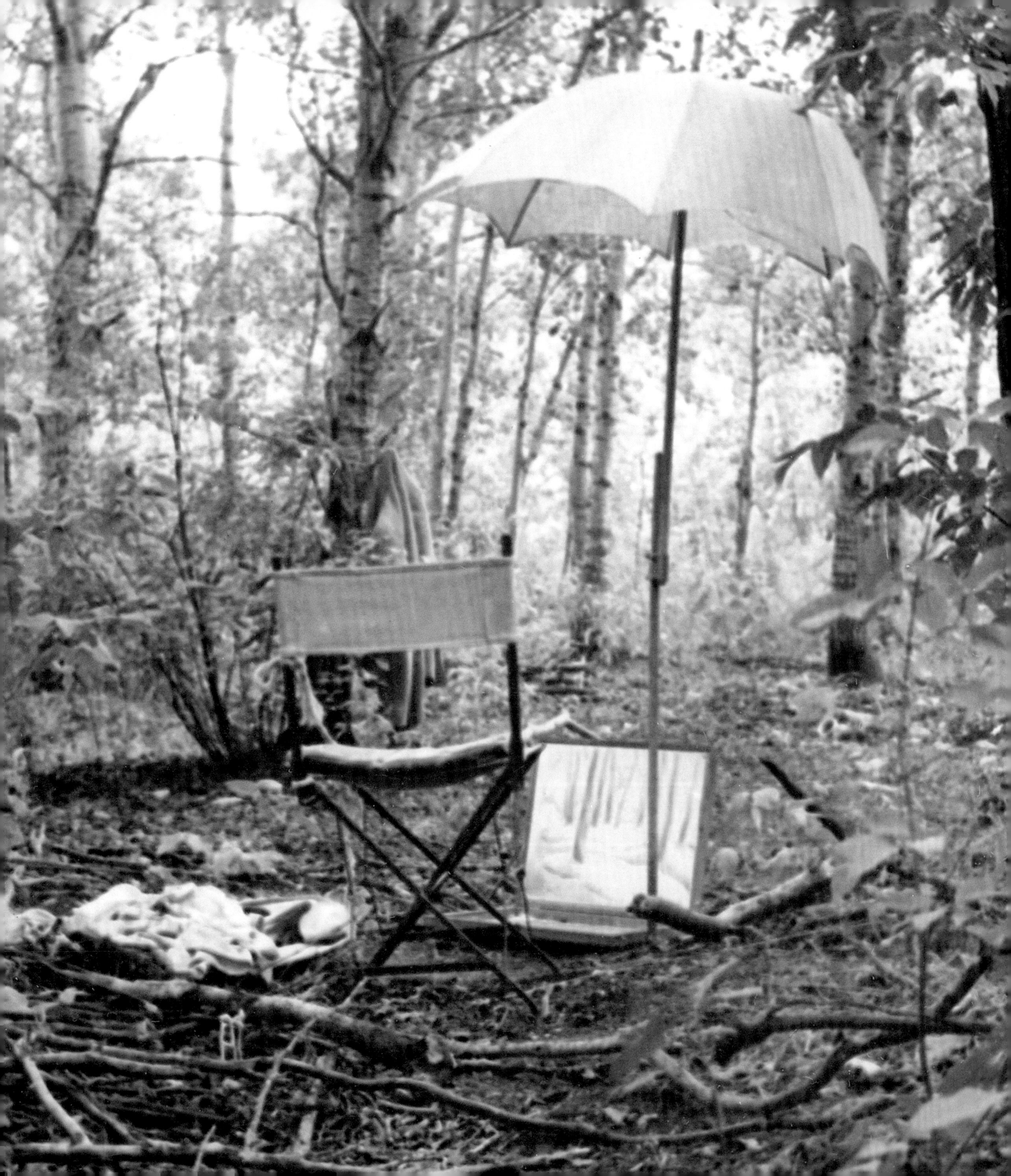

Further Reading

Baker, Marilyn. *FitzGerald in Context*. Winnipeg: Winnipeg Art Gallery, 2009. Exhibition catalogue.

Bovey, Patricia E. *L.L. FitzGerald and Bertram Brooker: Their Drawings*. Winnipeg: Winnipeg Art Gallery, 1987. Exhibition catalogue.

Bovey, Patricia E., and Ann Davis. *Lionel LeMoine FitzGerald (1890–1956): The Development of an Artist*. Winnipeg: Winnipeg Art Gallery, 1978. Exhibition catalogue.

Callahan, Maggie. *Lionel LeMoine FitzGerald: His Drawings and Watercolours*. Edmonton: Edmonton Art Gallery, 1982. Exhibition catalogue.

Coy, Helen. *L. LeMoine FitzGerald Exhibition*. Winnipeg: Gallery One One One, University of Manitoba, 1977. Exhibition catalogue.

———. *FitzGerald as Printmaker: A Catalogue Raisonné of the First Complete Exhibition of the Printed Works*. Winnipeg: University of Manitoba Press, 1982. Exhibition catalogue.

Eckhardt, Ferdinand. *A New FitzGerald*. Winnipeg: Winnipeg Art Gallery, 1963. Exhibition catalogue.

FitzGerald, L.L. "FitzGerald on Art." In *Lionel LeMoine FitzGerald, 1890–1956: A Memorial Exhibition*. Winnipeg: Winnipeg Art Gallery, 1958. Exhibition catalogue.

Harris, Lawren. "Lemoine Fitzgerald [*sic*]." In *Canadian Group of Painters 56/57*. Toronto: Canadian Group of Painters, 1956, n.p. Catalogue for an exhibition held at the Art Gallery of Toronto and the Vancouver Art Gallery.

Lalonde, Christine. *Beauty in a Common Thing: Drawings and Prints by L.L. FitzGerald*. Ottawa: National Gallery of Canada, 2004. Exhibition catalogue.

Parke-Taylor, Michael. *In Seclusion with Nature: The Later Work of L. LeMoine FitzGerald, 1942 to 1956*. Winnipeg: Winnipeg Art Gallery, 1988. Exhibition catalogue.

———. *Lionel LeMoine FitzGerald: Life & Work*. Toronto: Art Canada Institute, 2017.

Thom, Ian. *Living Harmony: FitzGerald's British Columbia Landscapes*. Vancouver: Vancouver Art Gallery, 1994. Exhibition catalogue.

Varley, Christopher. "Lionel LeMoine FitzGerald: Modernist in Isolation." In *O Kanada*, edited by Robert Stacey. Ottawa: The Canada Council for the Arts, 1982. Exhibition catalogue.

Wylie, Elizabeth. "The Development of Spirituality in the Work of Lionel LeMoine FitzGerald 1890–1956." MA thesis, Concordia University, 1981.

———. "The Prairie Art of L.L. FitzGerald." In Catharine M. Mastin, *The Group of Seven in Western Canada*. Toronto/Calgary: Key Porter Books/Glenbow Museum, 2002. Exhibition catalogue.

———. "A Picture as a Living Thing: Lionel LeMoine FitzGerald and Landscape." In *Embracing Canada: Landscapes from Krieghoff to the Group of Seven*. Vancouver: Vancouver Art Gallery, 2016. Exhibition catalogue.

OPPOSITE
FitzGerald's *plein-air* tools at Silver Heights, Winnipeg, August 23, 1934
Gift of Earl and Patsy Green from the Estate of Patricia Morrison / School of Art Gallery, University of Manitoba, Winnipeg / 1-0228
Photo: Arnold O. Brigden

Contributors

CURATORS

IAN A.C. DEJARDIN joined the McMichael Canadian Art Collection as Executive Director in 2017. Previously he was Director of the Dulwich Picture Gallery in London, UK. With Sarah Milroy, Dejardin curated the touring exhibitions *From the Forest to the Sea: Emily Carr in British Columbia* (2014) and *David Milne: Modern Painting* (2018). He was the lead curator of *Painting Canada: Tom Thomson and the Group of Seven* (2011).

SARAH MILROY is Chief Curator of the McMichael Canadian Art Collection. Formerly, she served as editor and publisher of *Canadian Art* magazine (1991–96) and as lead art critic for the *Globe and Mail* (2001–11).

MICHAEL PARKE-TAYLOR, former Curator of Modern Art at the Art Gallery of Ontario, is an art historian based in Toronto. Parke-Taylor curated *In Seclusion with Nature: The Later Work of L. LeMoine FitzGerald, 1942–1956* (Winnipeg Art Gallery, 1988) and is the author of *Lionel LeMoine FitzGerald: Life and Work* (Toronto: Art Canada Institute, 2017).

AUTHORS

STEPHEN BORYS is Director and CEO of the Winnipeg Art Gallery and an adjunct professor at the University of Winnipeg. He has held curatorial posts at the Ringling Museum of Art, Sarasota, Florida; Allen Art Museum, Oberlin College, Ohio; National Gallery of Canada, Ottawa; and Canadian Centre for Architecture, Montreal. He is a board director of the Canadian Museums Association, past board trustee of the Association of Art Museum Directors, and past president of the Canadian Art Museum Directors Organization.

OLIVER A.I. BOTAR is Professor of Art History at the University of Manitoba, specializing in early to mid-century Central European Modernism. He is the author of *Technical Detours: The Early Moholy-Nagy Reconsidered* (2006) and *Sensing the Future: Moholy-Nagy, Media and the Arts* (2014). He is co-editor of *Biocentrism and Modernism* (with Isabel Wünsche, 2011) and *telehor* (with Klemens Gruber, 2013). His current project is a history of art in Winnipeg/Treaty One Territory, 1913–60.

PIERRE DORION lives in Montreal, where he exhibited his work in the 1985 exhibition *Aurora Borealis* at the Centre international d'art contemporain. His 1994 solo exhibition there, *Autoportraits*, was followed by a touring exhibition organized by the York University Art Gallery in 1995. In 1997, Dorion was awarded the Prix Louis-Comtois by the City of Montreal and the Association des galeries d'art contemporain. His exhibition *Peinture et photographie* was presented in 2010 at the Montreal Museum of Fine Arts. In 2012, the Musée d'art contemporain organized a retrospective of his work that travelled to the Dalhousie Art Gallery, Halifax.

ROBERT ENRIGHT is a Winnipeg-based writer and curator. He is Professor of Art Theory and Criticism in the School of Fine Art and Music at the University of Guelph and the senior contributing editor and film critic for *Border Crossings* magazine. In 2005 he was made a Member of the Order of Canada.

ROBERT HOULE is a painter, writer, and educator and is a member of Sandy Bay First Nation in Manitoba. He studied painting and drawing at the International Summer Academy of Fine Arts in Salzburg, Austria. His work is held in collections throughout Canada and in several international institutions. Houle has received the Governor General's Award for Visual and Media Arts (2015), the Eiteljorg Contemporary Art Fellowship, and the Toronto Arts Award. He is a member of the Royal Canadian Academy of Arts.

GEOFFREY JAMES was born in Wales, studied history at Oxford, and began photographing in the early 1970s. He is the author or subject of more than a dozen monographs and has exhibited widely, with solo shows at the Palazzo Braschi in Rome, the Americas Society in New York, and the National Gallery of Canada. He is a Guggenheim Fellow and recipient of the Governor General's Award for Visual and Media Arts and the Gershon Iskowitz Prize. James lives in Toronto, where he was the city's first Photo Laureate.

ANDREW KEAR, former Head of Collections and Exhibitions at the Winnipeg Art Gallery, is Head of Collections, Exhibitions and Programs at Museum London. He has published essays and delivered papers on a range of topics, including abstract painting in Canada, German Expressionism, Conceptual art, official portraiture, and the social history of art institutions. Kear has published his writing in *Canadian Art*, *Border Crossings*, and *Sculpture*.

WANDA KOOP is a painter of large-scale atmospheric studies of light, landscape, and urban space. Her solo touring exhibition *Wanda Koop: On the Edge of Experience* was organized by the National Gallery of Canada and the Winnipeg Art Gallery in 2010. Her work is in many public and private collections, notably the National Gallery of Canada, the Musée d'art contemporain de Montréal, and the Dallas Museum of Art. Based in Winnipeg, Koop is also the founder of Art City, a storefront art centre for inner-city youth. She is a member of the Royal Canadian Academy of Arts, was appointed a Member of the Order of Canada in 2006, and received the Governor General's Award for Visual and Media Arts in 2016.

Published on the occasion of the exhibition
Into the Light: Lionel LeMoine FitzGerald

McMichael Canadian Art Collection,
Kleinburg, Ontario, October 12, 2019–February 1, 2020

Winnipeg Art Gallery, Winnipeg, Manitoba, March 7–July 12, 2020

19 20 21 22 23 5 4 3 2 1

Published simultaneously in French as *Vers la lumière : Lionel LeMoine FitzGerald*

Cataloguing in Publication data available from Library and Archives Canada

ISBN 978-1-77327-096-8 (hbk.)

Publication Manager and Photo Editor: Alexandra Cousins
Curatorial Research: Jacqui Usiskin
Design: Naomi MacDougall
Editing: Alison Reid, Linda Pruessen
Proofreading: Jane Broderick, Jennifer Withrow

Cover images: FRONT *Still Life: Two Apples* (detail), c. 1940, oil on canvas, 45.4 × 40.7 cm; Gift of the Women's Committee, Collection of the Winnipeg Art Gallery, G-56-28 / Photo: Lianed Marcoleta, courtesy of the Winnipeg Art Gallery BACK *Doc Snyder's House*, 1931, oil on canvas, 74.9 × 85.1 cm; Gift of P.D. Ross, Ottawa, 1932, National Gallery of Canada, Ottawa 3993 / Photo: NGC

Printed and bound in Canada by Friesens
Distributed internationally by Publishers Group West

Figure 1 Publishing Inc.
Vancouver BC Canada
www.figure1publishing.com

McMichael Canadian Art Collection
Kleinburg ON Canada
www.mcmichael.com

Winnipeg Art Gallery
Winnipeg MB Canada
www.wag.ca